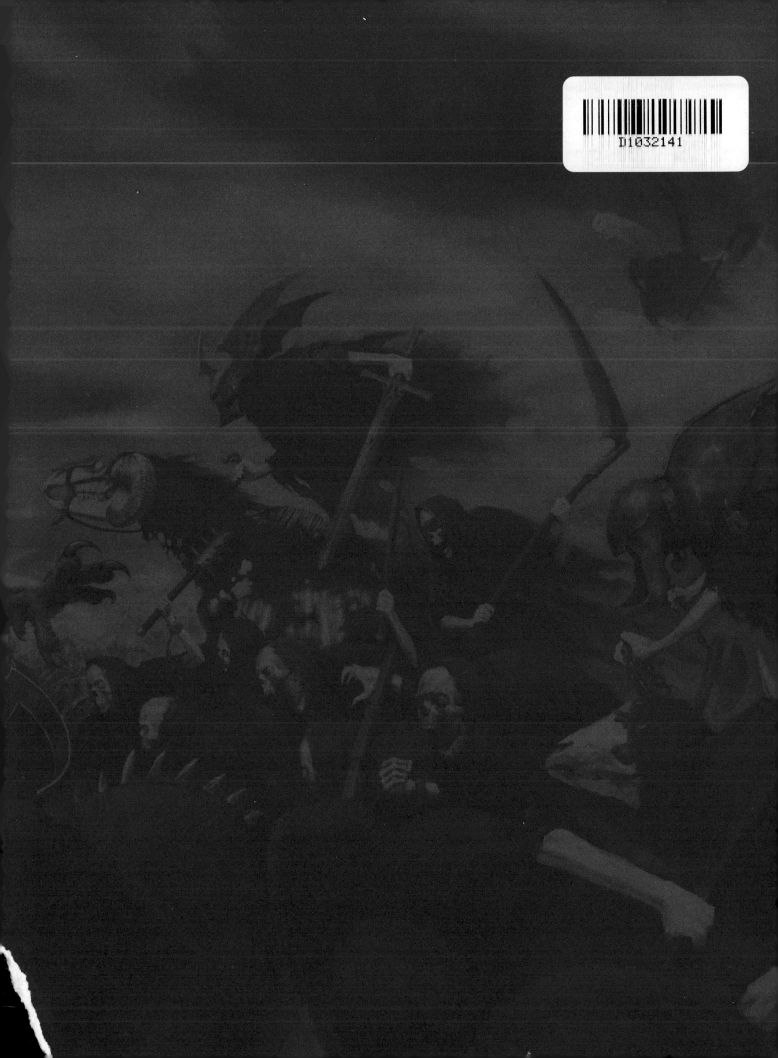

From the maelstrom of a sundered world, the
Eight Realms were born. The formless and the
divine exploded into life. Strange, new worlds
appeared in the firmament, each one gilded
with spirits, gods and men. Noblest of the gods
was Sigmar. For years beyond reckoning he
illuminated the realms, wreathed in light and
majesty as he carved out his reign. His strength
was the power of thunder. His wisdom was
infinite. Mortal and immortal alike kneeled
before his lofty throne. Great empires rose and,
for a while, treachery was banished. Sigmar
claimed the land and sky as his own and ruled
over a glorious age of myth.

But cruelty is tenacious. As had been foreseen,
the great alliance of gods and men tore itself
apart. Myth and legend crumbled into Chaos.
Darkness flooded the realms. Torture, slavery
and fear replaced the glory that came before.
Sigmar turned his back on the mortal kingdoms,
disgusted by their fate. He fixed his gaze instead
on the remains of the world he had lost long
ago, brooding over its charred core, searching
endlessly for a sign of hope. And then, in the
dark heat of his rage, he caught a glimpse of
something magnificent. He pictured a weapon
born of the heavens. A beacon powerful enough
to pierce the endless night. An army hewn from
everything he had lost. Sigmar set his artisans
to work and for long ages they toiled, striving to
harness the power of the stars. As Sigmar's great
work neared completion, he turned back to the
realms and saw that the dominion of Chaos was
almost complete. The hour for vengeance had
come. Finally, with lightning blazing across his
brow, he stepped forth to unleash his creation.

The Age of Sigmar had begun.

A thousand battle cries mingle with screams as they rise to the storm-lashed skies. Blades and hammers crash upon armour, sink deep into flesh, take heads from necks. Peril and strife are constants in these Mortal Realms, these tortured kingdoms that stand so close to the precipice of disaster. Only an army of demigods could hope to pull them back from the brink.

Such an army exists, forged for this very hour by Sigmar and his broken pantheon. That numinous host fights with every iota of its god-given strength to deny the final victory of Chaos, to save those pockets of humanity that can still be salvaged and bring them back into the fight.

Civilisation must rise again and, in places, it is taking root once more. But the towers and spires of progress cast long shadows of their own…

CONTENTS

DESIGNED BY GAMES WORKSHOP IN NOTTINGHAM
With thanks to The Faithful for their additional playtesting services

Games Workshop Ltd., Willow Road, Lenton, Nottingham, NG7 2WS, United Kingdom
games-workshop.com

WORLDS OF LEGEND

The Age of Sigmar is an epic setting populated by myriad armies, powerful heroes and magnificent monsters. It plays host to vast, realm-spanning wars between the forces of Order and Chaos, Destruction and Death. Read on to explore these battle-torn landscapes and learn of the many peoples and creatures of the realms.

GLORY COME TO LIFE

At the heart of the Games Workshop hobby lies a vast range of Citadel Miniatures. From shining heroes to lowly soldiers, virtually every daemon, warrior and creature depicted in the Age of Sigmar is represented in the form of a beautifully rendered model. Even the architecture of the realms is replicated in intricate detail, ready to take its place as a spectacular backdrop for your displayed miniatures.

The motivations behind each collection are as diverse as the models themselves. They are almost invariably a magical alchemy of the aspects that define the hobby – namely collecting, building, painting and playing games with Citadel Miniatures.

There are no guidelines to dictate how much time or emphasis to place on each – it's your hobby. So instead, we'll take a look at just what makes each facet so compelling. As you delve deeper into the unfolding legends of the Age of Sigmar, your collection can take you far beyond the vantage point of a mere observer. The fate of the Mortal Realms is far from decided, and your miniatures are the means by which you become both author and protagonist in that epic war. Your collection can be as expansive as you wish, drawing heroes, war engines and warriors from many distinct races. Alternatively, you may focus on a single element – such as a Stormcast Eternals Warrior Chamber – building it up, unit by unit, into a formidable tabletop force. As any seasoned collector will attest,

looking over the serried ranks of your freshly painted army is always a proud moment. Arranging them upon a lavishly detailed tabletop battlefield ready to face the foe is often the next logical step, and for many, this is the very essence of the Games Workshop hobby.

TELLING NEW TALES

Warhammer Age of Sigmar follows the realm-spanning wars between a dozen richly detailed factions and more. The Stormcast Eternals are striking protagonists, heroes taken from amongst the ranks of humanity and reforged as superhuman beings with celestial lightning running in their veins. Ranged against them are their arch enemies, the twisted armies of Chaos, mortal warriors and daemons alike given unnatural strength by the Dark Gods. All the while the forces of Destruction rampage across the lands, whilst the chilling necromantic hosts of Death emerge to claim the souls of all living creatures. These factions constantly vie for supremacy in the bloodiest era of battle yet seen – the Age of Sigmar.

Whether you take the role of avenging hero, bloodthirsty villain, rampaging raider or some more nuanced force of arms is up to you. Whatever you choose, once you've braved the maelstrom

of battle that is the Mortal Realms you'll find yourself wanting to return again and again. As you do so you will explore the rich landscapes of the Warhammer Age of Sigmar hobby – eight new worlds plunged into an era of battle, each with its own warriors, monsters, hazards and treasures. By delving ever deeper into this book, you will embark upon the adventure of a lifetime.

Exploring the background and character of your miniatures is a deeply enjoyable element of collecting an army. Throughout battletomes and campaign books, you will find in-depth accounts of histories and heroes, which between them weave a rich tapestry of the Mortal Realms and the races that war across them. Once you have learned about your chosen warriors, and played out the battleplans that epitomise their way of war, you'll be ready to write the next chapter yourself. There are no limits to the tales you can tell – let your imagination run wild!

This majestic, multi-level board represents a part of Glymmsforge, a city in the Realm of Death. A force of Stormcast Eternals rallies before its gates – only to be assailed by Nagash and a horde of his necromantic minions.

COLLECTING CITADEL MINIATURES

The worlds of Warhammer Age of Sigmar offer infinite possibilities for any avid miniatures collector. Their soaring landscapes, vast armies and fantastical battles will fuel your imagination – from your first few models and their journeys in the Mortal Realms to impressive collections and truly epic conflicts on the tabletop.

With such an array of incredible miniatures to choose from, how do you settle on which army, faction or characters to collect first? Sometimes you'll be drawn to a force through the books that recount the battles and tales of its most famous leaders. Alternatively, you may find yourself inspired by a particular army's colours and heraldry, or perhaps the wondrous creatures that fight for it.

Tabletop battles should always be friendly affairs, but at the same time, there's nothing wrong with wanting to emerge victorious from the games you play. Many collectors will look for inspiration in the rules for individual models or units – all

of which can be found on that model or unit's warscroll – gauging their capabilities on the field of battle. Others relish the challenge of piecing together the 'perfect' army, which is a hobby in itself. These sorts of forces yield the most competitive gaming experience when deployed, so for those with a taste for gritty warfare, this may well be the impetus that drives their collection. There's no right or wrong way, and it always boils down to whatever ignites your hobby spark.

You'll find as you delve further into the Age of Sigmar hobby that almost all factions have battletomes, exciting books that expand upon a

certain force. These are great sources of inspiration, and show a wealth of colour schemes and heraldry. They also include allegiance abilities – including battle traits, command traits and more – that lend new powers to your army. As you learn more about strategy and tactics, you may find that special rules and synergies between units inform your next purchases. Of course, there's no need to restrict yourself to a single army. You might be torn between the heroic Stormcast Eternals and the mercenary Fyreslayers, for example – in which case, just collect both! They look great alongside each other, and can easily fight together in your battles.

The Stormcast Eternals of the Sacrosanct Chamber are warrior mages, each adept at slaying supernatural foes. Just as well, for they face hosts of horrifying Nighthaunts.

It is quite common for collectors of Citadel Miniatures to arrange them on a shelf or in a cabinet, formed up on parade with just as much care as they were assembled and painted.

Warhammer World in Nottingham, UK, has an extensive museum full of displays and dioramas where thousands of expertly painted miniatures take pride of place.

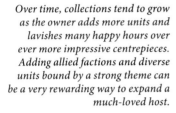

Over time, collections tend to grow as the owner adds more units and lavishes many happy hours over ever more impressive centrepieces. Adding allied factions and diverse units bound by a strong theme can be a very rewarding way to expand a much-loved host.

The army to the right includes mortal followers of Khorne bolstered by the daemonic allies they summon to war.

BUILDING AND PAINTING

The first steps into the Warhammer Age of Sigmar hobby usually involve building and painting your first model. Though you will not get perfect results straight away, with a bit of practice you will find that you have a fantastic band of warriors of whom you are rightly proud. So begins a voyage that can see whole legions brought to life.

One of the greatest joys of collecting Citadel Miniatures can be found in the modelling and painting of your collection, as you assemble and recreate all of the great heroes, terrifying monsters and amazing landscapes of the Age of Sigmar. Nothing beats seeing a fully painted army arranged in a carefully crafted setting – whether as part of an epic fantasy world recreated in miniature, with all the pageantry and spectacle that comes with it, or set up in a display case to be admired by all.

Before painting your models, you'll first need to assemble them. To begin with, you'll want to follow the advice given in the construction booklet supplied with your models, but as your confidence grows, you may find yourself trying more ambitious methods, leading to more personalised results.

There's real satisfaction to be had in making your miniatures your own, bringing them to life with a paintbrush and teasing out all of their finely sculpted details. Some people revel in treating each miniature as its own work of art, lavishing attention on every millimetre. Others prefer to assemble vast legions of warriors in matching liveries, focusing on the spectacle of massed ranks, armed and ready for war.

There's no right or wrong way to go about this – you should go wherever your inspiration takes you, and do whatever you think makes your miniatures look great. Take your time to consider; the paint scheme you select will help you to imbue your models with character and story, and to define who they are. Why has this particular chamber of Stormcast Eternals got pockmarked, battle-scarred armour? Why do they paint the shafts of their hammers in shining silver? What are they doing in a mysterious landscape of glowing ice sculptures and blue flame? With an ever-growing range of evocative Citadel Miniatures to choose from, the story is yours to tell.

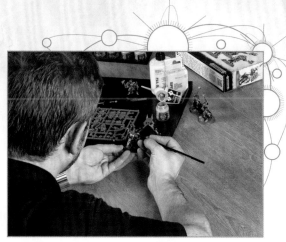

The first stage of bringing your miniatures to life is to have a really good look at the frames, absorbing all the cool details and deciding on how you want to assemble them. Then, whilst consulting the assembly guide, clip the right component parts from their sprues. After that you will need to put them together. Most models will need Citadel plastic glue – a dab or two on both sides of each join, and with a little practice the parts will bond perfectly.

Once the model is assembled and the glue is dry, you will need to undercoat it – this means painting it all one colour as a foundation on which to build your chosen paint scheme. Citadel spray paints are ideal for this. Then, once this undercoat is dry, use your chosen colours to paint on a basecoat. Advanced techniques include using layer paints, shades, highlights, glazes and technical paints to achieve truly stunning results.

WARHAMMER TV

Essential viewing, Warhammer TV's painting tutorials have insights for everyone. These guides are available for free on games-workshop.com and can also be watched via the Warhammer TV YouTube channel. Painting techniques for all kinds of models are covered, from individual warriors and squads to mighty war machines, monsters and even battlefields. And while the videos are a boon for newcomers, they come packed with a host of tips, inspiring ideas and handy techniques that make them equally popular amongst even the most expert miniature painters.

PLAYING THE GAME

The Mortal Realms are replete with tales of mighty heroes, bloodshed and betrayal. Your own games of Warhammer Age of Sigmar can evoke these epic stories upon the tabletop battlefield. Social, strategic and endlessly varied, the unique thrill of a good wargame cannot be overstated.

The rules presented in this publication give you a framework to make the tales of the Age of Sigmar your own. More than that, though, they enable you to tell your own stories set in the Mortal Realms, and to use your collection of Citadel Miniatures in glorious battles of your own devising. Some will fight to free the realms from the horror of Chaos rule, others to crush the upstarts who dare challenge the Dark Gods. Others still may be driven by personal agendas of conquest, glory, or simply the enjoyment of a suitably grand and violent clash. Whatever your goals, these rules allow you to play out one exciting tale of battle after another. Your exploits through

the fantastical landscapes of the realms can be as many and varied as you like. The only limit to the fun is your imagination. On pages 226-243 of this book are the core rules with which to play your Warhammer Age of Sigmar games. With these rules, you can pit any army against any other in whatever exciting scenario you choose. However, these rules are only the beginning of your journey. Games Workshop offers an ever-expanding range of battletomes, campaign supplements – such as the books detailing the tumultuous period known as the Realmgate Wars – and thrilling novels that tell tales from the Age of Sigmar. Whether by utilising the exciting battleplans

available in many of these publications, or drawing inspiration from the events they cover, you need never play the same game twice. The more games you play, the more ideas you will have for what to do next. From laying siege to towering Chaos Dreadholds or duelling with conclaves of wizards amidst the raging heart of a magical storm, to holding a perilous bridge over a river of boiling lava or fighting out the desperate last stands of ragged bands of bloodied heroes, your games will become more immersive by the day. Each new encounter will generate spectacular war stories that you and your gaming group will reminisce upon for years to come.

The Realm of Fire has long been in the grip of Chaos, but since the dawn of the Age of Sigmar, the Stormcast Eternals have begun to seize vital sites across the realm. This fantastical battlefield is hotly contested by warring factions, and resounds to the rattle of dice every week!

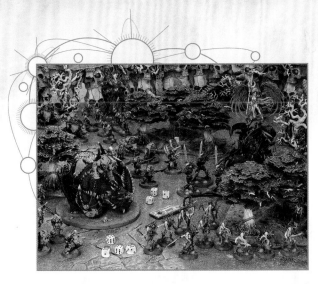

Some people become expert in using their collection on the battlefield, giving their units names and taking note of their victories and defeats over many years of gaming. You'll find the vagaries of fate make heroes of the unlikeliest characters – and betray the mightiest warriors at the most inopportune times! It is these stories that collectors and gamers love to swap over a beverage when the dust of battle has settled.

No gaming table is complete without scenery. The battlefield itself should be as fantastical and impressive as the armies that spill their blood upon it. To help achieve this, Games Workshop sells a variety of scenery kits ranging from simple Sylvaneth Wyldwoods to Realm of Battle boards and imposing Chaos Dreadholds over which many a deadly siege can be fought.

Some gamers have regular opponents with whom they build a friendly rivalry. Each hones their strategy against the other until they know their opponent's army almost as well as their own. Such a relationship can end in a kind of arms race where one gamer will add a new unit to their arsenal for the next game, only to find his nemesis has done much the same – but that's part of the fun!

Many see the peak of the wargaming experience to be a gaming tournament, where like-minded generals gather for a day or weekend of several close-fought games. The type of gaming known as matched play lends itself perfectly to this aspect of the hobby. In these gatherings, the standard of painting and the sportsmanship with which you play the game can be every bit as important as the results of the games themselves.

THE TALE OF AEONS

THE AGE OF MYTH

The breaking of the world-that-was, the Great Victory of the Chaos Gods, the End Times – that forgotten epoch has many names. Only the gods of yore and the inhuman slann remember it vividly, and the truth of its demise is buried in the dust of history. Yet there are those who still abide, their essence or spirit having survived the cataclysm that swallowed their world, or been resurrected by the powers bound to their soul. The God-King Sigmar is foremost amongst them. His world was shattered, its core hurtling through the aetheric void, but he clung onto it still, and was borne toward the Mortal Realms. In them he found a set of realities crystallised from the scattered energies of his world.

It is said Sigmar was awakened in the void by the Great Drake. Introduced by that zodiacal godbeast to the Eight Realms, he embarked upon many great voyages of discovery, exploring each in turn. He journeyed long and far, finding enclaves of natives and overcoming the monstrous beasts that preyed upon them. Sigmar taught the scattered tribes of mankind many things, and soon they worshipped him as a deity above all others. The light of civilisation was conjured from the stuff of the lands. Over the course of a few generations, nomads with flint-tipped weapons ceased their wanderings and instead learned to build. At first their efforts were just rough huts, but as the centuries slid past, they built townships, cities and teeming metropolises. Trade flourished, and spires pierced the skies in every Mortal Realm.

Guided by inner knowledge and fate itself, Sigmar located and awakened other gods – those he recognised from his former life – with mixed consequences. Using strength as much as wisdom he formed a new pantheon around himself. Amongst its ranks were the duardin gods Grungni, the Great Maker, and Grimnir the Furious. They were joined by darker presences – Malerion of the Shadow Realm, and even Nagash, the Great Necromancer, for they too desired worlds of order and progress over which to rule. Alarielle the Everqueen saw the hope of new life in Sigmar, and the twin-headed brute Gorkamorka was won over to the God-King's cause after a duel that flattened mountains. Each gave unto Sigmar a godly gift in return for giving them new life, and Azyr, the realm he had chosen as his own, thrived like no other.

But so disparate were these gods that their common causes did not bind them for long. Over time, the fractious alliances faltered and broke apart. Worse still, another pantheon had set their covetous eyes upon these fertile lands. Slowly, insidiously, the whispers and promises of these fell powers sowed division and treachery throughout the lands until they were ripe for conquest. Sigmar, bearing the light of civilisation ever on, did not see many of the dangers that coiled in its shadow until it was too late. Though that light can still be seen whenever some relic or crumbled architecture is uncovered, the secrets of such splendours have been crushed beneath the heel of Chaos oppression – or else hidden away by the gods themselves.

It was Dracothion,
the Great Drake, that first
beheld Sigmar. The God-King was
clinging to a lustrous sphere of sigmarite
that hurtled unchecked through the aether.
Entranced by its gleam, Dracothion chased the
careening orb, seeking to capture it and set it in the
heavens to better admire its beauty. Only then did
the celestial drake notice the battered form of Sigmar
gripping the pitted metal. Sensing a kindred spirit,
Dracothion revived the god with a warming breath.

Sigmar thanked his saviour, bestowing gifts
upon the Great Drake in gratitude. In turn,
Dracothion showed Sigmar star bridges and
crystalline passageways that led to each
of the Eight Realms. Thus began
the fabled Age of Myth.

The Age of Myth
is shrouded in legend,
remembered in song as a time of
great alliances, mighty works of magic,
the taming of zodiacal beasts and the founding
of colossal cities. Sigmar's claim to godhood was
unassailable, his twin-tailed mark made upon domains
still covered in the dew of creation. Yet he encountered
much that was ancient even then. He wandered in
amazement, finding portals between the realms and
exploring each in turn. There are many tales of his
supremacy: his slaying of the hydragors that guarded the
gates to Shyish, his overthrowing of the volc-giants that
once ruled the Great Parch of Aqshy, and the smiting
of Ymnog, grandfather of gargants and sire of
the godbeast Behemat. Even Auroxis the
World Beast fell to a blow from his
hammer, Ghal Maraz.

Despite their differences
an accord was struck between
the gods in those early days. Each of
the Eight Realms was appointed a divine
protector, and various oaths of domain and
allegiance were sworn. Grungni taught mankind
of metalcraft, and Nagash imposed order upon the
spirits of the dead whilst his lifeless thralls laboured
ceaselessly to build even grander edifices. Trade
flourished by means of portal-like Realmgates.
Even savage Gorkamorka worked long at his own
task – to clear the wilds of monstrous things
– for it suited him well, though ultimately
his quest was consumed by the
random violence so beloved
of orruk-kind.

Whilst exploring
Chamon, Sigmar climbed the
Iron Mountains and there freed two
gods enchained. Of how crippled Grungni
and raging Grimnir repaid their debt to Sigmar,
many songs are sung. Grungni joined Sigmar in his
quest to forge a world free of evil, but Grimnir wished
his debt settled then and there, and demanded Sigmar
name a foe worthy of his blades. That same night Grimnir
tracked Vulcatrix – the Mother of Salamanders and the
mythic creature that first birthed flame into the worlds – to
her lair. Endlessly, the wyrm uncoiled from her molten
abyss. Grimnir hefted his axes and charged. The titanic
clash that followed flattened hills and created the
Plains of Aqshy, but neither would submit. The
foes smashed into one another until god
and beast alike rained down as a
hail of blazing meteors.

The cities of that time were raised high, and the people that dwelt within their walls as numerous as the stars. For a while, those born into these worlds of wonder and possibility knew paradise. The God-King's might was beyond question, as was that of his immortal allies from the World Before Time. In Grungni's fair city of Elixia, in the Realm of Metal, the streets rang to the hammers of a thousand gifted artisans. On the balconies of Thyria's arboretums in the Jade Kingdoms, the flowers of Alarielle's magic bloomed in every archway. Grimnir's great lodges burned hot with the fires of passion, his duardin people hunting down monstrous beasts until the lands were safe. Even Nagashizzar in the Realm of Death was a place of order and progress, a city where anarchy and warfare were but distant memories.

In that era, many a weather-torn skald made the bold claim that he had visited each of the Great Wonders of the Mortal Realms in person. Through the magic of the Realmgates it was thought possible for a man to achieve such an odyssey over the course of a hundred years. The Crystal Spires of Thrense, the Spear of Mallus jutting from the Coast of Tusks, the Bone Pillars of Antghor, the peak of Deific Mons in the Shyish Innerlands, the Sky Bridges of Ghur – all these and more were visited by the traders and travellers of that halcyon age.

The Dark God Slaanesh, glutted on countless souls after the demise of the world-that-was, was chained by the magic of the aelven gods Tyrion and Teclis. Trapped between the Realms of Light and Shadow, no more could Slaanesh seduce the civilisations that sprung up across the lands. His lustful worshippers cried out in fear and anguish, for no longer could they feel their direct connection with the god that gave them meaning. But Tyrion, Malerion and their allies did not consider their work complete. By means of painstaking ritual, they used the arcane bindings that held the Dark Prince to siphon the souls of many of the aelves he had consumed, cleanse them of taint, and take them into the mortal lands of Ulgu and Hysh to be reborn.

THE
AGE OF
CHAOS

Already the pantheon of Sigmar showed signs of strain. Nagash sought to rule alone, creating strife and even open war between the living and the dead. Gorkamorka's warrior spirit drew him away from Sigmar's sage counsel, forever driving a blade of conflict between the savage and the enlightened. Lord Tyrion and Malerion abandoned their duties in order to capture the Dark Prince Slaanesh whilst he was still glutted with the aelven souls he had devoured. Elsewhere, stout Grimnir battled Vulcatrix until both god and monster were torn apart.

From beyond the haunted aether-void, the Dark Gods looked upon the discord of the Mortal Realms. In the peoples given civilisation by their old enemy Sigmar, they saw fresh prey. Their whispered promises and insidious curses turned men against one another, and in that strife they found their way in. At their command the Realm of Chaos spat forth its daemon legions once more in such numbers that all other hosts seemed trivial. Despite the great valour of Sigmar's followers, his civilisations were soon beset. So began the Age of Chaos – a time of death and deceit.

Though his enemies grew in power, and strife consumed the lands, the God-King Sigmar reforged old alliances and won many battles. It was not enough. United in conquest, the Chaos Gods had already proved far too strong. Sigmar was forced to lead a great exodus to the Celestial Realm, the last place of safety under the stars. The Gates of Azyr were closed behind him, and the seven realms that remained were left to their fate.

Life in the Mortal Realms became a living hell. All hope of peace was ripped away. Every race, people and settlement bled under the bite of the Chaos axe, their lands dominated by skull-clad fortresses and blasphemous temples. Even the realms themselves began to change, twist and fall away, in places corrupted beyond recovery. Though the descendants of the world-that-was clung to hope as best they could, only those that embraced the ways of their overlords survived for long. Honest men fought to the death in blood-pits for the amusement of their conquerors. Priests of dead gods turned their unheeded prayers towards viler powers. Wretches scraped what meat they could from the carcasses of the fallen. The spectres of betrayal and desperation turned brother against brother and father against son.

The Chaos Gods laughed in triumph, sure in the knowledge that there existed no force mighty enough to challenge them.

And yet, on the horizon, storm clouds slowly gathered…

In the Realm of Chaos, the Dark Gods reign supreme. Each has its own aims and obsessions, consumed by their ancient rivalry and the Great Game they play with the lives of nations, races and even worlds. Their twisted armies will fight alongside each other well enough, so long as they bring ruin to the Mortal Realms. Corrupted tribes worship these fell entities with maddened zeal, their humanity traded away for raw power. Encased in hell-forged armour, the champions of Chaos carve paths of slaughter through the realms. Mutants and monsters loom amongst their warbands, vying to catch the eye of the Chaos Gods. Savage Brayherds of beastmen dwell in the wild places, intent on tearing down civilisation and devouring its remains. The ratmen known as skaven extend their hidden empire, gnawing through the fabric of reality itself as they seek their own rise to dominance. Most feared of all the servants of the Dark Gods are the daemon hosts, for they are Chaos incarnate.

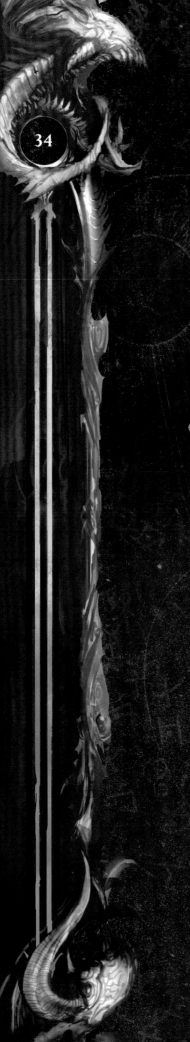

DAEMON INCURSION

As the kingdoms of the Age of Myth grew ever more powerful, cracks began to appear in the foundations of civilisation. Over time, those hair-thin weaknesses were widened and exploited by the agents of the Dark Gods until they allowed the hellish scions of Chaos to bleed into reality.

The eyes of the Chaos Gods came to gaze upon the Mortal Realms with terrible inevitability, for the attention of the Dark Powers are drawn to the energies of mortal ambition much as a shark is drawn to blood. Across the cosmos they stared with hungering intent, the glittering lights of grand cities reflected in their avaricious eyes. Here were fresh pastures, lands replete with magical power and the souls of mortal men. They were a source of endless energy and infinite entertainment – an arena in which their Great Game could be fought anew.

At first, the way in was barred to the agents of the Dark Gods. The strange realities of the Mortal Realms, when they first came to be, were gatherings of aligned magic so pure that the stuff of Chaos found it difficult to gain purchase there. The natives had no knowledge of the deities of Chaos, those fell entities that sought to force their way into the waking worlds; those exceptional few who had survived the destruction of the world-that-was kept silent, never speaking of their traumas lest they lend them strength – though for some, memories of carnage still haunted them in the dead of night. Only a handful of souls across the entirety of the Mortal Realms had come to learn that these eldritch powers could lend a supplicant physical might, skill at arms or the power of sorcery in exchange for his allegiance. Some amongst these cared not for the cost of such a bargain – in essence, the petitioner's immortal soul. These selfish few, these foolish ones, were the vectors by which the Chaos Gods made their play.

At first, the methods by which the Chaos Gods inveigled their way into reality were subtle. Treasonous schemers seeking to overthrow their rightful monarchs worked complex ploys against their betters, their prayers for change inviting the attention of Tzeentch – prayers that did not go unanswered. In Chamon's Hanging Valleys, courtly intrigues turned to slaughter when a meteor shower glimmered through the skies, granting the wishes of ninety-nine viziers and magi in a storm of contradictory change-magic that left golden palaces and gardens swimming in blood.

In Ulgu's Grey Paradise, listless nobles grew bored with the constant machinations of their shadowy realm. Seeking more intense pleasures yet finding themselves unable to enjoy simple things, they dabbled in dark arts to fulfil their exotic tastes – and in doing so, opened the door to orgies of destruction brought upon them by the daemons of Slaanesh.

Watching eagerly over fertile Ghyran, the Plague God Nurgle chuckled fondly when the Warlocks of the Seventh Mulch brewed a cauldron of pox, using it to poison the lands of their rivals in order to boast the bigger harvest. Other Ghyranite tribes, so beset by verminous infestation they were driven to their wits' end, began to worship the Great Horned Rat, for they saw his baleful eyes glowing in their dreams. These supplicants donned the bloody pelts and

In the Great Hospice of King Thanator, a healer was driven to distraction by the bone-eating plagues that had all but consumed her people. She prayed for someone, anyone, to help lift the curse. When a tiny fly descended from the void and whispered in her ear one night, she learned the name of one who could aid her – Nurgle.

The Plague God was already listening keenly, and in his generosity, he answered her next eventide prayer by unleashing seven diseases that were so strong that the bone-eating plague was eradicated in a single night. The surviving people of Thanator's Hospice, wracked inside and out by plague, were amongst the first to be known as Maggotkin. They were new believers of an ancient creed given fresh life, each riddled with a different strain of Nurgle's finest contagions. To this day, the Maggotkin march to war in Nurgle's name.

tails of the largest vermin they could slay, dancing on all fours around the burning corpses of local rat-catchers. When the gravid moon next rose green, their lands were drowned in furry brown bodies, and they too were consumed.

Though such freakish instances grew steadily more common, it was in the arid wastes of Aqshy that the strongest of the Chaos Gods made his mark with a daemon invasion. So important was that initial victory against the forces of Order, so symbolic to the passing of aeons, that word of it spread from one realm to another, shaking dozens of civilisations to their core. There, a rivalry between the forces of Khorne and Sigmar had begun – a bitter enmity that would define the long wars to come.

The sulphurous lands of Aqshy's Great Parch have a long history of violence. A volatile and passionate realm even in times of relative peace, Aqshy is famous for the vitriolic temper of its people. In prehistoric times its clans and tribes used any excuse to seek out war. Yet over the course of the Age of Myth, Sigmar's influence upon the citizens of the Great Parch saw them learn to sublimate their extreme emotions with competition, athleticism and regulated conflict.

As civilisation took root, their boundless vigour and drive saw them push each other to ever greater heights of progress. Yet their tinder-dry passions were to ignite like wildfire when rivalry inevitably turned to war. There were those in that land who could not put aside their pride and their aggression, who were so in love with violence they could not forsake it. Blood cults and murderous savagery became ever more common. At first, only the most primal barbarian tribes worshipped at the altar of carnage, but over time rituals of

bloodletting and cannibalism spread across the entirety of the Parch's Flamescar Plateau.

Where one savage religion took root, others were swift to follow. Shamans and seers turned to ever darker patrons as they sought to keep one step ahead. The civilised domains of Aspiria, Bataar and Vostargi Mont were content to leave the savage tribes to their dark work, instead concentrating on their own thriving trade and artifice.

Their complacency was to cost them dearly. When a warlord known as Korghos Khul rose to prominence, he led his battle-hungry tribes in an endless contest of bloodletting that

became a way of life. Those who did not join his cause, those who refused to devour the slain after battle's end, were cut down and added to the corpse-feast themselves. The intense violence of that time reached such dizzying peaks that reality was stretched to breaking point. Khorne's hot breath thinned the veil in his anticipation of the red work to come. Then, one fell night, the daemons of the Blood God broke through from the Realm of Chaos, invading the Great Parch amidst a maelstrom of magic. For whole generations the once-fertile and painstakingly irrigated lands ran with rivulets of gore. It was the beginning of a dire epoch of Chaos ascendancy.

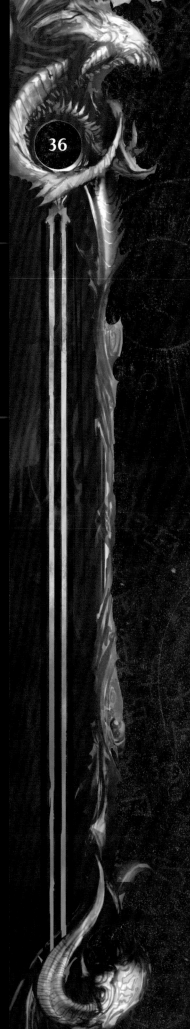

THE BREAKING OF THE PANTHEON

For a time, Sigmar's alliance had been a force powerful enough to reshape the Mortal Realms. The fact the gods shared a commonality of origin – the world-that-was – proved a strong bond. As the rise of Chaos slowly put their kinship asunder, however, disaster loomed.

For a long and productive period, Sigmar's Pantheon of Order met in the grand conclaves of Azyr. Their heated debates and miraculous interventions shaped the realms into places where native cultures and survivors could thrive. Yet the insidious lure of Chaos proved hard to deny, as it had ever been, and over time its tendrils corroded the integrity of the pantheon just as they tore at the stuff of reality itself.

Alarielle had long proven a powerful ally to Sigmar, for wherever she sowed the seeds of growth and strange harmony, those lands remained fertile and verdant forever more. Wherever she walked, the ground blossomed and became lush. Even the most hostile realmscapes were rendered habitable in the wake of her footsteps. Flesh-desiccating deserts became oases of exotic life and sentient plants; arid salt flats became tillable fields that sang with life. At Sigmar's behest she ventured far and wide, and where she passed new civilisations were founded in her wake. But as the seasons changed, and her sojourns became longer as she sought peace amongst the lifeblooms, the heartlands of Ghyran came under attack.

The Plague God Nurgle had long coveted Alarielle's paradises of fecundity, seeking to infest them with grotesque forms of life that they might become part of his vile garden in the Realm of Chaos. By the time Alarielle returned and truly began to fight for the lands of Ghyran, the realm was already infected. Her guilt and

anger were so profound she slid into despondency and decline. Alarielle blamed Sigmar as much as herself for the disaster. She became a recluse, retreating to those remote areas of Ghyran still untouched and resolving to die there if she must. She led the resistance against Nurgle's invasions, but always foul forces found her sites of power. Over the centuries, Nurgle's influence waxed mightily, and the battle for Ghyran was slowly lost. Using all her enchantments, Alarielle withdrew to the hidden vale of Athelwyrd and prepared for the worst.

Gorkamorka, that primal force of destruction that exemplifies the battle-lust in the heart of every greenskin, was a reluctant member of the pantheon at the best of times. He had been freed by Sigmar when the God-King and his ally Dracothion had encountered him trapped within the mountainous glacier of primordial ooze known as Drakatoa, the living avalanche. In shattering that vast entity even as it held Gorkamorka prisoner, Sigmar freed the greenskin god, but inadvertently caused him to vent his pent-up anger on those closest to hand. Within seconds, Dracothion was struck down. Sigmar, enraged, fought Gorkamorka in a colossal

brawl that shook the earth of Ghur for twelve days and twelve nights. When the dust settled, the two laughed long and loud, for they recognised in one another an indomitable warrior spirit that could not be extinguished.

Gorkamorka, indebted to Sigmar, agreed to direct his temper at the enormous predators that roamed the Hinterlands of Ghur, the better to give the tribes of men a chance to thrive. The titanic skeletons that dot the Realm of Beasts from end to end are said to date back to that long rampage. So much blood was spilt, so massive were the skulls littering the land, that Khorne could not help but look upon Gorkamorka's grand hunt with approval. But when the Blood God learned that Gorkamorka was doing the bidding of Sigmar and the Pantheon of Order, the skies boomed with mocking laughter. It was not long after that Gorkamorka, frustrated beyond measure by the debates and politics of the Azyrite councils, roared suddenly in animalistic wrath and left Azyr forever, launching into a violent crusade that stormed across reality with the force of a hundred natural disasters. He led the Great Waaagh! from one side of the cosmos to the other, leaving utter mayhem in his wake.

Grungni had his own reasons for working so long at Sigmar's side. The duardin never forget a debt, and the same can be said of their stalwart gods, but so long did Grungni work to further the goals of Azyr that he repaid that debt three times over. By the forge-god's hand was the Sigmarabulum raised to embrace the core of the world-that-was; by his hammer was the Anvil of the Apotheosis hewn and the Crucibles of Reforging brought into being from void-cold nothingness. His breath mingled with the metallic by-products of his godly work, forming aether-gold, the arcane element that would become so central to the existence of his Kharadron children.

Grungni stayed long at his work. He knew his people, like the coal of the earth, became hardiest and shone brightest under extreme pressure – as the duardin say, peril is the father of success. He let his sons and daughters fend for themselves even when the scourge of Chaos saw every mountain kingdom toppled, every hold shattered and bled dry. Many of the survivors took to the skies, becoming far more successful in their endeavours than they had ever been as people of the mountain, but they bore scars in their souls from their race's long trauma. Grungni could never tell them how he had aided them in not helping them, for the grudge his people held against him ran too deep. In the end, the guilt he felt at turning a deaf ear to his people's desperate prayers overcame him. He passed his duties onto the Six Smiths that he had assembled to work alongside Sigmar, and from there he faded into legend, for it was beyond his ability to mend the wound in his mighty heart. Not even the most intrepid duardin explorers know where he is now.

The aelf gods Tyrion and Teclis had rejoiced to find Sigmar – and later his aelven allies in Azyr – after their long travels. For a time, the gods of light lent him the aid of their matchless minds, with Tyrion teaching the people of Azyr in military acumen, athletics and philosophy as his brother Teclis taught them the arts of science and magic. When the twin brothers found their own arcane studies leading them towards the fringes of reality, and more specifically the region where their nemesis Slaanesh could be found, they spent less and less time working with Sigmar, instead joining forces with Malerion to locate and perhaps even rescue the lost souls of the aelven race.

As for Malerion, the shadow king needed little coaxing to split away from Sigmar's Pantheon. He had laboured hard to create his gift to the God-King. The Gladitorium it was called, a many-layered arena of illusion so vital and convincing that the Azyrite warriors that trained there could fight at full tilt, even slaying one another in battle, only to walk out unharmed at day's end. Malerion knew well how valuable a gift this was. Seeing his duty as done, he was the first to distance himself from the pantheon in order to pursue his own agenda – reclaiming his aelven kin from their demise.

The alliance between Nagash and Sigmar had once been strong, for both gods recognised in one another a major force in the cosmos. Without the tireless work of Nagash's thralls, there was no way their respective civilisations could have grown so strong so fast. Those tribes that came upon empty towns and cities ready for settlement did not ask too many questions, though there were dark whispers of skeletal figures stalking in the night. But when the Realm of Death came under attack by Chaos forces, Nagash was quick to defend his holdings, and the building of the cities slowed to a crawl.

Seeing opportunity, Archaon had invaded Shyish by forcing tens of thousands of enslaved barbarians to fight to the death, drown in lakes of blood, or slay one another in ritual combat so they might reach the underworlds of Shyish en masse. Archaon led his Varanguard elite through the Gate of Bones, with them the skaven clans that gnawed their way into the Outerlands, and the daemon legions called forth by the Gaunt Summoners. This grand host proved unstoppable. Sigmar, ostensibly Nagash's ally, was nowhere to be seen.

Though the Great Necromancer Nagash ultimately forced many of these Chaos hosts from Shyish at great cost, his slow-burning anger at what he saw as Sigmar's betrayal was undiminished. This came to a head at the Allpoints, that interstitial zone in the aether-void where eight vast portals allowed the passage of entire armies to the heart of each Mortal Realm.

The Allpoints was a location key to the battles to come. Alongside Nagash's legions, Sigmar had sent a great host of his Azyrite armies to lay claim to it in the name of the Pantheon of Order. Yet the forces of Archaon were there already. There, even as the battle against Chaos hung in the balance before the great portal known as the Shyish arcway, the hosts of Nagash turned upon the Azyrite armies without warning. This betrayal was to send Sigmar into a rage. In his blind anger he took his warrior aspect, and battered a path across Shyish in search of retribution. He did not find it.

In leaving his warriors to the mercy of Archaon's blades, Sigmar set in motion events that would see the Allpoints conquered by Chaos entirely. Chaos threatened to consume the Mortal Realms. The fulcrum of destiny was nigh, cemented by the calamitous clash known as the Battle of Burning Skies.

THE BATTLE OF BURNING SKIES

Where one daemon infestation flourished, more sprang up nearby. Many mortal cultures turned their coats purely in order to survive. As years slid by, hundreds of Realmgates were claimed by the Dark Gods, opening new portals for the daemon hordes. Sigmar's wrath was thunderous.

The God-King Sigmar had long dwelt upon the nature of the Chaos Gods, and how best to defeat the daemon hosts and mortal worshippers that served them. In person he was unstoppable, glowing visibly with the magical energies of the Broken World that he had called his home for so long. When his innate power was focused through the ancient hammer Ghal Maraz, Sigmar could hurl back armies with a bellowed war cry or flatten mountains at a stroke. Yet the struggle against the Ruinous Powers already took place on a thousand battlefields. Even as he secured a lasting victory in one theatre of war, a dozen more fell to the ever-growing numbers of his enemies. Whilst manifest physically in the vastness of the Mortal Realms, he could no more coordinate an eightfold campaign than he could slay the gods themselves. Worse still, Sigmar's alliance had shown the first cracks in its foundations, for even the deities of Order had their own agendas and obsessions. Still the God-King fought on, alone when he had to.

The first daemonic incursions to make their mark upon the Mortal Realms saw cities, nations, even whole sub-realms fall to the onslaught of Chaos, for not even the greatest warrior nation could stand before the relentless attacks of the daemon hosts. Soon after disaster came revenge, for the armies of Azyr – largely untouched by Chaos invasion – were swift to reinforce their embattled kin. The greatest assemblages of Chaos were led by the daemon kings known as the Tetrarchs

of Ruin. Amongst the flames of Aqshy, Sigmar cast down the Exalted One, An'ggrath, and destroyed his armies of Khorne. He hunted the Great Unclean One Feculox to the City of Branches in Ghyran, following the trail of slime before dealing him a debilitating blow. With the God-King on the rampage, the Lord of Change known as Kiathanus eschewed a direct fight, but bound Sigmar in a loop of deception that would condemn him to search the same labyrinth for the rest of time. Through the steel of his warrior soul, Sigmar broke the spell.

Luxcious the Keeper attempted to seduce the God-King with worldly desires in the name of Slaanesh, but Sigmar's loathing for Chaos kept his will strong, and ultimately the Keeper of Secrets found herself withering in the face of his contempt. With each victory, however, Sigmar made a powerful enemy.

Archaon the Everchosen, Chaos warlord supreme and a conqueror of great vision, saw in these defeats an opportunity. Though it took long decades to achieve, he united the daemon

lords in a common cause. They had been beaten when apart, but together they would become unstoppable.

At the Battle of Burning Skies that alliance was to bear fruit. Upon Aqshy's endless Fireplains, each of the thwarted greater daemons met Sigmar in battle once more. United by the leadership of the grand marshal Archaon the Everchosen, the size of their hosts blackened the earth. The sorcerers in Archaon's employ had wrenched open a rift in the air itself – a portal to the Realm of Chaos through which entire armies of daemons could pass.

Against this daemonic alliance stood Sigmar and the twelve mortal tribes of Bellicos. The fiery nomads and barbarians that had stood against Chaos from the beginning had taken up arms once more and gathered behind the banner of their godly liege, Sigmar Heldenhammer. With them were oath-bound duardin, aelves in glittering armour, battle-hungry orruks, ranks of living dead and stranger things besides, for Sigmar had many allies of his own to call upon.

As the sonorous call of war-horns rang out in the hot, ash-choked air, the Battle of Burning Skies began. On raged the conflict, with no quarter asked nor given. Dusk led to dawn and to dusk again. So great was that clash of mortal, monster and daemon that the pyres of skulls raised to the glory of the Dark Gods were as mountains. So relentless was the carnage that for a year after the battle, the seers of the other realms saw a burning death's head when they looked to Aqshy in the night sky.

Though he did not fully commit his strength, Nagash summoned vast necromantic armies from the battlefield dead. Gorkamorka raged unstoppably, clubbing gaping holes in the oncoming hordes. The burning light of Teclis banished foes unnumbered, yet it was mighty Sigmar, always at the pantheon's fore, who turned the tide again and again.

Crowned by thunderheads, titanic in his rage, the God-King could not be stopped. Each swing of Ghal Maraz hit with meteoric force. The hurricanes that swirled from every impact swept foes aside in waves and banished daemons howling back to the Realm of Chaos.

Seven times Sigmar led the charge, his coalition crashing deep into the enemy ranks that passed beyond the horizon. Seven times they threw back their Chaos foes, reaping a great tally with each clash. On the eighth time, Sigmar shouted his earth-shaking war cry and charged forth to meet the four greater daemons he had defeated long ago – the Tetrarchs of Ruin.

Sigmar bore down on the daemonic commanders, a killing light blazing in his eyes. One after the other the Tetrarchs tasted Ghal Maraz's wrath, for in their monstrous pride, they still would not fight as one. But there remained another who would challenge the God-King, one whose cunning had undone entire worlds.

As Archaon the Everchosen rode to oppose Sigmar, the God-King hurled the hammer Ghal Maraz – for he knew of old that Archaon's blade, the Slayer of Kings, could kill even a god should its wielder get

close enough to strike. It was a mistake with consequences that would ripple through the centuries.

An illusion conjured by the Everchosen as he drew close had tricked Sigmar into throwing the warhammer not at Archaon as he intended, but into the very rent in the reality from which the daemon hordes had invaded.

The skies cracked and boomed as Ghal Maraz the Great Shatterer ploughed from one realm to the next, waves of destruction spreading in its wake. Through space and time Ghal Maraz hurtled on, leaving ripples in the aetheric void that would spread out through all the realms. Its passage left a series of cosmic fault lines that would one day be exploited in the name of conquest. The hammer eventually came to rest in distant Anvrok, attracted to the dense magic that flowed through the strange valleys that hung in Chamon's edgeward skies. But already it was hidden from Sigmar's sight. The God-King felt his heart grow cold with a sickening feeling of doubt as the calamity became clear to him.

Archaon's laughter was long and cruel that day, for bereft of that relic Sigmar was much diminished. The God-King despaired as the thunder of the Dark Gods' triumph rang in his ears. Without his mighty hammer, the battle was all but lost. He fought on, but his armies were slowly decimated.

Seven steps took Sigmar, striding as a giant;

None could stay him, nor stand before his wrath.

Again and again his foe-cracking hammer wrought crimson wreckage.

Yet Archaon, the Three-Eyed King, the World-Ender, had united the Four Foes of Old, the greatest of their kind.

Across the aeons Sigmar had vanquished each before, as well they remembered.

So great was that battle, it set the skies aflame;

So began the red dawn, the sword time, the wolf age.

- Excerpt from the Saga of Burning Skies

Near endless was that day's slaughter, so great that it ushered in a new era. Sigmar blamed his allies as much as himself for the ruinous defeat of that day, and channelled his anger into a series of desperate clashes. The disasters of the Nexus Wars, which culminated in the War of the Allpoints, ensued soon after.

The crowning victory of the Dark Gods came when Sigmar, seeing no other option, retreated to the Realm of Heavens and sealed the gates of Azyr behind him. Only by laying down the mantle of the warrior-god and embracing the sceptre of the godly monarch could he succeed.

For years Sigmar dwelt upon his losses, his rage simmering as he brooded on how best to retake the Mortal Realms. None could have foreseen then just how far he would go in order to succeed.

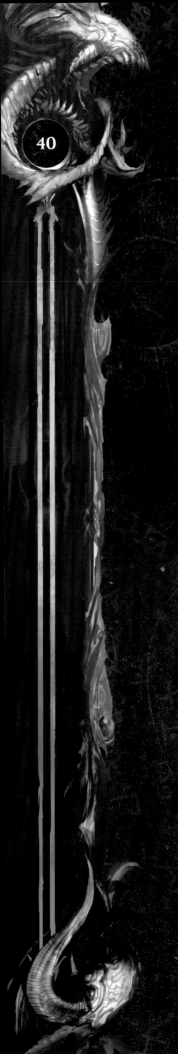

DOMINION OF CHAOS

Without Sigmar to hold it back, the scourge of Chaos spread across the Mortal Realms like an uncontrollable infection. As decades stretched into centuries, the lands themselves twisted into terrifying new vistas – and in places crumbled away entirely. To live in these terrible kingdoms was to know purgatory beyond tolerance.

The corrupting touch of the Dark Gods had seeped into the Mortal Realms through the tiniest cracks at first, exploiting the ambitions and passions of the common folk as well as those born into wealth and power. Over time these cracks widened, allowing trickles of Chaos energy to manifest in reality. Via tainted Realmgates and the haemorrhaging spells of incautious wizards, great rivers of daemonic filth gushed through. As more foolhardy mortals opened the way, these rivers joined together to become a flood. Those who had once claimed ownership over the lands paid the highest price, their legacies torn apart and swallowed by a rising tide of unrelenting anarchy.

It was not just the legions of the Dark Gods that invaded, not only the daemon, the traitor and the monstrous beast that wrought such violent change upon the prosperous nations. It was the raw stuff of Chaos itself. As the years trickled past, the domains of men became ever more like the surreal, hellish dimension from whence the daemons had emerged.

In many of those places infested by the crimson hosts of Khorne, the rivers that had once irrigated the lands ran red with gore, fast-flowing at the centre, clotted and stinking near the banks. Wherever there was little to no potable water left, the folk of those lands slowly died of thirst, or else gave in to their growing rage, lashing out in murderous, despairing frenzies and in so doing adding their own tributes to the skull throne. The most cruel of tyrants hoarded the water for themselves, the populace of the arid lands

forced to do their bidding in exchange for a handful of brackish liquid. The earth of entire nations became hard as brass, unyielding to the spade and the ploughshare, for the faithful of Khorne are sustained by the flesh and blood of their victims, and have only contempt for such luxuries as bread, fruit or crops. Where once wheat and maize had swayed in the summer breeze, the land was flattened, scorched and bled dry. Grand engines of destruction and skull-lined fortifications were raised upon the sites of shattered temples by corrupted, metal-masked duardin and the human work-gangs that toiled beneath their whips. As the decades slid past, the sovereign lands of the Blood God were wrought anew, a hundred empires of pain and misery founded on the bones of the pure.

The lands in the wake of those that scoured for signs of their errant god Slaanesh were perverted by the clawed feet and cloven hooves that danced upon them. The ground became fleshy, pallid and soft, splitting here and there to form tooth-lined fissures and chasms that yawned like open wounds. Obscene flowers pulsed soporific musk, rendering their prey lethargic before burying needle roots into the fallen. Maddening music filled the air, the trills and hoots of Slaaneshi daemons mingling with the maniacal piping and shouted blasphemies of their acolytes to linger long after the Seekers had passed. Those who heard such strains upon the breeze found the serpentine melodies winding into their minds, where they could not be dislodged. In time, they too found themselves dancing,

laughing manically and crying in despair all at once as they carved the symbols of Slaanesh into their bare flesh. These playthings begged to join the carnivals they had once avoided at all costs, and found themselves received with cruel pleasure.

The Plague God seeks always to expand his domain, to push the tendrils of his daemons' paradise into new territories the better to increase his power – for he had always sought to claim the lands as much as the people who populated them. His repugnant generosity was boundless. At first, the signs of supernatural plague were few in number, though they grew as steadily as a pimple swells to bursting point. Cattle were born covered in foul buboes, or with heads at either end of their bodies which vomited noxious fluids. Entire tribes would rot from the inside out, melt away into slurry in their sleep or swell to become grotesquely obese, bloating horribly with each morsel they consumed. Arable fields and bluebell woods in which lovers had once strolled became noisome swamps, each filled with grasping, spit-slick pseudopods that snatched the unwary under the surface.

In the places closest to the corrupted Realmgates that led to Nurgle's realm, poisonous miasmas and waves of raw toxicity rippled across the lands. Even the most beautiful citadels and towers crumbled under the slow but unstoppable onslaught, their foundations undermined by the questing roots of diseased plants, and stinking puddles of slop that grew with each downpour of oily, infected rain.

Where the lands under Nurgle's baleful influence were fecund and overgrown, those claimed by the Horned Rat were dusty wastelands where the ash of fallen empires was carried on the breeze. The scars of pestilence dug deep; in places not even a single blade of grass could be found that was not yellowed and gnawed by vermin. Dagger-toothed rats and twisted insects scurried through the ribcages of those that had starved to death; even those who somehow clung to life were skeletally thin and eternally ravenous, cursed never to be sated in their hunger even should they fight their way to the table of a noble's feast. Everywhere skaven of all sizes scampered, hunted and roared in triumph; those that worshipped them as gods were allowed to live for the sake of amusement, but even they were put to death or used as fodder for hideous experiments before long.

Most surreal of all were those domains claimed by Tzeentch. Without Sigmar to bind the lands under the rule of Order, the mages that worshipped the Architect of Fate had wrought dramatic and hallucinogenic change wherever their spells were unleashed. Rock formations and even entire mountain ranges were reshaped into mazes of mirror-like crystal that refracted every doubt and fear, and brought the nightmares of the viewer to life. At dusk, sky-rays of every hue and size screamed the last words of those mortals they had chased down and slashed apart, feeding on life energy as a flock of swallows feeds on the insects at the day's end. The glittering fronds of sentient plants snared the thoughts of those who sought to escape these lands, stealing their intent and sending them staggering back into the hellscape. Those who fell under the shadow of the Gaunt

Summoners' Silver Towers found themselves plucked from reality and thrust into a labyrinth of ever-escalating terror, their lives begun anew as puppets for the dark amusement of their captors.

Over it all reigned the Three-Eyed King, Archaon, he whose sadistic genius had brought about the death of worlds. His Varanguard agents loomed at the side of almost every tyrant and dark king in the lands. Perhaps there was some grand design behind his great work, his orchestration of the downfall of the Mortal Realms and the slaughter and enslavement of its peoples. But even to those who had somehow escaped or endured the curse of Chaos – to those men and women still eking out a semblance of a normal life – there was but one immortal truth: Chaos had come, and it had claimed a victory that could never be undone.

The talons of Chaos dug hard into the peoples of the Mortal Realms. In every land, across every generation, those who had grown strong under the rule of Sigmar's Pantheon found themselves cast into the dirt to grovel under the iron heels of their oppressors. As easy as it was to see the terrors inflicted upon the people as gross misfortune, or as the act of a malevolent outside force upon an innocent populace, the wise knew that was not the case at all. Here was the darkness in the hearts of every man and woman made manifest, the nightmare lurking within every soul given form and set against the people they once called kin. For the Chaos Gods were formed of the hopes, lusts, fears and urges of mortal souls. Their worshippers too were people; those who not only turned from their own kind, but who sold themselves to eldritch forces so they might gain instead of suffer from the onslaught.

Amongst the nations of men were those who fought back with blade, spear, hammer, even tooth and nail, refusing to give in. Most ended their lives impaled, hung as grisly adornments, or beheaded in the dirt, their pike-mounted skulls a warning to those who would rebel against their masters. The most tenacious of these warriors, those that spat in the face of Chaos even unto death, would one day meet a different fate – but for many decades these doomed heroes were visited by the worst punishments of all.

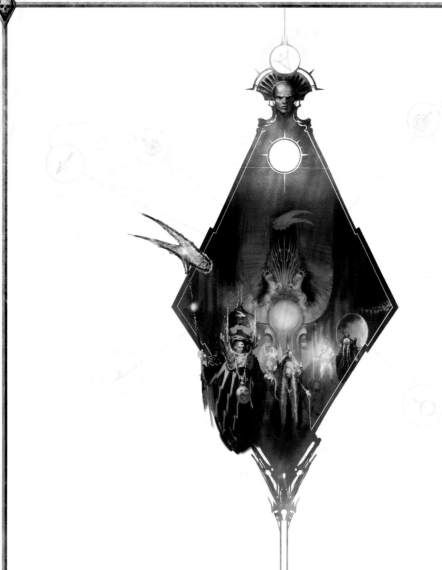

THE AGE OF SIGMAR

Sigmar's vengeance against the Chaos Gods was slow in coming, but when it arrived, it did so with epoch-shattering fury. From the threshold of disaster had Sigmar snatched those champions strong enough to defy Chaos, and in Azyr he had remade them. One by one these heroic souls were reforged as warriors of storm-wrought fury. The first amongst them had to endure centuries of anticipation, meditation and training, readying for a moment of revenge that seemed never to come. Painstakingly had Sigmar worked to create his new armies, and with the greatest artifice had Grungni laboured to forge the divine lightning that would carry them.

On the day of reckoning, the skies of every realm were lit by Sigmar's Tempest. Down from the heavens came the chambers of the Stormcast Eternals, warrior hosts borne within each blast of lightning. Columns of heavenly energy slammed into the bloodstained earth of the ravaged Mortal Realms. They each struck near the long-sealed Gates of Azyr, for those barred portals could not be opened from one side alone – the Reforged warriors of Sigmar would have to cast them open from without as well as within. Each bolt of celestial force sent to the Mortal Realms faded in a glow of azure to reveal a retinue of champions, each clad in shining battle plate.

Straight into battle charged the Stormhosts, joyous war cries upon their lips. The Long Wait was over. These warriors had been made not to negotiate or build, but to slay those with evil in their hearts. They proved perfectly suited to the task. The lightning hosts had been hurled by Sigmar's hand into the most desolate of lands, the better to strike at the architects of their ruin. Sigmarite hammers and swords clashed against ensorcelled blades and axes carved with dread runes – and for the first time in living memory, the hordes of Chaos knew fear.

Time and time again the Stormhosts hurled back the minions of the Dark Gods. Each Realmgate they flung open saw the armies of Azyr march forth, not only reinforcing the chambers of the Stormcast Eternals but consolidating and building upon those lands they had emancipated. As the new era dawned, fortified cities and civilisations were built upon foundations of broken bone and shattered keeps from the Age of Myth.

The fate of the Mortal Realms had been changed forever more. Together, Sigmar and Grungni had crafted an army of miracles, a host of armoured angels created from the souls of the finest men and women the Mortal Realms could provide. Their devotion, their singular vision, had been so powerful it had proven enough to challenge the dominion of the Dark Gods.

Only later did the cost of that godly ambition become clear.

THE TEMPEST BREAKS

46

The first of the God-King's hosts, the Hammers of Sigmar, manifested upon the Brimstone Peninsula in the south of the Great Parch. There began a deadly rivalry between the immortal warriors of the God-King and the flesh-eating maniacs of Khorne.

By the time Sigmar's Tempest gathered over Aqshy's Great Parch, the continent was all but lost. Even the warrior smiths of the Direbrand Tribe, most redoubtable of all the Flamescar Plateau's kindreds, had their defiance finally broken at Scorched Keep. Only scattered remnants of the once-great societies were left. They fought or fled each day before an ever-growing throng of Korghos Khul's followers – known as the Goretide for their habit of turning the lands red in their path. Those who once prayed for deliverance had given up hope, for even should their prayers somehow be answered, the people of those lands were too broken in body and spirit to be worth saving.

That salvation came nonetheless. Vandus Hammerhand – formerly Vendell Blackfist of the Direbrand Tribe – was the first to lead the Stormcast Eternals to battle. The golden armour of the Hammers of Sigmar gleamed as heavenly energies bore them to war. Soon enough, that burnished sigmarite was splashed with hot blood.

The Hammers of Sigmar were not alone in taking the war to the Bloodbound servants of Khorne; helping forge their beachhead upon the Brimstone Peninsula were the Anvils of the Heldenhammer, the Lions of Sigmar and the Celestial Vindicators, who were to become close allies over the coming years. Vandus' fellow Lord-Celestant, Jactos Goldenmane, paid dearly for his headlong assault upon Khul's warbands, meeting his end upon the blade of Khul's reality-splitting axe. His sacrifice was not in vain.

The pincer attack that Vandus coordinated with his Lord-Relictor, Ionus Cryptborn, saw Khul's brass towers torn down. The Bloodbound warlord himself was brought to bay atop the pyramid of skulls he had raised to Khorne's glory. On the cusp of winning his ascension to the rank of Daemon Prince by using Jactos Goldenmane's decapitated head as a capstone, Khul found he could not refuse Vandus' challenge to single combat. Khorne has only contempt for cowards, after all.

The Lord-Celestant was on the brink of death at Khul's hand for the second time – for Khul was strong, and had slaughtered the Direbrands long ago. Vandus called upon Sigmar's lightning to strike hard at the Gate of Wrath, that dread portal his nemesis was using to summon his daemonic allies. Sigmar heard his plea that day. A great skybolt blasted down, tearing apart the Gate and the Red Pyramid alike. Without recourse to his daemon hosts, and with the heart of his Bloodbound armies torn out, Khul was forced to cede the Brimstone Peninsula to the Stormcast Eternals.

THE QUEST FOR GHAL MARAZ

In Chamon's Hanging Valleys, the Celestial Vindicators – most vengeful of all Sigmar's hosts – sought signs of the God-King's ancient ally, Grungni. They found not duardin in the deserted mountains of Anvrok, but the taint of the Tzeentch-worshipping forces that had driven them away and caused the land to be in thrall to the corrupted godbeast Argentine. There, under the skyborne glow of the silver drake's fires, lay the ruins of the once-great metropolis Elixia.

At the heart of that tumbled city was a dread fortress of impossible scale, and Thostos Bladestorm, Lord-Celestant of the Celestial Vindicators, was quick to attack. His impetuous assault led him to disaster. After wrenching a breach in the walls of the Eldritch Fortress, he was blasted by the change-magic of the sorcerer Ephryx, turned to living metal, and slain. Yet he was reforged in glory. Through that breach Thostos had witnessed the light of a divine artefact – nothing less than Sigmar's lost hammer, Ghal Maraz the Skull-Splitter.

So it was that both Vandus and Thostos were sent by the God-King himself to reclaim that most divine of artefacts. At the head of the Heldenhammer Crusade they returned to Anvrok, only to find the fortress wrenched from the lands by Chaos magic and transported to a crucible-like crater of molten metal heated by Argentine, a shimmering Tzeentchian godbeast that coiled in the skies high above. The Stormcast Eternals fought through embittered ghosts, Slaves to Darkness and ambushing skaven that scurried out from gnawholes in reality, but only won through by convincing Dracothion himself to intervene in order to fight the drake Argentine. Whilst the sky burned above, they reached the Eldritch Fortress. There they found not only Ephryx but also Korghos Khul awaiting them – he too was an agent of the gods, and hungry for revenge. Once more Vandus matched wits against his nemesis, and once more Khul was overcome, this time by his own rage. The Lord-Celestants fought on through daemons and warlords until they saw the divine light of Ghal Maraz. The magic of Sigmar's hammer was being used to spirit the Eldritch Fortress from Chamon into the Realm of Chaos.

Vandus, given time by Thostos Bladestorm's headlong assault, took up Ghal Maraz and smote the Tzeentchian lords that sought to pervert its power.

That hammer, returned to Azyr against impossible odds, was presented in great ceremony to Sigmar. The God-King gave it the next day to another, for the purpose of a weapon is to be wielded, not be used as a symbol of rulership. Though none knew it, Sigmar had long ago created the hand that would bear it in his name. From a hidden chamber was summoned the Celestant-Prime, first and most puissant of all Stormcast Eternals. Finally revealed, he was given the Great Shatterer, and entrusted with a most sacred duty – to lead the war against the scions of the Dark Gods.

'This night we ride the storm. This night we smite the savage and the daemon. This night, we fling open gates long closed.

The fallen will be avenged a hundredfold, and the Dark Gods themselves will feel our fury.

This night, brothers, we bring war!'

- Vandus Hammerhand, Lord-Celestant of the Hammers of Sigmar, before the invasion of the Brimstone Peninsula

WAR UNBOUND

In loosening the stranglehold the Dark Gods had upon the Mortal Realms, Sigmar opened a new chapter in the history of mankind. Old allies and former nemeses alike rejoined the fight, invigorated by the thrill of war and conquest – or by a much-needed breath of hope.

The successes of the Stormcast Eternals in Aqshy and Chamon were remarkable indeed, but perhaps more so were the actions of the Hallowed Knights in Ghyran. Here, that purest of all Stormhosts went to war against the scions of Nurgle that were suffocating the Jade Kingdoms. Their duty was to find Alarielle the Everqueen, and to convince her that the time was right to put aside despair and strike back against the dominion of Chaos. For her part, Alarielle did not wish to be found, for she was lost in the winter of her desolation, and wished only to hide away. There were those amongst her legions, however, who would see the pall of Chaos lifted from Ghyran – foremost amongst them the Lady of Vines, a Branchwraith grown from Alarielle's own severed right hand.

The first Stormcast strike in Ghyran saw the Hallowed Knights attempt to seize the Gates of Dawn from the forces of the Plague God. They took on seven Great Unclean Ones in the process, and would have been doomed but for the fact the Stormcast leader, Lord Gardus, ventured into the noxious Garden of Nurgle in order to lure the titanic daemon Bolathrax away from his men. Such was Gardus' purity that he made it out of the garden alive, if forever changed. The Lady of Vines saw him reunited with his kin, in doing so establishing an alliance between Stormhost and Sylvaneth that persists to this day.

Armed with knowledge he had gathered during his arduous exile in the Garden of Nurgle, Lord Gardus led the Stormcast Eternals to Alarielle.

In reaching the Everqueen's haven, the Lord-Celestant and his Hallowed Knights succeeded where the forces of Nurgle had failed. The invaders had long searched in vain, but those with the taint of Chaos upon their souls could not even perceive the Everqueen's sacred retreat of Athelwyrd. However, as ill fortune would have it, the Stormcast Eternals had inadvertently led the armies of Nurgle straight to their quarry – for the skaven spies and beastmen trackers of the Plague God's forces were tenacious. Into the once pure River Vitalis ventured the armies of Stormcast and Chaos worshipper alike, and battle was joined in the other-world beneath. Leading the Nurgle hordes were the Plague God's favoured generals – amongst them Torglug the Despised, former guardian of the Lifewells, and the diseased mutant triplets known as the Glottkin.

As her enemies breached her sacred stronghold, Alarielle faced the crisis she had long avoided. She could hide no more from the fate of her realm. The Everqueen fought hard for her refuge, but with the rains of Nurgle's Deluge filling the valley, she had no option but to flee. In her despair, she took the form of a gestating seed, and was borne from Athelwyrd by the Lady of Vines. Seeking to make amends, the Hallowed Knights formed her escort. The Sylvaneth and Stormcast Eternals fled with the armies of Nurgle hard upon their heels. The running battle that followed saw many gruelling days and nights of fighting, crossing frozen seas, living glaciers and foetid forests.

The allies' numbers dwindled with each engagement. Only when the Celestant-Prime descended in a storm of energy did the Stormcast and Sylvaneth forces find the flames of their defiance blazing anew.

Torglug the Despised was laid low when the Celestant-Prime struck him with Ghal Maraz. In that moment, the part of his soul that was still pure was snatched from his rotting body and taken up to Azyr. There he was reforged into the winged Knight-Venator known as Tornus the Redeemed. He was to be the first of a new breed of warrior – those whose essence still had a glimmer of valour within them. Here was hope that even corrupted souls may be reborn in glory by the power of Sigmar.

The Chaos Gods looked in anger upon this new force in the Mortal Realms, this new challenge to their rapacious intent to claim or devour every land and kingdom they could find. In this they were not alone. Archaon the Everchosen, the Three-Eyed King, architect of a thousand wars and mastermind behind the fall of the world-that-was, saw the threat of the Stormcast Eternals clearer than any other.

The Storm of Sigmar represented the first real challenge to the stranglehold of the Chaos Gods. Though Khorne's followers had been struck hard, the Blood God was greatly pleased by the eruption of battle and strife across the cosmos. He hungered only for blood, no matter its provenance. Archaon, meanwhile, saw a great deal of opportunity for his own ambitions in the new era.

Before he put his plans into motion, Archaon sought a magical boon that would ease his path to victory. He knew that inside the hollow world of Golgeth was a land so redolent with transmutative energies that time itself flowed in anarchic eddies. There, atop the peak known as Mount Kronus, was a temple to the Oracle Kiathanus, the Lord of Change that had matched its powers against Sigmar at the Battle of Burning Skies. By gathering the syllables of its true name, Archaon sought to bind the

daemon into his service as his personal soothsayer. Vandus Hammerhand and his warriors, sent by Sigmar, rode to stop him – and met their doom.

Atop the peak the generals duelled, but the Lord-Celestant could not truly hope to match Archaon. Vandus was bodily ripped apart by Archaon's fabled daemon sword, the Slayer of Kings. His essence returned to Azyr, but such was the violence of his death it would be long years before he could be properly reforged.

Archaon led his Varanguard in the slaughter. In a single bloody day, every one of the Hammerhands was slain. Archaon bound the Oracle Kiathanus into the form of a bracelet, and in doing so partook of the daemon's knowledge. Even in the face of Sigmar's finest, the Everchosen had proven all but unstoppable. But the Hammerhands' sacrifice did not go unnoticed. Their deaths roused wise Dracothion to action, and saw the Extremis Chambers opened in Azyr for the first time.

THE GODBEASTS ARISE

Many would-be conquerors yearn to rule over neighbouring kingdoms, or even to subjugate entire civilisations, but only the Everchosen sought to bind every realm and domain to his command. To break open even Azyr itself, he aimed to enslave zodiacal beasts of terrifying size to his cause.

Sigmar's grand strategy seemed to be working. In several Mortal Realms his warriors had consolidated their early gains. Some had even started to build cities around those vital Realmgates they had seized. Though each was but an island of Order in a sea of mayhem, they were growing fast. But in putting all his hope, all his efforts, into his great crusade, Sigmar had nearly emptied the Heavens. With the Stormhosts abroad in the Mortal Realms and the free armies of Azyr fighting in support, the walls of Azyr were largely denuded.

Herein lay an unprecedented opportunity for Sigmar's enemies to land a telling blow. It was Archaon's intent to invade Azyr itself, that realm so long barred to the hordes of Chaos, even as his chosen champions crushed the warriors of Sigmar's Tempest into the dirt upon the battlefields of the realms. To breach the walls of the Realm of Heavens, he intended not just to summon chosen warriors to his banner, but also to bind titanic beasts – mythical terrors that could each rival the power of a deity – to his will.

Near the Realm's Edge of Aqshy lay the Ashlands, a region of islands floating on an acidic sea. Above them hovered the Land of the Chained Sun, a floating crescent-shaped isle bound to the lands below by titanic chains. It was lit by the godbeast Ignax, the Solar Drake, whose fire burned so bright that many on the lands below thought her to be a sun.

She too was chained, bound to the crescent isle by Grungni himself so that the duardin below might live in eternal illumination and thereby escape the ghoul-things that prowled the humid night. It was Archaon's intent to break those huge god-chains, and to corrupt Ignax's mind so that she would fight at his behest.

Archaon sent two of his champions to pave the way for his conquest. Appearing from a cloud of flies, the maggoth-rider Bloab Rotspawned spread a vitality-sapping plague across the Ashlands. The disease was designed to subdue the native populace and any warriors hoping to defend the region. Ultimately, however, the Nurgle sorcerer failed in his mission, his plagues burning away when Lord-Relictor Ionus Cryptborn and Lord-Celestant Victrian Cyrocco of the Tempest Lords harnessed the fiery rage of the daemon Skarbrand against him. In fleeing to Ghyran, Bloab instead spread his plagues to new lands – the Scabrous Sprawl.

Meanwhile the mighty lord Korghos Khul, second of Archaon's emissaries, took his armies to the Orb Infernia. This was a cadaverous once-world that hung above the Ashlands, upon which four Chaos nations vied for supremacy. Khul aimed to unite these warring factions and, in doing so, amass a world-conquering army.

Khul first took his axe to the warhosts of the Daemon Prince Skinskein. By feigning weakness in a duel with the Khornate lord, Khul found an opening – with a blow from his enchanted axe, he broke the towering fiend's power. The Khornate legions bowed to him as their new leader, and with sheer force of will and unremitting violence Khul united the daemon hosts of the Orb. Next, he struck against the Seraphon that had long harried that world, and then against the denizens of the Ashlands below. When Khul's invasion reached the Land of the Chained Sun, Archaon's long-running scheme came to fruition. There the Fyreslayers of that region found themselves caught between the heavy cavalry of Archaon's Varanguard and the daemons under the banner of Khul. They fought hard, but were already doomed to defeat.

In desperation, the Runefather of the Austarg lodge allowed his hot-blooded sons to make a grand sacrifice. Climbing Ignax's titanic chains upon their Magmadroth steeds, they hammered an ancient Rune of Binding into the Solar Drake's hide, even as their flesh melted away. Ignorant of their sabotage, Archaon corrupted the godbeast's mind and caused her to break her bonds by plunging the Slayer of Kings into her vast cranium. With his goal complete, Archaon made for the Allpoints. He knew not that another's mark had already been made upon his victory.

'Gather to me, children,' said the half-crone. The wizened side of her face puckered as she was jostled by the traders bustling behind. 'Gather and learn. This great ribbed vault, this pillared cathedral of trade and opportunity, once held the heart of a giant.'

The swamp urchins, each of whom bore his or her own strange disfigurement, feigned indifference. But none of them left. The child-teller continued.

'He was called Behemat, the World Titan. He walked this land even before Sigmar the Thunderer brought light to the Scabrous Sprawl.' The hag bunched her hands, knuckles popping. 'His fists were mountains, and his bald head touched the sky.'

One of the children snorted in disbelief and picked his nose, only to be elbowed sharply in the ribs by his little sister.

'When he opened his cave-like maw, out from his throat crawled the fathers of the Swamp Tribes,' continued the half-crone, gesturing at a gargant lumbering drunkenly through the eastern halls. 'It was the Giant King Brodd that took the monolith from the Temple of Tor Crania,' at this, she pointed at a distant hill, 'and he that struck down the Umbilicus pillar leading to the Great Green Torc. But why?'

'To stop the Three-Eyed King,' said the girl reverently, eyes wide in her rot-smudged face. 'That's right, my sweet,' crooned the hag. 'The Everchosen wanted to enslave Behemat with the Torc as a chain-collar, for he wanted to conquer all. He sent Bloab, the Lord of Swarms, to sap the energy of Behemat as he slept, infecting him with an insect-borne plague. But he had reckoned without the Hosts of the Tempest.'

'The Storm Kings!' shouted one of the urchins, smiting the air with an imaginary hammer. The crone grinned, exposing a rotten graveyard of brown teeth. 'Yes, greenling. Down they came from the skies, with lightning in their eyes and thunder in their fists. The Stormhosts drove back Bloab and his maggoth even as Behemat awoke. They were too late – the World Titan was already infected. It was the Knights Excelsior that dealt the deathblow, summoning Sigmar's Great Bolts to blast Behemat's mind apart,' the half-crone flicked the nose-picking urchin hard upon the forehead, 'and deny the Three-Eyed King his prize. He fell down dead. Time claimed his life, as it claims all of us.'

Black spots of rain began to fall from the Torc, and the children slunk away. The crone smiled, then coughed wetly as she shuffled on, a fat fly crawling from her bloodied lips.

GATES ARE LOST AND HELD

The grand invasions of Chaos that had seen so much of the Mortal Realms conquered owed much to the strange island of reality known as the Allpoints. Through its mighty portals marched armies of world-breaking size. Both Archaon and Sigmar knew it was key to any lasting victory.

The arterial Realmgates that led from the Eight Realms to the Allpoints – or the Eightpoints, as it had been known since Archaon's conquest of that place – were called arcways. Each was protected by a fortress known as an All-gate. Here was war writ large, a struggle for ascendancy that would forever recast the Mortal Realms and the balance of power amongst them.

Across eight vital battlefields within the Mortal Realms, war raged on the far side of the arcway portals as the Stormcast

Eternals and their allies sought to win lasting supremacy. The victors at each gate would travel through the arcways to reinforce their allies at the Eightpoints, under the shadow of the Varanspire. If fate was with them, they could align the gate's innate magic so that only they and their kin could pass through it from then on.

At the Mercurial Gate of Chamon, Thostos Bladestorm and the Celestial Vindicators attacked the impregnable Ironholds from below, tunnelling under their serried

walls using the lava-magic of their Fyreslayer allies. There Archaon himself rode his monstrous steed Dorghar into the fray. Thostos wounded the Chaos warlord in a duel, only to be ripped apart and devoured by Dorghar, never to return.

In Aqshy, the Brimfire Gate was closed to the scions of Chaos. Archaon unleashed Ignax the Solar Drake, but the Fyreslayers triggered the secret Rune of Binding that they had hammered into the godbeast's hide, turning Archaon's slave into a deadly

enemy at the moment of his triumph. Vandus Hammerhand fought the exiled Bloodthirster Skarbrand as the forces of the Blood God matched their might against the Stormcast Eternals and their allies, but through valour and strength Vandus emerged triumphant. That realm still belonged to Khorne, but the Blood God suffered a major defeat in failing to control that vital gate.

Nurgle, too, found his prize snatched from his clawed grip at the last. In Ghyran, the sacrifice of the Hallowed Knights won the beleaguered Sylvaneth a chance to rally. From the brink of disaster, Alarielle's mood turned from a winter of despondency to the rage of a spring tempest. Resurgent, she cast down Nurgle's champions – the Brothers Glott – and her crusade began in earnest.

In Shyish, the Endgate remained in Archaon's hands. Though the Anvils of the Heldenhammer believed they had re-established an alliance with Nagash, history repeated itself when the Great Necromancer forsook Sigmar's armies in their time of need. The Realm of Light had seen wars beyond counting, but no aid came from there to the Eightpoints. The strange denizens of Hysh had their own dire wars to contend with.

Ulgu, the Realm of Shadow, was difficult to perceive as ever. Of whether Malerion and Morathi had won their own long war against the forces of Chaos, there came no word. In Ghur, the Realm of Beasts, the forces of Destruction and Chaos clashed over the Mawgate – no normal portal, but the yawning gullet of a segmented, crawling godbeast

known as Fangathrak. As the violence of the Megaboss Gordrakk's orruk attack escalated, Fangathrak was battered, hewn and unchained from the fetters with which Archaon sought to control it. When the dust settled over a corpse-strewn wasteland, the gate remained unclaimed.

Whilst gods, tyrants and lords of fate consolidated their gains and planned their next moves, the cosmos aligned to the new order that Sigmar had brought. In lands broken free of the shackles of Chaos, new civilisations rose from the ashes like phoenixes given fresh life by the flames of their demise. The forges of the Sigmarabulum rang loud with the energies of reforging, for Sigmar did not rest idly. The true battles for control of the realms were only just beginning…

THE SEEDS OF HOPE

The Realmgate Wars had seen the choke-hold that Chaos had established broken apart in a hundred war-torn kingdoms. Sigmar and his pantheon wasted no time in raising new cities, each as much a statement of defiance as a practical power-base around which to shore up the war effort.

From prophecy-rich Excelsis in the Realm of Beasts, to volcanic Vindicarum in the Realm of Metal, the cities of Order were many and varied. Most took decades to build, growing slowly from fortified encampments to huge and bustling hubs of civilisation. There were three cities that sprung up far more swiftly, however, known as the Seeds of Hope.

In the Realm of Life, with the Season of War burgeoning, the forces of Order sought to follow their victory at the Genesis Gate with swift and purposeful construction. Much of the realm still festered beneath Grandfather Nurgle's rancid touch, but with the Everqueen's armies driving the pestilent hordes back every day, the forces of Order were filled with confidence.

It was Alarielle herself who raised the first of the Seeds of Hope. In the Jade Kingdom of Thyria, the Everqueen defeated the skaven swarms of Clan Morbidus and drove them from the Hollow Forest. Once a trackless ocean of vibrant flora, this immense woodland had come by its bleak name after the Clans Pestilens gnawed away its roots and left it to desiccate and die. The Everqueen restored it to life, her purifying energies flowing through the rattling husks of ghost-elms and sighing willows. Amidst the reborn woodlands, Alarielle raised a mighty city through the power of natural magic. Her song soared high and lilting as it brought forth bulwarks of ironoak and bedrock. Towers and fortifications she fashioned from thorn-studded vines and seams of song-forged metal.

For fourteen days and nights, the ground shuddered and the forests swayed as Alarielle went about her work. Eventually, a new city of prodigious size stood atop the plateau, a mighty fastness to watch over the Hollow Forest. Alarielle knew that her children were too fey and mercurial to be confined as the garrison for such a place. Instead she offered it to her mortal allies, a place of safety to call their own in exchange for watching over the Everqueen's wondrous forest. Though some feared this city of plant and stone, many accepted Alarielle's offer and became wardens of the Living City.

The second of the Seeds of Hope could not have been more different from the first. Led by the visionary architect Valius Maliti, a collective of artisans and labourers poured through the Festermere Realmgate into Greywater Reach, ready to build a fastness against the powers of Chaos. Guarded by the Anvils of the Heldenhammer, the spellcraft of the Eldritch Council and many regiments of Freeguild soldiery, the work began in earnest.

Throughout the Mortal Realms existed concentrations of raw magic, coalesced into disparate substances known collectively as realmstone. Whether the burning coals of primordial anger found in Aqshy, the meteoric stardust of Azyr, or the steaming, jade-hued ice found in Ghyran, realmstone had always been seen as volatile. It was Valius Maliti who first made the intuitive leap of suggesting that its hazardous manifestations could be used as a source of power. Between the architect's

genius, the boundless wisdom of the aelven enchanters, and the pragmatic skill of the Ironweld engineers, history was made in Greywater Reach as a deposit of Ghyranite realmstone was harnessed with arcane machinery.

Suddenly, the forces of Order had all the power they needed and more. The bog-grot tribes that had harassed their stockades were driven back by crackling war machines. The swamp waters were drained away in a matter of days, and the land baked to hardened clay. Walls rose. Towers spiralled upward. Trees were felled by the hundred, and the region's resources were plundered to fuel the lightning-fast growth of the Greywater Fastness. The children of Alarielle looked on in horror at this rapacious industry, some even coming to blows with their erstwhile allies in their sorrow and anger. Yet still the Fastness rose, a towering stronghold of ironclad walls, roaring furnaces, sorcerous wards and lowering cannon batteries that dominated the region all around.

The third of the Seeds of Hope was the Phoenicium. Before it became a symbol of rebirth, the Phoenicium was a vast and sprawling ruin that dated back to the Age of Myth. Ancient and enigmatic, it sat at the foot of the tree-like Arborean Mountain, its structures haunted by strange entities and inhabited by bands of brigands and wanderers. During the early stages of the Chaos invasion, a fierce battle was fought amidst the nameless ruins and a terrible catastrophe engulfed everyone involved. Whether by some mighty spell or weapon, the wooden slopes of the Arborean Mountain were torn open, and an oozing tidal wave of sap was released. The sap-tide rolled inexorably down upon the nameless citadel, immersing it entirely before setting as a glacier of amber. So was the nameless citadel preserved, like some prehistoric insect, for hundreds of years. Perhaps it could have stayed that way forever, untouched by both the corrupting power of Nurgle and the healing magic of Alarielle, but such was not the ruined city's fate.

It was the Anointed of the Phoenix Temple who found the preserved ruins, after their defeat of a Rotbringer host at the Dreamloss Realmgate. Battered but victorious, the aelves marvelled in silence at the incredible spectacle before them. It was then that their Flamespyre and Frostheart Phoenixes took to the air, crying out to one another as they began a mystic aerial dance. Back and forth the magical creatures flew, sorcerous fires and whirling cold trailing across the encased ruins.

Slowly, impossibly, the amber began to melt away, becoming a beautiful golden mist that rolled out to surround the ruins. Though it took many hours, and the Phoenixes were exhausted by the time they were done, the nameless ruins were fully revealed, empty and ready to be reclaimed.

Aided by the children of Alarielle, Sigmar's Stormcast Eternals and many of the Azyrite peoples, the Phoenix Temple resettled the nameless city and raised it up from the twilight limbo in which it had languished for so long. So did it become the Phoenicium, a city where the inner ruins and deep tunnels still harboured many strange secrets, and whose borders were veiled in a magical golden mist.

The Seeds of Hope had been planted, and though each was different to its counterparts, all three cities were enclaves of civilisation amidst the war-torn bedlam of the Realm of Life. They swiftly became symbols of what the forces of Order could achieve in spite of the Dark Gods' malice.

In founding the Seeds of Hope, however, Sigmar and Alarielle had overreached themselves. Where most of the new cities of Order were built steadily, carefully, under the watchful eye of countless Stormcast Eternals, this trio of enclaves had risen with breathtaking speed. Each was isolated, so far away from the others that the cities might as well have been in different realms. Though they could be reached by forces moving through Realmgates from Azyr, the lands around the cities were still corrupted by the touch of Chaos and swarming with myriad foes. Those dwelling within the Seeds of Hope found themselves fighting daily to repel attacks not only from the servants of Chaos, but from other powers also.

These new cities were a statement of intent, symbolic of a new order. They were enough to kindle the flame of hope in the hearts of some, and of jealousy in others. The storied annals of their histories were to be stained red with blood over and over again in the coming years.

GREYWATER FASTNESS

LIGHT IN THE DARKNESS

Though the lands remained in the grip of Chaos, Stormcast Eternals raised towering Stormkeeps to watch over key Realmgates, whilst processions of the faithful and arcane cleansed the land through their blessed blood and magical skill. The greatest of all the new cities was Hammerhal.

Amongst the cities built by the forces of Order following the Realmgate Wars, none was greater than Hammerhal, the Twin-tailed City. The Cities of Sigmar – as they came to be known – were mostly built around fortified Realmgates, claimed initially by chambers of Stormcast Eternals.

It was not uncommon for the cities to be named to honour those immortal heroes. Thus was Hammerhal originally named for those Hammers of Sigmar who claimed the Stormrift Realmgate. To ensure their people's safety, Sigmar's warriors crushed the vast orruk tribes that had long launched savage attacks through the Realmgate. The greenskins were purged in both Aqshy and Ghyran for leagues around that mystic portal. Amongst the ashes of the greenskins' territories the Stormcasts raised the first foundations of what gradually grew into a singularly spectacular city.

Hammerhal is named the Twin-tailed City because, to all intents and purposes, it is two metropolises ruled as one. The great city sprawls out on both sides of the Realmgate, occupying both the Ashlands of the Realm of Fire and the Jade Kingdom of Verdia in the Realm of Life.

Hammerhal Aqsha is a harsh and heavily fortified place, its myriad banners and pennants dancing on hot, angry winds. The Ironweld Arsenal maintain a strong presence amongst Hammerhal Aqsha's towering bastions and batteries. Their genius maintains the city's crackling lightning shield and keeps its mobile forts lumbering ever outward to extend Hammerhal's boundaries, while the self-flagellating throngs of the Devoted cleanse the hard lands around the city.

Hammerhal Ghyra is a stronghold of aelf-kind, though it houses many other Free Peoples besides. To hold back the aggressively exuberant growth of the Realm of Life, this side of the city channels lava through the Realmgate from Hammerhal Aqsha. The molten rock flows along carefully cut trenches and forms a wall of fire that protects the city's celestial spires and golden domes. In return, a steady supply of water and food flows through the Realmgate from Hammerhal Ghyra, the endless abundance keeping its Aqshian districts fed.

Hammerhal is governed by a Grand Conclave of lords chosen from amongst the best and brightest of Azyrheim. It is defended by countless armies – including no less than twelve chambers of Stormcast Eternals. Without doubt it is the spiritual capital of the Cities of Sigmar and the greatest of their number.

CLAWS OF CHAOS

Sigmar had hurled back the encroaching darkness in many lands and kingdoms, and new civilisations blended with the remnants of those from ages past. Alliances were forged, and hope rekindled. Yet the Dark Gods were mustering their strength for a devastating counter-blow.

The deities of Chaos, having been so close to their ultimate victory, found their plans in disarray. The balance of power between them had shifted massively, and a new phase of the Great Game had begun. Arguably the one to profit most from the turmoil was Khorne, the Blood God, whose meat is warfare and whose drink is spilt blood. In Aqshy, his followers had spread so far, and grown so strong, that none had been left to oppose their supremacy. Many warbands hunted day and night without finding any centres of resistance, and had been forced to make war upon themselves; with the lands reduced to gore-clotted wastes and the mortal kingdoms laid low, the chances of finding a glorious war had become vanishingly small. In rising to the utmost heights of power, Khorne had risked his own dizzying descent.

The coming of the Stormcast Eternals had changed everything. Now every realm resounded to the din of clashing battle lines, every land was stained once more with fresh blood. A new age of war had begun. Khorne frothed with anticipation at the slaughters to come, for in Sigmar's armies he had found a worthy foe once more.

Tzeentch also profited from the age that was dawning across the Mortal Realms. His agents had met violent ends in a hundred new wars, and Sigmar had reclaimed Ghal Maraz from the Tzeentchian strongholds of Anvrok, but the Architect of Fate had no equal when it came to turning misfortune into advantage. Every city and culture that sprang up in the wake of

Sigmar's conquests was fertile ground for his insidious schemes and manipulations. Every pauper praying for a better life, every refugee or downtrodden soul who looked for an easy solution to his predicament could find one in Tzeentch – though it would cost him dearly. Slowly, the Great Conspirator inveigled his tendrils of influence into the new cities as he had with those that came before. Hidden cults met in basements, secret societies thrived beneath the masks of aristocracy, and lunatic scholars penned arcane tomes that could drive the reader to madness.

The architect Valius Maliti, under the cover of his sheer competence and unalloyed genius, worked the designs of his secret patron Tzeentch into a dozen free cities. The Enemy Within had a thousand faces, but invasions of robed Acolytes, shrieking Tzaangor beastmen and kaleidoscopic daemons were never far behind. Tzeentch would have his prize, for the lands were rich in the stuff of magic. But first he would show Sigmar that nowhere was safe from the predations of the Dark Gods.

Nurgle had suffered a crushing setback in the Realm of Life, for the goddess of Ghyran had spurned his generous gifts and cast aside much of his hard work in the process. The glorious annex to his garden was withering on the vine as the Sylvaneth and their Stormcast Eternal allies fought back from the brink of disaster to win dominance in one Jade Kingdom after another. After a long period of sullen introspection at this rejection, Nurgle gathered his spirits once more and embarked upon a new crusade – to deliver his vile blessings across all the realms, conquest by conquest, until every land bore the stigmata of his virulent touch.

The Great Horned Rat, least of the Chaos powers in strength but by no means in cunning, followed his own path. The skaven spread starvation and blight wherever the people of the Mortal Realms dared to believe themselves free of hardship, turning once verdant lands into lifeless sprawls of twisted stalks and rotten vegetation that teemed with vermin. Swarms of ratmen, left to multiply as the great and the good warred amongst themselves, bred until they were beyond counting. All the while they gnawed at the roots of existence, working towards an uprising that would overturn every realm at once.

Though they would never admit it to themselves, each of the Dark Gods was united in a single goal – to divide and conquer the Mortal Realms, pouring their malevolence through every portal they could seize or fashion until their anarchy and horror capsized reality entirely.

A HIDDEN WORLD

Whilst Sigmar capitalised on his new victories, Malerion and Teclis travelled at will between the lands of light and dark. Long ago, during the Age of Myth, they had found a region called Uhl-Gysh, the Hidden Gloaming. It was this strange cosmic anomaly they had used to entrap Slaanesh, and rescue the souls of their kin.

By the time Sigmar's Tempest broke across the Mortal Realms, the magic of the aelves had seen many of their number saved from the most terrible of fates. By using the magic of Ulgu and Hysh as one, the aelven gods had extracted the souls of their lost kin from within their nemesis, the Dark Prince Slaanesh – though those that emerged from this ordeal had been changed irrevocably by the unimaginable trauma.

*L*ong ago, the gods Tyrion and Malerion had been borne to the Mortal Realms as beings of light and shadow respectively. So anathema were these energies that one could not enter the other's domain for more than a few moments. Yet with the aid of their closest kin – Teclis, who acted as confidante and advisor to Lord Tyrion, and Morathi, who fulfilled a similar function for Malerion – they located a middle ground within which they could meet.

Having searched the length and breadth of Hysh for signs of aelf-kind, yet finding nothing, Tyrion and Teclis had come to believe that their people had met a final demise. Thinking to find them in the Realm of Death, Tyrion climbed the highest dune of Hysh's Desert of Ending – and descended the other side in Shyish. But the missing aelven souls could not be the found even in those desolate lands.

Malerion had a similar experience in Ulgu, Realm of Shadow. There he had found only his mother, Morathi. They too ventured into Shyish in search of their aelven brothers and sisters, emerging whole from the Pool of Midnight in a slick of iridescent oils. They roamed the underworlds for many years, hidden from Nagash's far-seeing gaze by a pall of magical shadow. It was in the distant reaches of Bonehallow that Malerion found hope. There lived an order of raven-worshipping monks that had recently offered aid to Tyrion and Teclis. Willingly, these monks led the aelf gods to one another, and spoke of their order's secrets.

Only after much debate did Tyrion and Malerion find common ground. They combined the knowledge they had gleaned from the raven monks and the other ancient peoples of Shyish, and in doing so uncovered a secret that had been buried deep. Forgotten by almost all, that knowledge had drifted into Shyish, where all things find their end. The secret was the truth of Uhl-Gysh, the Hidden Gloaming – a sub-realm that was neither of light nor of darkness, and yet of both at the same time.

Existing between Ulgu and Hysh, the Hidden Gloaming occupied a place in the cosmos between the two great realmspheres that formed its constituent parts. That penumbral state of half-shadow is the meeting point of lucid wakefulness and dark dreams, the state in which something is simultaneously known and unknown.

In learning of this ephemeral non-place, Tyrion and Malerion found a way to consult with one another on neutral ground, for in this interstitial twilight they saw great potential. Here was a place

only they and their chosen acolytes could reach, for only the aelves had the spiritual focus to pass their minds into such an eldritch place. They spoke long upon the matter of their mutual nemesis, Slaanesh, and together devised a plan.

Over the course of the Age of Myth, Tyrion and Malerion became practised in casting their minds into the twilight of the Hidden Gloaming. In their searching of the realms, they had at last discovered a few aelven souls, mostly in Azyr, and they gathered the magically adept of these and tutored them in the same arts. Together with these protégés, they raised a great arcane engine of mathematically precise construction, using not stone or metal but the energy of that secret place and the power of their own minds. Decades rolled past. On the eve of the sixty sixth new year, they worked a great spell that would change the cosmos forever.

Slaanesh, still gorged on soul energy after the demise of the Broken World, was glutted and all but insensible. He had ventured into the aetheric void between realities, the better to digest the souls of his victims. There he had become so vast he was effectively immobilised by his own gluttony. The prospect of a princely feast would stir him into motion once more, however, for to consume the most powerful of aelven souls would form the crowning glory of his conquest over that proud race. And in the far distance, there they were – glimmering within wisps of light and shadow in the darkness.

Slowly, longingly, the Dark Prince moved closer and closer towards Uhl-Gysh. There he could make out the souls of two young gods, lithe and potent, each a delicacy that would empower him beyond measure. Around them a small constellation of talented aelven souls added their power to that of their masters, engaged in some mystical process that they likely believed hid them from their enemy's attention. Slaanesh's predatory hunger could not be held at bay forever. In slid the Dark God like a serpent, taking an approximation of physical form with jaws yawning once more to consume

Tyrion, Malerion, Teclis, Morathi and their allies in one single gulp.

The realmstone obelisks imbued with soul-stuff that Tyrion had prepared, each standing upon a levitating island within the Hidden Gloaming, flared bright as Slaanesh grew close. As one they sent out binding, luminous light-nets of Hyshian magic. At the same time, the grey web-like tendrils of Ulgu blossomed from spheres of distilled darkness, reaching out to wrap themselves around the energy-rich incarnation that was Slaanesh. The distilled magic of the two realms mingled, each unleashed in exactly the same measure by the aelven monarchs who had laboured so long to construct them.

Caught in the paradoxical trap, Slaanesh was held fast. In that moment, the Dark God found that his power had been undone. With a scream of rage he fought against his bounds – but to no avail. He was captured, and his worshippers the realms over were thrown into turmoil at his loss.

THE QUEST IMMORTAL

The Stormcast Eternals are shining angels of the tempest, this much is known. What did not come to light until years later was the price they paid for their immortality. Over years of war unending, Sigmar came to recognise the flaws in the reforging – and sent forth new agents to find the cure.

When a Stormcast Eternal dies, his essence is snatched up into the heavens by the magic of Sigmar and the art of the soul-smith. In Azyr it will be reforged anew, an agonising process that may take hours, or may take years. Upon each reforging there is a chance the Stormcast Eternal may become less human. Over the course of several deaths, many of those reforged become numb to the horrors of war. They lose sight of subtler virtues – concepts such as compassion, pity and mercy become eroded by the burning heat of the forge. This makes them daunting opponents indeed.

Though the God-King Sigmar knew that the reforging may carry a cost, he did not realise the full scope of the strange curse that would come to afflict the Stormcast Eternals as their reforgings became ever more frequent. Known amongst the Lord-Relictors as the transfiguration, this phenomenon became ever more pronounced in those warriors who were reforged time and time again.

Something had been lost in the process. Over time, many of those who had been reforged too many times were altered in body as well as in spirit, whilst others became ever more powerful creatures of the storm. For long years none spoke openly of their fears, for it is all but forbidden to doubt the God-King. Vandus Hammerhand was the first to put into words his concerns of the dire future that awaited him. He was plagued by visions of a soul he came to think of as the Lightning Man – a figure of crackling energy that he feared represented his future self.

In Sigmar's cities, those who had been reforged too many times became totems of awe and fear. Though they were fierce and determined, they had lost much of what it is to be human, and with that, any sense of judgement or discernment regarding right and wrong. For these post-human beings, only an existence of black and white remained, of Order and Chaos, with no shades of morality in between. They existed only to oppose darkness and corruption, no matter how fair a form it took. Though these transfigured warriors made for excellent shock troops in the war against Chaos, their reduced humanity made them very dangerous for those who strayed from the true path of Sigmar's teachings – and of these, there were many.

When the great new cities of Order were painstakingly built across the Mortal Realms, each with a Stormhost's keep at its heart, the terrifying implications of the transfiguration became clear. Humanity is complex, and its morality more so. When murmurings of unrest inevitably began within these new-found settlements, not all of the Stormcast guardians were best equipped to deal with them. In places, murmurings led to riots. These were viciously put down by the more hard-line chambers, who saw them as precursors to Chaos cults and uprisings. So began a cycle of retribution and rebellion that led to many cities being riven by civil war and brutal suppression. The Chaos Gods stoked the fires where they could, but in many places they simply watched in sadistic glee.

Sigmar dwelt long on the dilemma that had befallen his chosen warriors, for it galled him to admit he may have been too hasty in his reforgings. Already the implications were unfolding across the realms.

In Vindicarum, the sparks of conflict became a raging bonfire. Singing as they slew, the Celestial Vindicators brought a terrible judgement against those citizens that harboured even the smallest seed of corruption in their souls. A full three-quarters of the inhabitants were slain in a single night, rivers of blood trickling down the volcano city's caldera. That event became known as the Purge of Vindicarum, and its implications have echoed through time ever since.

Those who survived the purge banded together into an army of zealous faithful, marching to war alongside the wrathful warriors that had let them live. Yet beneath that solidarity, there was a hidden undercurrent of fear. Stories of extreme measures abounded. Excelsis, guarded by the Knights Excelsior, was said to be surrounded by chains of celestial lightning through which only those of pure soul could pass. Was this, too, a kind of slavery?

Sigmar ordered the upper echelons of his temples to investigate further. To bolster them, the Sacrosanct Chambers were sent forth from their guardian duties at the Anvil of the Apotheosis. They were reforged not from the ranks of savages and tribesmen, but from the finest battle sages and warrior mystics in the realms, and they were wise indeed.

Somewhere in the divine process of reforging, a small portion of each soul was escaping into the aether. It was the appointed task of these arcane brotherhoods to solve this quandary – or at least allay it for a time. They theorised that some of those mortals the God-King had taken to Sigmaron were strong enough to withstand the process of reforging once, but not adamant of spirit enough to pass through the apotheosis over and over again.

Perhaps Sigmar had known this all along, but had no other choice – had he not mustered such numerous armies when he did, the Mortal Realms would likely have been lost forever. Only now was the cost of his last-ditch attempt to save them becoming clear.

In secret the Sacrosanct Chambers searched every corner of the Mortal Realms for knowledge of soul-stuff, monitoring not only the forges of Azyrheim but also the translocation that occurred whenever a Stormcast died in battle. To fully understand the magic of the soul and the cycle of life and death, the storm-sages dabbled with matters best left to the necromantic arts. In doing so, they risked the wrath of Nagash. That ancient liche-god considered the dead his sole province, and had long harboured a grudge against Sigmar. The existence of this new breed of warrior mystic would be seen an insult, for the war sages strayed upon Nagash's territory, fighting hard against all manner of unquiet spirits. In this, their story was only just beginning.

Many paid the ultimate price, their souls snatched away by Nagash's ethereal agents. It was a willing sacrifice, for should the curse of transfiguration continue unabated, every Stormhost of the Stormcast Eternals would slowly drift further from humanity until they were truly lost.

The transfigured were growing too stark in their demi-godhood. In becoming both more and less than human, in so thoroughly embodying all that was ordered and lawful, they had abandoned the ways of normal men and become pitiless killers. A question hung in the air, though none dared to ask it out loud. Was it possible for a warrior to become so pure, so holy, that to the eyes of the mortal man, he would be the embodiment of terror?

THE STOLEN SOULS

It was not only Sigmar who had taken souls from Nagash's clutches as the aeons slid by. Some amongst the gods had defied him long before Sigmar visited the Mortal Realms for the first time, whilst others had stolen from him in the ages of Myth and Chaos. And all would pay, in time.

In the Mortal Realms, magic saturates reality. Those who can manipulate it find there is little they cannot do; even the power of life and death can be bound to the desires of a magical adept. Yet doing so carries many risks – mishaps that can leave an individual trapped between life and death, bestow an eternity of raw madness, or turn the would-be conjurer of souls into a wraith that howls in pain and frustration forever more. But even the most dire spell, the most grievous curse, cannot compare with the fate of those who draw the pitiless gaze of Nagash.

CALL OF THE HEAVENS

Scholars, bards, shamans and skalds in every realm have heard tell of the Stormcast Eternals. Word has spread far since their tumultuous crusade against the forces of darkness began – and in the wake of each story, hope has blossomed. Though Chaos still rules the vast majority of the lands, over time, parts of Sigmar's grand scheme have fallen into place.

Yet not everyone has welcomed Sigmar's intervention. The most bitter of elders and rabble-rousers claim there is treachery in the God-King's methods, for it was he who stole away the heroes of the realms as they defied Chaos, and in doing so brought an end to many mortal bloodlines and settlements.

None have learned so well of these acts, nor paid such obsessive attention to the details, as Nagash. From the very first soul Sigmar snatched from the threshold of death, the Great Necromancer has been watching. The souls of

truly great men and women are the strongest in the afterlife as well as the living world, and the finest of Nagash's captains and lieutenants are those who led their kin whilst still mortal. Nagash was at first content to keep a tally, knowing that one day the bill would be called past due, but as Sigmar denuded the realms of its finest warriors, Nagash set in motion a dark mirror of the Azyrite muster.

The Great Necromancer sent forth his shambling legions to find the greatest mortal heroes, not only in the Realm of Death, but further afield, and had them cut down the champions of men wherever they could – for even the most proficient swordsman can be brought low if enough undead are sent against him. These champions too were reforged, after a fashion – not into shining heroes, but into mindlessly obedient thralls, living dead that were ready to fight in the retributive wars to come.

OF LIGHT, SHADOW AND DEEP PLACES

Humans were not the only folk in the realms to defy Nagash's claim upon the dead. In Ulgu and Hysh, the souls of those aelves rescued from Slaanesh's essence were given focus, taking form once more. Many of these aelf-things were humanoid, appearing much like their former selves but for a faint glow of lambent energy. Others were remade in stranger forms, the magic that coursed through their being writ large. Some of those born to the Realm of Light were luminous beings, angelic creatures of pure reason. Those given new life in Ulgu were majestic and terrible all at once.

Though not even Malerion truly realised the extent of her subterfuge, his mother Morathi was drawing souls from Slaanesh's recumbent form in her bid for true godhood. Her skills in the arts of illusion saw her create whole armies of aelven soul-hybrids without coming to the notice of Lord Tyrion and his kin. Unfortunately her secretive deeds bore a terrible cost, for the roaming scions of Slaanesh were drawn to Ulgu, attracted by the concentration of souls that had been stolen from their missing lord and master. They fell into an obsessive frenzy of ecstasy at finding the scent of the Dark Prince upon the winds. Their heated excitement stood in stark contrast to the cold-burning hatred of Nagash, for in taking those souls, Morathi had invited retribution from not one, but two deities.

In the deep places of the realms dwelt the mysterious Idoneth, amongst the first aelves to have been torn from Slaanesh's immense godhood. Free from a nightmarish existence, they fled even from their saviour Teclis, seeking the darkest and coldest realms they could find – for what better place to escape the god of sensuous excess than a place where sight, sound and even touch were all but impossible to experience? The Idoneth sequestered themselves in the abyssal depths of seas and oceans so deep and remote that not even Nagash thought to look for them there. But they could not remain hidden forever.

When the ploys of the Dark Gods thrust the Idoneth into the light, the Great Necromancer turned to look upon that most well-hidden of aelven kindreds. To his mind, by escaping the pull of the grave and the afterlife that followed, even they had defied his claim upon their souls. They too would answer for their crimes.

THE ESSENCE OF GODS AND MEN

In each realm the story was much the same, for in every race, there are those who seek to cheat death. The shards of Grimnir's soul, shattered by Vulcatrix and reduced to the priceless material ur-gold, are jealously hoarded by the lodges of the Fyreslayers. The Seraphon are a race long departed from the physical plane, yet their Starmasters keep them from oblivion with memories so powerful they can cause corporeal echoes to manifest at will. Even the Chaos Gods impinge upon Nagash's rightful tithe. Their minions willingly sell their souls in exchange for power and long life, and in doing so either damn themselves to an existence of surreal horror, or ascend to the immortal rank of Daemon Prince. Even the least of those so corrupted are ultimately bound not for the Realm of Death, as is the proper order of mortality, but for the Realm of Chaos.

Each anomaly, each exception, Nagash took personally. Was he not the Lord of Death? Was he not the master of the afterlife? Soon enough, there would be a reckoning, for though Nagash has the patience of the grave, even he would not wait forever.

'The Mortal Realms are known as such for good reason. Those that live there may do as they please with their natural span; that too is worth fighting for. Yet each thing that lives, from the merest insect to the mightiest behemoth, must ultimately meet the end of its days. When it does so, it becomes one with death. At that point it is the property of one being, and one being alone, to do with as he sees fit for the rest of time.

That being is named Nagash.'

NAGASH'S IRE

Though the Great Necromancer has a hundred dire spells at his command, and though his mighty blade has slain kings and warlords by the dozen, some say his most potent asset of all is his ability to wait entire generations for the right moment to strike.

The being known as Nagash is a true immortal, a god-eating horror who has died over and over again. He resurrects after each demise, coalescing once more into another ghastly form, even if it takes millennia to do so. To Nagash, the passing of the centuries is as the passing of years to a mortal man.

However, his patience is not infinite.

When the spiritual essence of Nagash solidified in the Mortal Realms after the destruction of the world-that-was, the Great Necromancer was immediately convinced that he had finally come to his birthright. Here was no solitary paradise like those once promised to the nobles of Nehekhara, land of his birth. Nor was it a singular purgatory devised to punish former sins. Shyish was a reality that revolved around a hundred different afterlives, each built to a greater or lesser extent upon the energies of death. Visiting each of the lands in turn, Nagash laid his hollow eyes upon every corner of Shyish, and everything that dwelt there, and considered it his. Even the gods that ruled over each underworld of the realm he considered his property, there to be consumed at leisure after he had raised his undying legions once more.

When divorced from the flesh and blood of its mortal incarnation, the spiritual essence of each dead mortal entity – often known as the soul – will usually find its way to one of the Shyishan underworlds. In the act of dying, it is drawn irrevocably to the Realm of Death, there to while away the aeons until

its energies dissipate or it is somehow returned to life. All things must end in Shyish, it is said, even the energy of souls, though it may take centuries or even millennia for a spirit to fade away completely. The energy of a normal spirit, the animus of each departed soul, can vary wildly. A basal coward from a backwater human village may have little in the way of spiritual energy, his ghost no more than a faint and moaning shade. A martyred hero – especially one of potent lineage, such as an aelven or duardin warrior – glows bright with immortal power, its spirit a powerful essence in its own right.

These were the souls that Nagash coveted the most, and the souls that were stolen from him by the deities that the Great Necromancer saw as his rivals. The vast majority of aelven souls were absent from Shyish, for they had been consumed by the Dark Prince in a gluttonous feast that had seen Slaanesh rendered insensible by his own greed. Others had sunk into the black depths, passing through sea-portals and escaping

the hunger of Slaanesh as well as that of Shyish. Most other aelven souls had been sequestered or stolen away by the aelf gods Tyrion and Malerion, each seeking to rebuild the societies over which they once ruled.

Perhaps the most grievous offender was Sigmar of Azyr, the Soul-Thief, Taker of Heroes and Betrayer of Trust. The God-King had convinced Nagash to join the Pantheon of Order in the name of bringing civilisation to the realms and, reluctantly, Nagash had agreed – up to a point. He had no intention of engaging in direct conflict with the Ruinous Powers, who together could undo even his great works. After the Battle of Burning Skies, where Nagash's absence angered Sigmar greatly, the God-King usurped the Great Necromancer in the most grievous way. Whenever a heroic soul was upon the threshold of death in the fight against Chaos, Sigmar would snatch that being away in a flash of divine lightning. In doing so he stole one of the mightiest assets that Nagash could hope to bind to his own cause. The Great Necromancer watched this happen again and again. Worse still, Sigmar had the audacity to take a number of souls who had long dwelt in the Realm of Death. In fact, the God-King created an entire Stormhost from the heroes of ancient conflicts – the Anvils of the Heldenhammer, who were forged under a dark moon. To Nagash, this pillage of Shyish's finest souls was blatant theft, a calculated insult for which Sigmar would be made to pay. Yet Nagash knew better than any other that revenge was a dish best served cold.

The Great Necromancer seethed in silence over Sigmar's insolence, but he did not intend to do so forever. Behind a shroud of secrecy, he had his followers labour ceaselessly, day and night, on a great work of surpassing potency. Nagash had long ago devised a method to harness the darker forms of magic, and the building of great black pyramids was a hallmark of his art. In the very centre of the Realm of Death he had his minions construct a vast inverted pyramid out of monolithic blocks, each made from Shyishan sand that had been vitrified by necromantic witch-fire to appear much like volcanic obsidian. No normal sand was used in the construction of these giant segments, but the magical substance that some call grave-sand, or the sands of time. The purest deposits were used to make the capstone of that inverted pyramid – that which would one day form an awl to burrow through the substance of Shyishan reality.

GRAVE-SAND

Grave-sand is the naturally occurring realmstone of Shyish, a granular crystalline substance that once trickled down the dunes of the lonely deserts and bluffs at the Realm's Edge. Each stream and rivulet of grave-sand is said to be attuned to the lifespan of a living creature – once every single grain of a particular trickle is still, the lifespan of that mortal being is over. Some say it is possible for a being to extend their own lifespan by seeking the Realm's Edge, finding their personal stream of grave-sand, gathering up the grains in an enchanted hourglass and inverting the artefact so the sand flows back upon itself. Very few know the truth, for to strike out for the Realm's Edge is to seal one's own fate – it is a place of raw death magic, and for a mortal to dabble with those

energies is to invite all manner of catastrophe.

To one such as Nagash, who embodies the energies of undeath, grave-sand is but another kind of clay with which to build his empire. His numberless skeletal minions stalked slowly to the Realm's Edge, walking through hurricanes of amethyst energy that would have flayed a mortal man in seconds. Amongst the dunes they gathered every deposit of the realmstone they could find, often one grain at a time, going to and fro in long thin processions like ants gathering sugar to take back to their nest. Over long generations, Nagash ensured the greatest concentration of grave-sand in Shyish was no longer at the edge of the realm, but at its centre.

As the centuries rolled by, the Great Necromancer's fortress, Nagashizzar, was steadily piled with mountains of granular realmstone. In this manner Nagash was able to build his finest masterwork. It was to be an echo of the Black Pyramid he had once raised in the arid lands of Nehekhara, the most evil structure ever to mar the surface of the world-that-was. Yet this, the greatest of all black pyramids, was built inverted – its capstone, and the energies that poured into it, was to pierce Shyish entire.

THE GREAT BLACK PYRAMID

As his numberless minions retrieved the stuff of Shyishan magic, Nagash laboured night and day upon his defining monument. It would be imbued with a grand spell that would eclipse even that which had stripped all life from Nehekhara. This endeavour was no ode to pride or vaunting ambition, but the beginning of a carefully planned arcane coup. The structure was hidden amongst the ruins of Nagashizzar's citadel keep, that immense reflection of Nagash's immortal ego that had been toppled by the forces of the Dark Gods during the Age of Chaos. The monolithic wreckage of shattered libraries and broken palaces had not been rebuilt, but instead winched into place to form the pyramid's scaffold. The bones of a million broken skeleton warriors, those who had failed to defend Nagashizzar against the forces of Chaos, were repurposed as mortar. No sacrifice was too great, for the pyramid's construction was a work of such surpassing artifice that all in its shadow was rendered irrelevant.

Though Nagash had created black pyramids as centres of dark energy before, this was undoubtedly the grandest. It was also the most geometrically perfect. Every tunnel, every corridor and finger-thin conduit inside it was shaped to the most stringent arcane formulas known, for Nagash had long ago mastered the hermetic arts of his birth-land. With an eternity in which to perfect them, he had raised his arts to hitherto unheard-of levels, and with legions of mindlessly obedient skeletons working tirelessly to fulfil his every exacting specification, he had the means with which to put his knowledge into practice. Chip by chip, chisel-blow by chisel-blow, the black pyramid took shape.

At all times this monolithic edifice was inverted, held aloft by complex energy fields. Its tip hovered but a hand span above the earth, while its immensity loomed upward so high it made even Nagash himself seem like an insect by comparison.

THE DRAINING OF THE KHAPHTAR SEA

The construction of this colossal site of power caused fluctuations in the aether-void, ripples of events to come that haunted those with the power to scry the future. Amongst them were the Warpseers, monstrous daemonic skaven that constantly sought ways to advance the agendas of the Great Horned Rat.

The skaven race know well the value of realmstone. Their stronghold sub-realm is so vast it has its own crystalline equivalent, the malignant green-black substance known as warpstone, which they use to fuel their arcane inventions. The Warpseers reasoned that if a treasure trove of realmstone was somewhere at the heart of the Realm of Death, they could snatch it away from its dim-witted undead keepers, and in doing so earn great power. The Warpseer council gave their orders to the rest of the Masterclan, who in turn brought their fearful influence to bear upon the other great skaven clans. Before another new moon had passed, the ratmen of the half-real verminopolis known as Blight City were burrowing their gnawholes through the aether once more, this time bound for Shyish.

This endeavour, as with so many others undertaken by the skaven, proved to be far more ambitious than it was practical. The first skaven gnawhole, tunnelled by drill-armed Stormfiends and a menagerie of burrowing machine-beasts, breached the underworld of the Khaphtar Sea – also known as the Sea of Suicides.

An ocean so titanic it held the floating, ever-damned corpses of every soul to have drowned itself in despair, the Khaphtar Sea had become populous indeed since the Age of Chaos bit deep. Nagash had defeated that underworld's deity, the Brine-God, and taken the entire domain for himself. Shortly after, the pallid corpses that floated there came to life, grasping at nothing in the cold and inky depths.

By burrowing into that sunken underworld, the skaven caused the Khaphtar Sea to flood back into their gnawhole network. The waters crashed and seethed through the gnawholes,

drowning entire generations of skaven and carrying a billion bloated sea-zombies along with the ratmen's wet furry bodies. Eventually, a tsunami of filthy, corpse-choked water burst into the workshops of the Clans Skryre in Blight City. On that day the Year of the Drowned Rat began, and the ensuing battles of extermination still rage on in parts of the skaven capital even now.

By undermining the Sea of Suicides, the skaven had done more than empty an underworld of its rightful souls. Hidden away in the impenetrable depths of that strange ocean was an enclave of Idoneth Deepkin. For well over a thousand years their borders had been kept safe from sea-zombie attack by circling patrols of eel-riders. So adept were they at stealth, and so powerful was their shrouding memory-magic, that even Nagash had been unaware of their existence – until now. With one of the Great Necromancer's demesnes all but emptied, and the Idoneth city upon its bed soon to be exposed, the Deepkin courted disaster.

One of the aspects shared between the aelves of Ulgu and those of the deep places was an aptitude for distraction. Running out of time, the Idoneth of Khaphtar sent a diplomatic delegation to their cousins in the Laebrea Basin. The basin was another underworld – not of men, but of great beasts – that took the form of an ocean of peaty tar. There the great mammalian titans of Ghur emerged whenever they passed through one of the pitch-black pits that formed the primal Realmgates of the Ghurish Hinterlands. Upon the basin's clotted bed dwelt the silent, pallid Idoneth known as Laebreans, whose eyes and mouths bled thick tar whenever they ventured into Ghur on their soul-raids.

An accord was reached after the Khaphtar Court pledged allegiance to the Laebreans – together, they would direct the Great Necromancer's indignant fury before it was too late. It would not be their people that felt the brunt of Nagash's wrath.

The Laebreans had long grown wise to the ways of the Ghurish tribes – in truth, there was not that much to learn. If they stayed out of the way of the fierce Hinterland orruks, troggoths and ogors, they could raid the human tribes with impunity. This time, however, the Laebreans ventured forth from the slick black pools of the primal Realmgates in search of direct confrontation, the better to lure the bestial tribes to their doom. This time, it was not the Hinterland orruks who made use of the tar pits, but the Idoneth.

Over a harrowing month of ghastly visitations, insidious lures and black drownings, hundreds of thousands of Hinterland orruks and ogors passed through the tar pits in the same manner as the mammuts and the rhinoxen they once hunted. Having met a suffocating demise by sinking into tar, the bestial tribes passed through those strange Realmgates – but their journey did not end there. Using the magic of their Tidecasters, the Laebreans sculpted the tar to form a sticky, stinking pathway leading out of the basin's depths and into the underworlds nearest Nagashizzar.

The greenskins' rage and lust for battle did the rest. Having seen Nagash's citadel on the horizon, the orruks and their ogor allies made haste out of the basin and onto the dry, crumbling land that was home to Nagash's greatest stronghold. They were met with phalanxes of Nagash's finest garrison troops – creatures made from refashioned bone and sinew,

each larger and more bizarre than the last. Yet the stouter the resistance, the louder the din of battle became, the more orruks headed for the front line.

Through the dreams and visions of orruk Shamans back in Ghur, word spread of the Fight at the End of the World. Ever more tribes sought ways into Shyish, either through deathly Realmgates or the act of dying en masse in ever bloodier civil wars. By the time the briny, decomposing depths of the Khaphtar Sea had drained completely into Blight City, Nagash's holdings were under attack from so many greenskins that the Idoneth enclave escaped his attention entirely.

Yet Nagash's master plan had been well prepared. Not even the combined assaults of skaven, aelf and orruk could stop the coming disaster.

THE CATACLYSM OF SHYISH

When the day of the pyramid's completion grew close, the dust of battle was already clogging the horizon. So delicate was Nagash's work, the painstaking finale of his great ritual, that he could not afford the disruption of open war on his doorstep. Perhaps it was the avalanche of destruction grinding ever closer that caused his lack of focus at the last minute, perhaps even one as intelligent and focused as Nagash can make mistakes. But on that day, on the hour in which the final rune-carved monolith was laid in place atop the pyramid megastructure and the last stanzas of the great ritual spoken, the Great Black Pyramid played host to a critical impurity.

When the Clans Skryre had burrowed into Shyish's underworlds, causing the Sea of Suicides to drain, they had opened a pathway to the

Realm of Death that few had the courage to exploit. Yet if the skaven have one emotion even stronger than their innate cowardice, it is sheer greed. With word of mountainous deposits of realmstone deep in the heart of Shyish, the skaven sent their agents back along the brine-swilling gnawhole that led from Blight City to the Khaphtar Sea, determined to seize it all.

This time it was agents of the Clans Eshin that made their way into Shyish, entire leagues of the verminous assassins shrouded in shadows. Slinking past the undead guardians of Nagash's masterwork within palls of enchanted gloom, they dived into the larger tunnels and crawlspaces of the Great Black Pyramid, trusting their uncanny senses and twitching whiskers to see them to the treasure trove they believed lay at its heart. Yet the labyrinth inside the pyramid did not conform to physical laws. One by one, the skaven agents squirted the musk of fear as they realised they were utterly, irredeemably lost.

When the final stone of the Great Pyramid was put in place, and the masterwork ritual was completed, the shadowy agents of the Clans Eshin were still trapped inside. It was too late for them – and for the chance of Nagash's great ritual to proceed as he had planned. Whether their corruption of Nagash's masterwork was a blessing or a curse, none can say.

A howling hurricane of unstable magic raced throughout Shyish's many underworlds, summoned to the heart of the pyramid and converging on a single point. With a thunderous, mind-splitting boom, Shyish underwent a magical inversion, a change of polarity that would redefine it forever.

The arcane energy of the Realm of Death, so famously difficult to manipulate, was suddenly, irrevocably drawn to a single location. Slowly at first, Nagash's inverted pyramid began to revolve, getting faster with each gale of eldritch power it absorbed until it span with whipping, killing speed. Its dark energies pulsed, blinding in their blackness. The lands nearest the heart of Shyish were drained of all colour and life, leaving only bleached wastelands behind, and every creature for a hundred leagues was blasted to dust.

As the Great Black Pyramid became heavier with magical energy, it began to sink into the heart of the realm, not so much drilling into it as buckling, stretching, drawing the lands of Shyish down around it, like an iron cannonball placed on a sheet of tanned human skin. Around the inverted pyramid was a maelstrom, a vortex, a hungering whirlpool of energy that gathered in everything – be it living or dead, earthbound or aerial, physical or ethereal – and drew it ever downward. At the very bottom was Nagash, drinking in every mote of power and every soul that slid down into his clutches. The magical energy of Shyish converged on this site, pulled down into the infinitely dense point known thenceforth as the Shyish Nadir, the End of All Things.

NECROQUAKE

With the skaven agents bodily corrupting Nagash's ritual by the virtue of their presence inside the pyramid, the energies of the Shyish inversion were far more destructive than even Nagash had envisioned. The bow wave of energy that spread out into the void crashed across each of the Mortal Realms in turn. The cataclysm's energies spread throughout time and space, and with them went a strange and deadly disruption to the fabric of the Mortal Realms, for with the skaven's interference the ritual was tainted with Chaos. Everywhere, the ordered energies of death went wild as the metaphysical backlash cascaded across the cosmos. Twisted gheists of all descriptions burst from the mortal clay they had once inhabited as one domain after another was visited by the risen spirits of a billion dead souls.

The mages and wizards of the realms found their powers increased markedly by this realm-wrenching phenomenon, and many sought to harness the strange abilities that blew into their minds upon the gales of invisible force. Most of them paid with their lives within an instant. None save Nagash could hope to harness the colossal energies he had unleashed, and even he was stretched to the limit.

As for Shyish, the pyramid changed it beyond even Nagash's expectations. No more would the souls of the dead escape the Great Necromancer's clutches so easily – from then on, everything that made its way to Shyish would ultimately be devoured by the eternal hunger of the Nadir. Some of those mortals with the wit to comprehend what had happened dared to hope that the Great Necromancer's gambit would see him harness too much power, and in the end bring about his undoing. Their hopes were not unfounded.

The Nadir was so incredibly rich in energy, so potent in the raw stuff of endings, that even Nagash could not dwell there indefinitely. Corrupted as it was by traces of Chaos magic, it became a place of insanity as well as death. Even the vampires and liches that strayed there felt skeletal fingers raking down every inch of their skin, and the freezing silt of underworlds ground to utter destruction pressed down upon them. In the visions of mages and madmen, it appeared as a pitch-black deathscape crushed beneath the weight of eternity. Any who spoke of it had years stolen from their lifespan, for its hungry curse crossed reality.

A new evil had come to the Mortal Realms, as inescapable as time itself – and with it, a new era of death ascendant.

MAGIC WITHOUT END

The coming of the Shyish Nadir not only caused a mass resurrection of undead, but also saw the stuff of magic itself billow and cascade across the cosmos. Those with the power to channel that energy found themselves able to cast devastating and predatory spells that lasted in perpetuity.

As the lands were assailed by baleful phantasms and the spectres of the past, mages of all kinds found boundless power at their fingertips. Many a gheist was banished by their destructive emanations, but always more were there to take their place. Desperate, sorcerers reached for ever more ambitious spells and incantations. These mages drew to themselves the anarchic power rolling across the cosmos, shaped it into forms that resonated with their nature, and hurled it back out, more deadly than ever before. These spells manifested physically, not for a single lethal moment – nor even an hour or day – but indefinitely.

The magic of a spell usually dissipates over time. With the right incantations, artefacts and gestures, a wizard can draw motes of a certain type of eldritch energy into a coalesced form, but those sorceries will soon be pulled apart once more by the irresistible draw of the Realm's Edge. However, the spells borne on the bow wave of the Shyish necroquake were unaffected by this process. Shorn of their due demise by the backlash of Shyishan energies, these spells had no end. They continued to assail the Mortal Realms long after they were cast, with many feeding on the energies of the living in the manner of an arcane predator or vampire.

A cackling skull of flame shaped from the energies of Aqshy would burn on and on, seeking out ever more victims as it scorched a path across the lands. Eventually such a hazard would become known to a region's native people, named for its peculiar dangers, and avoided at all costs. Though the caster might have initially felt a thrill of raw power as he unleashed such a spell against his foes, it would soon escape his control, consuming his allies and perhaps even himself.

Many of the spells granted terrible permanence by the necroquake's energies were intrinsically linked to Shyish, for after Nagash's great spell,

those energies were in the ascendant. Hurricanes of raw magic whirled across the lands, shaped into sentient tornadoes by those with the skill to bind them. The Purple Sun, a form to which baleful Shyishan energies are easily drawn, was conjured on a hundred battlefields; those touched by the giant spined sphere were instantly transformed into statues of soulless amethyst. Wherever Nagash's foremost servants walked, empty sepulchres were given horrible life, hungering for creatures to bury alive. Entire graveyards ruptured and began roaming the lands to crush the living under seismic waves of earth, tomb-slabs and corpseflesh. Discoloured shackles burst from the land at the whim of spiteful Necromancers, their pincer-like manacles grabbing hold of souls, rather than bodies, so they might tear them down to the Great Oubliette.

But Nagash's masterwork had stirred up every form of magic, not just the macabre energies of the Realm of Death. Gnashing maws large enough to swallow a Dracoth emerged from Ghur to ravage the lands. Chronomantic cogs from Azyr appeared in mid-air to wreak havoc on time itself. Prismatic walls of purest Hyshian crystal burst from the ground to dazzle and blind those nearby.

The sages and seers of the free cities swiftly learned the dangers of these rogue spells. After the disastrous Living Inferno of Hallowheart, the battle wizards of the Collegiate Arcane combined forces with the Swifthawk Agents of their cities, sending covens of Bright wizards to channel and dissipate rogue Aqshian spells and cabals of Shyishan adepts against the roiling energies of the Realm of Death. The Eldritch Council convened

whenever a spell proved too powerful for human minds to banish, riding enchanted steeds and sinuous drakes to hunt down those spells that crackled beyond the reach of men.

Though hundreds of talented magic users met spectacular ends for their trouble, the finest minds found their efforts rewarded. Some of those spells that could not be banished were instead channelled and siphoned into enchanted relics, bound to those ensorcelled artefacts that had long held a magical charge – and were now given all the more power. Yet for every spell dismantled and dispersed to the edges of the realms through sheer willpower, for every sorcerous manifestation placed in a solid physical form, a dozen more arcane phenomenons raged on across the realms, killing or eternally cursing those foolish enough to approach them.

The creation of the Shyish Nadir changed forever the connection between a cadaver, no matter its state, and the spirit of the entity that had departed it. The cosmic distortion caused by the Nadir's power strengthened the silver cords of soul-stuff that stretched between every corpse in the Mortal Realms and the animus that travelled from it upon the moment of its death. A trillion gossamer threads twitched and vibrated across the void as the Shyish necroquake shook the Mortal Realms to their foundations, like a spider's web set alive by the deathly monstrosity at its heart. Along millions of these silver strands flew tormented gheists, making haste back to their bodies and using their own mortal remains as a portal to the corporeal world. Nagash's eyes glowed with satisfaction as spectres burst forth from every grave and ash-field.

The War of Souls had begun.

THE
MORTAL
REALMS

78

REALITY UNDER SIEGE

The Mortal Realms are near infinite in scope, with every conceivable landscape somewhere within their reaches – from the most dire hellscape to the most gorgeous paradise. Not even the gods themselves can claim to know every aspect of their grandeur. Yet they remain united by laws of reality that are nigh impossible to break.

The Mortal Realms are vast beyond the ability of the human mind to comprehend. Each exists in the aether of the cosmos, a great sphere-shaped concentration of magical energy that in places has crystallised into landscapes of impossible majesty and scope. In these Mortal Realms, motes of magical energy can be found in every pebble and leaf. At the core of each realm, where that energy is the least volatile, this aetheric power is thin indeed, and all but imperceptible even to one gifted with the witch-sight. At each Realm's Edge, reality is so saturated with magic that even a curse spoken in jest can kill a man, and a careless sweep of the arm can send bolts of energy crackling all around.

The lands of the Eight Realms are linked, within themselves as well as one to another, by magical portals known as Realmgates. Most of these already existed even when Sigmar laid the seeds of civilisation across those regions he saw as fertile ground for his new order. Since then, many more have been constructed by those godly powers that understand the weft and weave of the cosmos and the aetheric links that bind it.

Over time, Sigmar learned well of the pathways that spanned the Mortal Realms. He had the Mallus Portals built to lead to and from the Realm of Heavens – for that realm Sigmar chose as his stronghold. The wise and the brave use them still, for these are portals of such divine artifice and power that even Chaos can neither corrupt nor destroy them. They too have their dangers, however, for not all that glitters is gold, and a soul passing through might not emerge where they intend.

The daemon dimension, known only as the Realm of Chaos, is a domain apart. It is amorphous and unimaginable, beyond all notions of order and the attempts of intelligent beings to depict it. Seeking to grow ever larger, it consumes the Mortal Realms wherever the Dark Gods can force an entrance, seeking ingress through tainted Realmgates and daemonic infestations. Inside that dark reality – and those domains already conquered – the Chaos Gods wage war in their perpetual battle, each striving to conquer the others' territory in the Great Game. Thus far they have met with great success. Every Mortal Realm has felt the touch of madness, every peripheral land has felt the bite of Chaos energy gnawing at its fringes. It remains to be seen if Sigmar's great crusade can stop the Ruinous Powers from devouring reality entirely.

'We die over and over, and for what?' said Derrus of the Hallowed Knights. His sundered sigmarite breastplate slowly healed under the light of Lorrus Grymn's long-hafted warding lantern. 'One pocket of resistance is saved, even as another is swamped behind us. When will this ordeal end?'

The Lord-Castellant scowled. 'Do not doubt the God-King,' he rumbled. 'He has his plan.'

'But what is it? How do we finish this? The hooks of Chaos are embedded too deep for us to save the realms through simple war.'

'None truly know,' said Grymn. 'But I have noticed it is easier to pass through those Realmgates that we have claimed than those left wild.' The Lord-Castellant sighed. 'Perhaps Sigmar has us secure the Realmgates in order to bind the Mortal Realms together, using each link as part of a chain. The more we fortify, the more the forces of Order harden that link, the more the chain contracts. Perhaps...' Grymn paused before continuing, and Derrus looked up curiously.

'Perhaps if those chains contract enough,' he continued, 'the realms will come together as one, forming a single great realm freed from the scourge of Chaos.'

'That sounds a glorious place,' said Derrus.

TEMPEST'S EYE

ANVILGARD

HALLOWHEART

THE COSMOS ARCANE

Many strange worlds comprise the domain of the God-King Sigmar. The largest by far are the eight Mortal Realms. These elements of existence can be imagined as spheres of reality, coalescing and breaking apart within the void.

Each realm is made from the raw energies of creation, with different magic in each. In the spaces between them drift motes of unaligned magic – much weaker in power than the aligned energy of the realms. This null-space is known as the aetheric void, the Great Nothing, or the Darkness Without. It is this non-realm that forms the sky of the realms.

Not all the realms appear the same, or obey the same laws. Chamon, for instance, can be seen as a shifting collection of strange sub-realms – somewhat like the laboratory of some godly alchemist constantly striving to find the perfect creation experiment. Azyr glitters above all, a swirl of heavenly energy. Stranger still are the shadow realm of Ulgu and the light-realm of Hysh. They are inextricably linked, for shadow cannot exist without light, and illumination cannot help but cast a shadow. These two realms revolve around one another in an endless orbit, chasing their opposite number in a stately celestial dance. In doing so, they shed light, then darkness, then light again across the other Mortal Realms. Between the two orbits there exists Uhl-Gysh, a penumbral sub-realm that has been used by those of surpassing power to hide away their victims.

The Mortal Realms have many habitable regions, some of which are linked by Realmgates. These portals can either lead from one location to another within a single realm, or from one realm to another. Over time, the forces of Chaos have corrupted many Realmgates. These tainted passageways might take literally forever to cross, lead to the dread Realm of Chaos, emerge in the fabled Silver Towers, or even lead to the nothingness of the aetheric void.

HYSH, THE ILLUMINATING

SHADESPIRE

SLAANESH IMPRISONED

ULGU, THE SHADE REALM

UNDERWORLDS OF SHYISH

REALM OF CHAOS

HIGH AZYR

JADE KINGDOMS OF GHYRAN

REALM OF CHAOS

THE AETHERIC VOID

SAVAGE LANDS OF GHUR

VARANSPIRE,
CITADEL OF THE
EVERCHOSEN

THE ALLPOINTS

REALM OF CHAOS

GOLDENREALM OF CHAMON

AQSHY, THE BRIGHT

BLIGHT-CITY

SPHERES OF EXISTENCE

Long ago, the eight types of magic gathered separately in the aetheric void, for kindred energies are attracted to one another by cosmic law. In doing so they made orbs of energy known as realmspheres, within which lie the Mortal Realms.

Realmspheres are not technically infinite in size, but to a mortal they may as well be. A traveller could spend a lifetime crossing Aqshy to reach the pure and searing fire magic that forms its outer edge, only to be incinerated long before reaching their intended destination. The habitable parts of the Mortal Realms are crystallised from the aligned energy of each realm. They were long ago crushed together by cosmic forces into a collection of landscapes redolent with motes of magic. Many of these can be imagined as huge plates of land that linger within a sphere of pure essence. These slabs of solid matter hang in a rich gaseous swirl, sometimes orbited by smaller satellite worlds. In truth, each realm has its own logic of form.

At the heart of the realms are the kingdoms of mortal humans, founded during the Age of Myth. Towards the perimeter of the realms, the magic that forms them becomes wilder and more intense. Some unwise men have launched expeditions to the edge of their realm in order to harness the intense magical energy – spellcrafting becomes almost too easy there, but so do the inherent dangers increase. Each Realm's Edge is inimical to mortal life, but is not always a literal barrier; some areas are endless deserts, others misty seas. Much of the Realm of Life's perimeter is a jungle of jade so thick with magic it is impenetrable – those who approach it may sprout foliage all over, perpetually give birth, sire new forms of life, or take root entirely.

Though vastly different, each of the eight Mortal Realms is governed by the same cosmic order. But there exists another, a domain of pure anarchy – the predatory dimension known as the Realm of Chaos.

THE GREAT PARCH

THE AETHERIC VOID

CORRUPTED REALMGATE

THE REALM OF CHAOS

AQSHIAN VAULT

SKAVEN
GNAWHOLES

SIGMAR'S
TEMPEST

ORB INFERNIA

REALMGATE PATH
(INTER-REALM)

THE GREAT PARCH

REALM'S EDGE

MANY
HUNDREDS OF
REALMGATES
SPAN THE
COSMOS

ORBITAL PATHWAY

THE PERIMETER INIMICAL

THE REALM OF AQSHY

AQSHY, REALM OF FIRE

Aqshy's many land masses are places of raging passions and volatile horizons. In this realm aggression is born and carried afar on hot, gusting winds, and life is lived to the full. No realm has a fiercer outlook, no lands have cultures harsher or more littered with invective – especially since the forces of Khorne invaded. That dire fate struck first at the Great Parch.

The lands of Aqshy, known as the Bright Realm, are formed of dozens of continents. Each is replete with its own cultures and history. These continents hang suspended in the midst of the Aqshian realmsphere. Though once they were joined by the same bodies of water, over time the energies of Chaos have splintered many of them apart into islands of reality all but impossible to reach without passing through specific Realmgates. No map details them all, yet some commonality still binds them.

There is a widespread philosophy among the tribal people of Aqshy to burn brightly and well – life is to be lived fast, hard and violently. Coming of age rituals, such as cliff diving and sulphur running, kill the aspirants as often as they harden them into better, braver warriors. Those that live long enough to rot and decline are seen by some younger folk with pity and even scorn. However, the more mature souls realise that the elders in their midst are to be celebrated – they have passed through the fires of conflict and lived to be tempered by them. The gnarled and scarred warriors that lead the tribes have earned their position a hundred times over, as any would-be challengers soon find out. Though civilisations have been laid low and fallen into disaster across the breadth of Aqshy, even Chaos could not extinguish their spark entirely. With the return of Sigmar in the form of the Stormcast Eternals, the hopes and dreams of the mortals in this realm have been reignited, as bright as flame in the darkness.

THE GREAT PARCH

FLOATING CITY OF BATAAR
A traders' armada held aloft by limitless wealth and resource

COTHAL

RESINWOOD COAST

ARMADA'S BANE

BETRAYER FJORDS

CAPE KNIFE

CRACKLING COAST

VALE OF CURSED BEASTS

SILKER'S RIDGE

FLAMESPIDER WOAD

LAKE OF DARK PACTS

THE BLOODIED TRACK

ISLE OF TRYSTS

SKYHEIM PEAKS

GOLVARIA

CASTLE DRAKESBANE

THE BEATEN MEN

VENAL PEAKS

THE SEA WOUND

FURY STRAIT

VENDETTA BRIDGE

HAG'S DELTA

PORTS OF COMMERCE

BROKER'S BAY

BATAAR

THE NARROWS

WRETCH SEA

HALLOWHEART

BRIGHT MOUNTAINS

THE GATELANDS

VITROLIA

OPAL ISLE

OCEAN OF SWORDS

DISINTEGRATING SHORES

AGLORAXIAN CITADELS

ISLE OF EXILES

THE BEASTBRIDGE

KINDLING FORESTS

SACRED LAKE

PASSION'S GATE

ASPIRIA

POLYCHROMATIC SEA

STEEL SPIKE

TEMPEST'S WATCH

THE ASPRIDES

VOCIFEROUS DELTA

BRIDGE OF BRINE

TEMPEST'S EYE

OBSIDIAN FORTRESS

LUCID COAST

THE FLAMESPIRES

SHATTERED FORTRESS ISLES

GOLDENMANE MONUMENT

VANX LITTORAL

KHUL'S RAVAGE

SERRIED PEAKS

WRECKER'S ISLE

BLOODWARM WATERS

BLEACHED FOREST

HAMMERHAND COAST

JAGTOOTH FORTS

VANX

DRIZZLING ISLES

STEEL SPIKE
Fortified promontory and bulwark of sorcerous defiance

VOSTARGI MONT
City of Brimstone, vassal keep of the Fyreslayers

CHAKRIK'S FOLLY
Skaven undercity wracked by deadly earthquakes, but thriving still

THE JUTTINGS

THE CRIMSON TWINS

CUPRICON RANGE

SEARING SEA

BRAZIER PROMONTORY

BRIGHTMAN COAST

THE BROKEN KEYS

PEPPER WOAD

SPLINTERING ISLES

THE LEAPING TONGUES

MAGMAR FJORDS

THE STAIN

THE SMOULDER ISLANDS

CHARRWIND COAST

GRIMNIR'S FIREHOLD

ANVILGARD

SOOTSTAIN HILLS

THE FORGE ANATHEMA

BRAZENSKULL VOLCANO

THE RECLAIMED DEMESNES

CALLIDIUM

ARIDIAN

CHARCOAL SCORCH

BRUTOS HILLS

ADAMANTINE CHAIN

HEL CROWN

REAVER WASTES

VOSTARGI MONT

RUINS OF AHRAMENTIA

PYROC PLAINS

TRIBAL HEARTLANDS

THE VEINS OF GRIMNIR

COAST OF A THOUSAND EYES

PRISMATIKOS

BLOODSHOT PLAIN

ANVALOR

LAVA BLEED PORTAL

ONYX GATE

TALON OF IGNAX

CRUEL SPREAD

VULTUR SANDS

FLAMESCAR PLATEAU

SPLITBROW LAKE

SNOW PEAKS

CAPILARIA

CHAKRIK'S FOLLY

SORROW-PEAKS

INFINITY GEARS

THE ARTERIALS

GATES BELOW

THE TALONS

JAGGED ISLES

SCATTERING ISLANDS

WEBWOAD

OCEAN OF TEARS

SKULPILE

CAVERNS OF FULMINAX

KLARIKKAZ EARTHSCAR

HAMMERHAL AQSHA

HEARTBLOOD SEA

VITAE DELTAS

VANDIUM

SPORE HOLLOWS

EMBERKELL VOLCANO

INLETS OF DRIED GORE

SWELTER GULF

RONDEL WICK

UNTH

DAGGER STAB

RIVEN DEPTHS

CAUSTIC PEAKS

THE SETTLED LANDS

RIPPLEGHAST SOUND

THE FIREFANG

THE SHARDS

CRESCENT SEA

CLAVIS RIFT

COAST OF BONE

THE SCABLANDS

THE HORN OF IGNAX

CHRONOS GATE

IRRIGATION KEEP

THE EYE

VIRGIN PEAKS

CAPE OF SPINES

MORDACIOUS SOUND

FORT DENST

THE FYRETINES

LOST ISLES OF GAITAN

AQSHY CLAVIS ISLES

DUARDINIA

SHATTERGLASS ARCHIPELAGO

BRIMSTEIN HEARTHLANDS

FORT IGNIS

EVERLYME POINT

IGNEOUS DELTA

BRIMSTONE PENINSULA

VITRIOLUS REACH

SIGMAR'S BOOTPRINTS

ISTHMUS LASH

VITRIOL SEA

HAMMERHAL AQSHA
Bustling metropolis and half of the Twin-tailed City

THE GREAT PARCH

The tribes of the sprawling continent known as the Great Parch are bombastic and reckless. Tattooed with scenes of their own victories, they live to fight, to love and to feast as often as possible. These desert barbarians were the first to convert to darker ways when hosts of daemons began to infest the landscape during the Age of Chaos.

⚬ THE AGE OF MYTH ⚬

DUEL OF THE GREAT WYRMS

At the dawn of the Age of Myth, the Solar Drake Ignax fights the father of serpents, Great Nagendra, for domination of Aqshy's heartlands. The eastern isles are shattered, gnawed and scarred by their earth-breaking fight. Ignax shreds Nagendra's flanks, the flesh falling away to form the serpents of the south. Exhausted by her victory, Ignax is caught by Grimnir and shackled to the Land of the Chained Sun so that his people might always have light and fire.

RAGE OF GRIMNIR

After being freed by Sigmar, Grimnir fights the mother of salamanders, Vulcatrix, to the death. The volcano Vostargi Mont is formed from the falling embers of their mutual destruction. Ur-gold is scattered across the landscape, and the scorching of the lands cleanses them of the foul sulphurous dusts that had once rendered them barren.

RISE OF CIVILISATION

Sigmar's wanderings see order and culture brought to the Great Parch; crops take root and life begins anew as war and rivalry is put aside. Traders move further afield into different realms, and soon great cities are raised, especially in the western regions of Bataar and Aspiria. However, in the shimmering tracts of Brazier, Aridian and Capilaria, the populace is up in arms so often it falls backwards into atavism. Their barbarian tribes begin to worship Sigmar as a god of strength and self-sufficiency.

SEEDS OF EVIL

In the east, the Raging Tyrant Dromm reigns for eight bloody years before he is torn from his throne by his own sons and devoured. It becomes the way of Drommsend to eat their enemies' flesh in order to gain their strength.

THE TWIN NATIONS RISE

Bataar and Aspiria overcome their need to fight through heated negotiation, rivalry and athletic competition. Together they drive each other to new heights of progress. Soon the merchant kings of Bataar and the wizard lords of Aspiria are trading delicacies and artefacts ever further afield. The interior regions of the Great Parch are farmed for quaglid jerky and fever cactus, both excellent in a stew, and the spined fish known as the dappled efreet, which if prepared badly can cause the eater to literally catch fire. From the Adamantine Chain comes potent sulphur-vitriol, perfect for etching metal, and from Passion's Gate comes fine vellum.

THE WATERS OF LIFE

The central regions of the Great Parch are so arid that in some places fresh water is considered more precious than gold. Barrels full are imported from every domain that can provide it, especially vials of the life-giving, super-nourishing stuff of Ghyran, traded through the Realmgate around which Hammerhal will one day be built. Aqua Ghyranis, as it is known, becomes a mainstay currency of the region – ranging from phials that might cure a cold to vast greensteel

vats that can turn a farm's fortunes around in a single season.

SPIRITUAL SUCCESSORS

The Capilarian tribes, famous for smith-lords that fight with heavy iron hammers, are favoured by Sigmar as an echo of the world-that-was. The clans of Aridian, who instead make their spears and blades from Vostargi Mont obsidian, feel a fiery jealousy as a result. This spills over into border disputes and open war before Varrus Blackfist of the Direbrands brokers a fragile truce.

THE MARCH OF PROGRESS

In the west, Bataar grows ever more powerful due to its exceptional mercantile skills. The region's lucrative firesilker textile farms and mineral forges fund mining operations across the Venal Peaks. The Gilded Track is paved into Aspiria and Vitrolia via the Gatelands. Not content to wait for other nations to come to its bustling markets, Bataar builds a seaborne city of traders – known as the Floating Market. In a grand deal with Aspiria's mages, the fleet is ensorcelled, given the power of flight so it can trade in pastures new. Aspiria soon overflows with exotic goods in return, and grows powerful due to its high number of wizards and scholars of the exceptional arts. The sea to the north turns a rainbow of colours due to the alchemical run-off of their industry, and becomes known as the Polychromatic Sea.

A SAVAGE DIVISION

The land bridge that links Bataar and Aspiria to the tribal grounds of Vitrolia, Golvaria and Aridian is conquered by orruk warbands. The greenskins set out to slay the giant beasts that cross the bridge in search of greener pastures, but are happy to fight anyone they can find. Some bother to tax and extort their victims, others just slay for the thrill of bloodshed. Only when the Aspirians ignite the Kindling Forests

– thereby consuming many of the orruk tribes – is the Beastbridge re-opened for commerce between west and east.

THE BURNING BRIDGE
Without the civilising influence of Bataar and Aspiria, the hot-headed tribes of the middle reaches descend into civil war. The traders and wizards decide to leave them to it, a decision which proves crucial in the years to come. The Kindling Forests burn on, a permanent barrier sustained by magic. The only other crossing, the Bridge of Brine – a short sea voyage between two peninsulas – is fortified and defended by the Aspirian military. The area becomes known as Steel Spike.

BLADES AND BONE
Soon after, Aspiria opens trade with Vostargi Mont, securing a source of powerful magic weapons by walking through the fires of the Beastbridge to deal with the famous blacksmiths of the Direbrand Tribe and their duardin allies in Vostargi Mont. Jealous of their power, the necromancers from nearby Golvaria seek to disrupt this trade route, but the wizards of Aspiria are always one step ahead. Golvaria becomes the butt of jokes and humorous tales across the Great Parch.

The Golvarians make an alliance with the red-headed tribes of nearby Vitrolia, and cross the Skyheim Peaks to slaughter an Aspirian caravan with a tide of living skeletons. Battle lines are drawn. The merchants of Bataar, old allies of the Aspirians, purchase fickle Vitrolia's allegiance with gold. This causes the latter to turn upon the Golvarians at a critical moment, and a deep and abiding grudge is formed.

A GRIM HAVEN
The Golvarians are edged out of their lands by fierce magic-wielding undead-hunters from the Aspirian academies. They flee to the eastern Isle of Ghouls, and for a while make common cause with the degenerate feudal courts that live there – an offshoot of an ancient dynasty whose generations of inbreeding have taken a terrible toll.

◉ THE AGE OF CHAOS ◉

THE RED FEAST
A challenge of bloodshed is proposed by the Vanxian warlord Threx Skullbrand. Capilaria, Aridian, Demesnus and Flamescar, seeking an end to wasteful tribal war, send their champions to the contest upon the Aqshy Clavis Isles. However, Skullbrand has an ulterior motive. The Red Feast goes on and on, with the mighty lord Korghos Khul of Aridian gradually fighting his way to the top.

When the death toll rises to eight hundred and eighty-eight barbarian champions, the air screams, the bloodied water boils, and a great cataclysm erupts. So catastrophic is the maelstrom of blood and death that the Realmgate at the centre of the Aqshy Clavis Isles explodes, leaving a gaping hole in reality through which legions of howling daemons emerge.

THE GORETIDE RISES
The daemon hosts invade the Great Parch as the Dark Gods seek new conquests. Khorne is the most prevalent, as he lays claim to the warlike nations and emotional turmoil of Aqshy; he even attacks Nurgle, Tzeentch and the Horned Rat to ensure his supremacy. The tribes of Golvaria, Capilaria, Aridian and Flamescar are brought to battle by the daemon armies of Khorne. Protected by their walls of fire and steel, the horrified lords of Bataar and Aspiria leave them to their fate. In desperation, many tribes turn to the worship of these 'red gods' in the hope of surviving the slaughter. Others turn quite willingly, seeing an opportunity to sate their savage lusts. First amongst these barbaric hordes are the warriors that call themselves the Goretide, led by the champion Korghos Khul. By forcing their victims to choose between dying and partaking in the dark cannibalistic feast that occurs every eventide, Khul and his man-eating fellows ensure their legions grow ever larger.

PLAGUE AND STRIFE
In the far west of the Great Parch, the forces of Nurgle invade from the hard-bitten northern land of Cotha – a region which has at its frozen heart a Realmgate leading to the now infested reaches of Ghyran. The Floating Market of Bataar, along with its escort fleet, the Iron Armada, is attacked by a vast Plague Fleet and its loyal pod of rotting great cetaceans from the depths of the Bladewhale Sea. The Bataar navy is destroyed in a week-long sea battle. Its wrecks line the coast in such number the region is known forever after as Armada's Bane. Weeks later, the vials and urns of sacred water imported from Ghyran and transported by the Floating Market wash up on the shores of a dozen regions. They are recovered eagerly, but some have become tainted, spreading disease across the lands.

THE TEETH OF TYRANNY

The lands south of Godbeast's Bite, lightly defended by the tribes that hunt there, are conquered by an army of brass-clad killers. The region is decimated, its surviving indigenes enslaved and forced to build strings of Chaos fortifications – the Dreadfort Spines – and the sadist's paradise of Calder City.

AN EMPIRE OF BLOOD

Khul's vicious tactics see him take a great swathe of land from Vostargi Mont all the way down to Vitriolus Reach beneath the Brimstone Peninsula. The southernmost regions are renamed Khul's Ravage. The Isles of Gaitan – once the home of warrior monks who sought enlightenment through fury – are ransacked, and their ever-flaming pagodas extinguished with the blood of their keepers. Unopposed, Korghos Khul stacks the bones of his victims high. He raises the Jagtooth Forts along the coastline of Khul's Ravage in order to reinforce his coastal slave routes and protect his power-base from invasion via Vitriolus Reach.

The Red Pyramid of Khul is raised, a structure made from millions of skulls taken from the tribes north of the Brimstone Peninsula. The lands between the Duardinia mountains of the Brimstein Hearthlands and the Flamescar Plateau become tough, cracked and brown due to the lakes of blood spilt there. They are known thereafter as the Scablands.

ASPIRIA BESIEGED

Far to the west, on the shores of Aspiria, a magical war rages between the scions of Tzeentch and the spellmasters of the native magocracy. The fighting is so intense that the land itself begins to crumble under the ceaseless onslaught. All along the cliff-line watched over by the Agloraxian Citadels, the land crumbles away, known ever after as the Disintegrating Shores. Aspiria itself is diminished, physically eroded by the violence of Chaos. Less than a week later Aspiria comes under attack from the legions of Khorne that have marched past the Obsidian Fortress to cross the Bridge of Brine. Steel Spike is besieged just as the invasions from Tzeentchian

forces intensify. The magocracy finds it cannot fight on both fronts at once, and is forced to retreat to high ground, locking its citadel-cities behind magical wards and trusting to fate that the storm will soon pass.

THE RED CENTURY

The war between the traitorous Bloodbound hosts and the barbarian tribes of the Great Parch reaches fever pitch as the daemons of the Clavis Eye wade from the Vitriol Sea. A hundred years of war stretch out, with the grinding attrition seeing the faithful of Sigmar slowly dwindling. Where once the seas teemed with aquatic life, now only waves of blood lap the shores, choking the beaches with grisly flotsam. Capilaria's irrigation networks – once laced with potent Aqua Ghyranis – run with gore, choking the lush plant life that once fed the native tribes. The channels come to resemble veins and arteries filled with clotting blood. Worse still, the heroes of the most bellicose tribes vanish in the midst of war, stolen away in a flash of azure energy. Bereft of their leaders, the starving and desperate people are easily conquered and forced to resort to cannibalism.

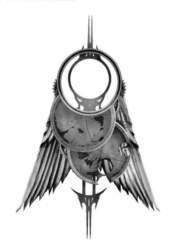

WRECKER'S ISLE

All along the coast of Vanx in the south-west, warbands of Chaos worshippers lure fleeing Aspirian vessels to their doom upon Vanx Littoral and the reefs of Wrecker's Isle. Emboldened, they join the fight to conquer Aspiria, taking many of the Aspirides islands on the south coast.

A ROAD SLICKED SCARLET

The Gilded Track, once the main arterial route of commerce across the Beastbridge, becomes home to countless Chaos warbands. The merchants of Bataar, held captive and driven by the lashes of cruel Bloodstokers, are forced to walk barefoot along its sharp volcanic stones carrying all of their carefully marshalled gold – a commodity once valuable, but now worse than useless. This road becomes known as the Bloodied Track.

WAR IN THE EARTHSCAR

Over the course of an especially ill-omened year, the Bonesplitterz of the Klarikkaz Earthscar engage in fierce fighting with the daemons spilling north from the Clavis Eye. The orruks are slowly driven back into the depths of their canyon. Fighting a guerrilla war as best they can, the Wurrgog Prophets of the Klarikkaz tribes pray to Mork for a way out.

THE BLOOD GOD STRIKES

Above the Flamescar Plateau, the mage elite of Ahramentia – a province in the west of Aridian – eliminates an entire army of Khorne daemons with a vast doomsday weapon they call the Prismatikon. Thinking themselves safe on their flying island, the Agloraxi are tragically visited by cataclysm when Khorne himself takes exception to their posturing. The Blood God manifests a giant red fist in order to strike their island, and it crashes spectacularly into the arid lands below.

Without the Agloraxi and their magical constructs to oppose him, Selpher Zaronax rises to prominence in the north-east of Golvaria after driving off the unquiet spirits there – even the dead fear the intensity of his rage. He begins a reign of terror under the title 'the Hand of the Everchosen', for it is none other than Archaon himself that has dispatched Lord Zaronax to keep a stranglehold over the Great Parch. Such is the success of Zaronax and his fellow lords that Khorne's minions are forced to hunt far and wide for their victims – and in places, turn upon themselves to sate their addictive blood-lust.

THE AGE OF SIGMAR

THE TEMPEST BREAKS
Sigmar casts his lightning over the lands of the Great Parch. Led by Lord-Celestant Vandus Hammerhand – formerly Vendell Blackfist of the Direbrand Tribe – and the Hammers of Sigmar, a dozen Stormhosts take battle to Korghos Khul and his Goretide. Khul's warriors are broken and the warlord himself defeated at the Red Pyramid, forced into exile by Vandus Hammerhand. Though the battle costs the lives of thousands of Stormcast Eternals, including that of Lord-Celestant Jactos Goldenmane, the Brimstone Peninsula is conquered and its Realmgates manned by the Lord-Castellans. By demolishing the Jagtooth Forts that secure the region and using the defensible peninsula as their staging post, Sigmar's armies take the fight to the Chaos scourge in a hundred different theatres of war across the Great Parch.

THE HAMMER STRIKES HARD
Through shock assaults, long-rehearsed tactics and raw skill at arms, the Stormcast Eternals retake swathes of Aqshy whilst the Chaos forces are still reeling. From the renamed Hammerhand Coast in the south all the way to the Reclaimed Demesnes in the north-east, the Stormcasts stake their territory.

Every Realmgate claimed by the Stormcast Eternals becomes the centre of a new fortified town, then a small city, as the Lord-Castellants of the Stormhosts perform their stalwart duty in conjunction with the Dispossessed duardin of Azyr and the Ironweld Arsenal. Soon, these centres of resistance become the crucibles in which new warrior tribes and foundling cities are forged – and hope with them. The cities of Hammerhal Aqsha, Tempest's Eye, Anvilgard and Hallowheart are founded.

A BATTLE TOO FAR
The courts of the Isle of Ghouls, now fully in the grip of the Flesh-eater delusion, sally forth against the Chaos oppressors. They intend to aid the Stormcast Eternals – seeing them as holy warriors and therefore potential kin – though in a tragic twist of fate, the Stormcasts attack them, thinking them to be yet more cannibalistic reavers. A powerful alliance turns into a deadly rivalry.

THE CLEANSING BEGINS
Wherever Chaos is beaten back, the citizens of the Great Parch petition mages of the Aspirian tradition to burn those regions clean with magical flame. In many places this works – with the lands scoured, new life can grow, like plants that germinate after a wildfire. The Jagtooth Forts, erected by Khul's bone masons and their legions of slaves, are replaced over painstaking years of labour by Azyr's stonecutters. The new lighthouse-style buildings are known as the Brimstone Keeps.

THE LEGACY OF GLORY
Statues to Vandus Hammerhand, Ionus Cryptborn and Jactos Goldenmane are raised across the land now known as the Brimstone Beachhead. The Stormcast Eternals consolidate their grip on the southern territories of the Great Parch. As the wars against Chaos proceed, some tribes see the Stormcast Eternals as abominations, for they do not truly die and turn to ash as all things must, but come back again. Others see them as saviours, and do everything they can to fight alongside them. Few indeed realise that the Stormcasts pay a hidden cost with each death and rebirth.

HOPE FROM THE ASHES
New cities thrive in those lands reclaimed by Order. Art, philosophy and fashion begin to develop once more, not just in Aspiria and Bataar but in Hammerhal Aqsha and Callidium also. The oranges, yellows and reds long favoured by the Great Parch tribes are still much in evidence, though the richest and most privileged dress in the whites, blues and silvers of Azyr in the hope of being thought as civilised and celestial rather than fiery and volatile. But whatever pretensions the city-dwellers might adopt, they find that Aqshian emotion still simmers beneath, their lives burning as bright and short as ever before.

THE LOOMING ORB
Just as civilisation is re-establishing itself, a terrible sight grows large in the skies – it is Orb Infernia, power-base of the once-banished Korghos Khul and his daemon legions. Blood rains across the lands as the forces of Khorne muster for a massive counter-offensive. Khorne does not really want the Great Parch utterly and completely for himself, but rather the war for it to continue indefinitely. In many ways Khul sees the coming of Sigmar's new civilisation and order as a boon – it gives his legions something to attack, and more blood to spill.

'*Ignax, she was called. A dragon so vast she coiled around the sun.*' Japeth the minstrel raconteur grinned, hot spiced ale swilling from his tankard. He posed heroically as people turned to listen at the sound of his raised voice, then gestured grandly at his embroidered waistcoat where godbeasts and stormbolts intertwined. '*If not for her, and the Lightning Warriors that rode alongside her, Aqshy would have burnt out long ago.*'

'*She was the sun,*' said a gnarled duardin at the back of the taverna, his face a mass of scars under a hood of sackcloth. '*And it was we duardin that did the saving, not just Sigmar's storm-whelps. Without the Rune of Binding, Archaon the Thrice-Damned would have had her turn us all to ash.*' At the mention of the Everchosen's name, many of the people recoiled and made the sign of the comet.

'*And how does a hideous beggar know so much about it?*' said Japeth, features twisting. He was fast losing control of the audience.

'*I was there, you prancing fool,*' said the elderly duardin, throwing back his hood to expose a face seared to the skull. '*I was there, I broke her chains, and I will see her burn bright once more.*'

GHYRAN, REALM OF LIFE

Ghyran burgeons with all forms of life, from the most massive gighemoth to the tiniest parasitic spore. Known as the Jade Kingdoms, the realm's people vary wildly in form and temperament. The Ghyranites have suffered much under Nurgle's invasions, and none more so than the denizens of the Everspring Swathe.

Once, the Jade Kingdoms were glorious to behold, wonders of verdant majesty enhanced still further by the seamless blending of civilisation with the natural world. Those areas nearest the core of the realmsphere were cultivated gardens and sun-dappled lawns, where the kingdoms at the edges of Ghyran's vastness were overgrown with lush jungle to the point of being utterly impenetrable by anything other than Ghyran's multitude of insects.

Even the richly scented air seemed to pulse and throb with glorious life force. The many seasons of the realm – not only spring, summer, autumn and winter but also the burgeoning, the reaping, secret remorse, the great lack and up to a dozen more – saw the cycle of existence revolve over and over again. This endless carousel of life drew the eye of the Father of Plagues; he coveted the Jade Kingdoms above all others, and sent the greater portion of his forces

to spread their foul taint across those lands during the Age of Chaos. Where once there was verdant harmony and rebirth, the power of Nurgle introduced blight, disease, and a vile fecundity that saw only foul things born, breaking down the most beautiful life forms and majestic living cities into repulsive, daemon-infested slop. The coming of Sigmar's Tempest has allowed Ghyran a reprieve – in time, it may yet heal from some of its wounds.

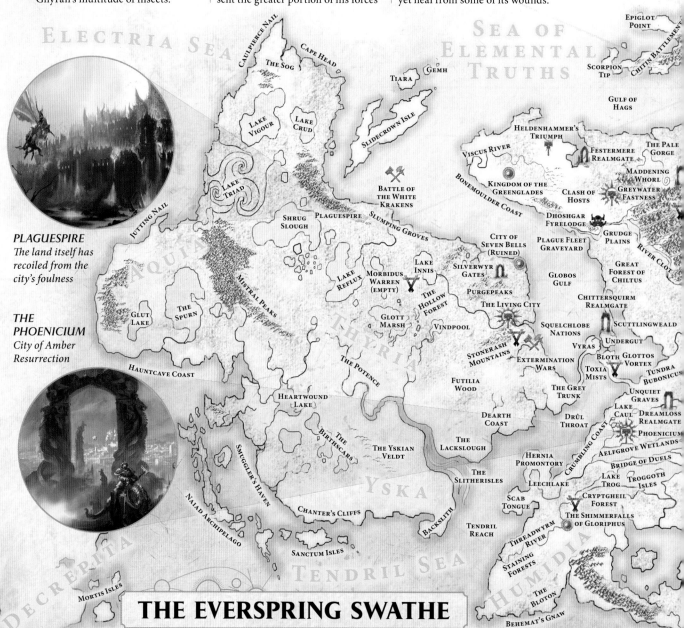

PLAGUESPIRE
The land itself has recoiled from the city's foulness

THE PHOENICIUM
City of Amber Resurrection

THE EVERSPRING SWATHE

THE LIVING CITY
Grown to glory in a matter of days by the magic of the Everqueen

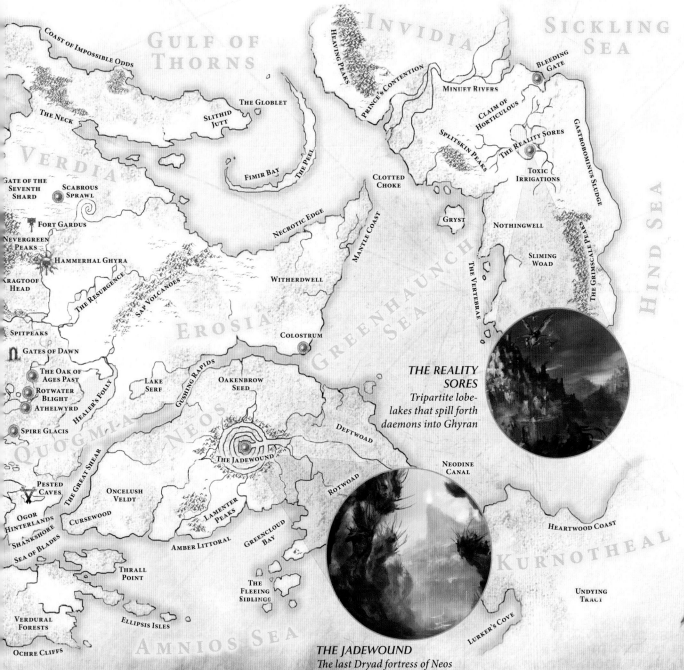

COAST OF IMPOSSIBLE ODDS

GULF OF THORNS

INVIDIA

SICKLING SEA

HEAVING PEAKS

PRINCE'S CONTENTION

MINUET RIVERS

BLEEDING GATE

CLAIM OF HORTICULOUS

THE GLOBLET

SLITHID JUTT

THE NECK

VERDIA

SPLITSKIN PEAKS

THE REALITY SORES

GASTROBOMINUS SLUDGE

TOXIC IRRIGATIONS

FIMIR BAY

THE PEEL

CLOTTED CHOKE

GATE OF THE SEVENTH SHARD

SCABROUS SPRAWL

FORT GARDUS

NEVERGREEN PEAKS

NECROTIC EDGE

MANTLE COAST

GRYST

NOTHINGWELL

THE GRIMSCALE PEAKS

HIND SEA

HAMMERHAL GHYRA

KRAGTOOF HEAD

THE RESURGENCE

SAP VOLCANOES

WITHERDWELL

SLIMING WOAD

THE VERTEBRAE

GREENHAUNCH SEA

SPITPEAKS

EROSIA

COLOSTRUM

GATES OF DAWN

THE OAK OF AGES PAST

ROTWATER BLIGHT

ATHELWYRD

HEALER'S FOLLY

LAKE SERF

GUSHING RAPIDS

OAKENBROW SEED

THE REALITY SORES
Tripartite lobe-lakes that spill forth daemons into Ghyran

DEFTWOAD

SPIRE GLACIS

QUOGMIA

NEOS

THE GREAT SHEAR

THE JADEWOUND

NEODINE CANAL

ROTWOAD

PESTED CAVES

ONCELUSH VELDT

OGOR HINTERLANDS

CURSEWOOD

LAMENTER PEAKS

HEARTWOOD COAST

SHANKSHORE

SEA OF BLADES

AMBER LITTORAL

GREENCLOUD BAY

KURNOTHEAL

THRALL POINT

THE FLEEING SIDLINGS

UNDYING TRACT

VERDURAL FORESTS

ELLIPSIS ISLES

LURKER'S COVE

OCHRE CLIFFS

AMNIOS SEA

THE JADEWOUND
The last Dryad fortress of Neos

THE EVERSPRING SWATHE

The twin Jade Kingdoms that form the Everspring Swathe were once a haven for the cycle of life. During the Age of Myth, Alarielle made her home there. The blessing of Alarielle's presence drives the twin isles into new heights of burgeoning fecundity, and a reproductive cycle takes place in the lands themselves.

● THE AGE OF MYTH ●

THE BIRTH OF NEW LANDS

Intrigued by the unusual quirk of Verdia's diverse ecosystem, Alarielle takes up residence within that sub-continent. There, all the life-forms are female, and every birth season they mate with the inhabitants of the land's counterpart, Thyria, where all the life-forms are male. Thyria enjoys divine patronage too, for this is a land where the Hunter God is often seen, migrating over from the eastern land of Kurnotheal. Each spring the lands themselves mate, and the seeds of new domains are planted, the sub-continent of Verdia making geological congress with its neighbour, linking with Thyria via the stamen-like promontories known as the Triske Isles. From this union is born the spring island of Neos, a thriving new kingdom that rises from the waters in the east to reveal at its heart a huge geomantic birthmark in the shape of Ghyran itself. That same season sees the rise of Neos' strange siblings – the Isle Decrepita, a land where the dwindling of years rules supreme, and the undulating island of Irridia, where even the soil itself is pregnant with new life.

ROOTS OF DISCONTENT

Though fertile Irridia is largely left to its own devices by Alarielle, the newborn nations of Neos and Decrepita are seeded with soulpods from the Everqueen's amphorae. They are soon inhabited by fresh glades of Sylvaneth – the proud Oakenbrow in Neos, and the shadowy Dreadwood in Decrepita. A rivalry quickly springs up between the two lands, for the cold-hearted humans and bitter Sylvaneth of Decrepita are jealous of the joyful, youthful tribes of Neos, who live in harmony with the Dryad groves that sprout there. Over the years, this rivalry is to turn sour, with the Princelings of Irridia caught in the middle.

TO STEAL AWAY THE YOUNG

In freezing Decrepita, few children are born. Every new year the ice-people of that realm take to the Tendril Sea and raid the shores of Neos, capturing newborns and soulpods with which to give life to their own barren shores. The doe-eyed people of Neos are usually kind, naïve, and quick to forgive – though the theft of their children they cannot ignore. Over time they learn to hate the gnarled warriors of Decrepita and to fear the sight of their wolf-ship sails.

THE OAK OF AGES PAST

Perhaps attracted to Alarielle as an echo of old realities, the Oak of Ages Past drifts through the void, coming to rest in the south of Verdia near the hidden vale of Athelwyrd. Sigmar sees this strange visitation from High Azyr and, recognising the great oak as a symbol of defiance, he makes haste to Verdia, bringing the gift of civilisation to the humans there.

A TIME OF PLENTY

With an ever-growing accord fostered between Alarielle's Sylvaneth and Sigmar's humans, great cities are built amongst the treetops and groves of the Everspring Swathe. The currency that comes into being across these nations is not that of coin, but labour. The people of the Swathe nations trade time – a minute, an hour, a day, or a week of hard work in exchange for goods and services, each promise kept by oral tradition and hearsay alone. At first, this loose honour system is all that is needed, such is the trust and harmony among the races.

FROM HARMONY, SLOTH

For a while, the Swatheling honour system works, but human laziness and complacency sees hostility break out amongst several tribes as trade-covenants are broken. Old debts and accusations resurface – in all five of the Swathe nations, the darker Sylvaneth kindreds are accused of stealing animals and even snatching away human children in the night. Cracks appear in the relationship between the races, and some tribes begin to mistrust or even bear hostility towards certain others.

INVASION OF THE DEAD

Decrepita, being a land where every living thing freezes and dies every year only to be reborn again each spring, is coveted by Nagash. Under the guise of a mass diplomatic visit he brings his armies to that region in person via the vast vertebral structures known as the Gates Mortis. At first, his vanguard is held at bay by the Dreadwood. However, seemingly endless undead pour through the gate and, ultimately, the Sylvaneth cordon is breached. A wide-scale eruption of violence is only halted by the direct intervention of Sigmar.

CELESTIAL ALIGNMENT

As the God-King spreads human civilisation across the lands, he enlists the aid of Alarielle and Nagash – albeit separately – as part of his Pantheon of Order. They both agree to his requests, but essentially for selfish reasons, doing so in the interests of fostering civilisations that they can later harness and mould in their own images.

During the dwindle-cycle after the summer of new growth, Alarielle seeks parley with Nagash. She points out they are both part of Sigmar's wider plan, and they agree to a compromise – Nagash will take Decrepita as his sovereign territory, but in return he swears to be content to keep his legions there and stray no further.

The spring isle of Neos, no longer raided and harassed by the wolf-ships of Decrepita, burgeons with new energies. The hyper-verdant realm gives rise to a thousand new species. Nourished by the Heaving Rapids, they cross the Great Shear to the motherlands of Erosia and southern Verdia. Alarielle's lush green continent sings with life more than ever before, and for a while, all is paradise.

THE HUNTER GOD

The far eastern island of Kurnotheal becomes the favoured haunt of Kurnoth – a land where he and his Wild Hunt can chase down spiralhorn, vernadyr and goliath alike, indulging their bloodthirsty instincts without fear of disapproval from his paramour Alarielle. Every spring, however, he makes his pilgrimage to Athelwyrd, the sacred valley where Alarielle makes her most beloved bower.

VIOLATION OF ACCORD

Neither Nagash's lieutenants nor the native Dreadwood Sylvaneth abide by their truce with Neos for long. Violence breaks out amongst the evergreen forests, and a battle for Decrepita's soul rages in the shadows. The shapeshifting dove-maidens of Neos watch with baited breath, fearing that the enmity that will emerge from the clash will be more terrible than ever before.

THE COMING OF BEHEMAT

Attracted by the rich herds of food that prowl Verdia, the titanic gargant Behemat strides through the sea to the Harmonis Veldt. He eats too much of the local fauna, bringing several bovine species to extinction. Stuffed to beyond even his capacity, he vomits forth entire tribes of wholly formed giants, known as the Sons of Behemat.

The Sons of Behemat make a civilisation of their own across the Harmonis Veldt, ruling from the Great Green Torc high above that swathe of land. Behemat himself, exhausted from his great feat of procreation, rests upon the land. There his lumpen form crusts over and hardens into several mountain ranges.

ERUPTION AND ENTRAPMENT

The giant geomantic birthmark upon Neos pulses with Ghyranite energy upon the Jade Equinox, causing life-quakes across the land and a rash of immaculate conceptions. In the north, the Sap Volcanoes of Erosia erupt, filling the skies with translucent tree-blood. In the west, the arboreal Quogmia Mountain heaves so mightily it splits its sides. Tidal waves of sticky amber entrap ancient Aelfgrove, a city elegantly built upon the mountain's flanks.

● THE AGE OF CHAOS ●

DIVINE VISITATIONS

The Plague Lord sets his rheumy eyes upon the Swathe nations, seeing a great crucible of life but a season's journey from a region of wintery death. Nurgle is jubilant, for he has found prime territory waiting to be annexed to the garden. The Dark God sends out swarms of spy-creatures, the compound eyes of plague flies watching with avid interest whenever a relationship between Sylvaneth, human and aelf goes sour. They largely go unnoticed, for insects of all kinds are ever-present in these regions, and not even the Sylvaneth are aware of the infiltration at first. Nurgle listens with curiosity as his spy-flies whisper and buzz in his ear.

THE DWINDLING BEGINS

As the season of the dwindling draws in, the invasions of Nurgle's forces are unleashed. At first, they strike through captured Realmgates and the reality-splitting gnawholes of the Clans Pestilens.

They gain a foothold with relative swiftness, for the lands have not seen their like, and Nurgle has learned well of the Everspring Swathe.

In a matter of scant seasons their influence is such that they can be summoned by means of a relentless downpour, the storm of tainted water with which the Lord of Plagues often favours his chosen ones. In northern Thyria, the blessings of the Great Unclean One known as Rotigus drench the lands. Such is the violence of Nurgle's Deluge that the once-sunlit upper lands, saturated with plague magic, crumble away to form the Slidecrown Isle. The land left behind is thereafter known as the Sog. Many human tribes, having long worshipped abstract rain gods as a source of fecundity, turn their loyalty to Rotigus within the passing of a single moon.

SWATHE NATIONS AT WAR

The Sylvaneth are the first to fight back hard against the Nurgle invaders. Bolstered by their allies, the human peoples of those lands and the aelves known as the Wanderers, their spirited counter-offensives cause tremendous damage upon the plague daemon hosts. However, when the Wanderers begin to contract Nurgle's Rot – foremost amongst a clutch of sickening and disfiguring ailments spread by the legions of Nurgle – many aelven tribes gather in secret far from Sylvaneth ears, and discuss taking a different path.

CURSE OF THE GLOTTKIN

The eastern reaches of the Sea of Elemental Truths become infested when Ethrac Glott, the sorcerous eldest sibling of the Glottkin triplets, releases a shoal of cursed hagfish into the water. The piscine terrors grow to a colossal size by feeding on the sacred Aqua Ghyranis of those waters, and they attack in a frenzy any who stray near the coast, even wrecking ships when they gather in sufficient numbers. The killer shoal interbreeds and spreads further, forming an impassable barrier of diseased sea life that prevents Verdia from being reinforced by its allies in the north. The area is thereafter named the Gulf of Hags.

THE SWARM DESCENDS

As Nurgle's curse spreads further, the isle of Irridia (soon to become Invidia) is surrounded by the sentient seaweed known as spinebladder. Its western sea-link to Verdia is clotted to the point that it flows no more, and the island is cut off.

COLD SEEDS BEAR NO FRUIT

The wintery land of Decrepita is assailed by Bloab Rotspawned and his plague fly swarms, accompanied by hosts of Plague Drones and Pusgoyle Blightlords. Decrepita's undead hold back the invaders whilst the still-living send their wolf-ship emissaries to the Dryads and nature tribes of Neos, seeking help in the face of a common enemy. The people of Neos turn a deaf ear – their habit of forgiveness has long been eroded by the violence of Decrepita's raids.

DIVIDED THEY FALL

Neos in turn is assailed, the south-eastern jungle becoming the Rotwoad when Morbidex Twiceborn summons a tsunami of Nurglings that turn the lush vegetation into rotting mulch. Without the tribes of the Everspring Sprawl standing united, the Nurgle invaders find them easy fodder for their rusting axes.

THE WANDERING

Those dissident Wanderers that believe the battle is already lost come into pre-eminence in Neos and Verdia, their arguments strengthened with each region overtaken by Nurgle. In the dead of night, they lead the population to the root-moulded Realmgate known as the Twining Portal. There they enter the Cascading Path, a mystical web of pathways that criss-cross Ghyran, and flee upon the hidden ways to Azyr. In doing so, they abandon the Sylvaneth to their fate. That slight is never forgiven.

THE CLAIM OF HORTICULOUS

With a great ritual of sullying, Horticulous Slimux turns the Hind Sea to gelatinous mulch and sends packs of Beasts of Nurgle across it. Kurnotheal is assailed by waves of the plague beasts. The creatures once hunted by Kurnoth become infected as Slimux's Beasts of Nurgle chase them down and slobber happily all over them. One dark night, the plagued herds turn upon those that once hunted them for sport. The invasion is timed perfectly, for Horticulous understands the passing of the seasons well – Kurnoth is in his wintering phase, and hence at his weakest right at the critical hour. Though he feels a great angst in doing so, Kurnoth withdraws to fight another day.

Even as the Beasts of Nurgle infest Kurnotheal, the Gravidian Gate is breached by the forces of Horticulous Slimux. The Garden of Nurgle begins to grow across the island, its curse so potent that the Realmgate buckles and splits into three pieces. In doing so, it becomes three massive sores in the crust of the kingdom, known as the Canker

Pits. The daemonic forces of Nurgle pour out from the fortresses that spring up around the Canker Pits like scabs around a wound. United behind the Grand Cultivator Slimux, they conquer the isle entirely. The kingdom is thereafter renamed Invidia, the Claim of Horticulous.

THE GIANT SLEEPS ON

In the area that has become the Scabrous Sprawl – formerly the Harmonis Veldt – Behemat the World Titan sleeps on. Learning of his presence through the sorcerer Kraderblob, Archaon the Everchosen makes plans to wake the godbeast and bind him using the Great Green Torc. The gargants known as the Sons of Behemat, driven from their holdings by Chaos attacks, are forced into hiding within the Sweatswamp by the massed attacks of the Clans Pestilens and their Rotbringer allies. The tribesmen that traded with the gargants are slain or driven into the sea. Only a handful of tribes survive the slaughter.

THE LANDS WRITHE IN PAIN

Repelled by the Hagfish Curse and the taint ravaging the forests of Slithid Jutt, a large fringe of coastline splits away from mainland Verdia. It forms the marshy crescent known as the Peel, and becomes a stronghold of the mist-dwelling Fimir race.

The Triske Isles – the stamen-like isthmuses linking Thyria to Verdia – become divided into three sub-realms. They transform into the tri-lobe structure now known as the Squelchlobe Nations, becoming Vyras, Bloth and Undergut. Each of the lobes is conquered by one of the three self-aggrandising sorcerers that call themselves the Sons of Putrefaction. With the Spirits of Durthu that guarded the sites slain and put to the torch, the sorcerers are free to pursue their own arcane agendas, and constantly vie for supremacy.

A DEADLY HARVEST

The War of Life intensifies as the Sylvaneth unite against the Nurgle invaders. The Glottkin and their rivals hunt for Alarielle across the lands, but she remains hidden in the under-realm of Athelwyrd.

THE OAK BEGINS TO ROT

As the war rages on, the Oak of Ages Past – a sacred link to the World Before Time – is defiled by Nurgle. The great lake around it is converted into a putrid, brackish slop, known now as Rotwater Blight. The once-pure waters of the River Vitalis that poured from the great tree's split trunk are tainted by the bathings of the Great Unclean One, Pupa Grotesse, and become the thick river of sludge known as Gelid Gush.

THE TOLL OF STRIFE

Across the Realm of Life the story is the same – with Nurgle's power waxing, there is little the heavily outnumbered Sylvaneth can do to hold back the tides of decay that assail them. Alarielle becomes despondent, retreating further into her malaise until her lands are all but abandoned to their fate.

THE BRINK OF UTTER DEFEAT

With his job done and a great part of the Everspring Swathe now in thrall to Nurgle, Horticulous Slimux departs for a new mission – to bring the garden to the Coast of Tusks in Ghur. In his wake, the forces of Chaos hunt every day for Alarielle, to no avail. They begin to war amongst themselves as they run out of natural enemies to fight. Guerrilla attacks from Sylvaneth continue, but it becomes obvious that Nurgle has dominance in every isle of the Everspring Swathe. Whole generations pass, with Alarielle's verdant fortresses found and conquered one by one. Only Athelwyrd is left, hidden under the waters out of the sight of its enemies.

● THE AGE OF SIGMAR ●

AT THE GATES OF DAWN

The Hallowed Knights are the first Stormcast Eternals to enter Ghyran, crashing down before the Gates of Dawn to destroy the host of the sorcerer Kraderblob and the seven greater daemons led by the rotting monstrosity Bolathrax. Gardus of the Steel Soul forces his way into the Garden of Nurgle, Bolathrax hard upon his heels – the gate crumbles under the Great Unclean One's bulk, preventing further Chaos reinforcements from coming through. Ultimately, it is Gardus' miraculous reappearance that turns the tide for the Hallowed Knights.

THE FADING OF THE EVERQUEEN

The Hallowed Knights search for Alarielle, entering the hidden valley of Athelwyrd at the end of their long quest – and in doing so, lead the warlords of Nurgle straight to it. A massive battle breaks out, culminating in Alarielle fleeing along the Cascading Path in search of safety. Such is her despondency that she becomes little more than a magical seed, borne by her handmaiden the Lady of Vines. Aided by a Jotunberg, a walking winter mountain, they stay ahead of Torglug the Despised's legions. By hastening across the frozen Sea of Serpents and shattering the ice floes behind her, she almost outruns her pursuers, but the sorcerous Slaugoth belches forth a bridge of frozen vomit across which the Nurgle hosts charge. Only the valiant efforts of the Hallowed Knights keep her from being overrun.

VENGEANCE LONG AWAITED

As disaster looms, Alarielle is replanted in the Grove of Heroes, and there gestates into her war form, ready to wreak a terrible vengeance on the followers of Nurgle. With Alarielle's resurgence and the defeat of the Glottkin at the floating Landshoals, the forces of Nurgle begin to break. Over the course of the now-fabled Season of War, the Everspring Swathe is painstakingly saved from the brink of utter damnation by the alliance of Sylvaneth and Stormcast Eternals. They take the fight to the Chaos intruders on a hundred different fronts, and though it costs millions of lives, islands of Order begin to emerge from the darkness.

THE SEEDS OF HOPE

The three cities known as the Seeds of Hope are established as Nurgle finds his power waning. Fast-tracked by Alarielle's life-magic, the cities of Greywater Fastness, the Living City and the Phoenicium spring into existence. Greywater Fastness becomes a centre of industry and an artillerist's haven, boasting more cannons per mile of city walls than anywhere else in the Jade Kingdoms. Valius Maliti, the famed architect, encourages the gung-ho attitude of the city's engineers, incentivising deforestation and thereby stoking the tension between the Free Peoples and Alarielle's forces. The militaristic, industrialist mindset of Greywater Fastness drives Alarielle to the point of rage.

A BRIDGE TOO FAR

When the inhabitants of Greywater Fastness level the verdant ground around the city during the Season of War and turn it into a desolate, chemical-ridden swamp, Alarielle sends forth a host of the Dreadwood to encircle the city and protect what is left – now known as the Ghoul Mere. Led by a Treelord named Pale Oak, the Sylvaneth refuse to let the people of the city into the despoiled regions, and the Ghoul Mere becomes a deadly no man's land. Only the Eldritch Council of Greywater Fastness are able to strike a deal to stop the city starving to death, ensuring that a single route in and out of the city can still be used without fear of reprisal. However, the region is shrouded in mist, and an unwary traveller who strays far from the heavily guarded trade road will be snatched away by vengeful woodland spirits, never to be seen again.

THE TWIN-TAILED CITY

Hammerhal Ghyra is established, becoming even larger and more influential than the Seeds of Hope due to its thriving trade with the other half of the Twin-tailed City, Hammerhal Aqsha. The magma streams channelled through the Realmgate from Aqshy keep back the endless growth of Ghyran, allowing the city and its lush gardens to be cultivated into one of the wonders of the Mortal Realms.

SHYISH, REALM OF DEATH

Shyish is the realm of endings and silent decline. It is not a contiguous domain, but a myriad of underworlds, all coalesced upon the same plane. They are crystallised into being from pure death magic, though both Nagash and the Dark Gods have sought to break them apart, the better to feed upon the richness of their amethyst energy.

Most understand Shyish to be a flat disc with a deep pit in the middle that pulls everything else in towards it, much as a whirlpool drains the flotsam of a shattered fleet into its depths. It can be depicted as a vast torus on which everything at the edge is pulled in towards the centre. However, some civilisations instead depict the underworlds of Shyish as continental plates suspended, one atop another, in an inverted pyramid of magical energy. Many ogor tribes see it as an impossibly huge mouth that devours all things, whereas the Spiderfang grots see it as the lair of a titanic arachnid that draws all mortal creatures into its web. Such is the nature of trying to define that which a mortal mind cannot hope to fully comprehend.

As a new mythical underworld gains ground in the belief system of a mortal society, the magical stuff of Shyish coalesces at the edge of the realm to form a reflection of that afterlife. Shapes crystallise in the amethyst clouds of the Shyish realmsphere, becoming ever more real until a new land is born, settled by the souls of those who believe in it upon their death. Though the nature of Shyish has been forever changed due to Nagash's baleful influence, this process continues unabated.

An underworld that thrives, grieves but a little and remains content in its fate can remain at the Realm's Edge almost indefinitely. One that is downtrodden will instead splinter and come apart until it is sucked towards the Shyish Nadir, ground down to little more than a silt rich in death magic by the unstoppable tidal forces that swirl and spin at the realm's heart.

LAKE LETHIS
Upon a shore caressed by enchanted waters, golden palaces once shone proud, but since the Age of Chaos they lie tarnished and strange.

ZHARR VYXA
The infernal industry of twisted duardin siphons the raw energy of death from within dark waters.

CARSTINIA
To approach the lands north-west of the Deserted Peaks is to witness Mannfred's morbid legacy writ large. Those who walk that road will pass scattered bones and once-cherished artefacts lying broken in the dirt.

THE PRIME INNERLANDS

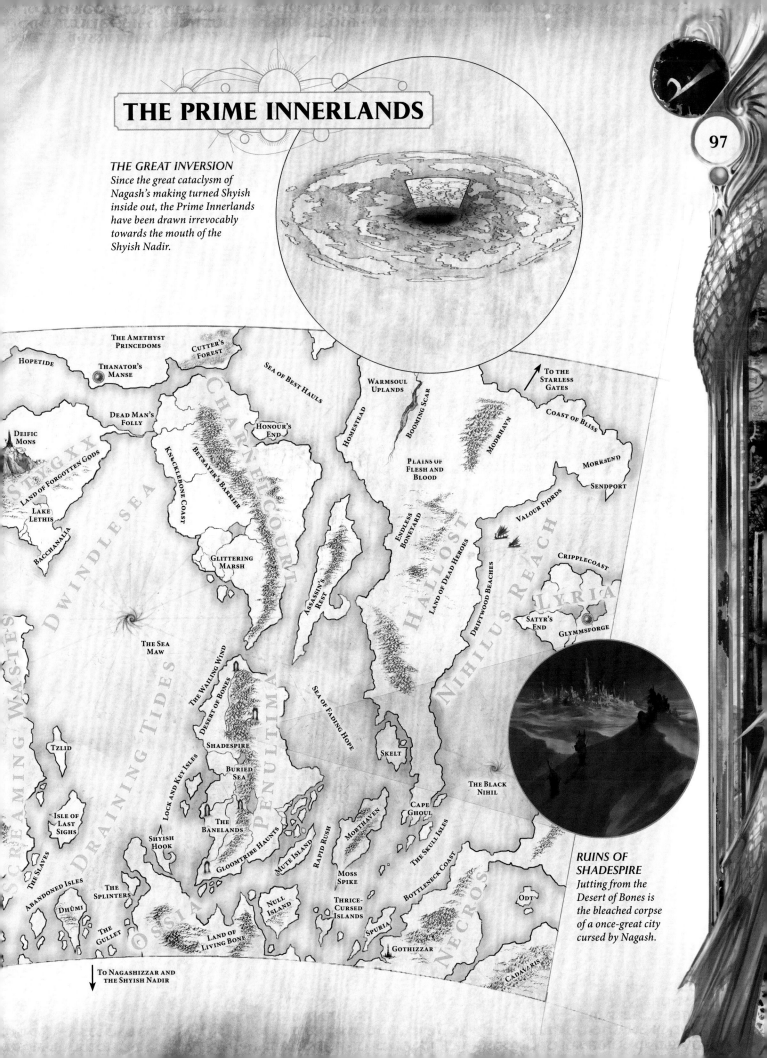

THE GREAT INVERSION
Since the great cataclysm of Nagash's making turned Shyish inside out, the Prime Innerlands have been drawn irrevocably towards the mouth of the Shyish Nadir.

HOPETIDE

THE AMETHYST PRINCEDOMS

THANATOR'S MANSE

CUTTER'S FOREST

SEA OF BEST HAULS

WARMSOUL UPLANDS

TO THE STARLESS GATES

DEAD MAN'S FOLLY

HONOUR'S END

HOMESTEAD

BOOMING SCAR

MODRHAVN

COAST OF BLISS

DEIFIC MONS

LAND OF FORGOTTEN GODS

KNUCKLEBONE COAST

BETRAYER'S BARRIER

PLAINS OF FLESH AND BLOOD

MORKSEND

SENDPORT

STYGXX

LAKE LETHIS

BACCHANALIA

DWINDLESEA

GLITTERING MARSH

ENDLESS BONEYARD

LAND OF DEAD HEROES

VALOUR FJORDS

CRIPPLECOAST

CHARNELCOURT

ASSASSIN'S REST

HALLOST

DRIFTWOOD BEACHES

NIHILUS REACH

LYRIA

SATYR'S END

GLYMMSFORGE

THE SEA MAW

SCREAMING WASTES

DRAINING TIDES

THE WAILING WIND

DESERT OF BONES

SEA OF FADING HOPE

TZLID

SHADESPIRE

BURIED SEA

SKELT

THE BLACK NIHIL

LOCK AND KEY ISLES

ISLE OF LAST SIGHS

PENULTIMA

THE BANELANDS

GLOOMTRIBE HAUNTS

MUTE ISLAND

RAPID RUSH

MORTHAVEN

CAPE GHOUL

THE SLAVES

SHYISH HOOK

THE SKULL ISLES

ABANDONED ISLES

MOSS SPIKE

BOTTLENECK COAST

ODT

THE SPLINTERS

NULL ISLAND

THRICE-CURSED ISLANDS

DHÜMI

OSSIA

SPURIA

NECROS

THE GULLET

LAND OF LIVING BONE

GOTHIZZAR

CADAVARIS

TO NAGASHIZZAR AND THE SHYISH NADIR

RUINS OF SHADESPIRE
Jutting from the Desert of Bones is the bleached corpse of a once-great city cursed by Nagash.

THE PRIME INNERLANDS

The Prime Innerlands are a swathe of Shyishan countries and island regions already in thrall to the Shyish Nadir. Though the edgeward lands – those furthest away from the Nadir – are temperate and, in places, even verdant, the coreward lands are moribund and lethal indeed. Only the dead can truly thrive there.

● THE AGE OF MYTH ●

THE STARLESS GATES

The First Great Change comes upon Shyish when the Starless Gates – defended against the living by giant skeletal hydragors – are flung wide by the God-King Sigmar. The hydragor guardians are shattered by the mighty hammer Ghal Maraz, opening the way into the underworlds for the living as well as the deceased. Gnorros, the Father of Hydragors, is so enraged by the slaying of his guardians that he stabs his claws into the Prime Innerlands in an attempt to slay Sigmar. The God-King escapes, but the indentations form the Chained Lakes, as well as the giant whirlpools known as the Sea Maw and the Black Nihil. Luckily, Gnorros, who has a very short attention span, leaves for pastures new.

THE QUICK AND THE DEAD

Under Sigmar's watchful eye, mortal folk settle and populate Shyish's Prime Innerlands – those least saturated in the energies of death. Slowly, cities are built and civilisations thrive. Great obsidian towers are erected, the finest tall and grand enough to rival even the star-spires of Azyr. Amongst the most impressive regions are those of Stygxx, a mountainous underworld where gods and mortals freely interbreed; Hallost, the Land of Dead Heroes, where those who believe in eternal battle are reincarnated with each new day; and Athanasia, where the mortals live only a set span before willingly going to their deaths in a great rite of ending – only to be reborn with the next rising sun.

The richest of the Innerlands are the Amethyst Princedoms – a domain where precious minerals glitter everywhere. The Amethyst Princedoms thrive above all, with the ven Denst dynasty acting as benevolent kings that trade through a well-defended Realmgate network.

Ossia, another underworld of the Innerlands, thrives. It is a place of peace, with the living coexisting in harmony alongside the dead. Many thousands of graveyards cover its lands, and every ghost-soul that travels there from the mortal lands of Fleizch finds an echo of their grave transported with them. They feel little grief, for they are often sought out by living relatives visiting their true graves in Fleizch, and take succour in hearing of those still living as the news echoes into Shyish.

BOUNTY OF THE SEAS

The waters of the Shyish Innerlands thrive with pale-skinned forms of life, amongst them massive eater-fish and greater scuttlefish that prey on all things that drift down to the sea bed. Though it takes the settlers of the Innerlands many perilous years to learn how to catch these omni-predators safely, they pull in hauls of such number that in the northern lands no soul need ever go hungry.

LIFE IN THE REALM OF DEATH

The people of the Innerlands, taught the arts of civilisation by Sigmar himself, thrive and innovate. Dirgesong, soulful music and amethyst sky-lanterns fill the underworld night. Gemstones, created from the crushing pressures of the subterranean strata and mined by gifted duardin and human guilds, become so commonplace that they are considered of less value than good meat – a fattened bull is worth a year's wages in the Innerlands, for fauna is scarce. Trade with the Realm of Beasts, established by the Amethyst Princes via the Penultima Realmgate network, sees much salted meat and livestock imported every year. For several generations, the Innerlands enjoy harmony.

THEN COMES NAGASH

In the course of his travels, Sigmar finds Nagash's soulless shell buried under a cairn of magical realmstone. After the demise of the world-that-

was, Nagash's essence had been naturally drawn to Shyish. Sigmar deliberates long upon the correct course, but sensing an opportunity he chooses to revive the Great Necromancer, just as Dracothion had revived him in turn. It is a decision he will come to regret.

Upon his awakening, Nagash swears to align himself with Sigmar's agendas, but in secret he covets the power of the underworlds and wishes to consume them all. He makes his home at the exact centre of the Shyish realmsphere, and builds the fortress complex of Nagashizzar at its core. For long centuries he crafts his armies with bone, spirit, amethyst and the stuff of death itself. When his legions reach the heights of magnificence, he sends his undead minions across the Innerlands to locate and gather as much Shyishan realmstone as possible. Over the course of long centuries, many monolithic deposits are unearthed by legions of skeleton slaves. Purple-black structures of vitrified magical sand take shape at Shyish's heart.

LANDS OF THE MORTARCHS

Nagash sends his lieutenants, the Mortarchs, to expand their own realms. Arkhan the Black takes a stronghold beyond the sight of mortal men, whereas Neferata extends her dominion to an unclaimed underworld, naming it Neferatia, and builds the city of Nulahmia there as a memento of her old strongholds. Mannfred von Carstein also annexes a part of the Innerlands, naming it Carstinia, but the land is a mere echo of his former glories. Mannfred sits on his overly huge throne, corpses fashioned in the likeness of Vlad, Konrad and Isabella at his beck and call, but in his heart he knows it is an artificial thing he has made, a reminder of his failure to claim the old Empire for his own. He soon abdicates, leaving a hollow mockery of Sylvania behind him.

THE FATE OF SHADESPIRE

Penultima is a thriving and populous land of mortal men. Its people revere their ancestors and build great cities of learning and understanding. One of these is Shadespire, where the civic luminaries known as Katophranes lead the pursuit of science, alchemy and magic.

The Katophranes even manage to harness the power of grave-sand, the near-black substance that is laced throughout the realmstone-dunes of Shyish, each rivulet representing the lifespan of a mortal creature in the realms. It is said that one who halts the flow of their personal sand-stream will put off indefinitely their own demise. The Katophranes succeed in this, vitrifying the sands of time into a brittle material known as shadeglass. With this invention, they live on in magical reflections long after their natural life's end, the better to teach their pupils the secrets they long ago uncovered.

Innovation and even technology becomes commonplace in Shadespire, as does the pursuit of the arcane. The city becomes famous, and its spires rise high indeed. Its thriving trade in ensorcelled items fills the city's coffers to bursting, but over time, Nagash becomes incensed by the arrogance of the Katophranes of Shadespire and their methods of escaping his clutches. He works a great spell to wrench the essence of the city from its physical incarnation and hurl it into the aether, where it will abide forever as a ghostly echo of its former self. The city's essence comes to rest in Uhl-Gysh, the Hidden Gloaming, the twilight realm between Ulgu and Hysh.

QUIETUS INTERRUPTED

Assassin's Rest, a land shaped like the hook symbol of Shyish, is home to the ghosts of some of the most notorious killers of the age. These souls roam the island eternally, each convinced by the island's peculiar magic that they are completely alone. They find a kind of peace as a result. Slowly, however, the land falls under the sway of Nagash's necromancers. With a legion of undead assassins at his command, he destabilises a dozen nations in a single night.

A DEADLY TOLL

Nagash's grip on Shyish becomes tighter and tighter. Many of the older, more traditional underworlds are conquered by legions of undead and their energies harnessed to feed Nagash's undying hunger. Across the Innerlands, primitive civilisations cower as Nagash hunts down the lords of each underworld and devours them, one at a time.

It seems that nothing can stop the Great Necromancer, for in the deathly lands of Shyish his power is magnified tenfold. The underworld nations pray, in their own ways, for something – anything – to break the curse of evil that has fallen across their homelands.

● THE AGE OF CHAOS ●

A TIME OF NEW STRIFE

The Dark Gods invade Shyish. Not content with his pre-eminence in Ghyran, Nurgle seeks dominance over the entire cycle of life and death, and sends his daemon hosts through the oceanic Realmgates that lead to Shyish. Plague fleets in great number emerge from the Sea Maw and the Black Nihil. Athanasia, the Amethyst Princedoms, Ossia and Stygxx are all invaded in one fell month as Nurgle's power waxes.

Khorne, for his part, covets the Land of Dead Heroes, and seeks an eternal war there. The quality of battle to be had in Hallost gives the Blood God a great source of power as deceased hero and daemon clash anew each morning in an unending war. Gravesites are raided, the heads taken from revered bodies and used to decorate the crenellated Chaos Dreadforts that are erected across the Innerlands. Some of the lands' departed gheists are even forced to exhume their own mortal remains and to place their skulls in the walls of the cities they once inhabited. All across the Innerlands the yoke of Chaos weighs heavy indeed, and all joy and life seems to flee these deathly territories.

The island of Ossia is invaded by the devoted of Nurgle, for the Plague God sees Ossia's endless graveyards as a fitting annex for his garden.

As the plague legions win battle after battle and the claw of Chaos grips the land, the once-vibrant populace of Ossia begins to lose hope. They are ill matched against the hosts of Chaos, and almost all of their warriors succumb to the daemon hordes. The remainder surrender, becoming slaves of the new order. Beneath Chaos oppression they become stagnant and mindless, trudging through each day without variation or rebellion. As the spined citadels of Chaos rise from basalt and ground bone, spirits and hopes sink ever lower. As the people of Ossia lose their will to fight, the land itself grows stale under the heel of Chaos.

THE WAR OF BONES

Nagash strikes back hard against the Chaos invaders and, for a time, he claims dominion over many fallen lands. The skaven, ever watchful and with an ancestral grudge against Nagash from ages past, counter-attack the undead legions from newly burrowed gnawhole tunnels. The War of Bones erupts across Shyish and, though it is ultimately fought to a standstill, it leaves Nagash further weakened.

Nagashizzar itself is toppled by Nurgle daemons immune to the morbid, desiccating curse of Shyish's innate magic. For a time, Nagash is forced to relocate to a secondary base of command in dank and clammy Stygxx. The deathly rage he feels at this dislocation is so strong it could freeze mountains. Nagash sends Arkhan the Black to oversee the building of the Great Black Pyramid, and the legions of Deathrattle slaves labouring at the heart of Shyish redouble their pace, working night and day to complete their master's grandest work.

BATTLE OF BURNING SKIES

The Amethyst Princedoms, holding out well in the battles against Chaos due to their wealth and infrastructure, answer Sigmar's call to action by sending a great many armies to the Battle of Burning Skies. The Princes of that realm acquit themselves well, but most are slain after Sigmar's forces are overcome – facing the forces of Khorne and Nurgle at one time, they are outmatched on a dozen fronts.

A STORM GOD'S WRATH

Enraged at the failure of his pantheon Sigmar thunders into the Innerlands in search of Nagash, seeking to call him to account over the perceived betrayal. Many of Nagash's lieutenants and heralds are obliterated at Sigmar's hand before he finally relents and heads back through the storm to Azyr, leaving the mortals of Shyish to their fate.

THE STOLEN HEROES

Sigmar musters a new army in the heavens. Hallost in particular provides the God-King with a great plunder of truly heroic souls

to reforge. However, with their brightest and best taken up to Azyr, the people of Hallost feel fear and doubt for the first time. They fight hard against the Chaos invaders nonetheless. For a time, they manage to keep from being overrun.

THE SCOURGE INESCAPABLE

Such is the strength and determination of the Chaos assault that they even hurl back the undead legions of Nagash. With the Dark Gods pouring their power into the realm through every Realmgate and summoning ritual they can utilise, the works of Nagash are torn down. Many of those lands in thrall to his magic are abandoned as a great exodus of people flees edgeward.

RAID AND PILLAGE

In the far east, the unending festivalia of Satyr's End is brought to a gory conclusion when the war for Hallost spills over onto that once-hedonistic isle. The sadistic warlord Thorro Splinterthigh turns to Khorne as soon as possible, and orders every captive crippled, rather than slain, that they might be bled anew each day. He rises high in the Blood God's favour, for he understands the value of spilt gore. A similar spectacle unfolds in Bacchanalia, at the southernmost point of Stygxx, though it is the Seekers of Slaanesh that bring doom to that land – and they do it through an excess of debauchery rather than its cessation. Bacchanalia becomes home to the court of the Great Pretender, a Slaaneshi warlord who hopes to wed the Stygxxian Goddess of Plenty and hence become the father of an entire tribe of demigods.

⊛ THE AGE OF SIGMAR ⊛

A RAY OF HOPE

Sigmar's Tempest breaks, and lightning strikes across the lands. The Hallowed Knights and the Anvils of the Heldenhammer invade in great strength, hurling back the legions of Khorne, Nurgle and Tzeentch on a dozen fronts.

As the Age of Sigmar begins in earnest, the God-King's debt to the people of the Innerlands is repaid in full – the Tempest strikes hard here, with Stormhost after Stormhost arriving to turn the tide wherever evil gathers darkest. In the northern lands of Stygxx, the Amethyst Princedoms and Hallost, Sigmar's legions prove so capable at hurling back the forces of Chaos that the mortals – and ghosts – of Shyish that fight alongside them begin to feel hope rekindling within them.

THE DEVIL YOU KNOW

The God-King seeks to re-establish the mutually beneficial alliance of the Pantheon of Order. Though he hates the Great Necromancer for his betrayal at the Battle of Burning Skies, he realises he cannot win against the Dark Gods without Nagash's help, and so sends the Hallowed Knights to treat with him. However, after dealing with the Mortarchs and reaching Nagash's stronghold, the Stormcasts leave without success.

THE TRUTH COMES OUT

After slaying a tide of monstrous Chaos beasts alongside the Astral Templars and Anvils of the Heldenhammer, the warriors of Hallost hold a great feast. There they find out that many Anvils were once Hallost warriors, and that they were torn away by Sigmar for this very counterstrike. The survivors of the original Hallost tribes feel a fierce hatred for Sigmar growing within their breasts upon learning this, and several tribes swear then and there to oppose Sigmar the Betrayer.

BACK FROM THE BRINK

The living fight alongside the dead once more as the Stormcast Eternals settle old grounds in the name of hope and progress. Chaos' grip on the Innerlands remains tight and unforgiving, but here and there the cracks begin to show as the forces of Order gain momentum. Realmgates are claimed and new cities are built in the far north of the Shyish Innerlands, while some of the more established underworlds begin to break free from the oppression they have endured for so long. A glimmer of civilisation is kindled, although the long dark night is far from over.

THE TRAGIC FATE OF OSSIA

Upon Ossia, the Stormcast Eternals appear in a storm of lightning. They launch scores of retributive strikes against the forces of Chaos, casting down their citadels and freeing the land. The spell of Chaos over Ossia is broken. However, in post-battle parleys with the few surviving mortal leaders of Ossia, the Stormcast Eternals are told that they are too late. If they had arrived fifty years ago, perhaps Ossia would still have had a chance of redemption – but now it is a place of dark and haunted pain.

BATTLE OF GOTHIZZAR

Chaos-seized Gothizzar is besieged during the battle of the All-gates. Nagash's forces do not arrive to reinforce Sigmar's hosts at the critical time. The Endgate remains in Chaos hands.

SINISTER OMENS

As Nagash's secret schemes near completion, echoes of the future ripple through the Mortal Realms in an escalating series of malign and ominous portents. Visionaries, heralds and emissaries from each of the Grand Alliances gather armies bound for Shyish.

A MAGICAL SINGULARITY

By channelling a great sorcerous spell through his carefully aligned black pyramid, Nagash reverses the flow of death magic so that it gathers not at the edge of the realmsphere, but at its centre. The hideous weight of all the gathered death energy collapses a hole in the centre of the realm, and the magical polarity of Shyish reverses completely.

THE SHYISH NECROQUAKE

As Nagash's great work is completed, a thunderous pulse of aetheric energy roils across the cosmos, causing the spirits of the dead to rise in every Mortal Realm. The lands of Shyish begin to move towards its core, pulled by the irresistible weight of concentrated death magic into the Nadir like flotsam to the mouth of a maelstrom.

THE END OF ALL THINGS

Those afterlives that have fallen into repetition and stagnation under the pall of Chaos slowly drift inward towards the Nadir. Most mortals are unaware of this at first – a man who is content simply to sweep the same floor day after day does not notice that his movements are becoming more synchronised and mechanical. Over time, he wastes away completely as his homeland is drawn closer to the Nadir. Eventually that man becomes little more than a skeleton with a broom, cursed to repeat the same task for eternity.

THE SEARCH FOR ETERNITY

Years after Nagash's act of betrayal left the Stormcasts without support at the battle of Gothizzar, Sigmar, having recalled his legions and delegations from the Anvils of the Heldenhammer, sends them to the Innerlands once more to enact a retributive strike against Nagash. This time, the God-King's wrath does not burn out so soon. A new era of war between the factions of Order and Death begins. Some whisper that there is more to Sigmar's agenda than simple vengeance, for the Stormhosts have a new breed of Stormcast with them. Appearing more wizard than warrior, they seek to uncover the true secrets of immortality in an attempt to perfect the reforging process.

THOSE WHO BURN BRIGHT

Hallost had long thrived above all as a vital and glorious place untouched by fear or doubt. Its warriors still fought the hideous creatures of Modrhavn every new day, and those who died were still reborn. Nagash once found he had little influence there – even his finest generals were seen as another military challenge for the fearless populace to overcome. Yet the Nadir's pull is irresistible, and over time even Hallost slips slowly southward.

Ossia also begins to descend to the Shyish Nadir, and becomes ever more terrible of aspect. In drawing nearer to that swirling, crushing vortex, the land becomes saturated with magic. Great armies of wraiths, banshees and spirits rise from the earth – the souls of those who called Ossia their home long ago – and attack their Chaos oppressors. Ill equipped to combat these ethereal hosts with blade and spear, the Chaos armies strike back with sorcery and daemonic power. Here and there the mortal populace rises up with blade and shield in hand, given hope by their ethereal ancestors, but most are too downtrodden and have already become half-dead husks. The fate of Ossia hangs in the balance.

'Sigmar was right to smash them cities down!' shouted Alaf, corded veins standing out on his neck. 'The Grave God betrayed him twice over!' Alaf's brother Doln had always said that Alaf could shoe horses with his own two fists, and right now he had them wrapped around Old Nicero's pale and wattled throat. It was all he could do not to squeeze the life out of the traitor.

Over Nicero's shoulder, Alaf could see a crooked, robed man emerging from behind the market square's corpse-stocks, stopping to delicately peel open the eyes of a gormless-looking cadaver as he went.

'But Sigmar broke his troth first, did he not, Fat Alaf?' said the newcomer. 'Gods are just as fickle as men. And men betray each other all the time.'

Alaf's eyes widened in recognition as a shout of pain and shock escaped his lips. Skeletal snakes were winding up his legs at terrifying speed, constricting as they flowed around his body to form a cage of bone. The last things Alaf saw were Nicero's smile and the glint of his long-lost brother's dagger.

CHAMON, REALM OF METAL

Full of transmutations and alchemical wonders, Chamon is a realm where impermanence is the only certainty. Blessed with riches beyond the wildest imaginings of misers and kings, it promises immeasurable power to those who can harness its resources. Tzeentch covets this realm, and the region known as the Spiral Crux in particular.

The Realm of Metal is ever shifting, but certain sub-realms abide, giving shape to the so-called Lands of Gold. Chamon is not a set of plates, islands or continents crystallised in the central plane of the realmsphere, but rather a dizzying variety of domains that hang in the Chamon firmament, each linked to the others by portals and mystical bonds. In Azyr it has been depicted as the laboratory of some godly alchemist, glittering with potential and hope.

Small wonder the realm's treasures are coveted by so many monarchs and warlords. Yet so mutable are its reaches that only those able to embrace change can thrive there for long – each of Chamon's tribes, cultures and civilisations has learned to adapt and evolve as the lands shift and meld, their fortunes rising and falling with every new generation.

Though much of Chamon is metallic in nature, it has verdant reaches and pure water in abundance, especially in those sub-realms nearest the realmsphere's core. Here and there the trees may have glinting, iron-hard bark, the earth may bear a ferrous sheen or the hues of exotic oxides in places, but by and large it remains habitable. On the outskirts of Chamon, however, the lands are ever changing to the point of madness. Many of these fantastical regions are further corrupted such that they are utterly inimical to life.

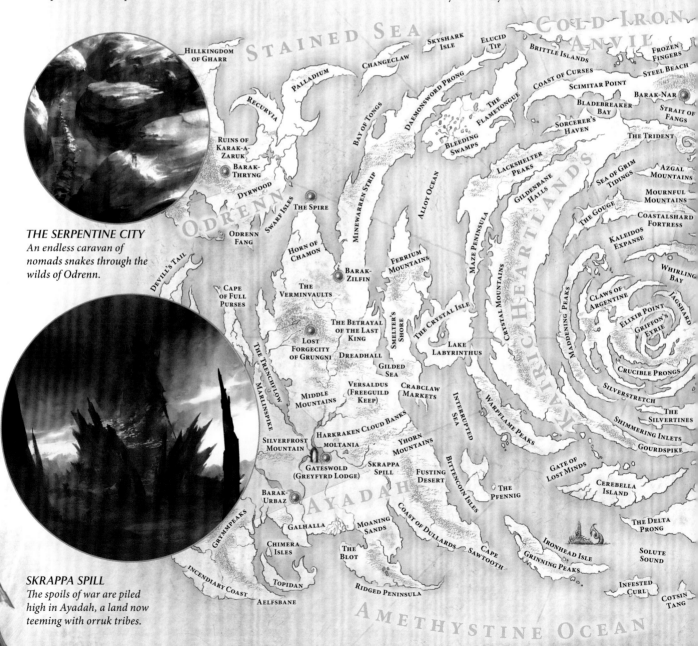

THE SERPENTINE CITY
An endless caravan of nomads snakes through the wilds of Odrenn.

SKRAPPA SPILL
The spoils of war are piled high in Ayadah, a land now teeming with orruk tribes.

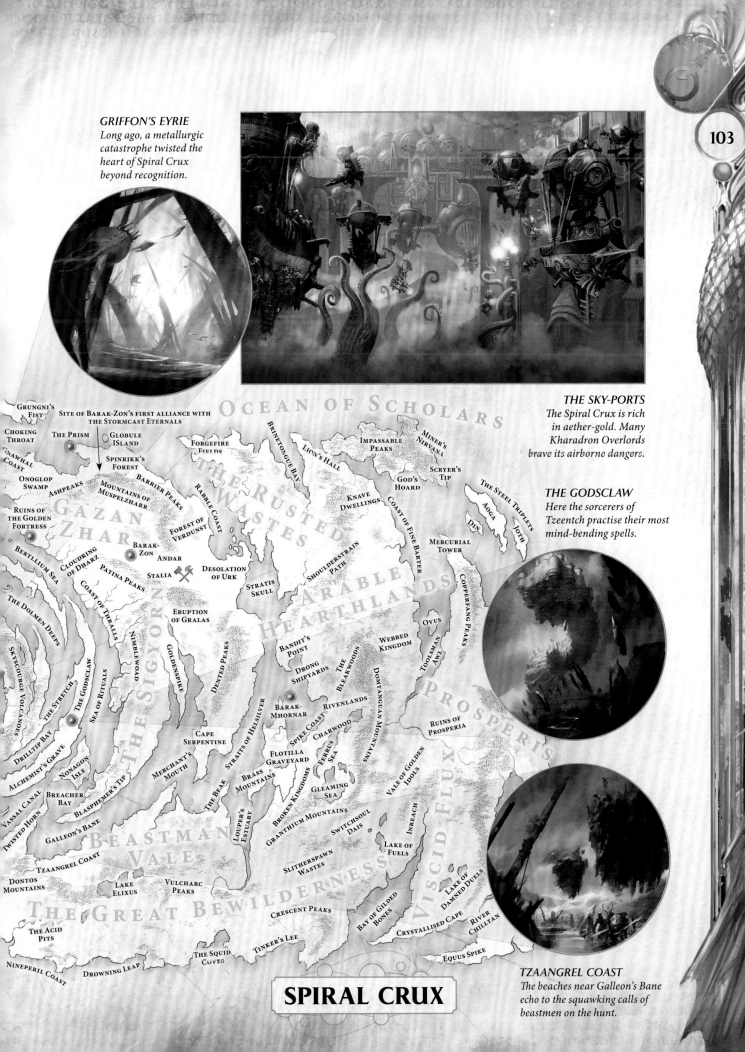

GRIFFON'S EYRIE
Long ago, a metallurgic catastrophe twisted the heart of Spiral Crux beyond recognition.

THE SKY-PORTS
The Spiral Crux is rich in aether-gold. Many Kharadron Overlords brave its airborne dangers.

THE GODSCLAW
Here the sorcerers of Tzeentch practise their most mind-bending spells.

OCEAN OF SCHOLARS

Grungni's Fist
Site of Barak-Zon's first alliance with the Stormcast Eternals
Choking Throat
The Prism
Globule Island
Spinrikk's Forest
Narwhal Coast
Onoglop Swamp
Ashpeaks
Mountains of Muspelzharr
Barrier Peaks
Forgefire Fields
Brinetongue Bay
Lion's Hall
Impassable Peaks
Miner's Nirvana
God's Hoard
Scryer's Tip
THE RUSTED WASTES
Rabble Coast
Knave Dwellings
Coast of Fine Barter
THE STEEL TRIPLETS
AOGA
DIN
IOTH
Ruins of the Golden Fortress
GAZAN ZHAR
Forest of Verdunst
Mercurial Tower
Beryllium Sea
Cloudring of Dharz
Patina Peaks
Barak-Zon
Andar
Stalia
Desolation of Urk
Stratis Skull
Shoulderstrain Path
ARABLE HEARTHLANDS
Copperfang Peaks
Coast of Thralls
Eruption of Gralas
Bandit's Point
Webbed Kingdom
Ovus
Toolsman Awl
The Dolmen Deeps
Nimblewoad
Goldenspire
Dented Peaks
Drong Shipyards
The Bleakwoods
Domtanguan Mountains
PROSPERIS
Skyscourge Volcanoes
THE SIGYORN
Sea of Rituals
Barak-Mhornar
Rivenlands
Ruins of Prosperia
The Stretch
The Godsclaw
Cape Serpentine
Spike Coast
Charwood
Drilltip Bay
Alchemist's Grave
Nonagon Isle
Merchant's Mouth
Straits of Helsilver
Flotilla Graveyard
Ferrus Sea
VISCID FLUX
Vassal Canal
Breacher Bay
Blasphemer's Tip
The Bear
Brass Mountains
Broken Kingdoms
Gleaming Sea
Vale of Golden Idols
Twisted Horn
Galleon's Bane
Louper's Estuary
Granthium Mountains
Switchsoul Dais
Inreach
Lake of Fuels
Tzaangrel Coast
BEASTMAN VALE
Dontos Mountains
Lake Elixus
Vulcharc Peaks
Slitherspawn Wastes
Lake of Damned Duels
THE GREAT BEWILDERNESS
Crescent Peaks
Bay of Gilded Bones
Crystallised Cape
River Chilltan
The Acid Pits
Tinker's Lee
The Squid Coved
Equus Spike
Nineperil Coast
Drowning Leap

SPIRAL CRUX

TZAANGREL COAST
The beaches near Galleon's Bane echo to the squawking calls of beastmen on the hunt.

THE SPIRAL CRUX

A land of jagged coastlines and sharp promontories, the Spiral Crux was once a land of Order and unbound creation. Since it caught the eye of the Dark God Tzeentch, the Crux has been visited by a grand cataclysm, twisted into a labyrinth of impossible landscapes long abandoned by the duardin empires who once called it home.

● AGE OF MYTH ●

GRUNGNI'S GIFTS
After being freed from his bondage by the God-King Sigmar, Grungni fashions the Nineteen Wonders of Chamon. His exertions are such that his breath mingles with the dust of his forges to form sky-borne clouds of aether-gold. Amongst his creations are the steel city of Maraz Drang, the cog-people of Odsin – later disowned after the Winding Storm – the World Hearth, and the perfectly straight Godwrought Isles. Each of these islands, pleasing in form and a rich paradise, is bestowed upon one of Grungni's worshipper clans. The linear isles and ordered mountains of this region are soon linked by curving bridges, each a glorious and perfect arc. Trade between the duardin and the human smiths that seek to learn from them begins to thrive, as do magma farms and burgeoning forms of technology. Satisfied that his folk are walking the path to self-sufficiency, Grungni departs to repay his debt to Sigmar. He joins the Pantheon of Order and dwells long in Azyr to forge the fabled Sigmarabulum.

Over eighty generations of prosperity and relative peace are to follow in the Godwrought Isles, but even Grungni could not fashion a society proof against the crippling curse of greed.

CHAMONITE
Across the most central regions of the Godwrought Isles, the globular, quicksilver-like realmstone of Chamon – known as Chamonite – is discovered in abundance. It is a source of near-limitless alchemical power for those with the art to manipulate it. After the invention of the syringe-like device known as the aether-glutton in the Azgal Mountains, Chamonite is harnessed in great measure. Siphoned, categorised and rationed by the gifted duardin aethermancers of Azgal and the Sigyorn, the ready

supply of Chamonite ensures every clan of the western isles – be they duardin, gholemkind or human – has an abundance of magic with which to power their forges. It becomes a widespread currency of sorts, with a single droplet roughly equal to a good-sized chest full of gold coin.

Claimant operations and land stakes reach fever pitch, with the tribal federations that shift and flow across the land competing and even warring amongst themselves to strip-mine the land of its magical resources before their rivals can do so.

THE FORGE TURNS COLD
The far northern land used for Grungni's forge finally cools from boiling volcanic heat to its former arctic climate. Only the strong survive as the lands of Cold Iron Anvil freeze over. Landmasses cleave off like ice chunks from a melting berg, forming the Brittle Islands. The tribes there are forced into a life of barbarism, hunting great white bears and taking their fur in order to survive the deadly cold.

TRADE AND PROGRESS
Around the circumference of the region, the art of endrin-barter and trade in pure metal ingots of all kinds thrives. The duardin strike

deals with the artisans of Azgal, the Sigyorn and the Crucible Prongs, collectively the most advanced engineers amongst all those who have made their homes in Chamon under the auspices of Sigmar. The ever-smiling Mintners of Azgal's Royal Orchard, they who specialise in harvesting coin from the Glinting Groves, spread their influence far and wide through the ignoble arts of money-lending. A contract is struck between the trio of flourishing regions, with the nations of Azgal, the Sigyorn and the Crucible Prongs now known as the Brothers Adamant. It becomes the fashion of the Adamants to wear garments of sheeted flowstone laced with beads of this glittering substance.

THE GAZE OF TZEENTCH
Tzeentch catches sight of Chamon, a collection of glinting sub-realms hanging like fruit waiting to be picked in a colossal realmsphere of heavy and potent magic. Perhaps if the rich people there had not revelled so much in their wealth and sophistication, the change-prayers of those less fortunate would not have been so fervent, and not attracted the eye of the Great Conspirator in the first place. But with so many flaunting their wealth, the poverty-stricken – the northern tribes of Cold Iron Anvil foremost amongst them – are quick to pray for change. As Tzeentch's eye lingers upon the Godwrought Isles, those who desire a new order hear the barely discernable whispers of daemons promising a better world at the cost of another's misfortune. The seeds of disaster are planted, yet it is the arrival of another godly force that twists the land beyond all recognition.

A GODBEAST DESCENDS
Attracted by the glamour of glittering clouds and the shimmer of so much unearthed Chamonite, the zodiacal beast known as the lode-griffon descends from the

void towards the Godwrought Isles. Chased from its home in the Hanging Valleys by the silver wyrm Argentine, the fortress-sized creature makes its nest upon the central island. The tremendous magical weight of the lode-griffon distorts the lands with pulses of raw magnetism. Over time, the straight landmasses forged by Grungni buckle and rip apart, forming the continental sprawl known as the Spiral Crux. As they change shape, every bridge and pipeline snaps and twists until it is wrenched into the sea, the molten realmstone they once transported floating free to gather as clouds in the Chamonic stratosphere.

REVERSAL OF FORTUNE
The tribes of Odrenn, Adayah and Viscid Flux – those islands furthest away from the site of the metallurgic apocalypse that surrounds the lode-griffon – capitalise on the downfall of the Brothers Adamant and the great reversal of fortune that has befallen the realm. Their artifice is largely unaffected by the coming of the lode-griffon, and their hallmarks become worth more than those of the Adamant Brothers in the space of a single moon.

By securing beneficial contracts with the desperate refugees of the inner isles, the artisan tribes of Odrenn, Adayah and Viscid Flux rise to ascendancy in the arts of forging and alchemy. The liquid-core blades of Odrenn's singing bladesmiths become famous amongst the warrior fraternities, second only in value to the living swords forged by Celemnis of Anvrok.

Settlers from Viscid Flux found the nation of Prosperis, building high with their near-limitless wealth. Their prosperous trade in clockwork automatons and fluid-metal pets – from giant ripple-skinned ferrosaurs to small tin-dogs – sees their fortunes eclipse even those of the Azgal Mintners.

The Fluxkin fund expeditions into the famously dangerous Impassable Peaks in search of yet more Chamonite. Their search is successful beyond their wildest hopes.

AN UNTENABLE CURSE
The Cruxian duardin, realising that their dream of a perfectly balanced society is in tatters, retreat to kingdoms high in the mountains to better escape the dread pull of the lode-griffon and the destructive greed of the human tribes. They become insular and divided, and trade amongst the duardin and human nations slows to a crawl. Coffers begin to empty around the Crucible Prongs, and tensions rise. With many tribes' financial survival on the line, this territorialism leads to open conflict.

To add insult to injury, the lode-griffon's magnetic blood drives the instruments of duardin artisans haywire. Many of the duardin, robbed of their livelihoods, consider how they might end the lode-griffon's curse upon the lands. As the moons above wax full, these dreams bleed into waking life. Vexed beyond measure, they gather their wealth and place a bounty upon the godbeast's skull. Within the week, warbands of duardin monster-slayers fight their way to the lode-griffon's lair and work to inflict *adaz kronn* – death by a thousand axes – upon the slumbering lode-griffon. Unfortunately, the metallic godbeast is all but impervious to mortal weaponry. Awoken in a rage, the beast slays its assailants and wreaks havoc on every tribe within a dozen leagues before retreating to its nest.

DEATH OF A GODBEAST
The nations of Azgal, the Sigyorn, Patina, Prosperis and Viscid Flux convene a great conclave of their mightiest aethermancers, hoping to find a way to slay the godbeast in the midst of their realm. Together, nine of their representatives make the perilous trek to Griffon's Eyrie. Each taking one of the points of a nonagonic ritual star, they work a powerful spell of transmutation. As the spell comes to its earth-shaking conclusion, a great avalanche is triggered, and eight of the nine magi are consumed in a wave of molten Chamonite.

The ninth mage, revealed by the haywire magic to be the Gaunt Summoner known as the Watcher King, flees on a flying disc-daemon to his Silver Tower in the far west. Yet the great spell is cast. The godbeast is transmuted to solid gold inside its lair, and its magnetic curse ended. Though the duardin aethermancers rejoice to see their instruments and war devices restored to normal function, the act carries a cost so profound that it alters reality across the Spiral Crux forever.

THE SKY-RIFT OPENS
The lode-griffon's death scream tears a hole in the sky high above the Crux, a rift through which spill legions of flying daemonic horrors. A new age of terror unfolds with horrible swiftness.

● THE AGE OF CHAOS ●

TZEENTCH'S HAND REVEALED

Though all the Dark Gods make their plays for regions of Chamon, Tzeentch concentrates his forces here more than in any other realm. He takes special interest in the sub-realms most saturated in magic – amongst them the Hanging Valleys of Anvrok, where the sorcerer Ephryx has hidden away the hammer Ghal Maraz; the Spined Sphere Golgeth, where time itself is malleable; and the Spiral Crux, where the air is laced with the stuff of change.

SLAUGHTER FROM ABOVE

With the daemon hordes spilling out of the sky-rift, every fortress and bastion wall created by the rich nations of the Crux proves worse than useless – for with the daemons swooping down everywhere they can smell the magical perfume of Chamonite, the defenders find themselves trapped within their own defences.

THE KHARADRON CODE

The duardin that escaped the coming of the sky-rift and the besiegement of their old mountain kingdoms spend years simply fighting for survival. At first, their insular defences hold back the scattered assaults, but over time Tzeentch's minions begin to coordinate their attacks from within the mountains as well as without. The infestation of the ancestral holds leads to many duardin factions taking to the skies, militarising sky-ports and Gyrocopter launch platforms until they can lay claim to the satellite kingdoms that stand apart from each mountain peak. The science of air travel, further bolstered by the aether-gold mined by the steamhead pioneers, progresses to the point that several duardin holds boast entire fleets of skyborne vessels. A new conflict erupts as the disc-riding vassals of Tzeentch and their winged daemon allies seek to prey upon the duardin air navies, but duardin war-technology has advanced by an incredible degree since the opening of the sky-rift, and the armies of Chaos find themselves hurled back on dozens of fronts.

Soon after, the disparate airborne forces forge a loose confederation for mutual protection. But, as the sky-ports grow, so too do their rivalries. All seek to mine the same aether-gold that has laced the skies ever since the coming of the sky-rift – it proves a versatile power source and, though no substitute for Chamonite, it keeps their societies flourishing and afloat, not to mention hidden from the warmongers on the lands below. The competition for aether-gold becomes so fierce that relationships between many of the duardin clans turn sour. On the verge of civil war, the leaders of each sky-port meet in council. It is this Conference of Madralta – named after the floating isle where the meeting takes place – that produces the document known as the Code. The predecessors of the Kharadron Overlords are born, and their ancient culture of statutes and contracts put into motion. They retreat high into the Chamonic stratosphere, and are not seen again by the eyes of men or mutant for long generations.

THE HAND OF THE CHANGER

Pleased by the Chamonite his followers have consumed in his name, Tzeentch himself works a great spell that rains transmutative warpfire from the skies in a terrible cataclysm. The aether around the Spiral Crux is shot through with multicoloured meteors of tainted crystal and bloodglass. Jagged knives of translucent stone claim thousands of lives, whilst Whirling Bay and the Kaleidos Expanse no longer provide fresh water, but run thick with molten metal that boils at the touch of mortal flesh.

THE LANDS TRANSMUTED

The Crystal Isle is wrenched into being around the island Realmgate of Seedgate. A huge landmass of shimmering kaleidoscopic crystal, it surrounds the Seedgate Isle, choking the passage from the Alloy Ocean to the Amethystine Ocean and forming the Interrupted Sea. The central isles of the Crux are further twisted by the terrible change wrought upon them, becoming a tangle of jagged coasts and curling promontories. Sky-sharks and flying chariots haunt the clouds, and beasts of the land

and sea are twisted into horrible new forms that take wing, or simply rise into the skies as if by invisible hands, to fall upon those duardin that have dared to stay and fight. A new age of oppression and madness takes root as Tzeentch claims the lands of the Spiral Crux with wave upon wave of daemon invaders, new tides of Horrors either tumbling from the skies or born from the still-burning warpfire at the heart of the lands.

A NEW WORLD ON HIGH

The Forge-City of Grungni is overrun with skaven when a gnawhole opens under the peaks now known as the Verminvaults. The last of the duardin's Great Karaks falls during the battle of Zaruk. Forcing themselves to look forward instead of back, the Kharadron Overlords ply the clouds near and far in their search for new seams of aether-gold, their ingenious constructions seeing them slowly but patiently found the six aerial cities that will come to dominate the region's skies.

Within the year, the Hydrox Wars are brought to a victorious conclusion by the fleets and new-found wealth of the sky-port Barak-Nar. The corpses of the many-headed aerial predators known as hydroxes are piled high in Barak-Nar's wake, though the fishy stench that results means they are soon jettisoned into the sea instead.

THE WARS OF MEN RAGE ON

The wealthy and well-armoured armies of Odrenn, Ayadah, Viscid Flux and Prosperis go to war against the daemon hosts, the traitorous humans of the Kairic hordes and Tzaangor warflocks that pour across the lands, sacking and setting fire to every city or township they can find. The Steel Dervishes of Scimitar Point hold out for months against waves of Chaos Spawn and the Horrors that create them from the beasts of the land. Their fate is twisted when the Argent Nail, the vast Silver Tower of the Watcher King, descends from the void to loom over the Alloy Ocean. The Gaunt Summoner that rules the Argent Nail rains curses upon the Steel Dervishes for nine days and nine nights. They die to a man before the month is out.

THE AGE OF SIGMAR

THE TEMPEST ROARS

Sigmar's Tempest roils across the skies of Chamon, driving potent veins of aether-gold before it. The Kharadron Overlords scramble to mine this bounty before the storm disrupts their plans entirely.

NOTHING BUT DUST

The agents of Sigmar seek the duardin across the Spiral Crux, hoping to reinforce ancient alliances that they might win a significant beachhead on the largest of the inner islands. Though they fight their way to the peaks of many ancient duardin holds, they find nothing but corpses and the echoes of an empire long forsaken.

VICTORIES HARD WON

The Stormcast Eternals strike the hateful tribes of Chaos with such speed and force that many strongholds are breached before their denizens can muster a cogent defence. The sorcerous warlords of Tzeentch are not wrong-footed for long, however. Working their arts of prophecy and foreknowledge, they anticipate where the next thunderous assaults will land and lay their traps accordingly. Teeming Tzaangor herds, armies of heavily armoured warrior thralls, and entire tribes of Ogroids rush from cave and swamp to fall upon the proud Stormcast Eternals wherever they appear, each cursed horde further bolstered by the pyrotechnic magic of the sorcerers themselves. Only when the sky is lit by dozens of columns of heavenly light do the Stormcast Eternals bring enough force to bear to scour the Tzeentchian legions from Scimitar Point, the Barrier Peaks and the Gnarwhal Coast, forming a strongpoint from which to expand their territory.

UNSTOPPABLE MOMENTUM

Sigmar's hosts are reinforced by those who fell in the first wave, reforged and sent back by Sigmar, but the grinding battle of attrition is only tipped in the God-King's favour when the survivors of the indigenous people – the warriors of Ayadah, Odrenn, Azgal, Viscid Flux and even Cold Iron Anvil – emerge from hiding to swell the ranks of the faithful. Together with a host of Free Peoples from Azyr, they muster strength enough to hunt down and surround the fractious Tzeentchian warbands. Slowly, as one Realmgate after another is conquered, the seeds of civilisation are planted and begin to bear fruit once more. New cities sprout up around each island of sanity and strength, and trade routes – although frequently embattled – are established across the isles.

ALL THE GOLD IN THE SKY

The Angelos Conclaves of the Hammers of Sigmar join the airborne wars that rage between the Kharadron Overlords and the flying daemons and Tzaangor disc-riders of Tzeentch. An alliance is struck between Captain Hrolf Alespitter of Barak-Zon and Vindt of the Gilden Pinion, Knight-Venator of the Hammers of Sigmar, resulting in the banishment of a large daemon horde from the skies above Spinrikk's Forest. Such compacts become more and more common, resulting in the newly coined Aetherstrike Force battle formation entering the legislation of the Kharadron Code.

FALL OF THE THANTANIK

The mighty super-ship known as the *Thantanik* is hit amidships by a devastating sorcerous strike when engaged in aerial battle with the Silver Tower of the Watcher King. Scuppered and sinking fast, the *Thantanik* rams the Silver Tower with such force that the Tzeentchian citadel's magical wards activate, sending it blinking out of existence as it teleports back into the void. The *Thantanik*'s pyrrhic victory ends with the colossal ship plummeting down to crash in the north-east of Moltania. It is used as a salutary lesson against the practice of building too large a vessel – as the Overlords have it, only a rube puts all his aether-gold in one aerostill.

THE GREAT SKY PURGE

Though the lands of the Spiral Crux are still infested by Tzeentchian daemons, cult uprisings and Brayherds, the airs above the inner islands are all but cleared of invaders by a united push from the Kharadron Overlords and their Hammers of Sigmar allies. Those duardin furthest from the war-fronts return to the business of sky-mining, abandoning most of the lands below to their fate.

BALEFUL REVELATIONS

The Kharadron of Barak-Zilfin discover a chain of crystalline sky-castles near the edge of the Crux's known atmospheric limits. The duardin high council's fears of a Tzeentchian plot in the making prove well founded as the sky-castles descend and the war for Chamon reaches new heights of violence.

'Ah, but this is a Celemnite blade,' said Odo Thring, eyes wide with false wonder. 'Forged by the Silver Banshee's own fair hand, and blessed by Lord Cryptborn himself.' The broadsword gleamed in the light of a crackling eel-globe from the Bataari markets. 'My contact went to great lengths to acquire it from the Hanging Valleys.'

'You take me for a fool? The sword-hag is a myth,' sneered the Odrennite duellist, feigning disinterest. 'The Anvrok saga is a fancy song to keep new recruits from soiling themselves when they see a Stormcast in the flesh.'

Odo smiled, gold glinting from every other tooth. 'See how well it handles, my friend,' he said. 'As if the sword-maiden were guiding your hand.' As he proffered the hilt, he saw the reflection of something moving in the sword's perfect surface.

Odo turned to see a puddle of what looked like spilt quicksilver sliding towards them through the forge. It flowed upward to form the gaunt face of a woman framed by long straight hair. A torso manifested beneath, reaching down to the waist. The thing distended its maw impossibly wide like that of a snake. The scream from its silvered throat rendered Odo deaf, blind and mute a moment, before his heart burst.

ULGU, REALM OF SHADOW

Ulgu consists of thirteen vast regions, each more distant and unknowable than the last. A realm of secrets and riddles on the wind, it is called the Grey Realm by many, for its true name can only properly be pronounced as a whisper – and never in broad daylight. Here, half-light and half-truth are the best a traveller can wish for.

Locked in a twin orbit with the realmsphere of Hysh, the lands of Ulgu have neither night nor day, but range from gloom to pitch black depending on region rather than time. This is the domain of secrets and lies, of twisted reason and mind-bending illusion, and it conforms not to the laws of logic. Ulgu can swallow an invading army just as morning mist obscures the dawn, and leave nothing behind but their screams. Not even those who have lived there since birth dare to trust their senses for long.

All the shrouded countries of Ulgu are saturated with illusion and lurking menace. It was not always this way – once, many of Ulgu's Thirteen Dominions were synonymous with refuge, philosophical introspection and the bliss of lucid dreams.

Over time, however, the lands have become changed by the invasions of Chaos, and they have changed for the worse. At first, Ulgu itself reacted to these incursions much as a living thing might react to a verminous infestation – by scouring it, drowning it, suffocating it and confounding it wherever possible. It is a testament to the hunger of Chaos that all thirteen of the Dominions are still scarred by the blades and bootprints of those who are in thrall to the Dark Gods.

Each of the Thirteen Dominions boasts many rulers, inevitably with viziers, loremasters and shadowy puppetmasters arrayed around them. They are tied together with invisible webs of intrigue and manipulation that shift with each new day. The closest thing to a supreme monarch is the godlike being Malerion.

Consumed by fell energies after the destruction of the world-that-was, the Shadow King was borne in spirit to Ulgu – for although Malerion is at heart a creature of Order, darkness and lies are like meat and drink to him. When he awoke in Ulgu, stirred to consciousness by Sigmar's presence, his physical form was gone. Only slowly did memories return to him. He could not control his corporeality, manifesting more as an inky black shade than as flesh and blood. How long he wandered across the forbidding landscapes he knew not, but he feared his fate was to forever be less than shadow. Yet as his anger and frustration mounted, his own rage gave him form. With fury came solidity and a measure of godly power.

Malerion discovered many strange creatures abroad in Ulgu, yet felt no true kinship with any of them. Only when he came upon a glade harbouring a writhing coven of shadow daemons did he feel a spark of recognition. At the centre of that bacchanal was his mother, Morathi – she too had transcended the fall of the world-that-was, but here she flickered in form between that of the maiden and the monster.

The reunion between mother and son was full of recriminations. Neither trusted the other, and the scars of their former sins and betrayals were not fully healed, but in this foreign land they at least understood one another. An uneasy truce was reached. Together, they put aside their tragic pasts, uniting under Sigmar as part of his Pantheon of Order – for a time, at least. With these two great minds to guide them, the mortal cultures of Ulgu thrived.

This realm of secrets and whispers proved alluring in the extreme to Tzeentch. Through the convoluted schemes and hidden societies that entangled the Thirteen Dominions, the Changer of Ways found his way

in. Slowly, insidiously, those who sought power through change spread their influence across the lands. They were the weak points in Ulgu's defences, and flung its gates wide.

When the Age of Chaos broke across the lands, Khorne was quick to invade Ulgu, hoping to steal a march on Tzeentch by sending his legions through Realmgates corrupted by secretive blood cults. His armies felt scorn for those that skulked in the mist rather than fought in the glory of the open field, but that contempt would be their undoing, for any who underestimates Ulgu's secrets does so the cost of their own life. Khorne's invading hosts were swallowed by Ulgu's magical fog banks, and when that miasma dissipated, all that was left was carrion.

Yet the forces of Chaos are legion. The disciples of Tzeentch brought the intrigues and arcane politics of the Thirteen Dominions to a violent climax, plunging dozens of civilisations into anarchy. The skaven, especially those of the Clans Eshin, sent their shade-scuttling hordes and shrouded assassins to every corner of the realm on fell missions that only the Masterclan claimed to understand. Though outnumbered, Malerion and Morathi waged a guerrilla war with such skill that the realm was not overrun entirely by Chaos. Even the coming of the Age of Sigmar has done little to break the deadlock.

THE AELVES OF ULGU

It was into Ulgu that many aelven spirits fled after being rescued from Slaanesh's endless thirst for souls. The first to be drawn from the god's immense, gluttonous shade were those straining to be free, those aelves most nimble of thought and razor-sharp of wit. Those taken by Malerion and Morathi were not humanoid in the way they once were, for they had been changed irrevocably. The first had bat wings, fine horns and long, dexterous tails, their devilish appearance hinting at the ordeals they had endured in the nether-realms – yet they had been cleansed by Hysh's light, and hidden from retribution by Ulgu's shadow. Morathi, as hungry for influence and power as a panther is for meat, has begun to secretly extract more souls for her own burgeoning priesthood than she stated in her Oath of Salvation.

HYSH, REALM OF LIGHT

The energies of Hysh shine so brightly they light up even the most distant parts of the cosmos. At its best, the Realm of Light is a place of unbound intellect and universal illumination. At its worst, its light is blinding and hypnotic – those dazzled by their own obsessions find a strange darkness there instead.

The history of Hysh is a peculiar one, and not truly understood by any mind save perhaps that of the Lord of Lumination himself. The realm was once as multifaceted and ordered as a finely cut gem or delicate paper structure, its many composite lands intersecting like wide shafts of light that could shift or flip with each leap of logic or pure thought made by its inhabitants. It was once the most virginal of all the realms, its white magic unsullied and free to shine out wherever there were mortal senses to detect it. Yet no realm save Azyr is safe from the greed of the Dark Gods, and even the Ten Paradises of Hysh have long suffered under the grinding maleficence of Chaos.

A realm of symbolism and mind-expanding arithmantic lore, Hysh's interlocking planes are inhabited by people elevated to higher thought by the very nature of their homelands. The most part of their number have a love for reason and symmetry. Even the wordless tribes of the crystal caves are given to long periods of introspection, and the walls of their artfully sculpted tunnels are covered with intricate images and diagrams.

Since the wakening of Lord Tyrion and his brother Teclis, and the spreading of their influence and dominion, the Ten Paradises of Hysh became home to many new cultures of aelves, while the empires and cities founded by Hysh's human architects and scholars were for a time the greatest in all the Mortal Realms. The tall pillars dotted across the deserts and alabaster plains were once legion, each topped with a cross-legged seer seeking enlightenment through denial and asceticism. Yet those cities have since been cast down, and those pillars toppled, by the anarchy and slaughter visited upon the realm by the savage hordes of the Dark Gods. Their conquest of Hysh was far more insidious than the blood-mad invasions of Aqshy, Ghur and Shyish.

The magical energy of Hysh does not coalesce into realmstone deposits as with the other realms, but travels the lands and skies as beams of pure yellow-white illumination. When the seers of Hysh learned how to harness these beams in magically translucent prisms, the composite realmstone-equivalent known as aetherquartz was devised. It quickly became a sought-after resource, and gem-like beads, jewels and necklaces strung with that incredible substance took the form of currency across the lands.

Those who wore jewellery made from aetherquartz found that they took its light into themselves, the gemstones growing dull as their intellects blossomed at incredible speed. Even their movements became swifter and more dexterous, for the stuff of Hysh lends the speed of thought to body as well as mind.

With unbound progress and success coming easily to the rulers and leaders of each paradise, the towers and pillars of Hysh were raised high. Amongst the most scintillating minds, however – the most inventive scholars and wizards of that realm – there was a certain level of competition. Some were above such mortal concerns, becoming so enlightened and pursuing their arts to such refinement that they transcended mortality entirely. So it was that the most advanced and heroic minds became numinous beings far removed from earthly concerns.

Others, however, found their personal weaknesses brought out into the light by the power they held in their hands. The lure of pride and the pursuit of perfection blended together to create a spectrum of unhealthy qualities. These were hidden at first, but as the contest to become the purest and most intelligent grew fiercer, they were soon revealed. At first, the friendly rivalry between two scholars might see them raise the pillars atop which they meditated to ever greater heights, or make their robes grow whiter and more luminous than those of their contemporaries.

As they became ever more self-centred and arrogant, as they leaned upon aetherquartz for ever greater leaps of mental agility and understanding, their noble quest became more akin to an addiction. Image was everything, and no trick or act of sabotage was off-limits in the crusade to appear the most enlightened. Such obsession drew the followers of Slaanesh, whose influence found its way into the hearts of those who dwelt in the Ten Paradises, and the corruption of Hysh's pure light began.

Since the coming of the Age of Sigmar, Hysh has gone from a land of logic and order to a wilderness of broken dreams and shattered statues. That which was not cast down by the subtle curse of Chaos has been smashed by the violence of open war. It is said that Lord Tyrion musters his forces for a great reconquest – but, as yet, salvation has not come.

THE ILLUMINATION OF THE GODS

The gods of the Mortal Realms are not omniscient – even Lord Tyrion, who is physically blind yet can reach out into the aether with a dozen other senses, cannot pluck visions from across the void. A deity cannot influence a realm without having some kind of presence there, and it is most commonly through their worshippers that they extend their powers. Faith is a two-way street, they say, for just as the worshipper is empowered by their deity in times of need, the deity is given power by the acts of belief and devotion practised by those who believe in him. The more people pay homage to a god – the more souls commit themselves to his creed – the more powerful that god becomes. Just as a Realmgate allows a person to move from one realm to another, a faithful soul allows a god to move a measure of his power into a mortal world. A shrine or site of worship might have a similar effect, but there is no substitute for the fiery faith of one who truly believes. Through such people the gods can work true miracles. More than that, they can see through their eyes – quite literally, in some cases. The God-King Sigmar could not well perceive the Tourmaline Spires, those blinding geometric pillars in Hysh, until the ever-faithful Lord-Relictors of the Tempest Lords braved the deadly beams of light that refracted between them. In bringing the faith of Sigmar to those benighted reaches, the priests of the God-King's creed gave him focus and extended his reach, allowing him to gather a mighty celestial tempest in that region. In doing so, Sigmar tipped the balance between aelf, Stormhost and Slaaneshi hedonist that had deadlocked the region for months. Similar bonds of spiritual energy bind every priest and deity in every realm. So it is that true faith can change a world.

GHUR, REALM OF BEASTS

The Realm of Beasts is a near-endless string of jagged continents, each awe-inspiring in its primeval splendour. Here, every creature is red in tooth and claw, and every animal, insect and plant is both predator and prey. Even the landscapes are possessed of a hungering animus. Primal violence lurks everywhere, in man and beast alike.

The prehistoric reaches of the Realm of Beasts tend towards rugged, wide open places where winged raptors wheel in the clear blue skies. Sweeping savannahs, craggy valleys and open plains are split by fierce white-water rivers and yawning chasms that open and grind closed like impossible mouths. Great migratory trails criss-cross the lands, made not only by herds of prowling megafauna and hunting behemoths, but by the features of the lands themselves. A traveller might seek refuge in a cave one night and emerge the next morning to find the horizon has changed, the landmarks having slid slightly, but discernibly, out of position. Here, the mountain moves in search of ice with which to armour its flanks, just as the open plain grinds the mountain's edge to sharp gravel, the better to protect its crust from the feet of those who seek to traverse it. The river conquers the hills, gradually carving them apart with the rocks it has ripped from the high peaks. The hills shiver free those forests that seek to take root upon them with avalanches of rubble and burrows of root-gnawing stonelings. In places the weather-beaten bones and ribcages of gargants and vast saurian monsters litter the lands, used as frameworks for everything from bivouacs to primitive townships. Strung with the furs of recent kills, they are daubed with charcoal, chalk and terracotta.

The larger settlements on the amber plains of Ghur tend to be surrounded by concentric rings of palisades where every stake is sunk deep to jut diagonally outward. A stone wall would soon be smashed down by a rampaging mega-beast, but a sharpened stake, at just the right angle and with the strength of stone behind it, can force even the hungriest creature to leave well alone lest its own charge be its undoing. Those too frenzied or dim-witted to learn the danger of such traps will spit themselves through in an instant – all the people of the settlement need to do is set a large bonfire beneath it and the creature will likely feed the whole tribe it intended to devour.

Gnawed, cracked and pitted bone is a common sight in the Realm of Beasts, for natural and unnatural creatures are in great abundance, and to die there is to be devoured. Even the realmstone of Ghur takes a similar form, the amber-hued substance naturally occurring like fossils in rock. Deposits that range in size from tiny magical phalanges no bigger than the finger bone of a bat, to huge thigh bone pieces like those of a Thundertusk, are sought after by the shamans and ambermantic seers of Ghur. Those who become attuned to these artefacts can unleash the beast inside, and even transform into massively muscled, primal versions of themselves that fight with the fury of enraged predators.

Where there's bone there's meat, as the hunter-tribes of the Great Coil say, and Ghur's is the best in any Mortal Realm. As a result, good quality sea salt is a hugely valuable commodity, as it is used by hunters and coal-claimers to preserve the vast slabs of meat they ship out to other, less bounteous realms. A good-sized rock-lion haunch fetches such a high price it can be traded for a batch of blades from the Realm of Metal, or a dozen barrels of flame-ale

from Aqshy – the real difficulty is keeping the would-be trader from eating the goods before the exchange can be made. In the Realm of Beasts, the demands of heart and stomach trump those of the mind almost every time.

The heartlands of Ghur are host to a great many tribes of savage and brutish species. Here the orruk and the ogor thrive more than anywhere else, their might-makes-right philosophy and reckless aggression lending them the edge they need to survive amongst the wilderness. Gorkamorka is worshipped in a variety of different ways across every continent, even by many of the human hunter-gatherers that eke out a nomadic existence there – entire wars have been fought over whether he is cunning but brutal, or brutal but cunning. Though the Ironjawz can be found enforcing their hierarchy of raw strength across every landscape of the pan-continental Ghurish landmass, the Bonesplitter orruks make up the majority of the greenskin tribes

in the heartlands. Ravenous ogors instead tend to migrate across the landscapes nearer the Realm's Edge – known to some as the Hinterlands – denuding the lands of sustenance as they go, before heading back to start all over again. Those known as the Beastclaw Raiders bring with them the Everwinter – a supernatural blizzard so intense the lands become icy and inimical to life in each tribe's wake.

The coming of Chaos to Ghur began first with the great skull-gathers and gore-hunts of those human tribes who worshipped Khorne, for though they knew not of that dread moniker, their behaviour opened the door to the Blood God's minions nonetheless. When Chaos daemons and their inadvertent allies claimed great swathes of Heartland and Hinterland alike, the tribes of Destruction met them with an avalanche of violence in return. Ghur still exists in a state of tension – with the Pantheon of Order joining the fight, there is no telling what fate is in store for the realm's reaches.

REALMSTONE

In places where there is great metaphysical pressure – usually because of some traumatic event – magical energy becomes compressed into realmstone. Every realm has a different version of this substance. In Ghyran, it takes the form of jade ice that constantly melts, turns to steam, condenses and then freezes once more. In Chamon, it is globular, something like quicksilver shorn of gravity. The quartz-like realmstone of Hysh is prismatic and can concentrate or dissipate magical energy. Ulgu's realmstone is a grey gossamer said to be lies given form. There are still stranger minerals mortals see as analogous – the malefic warpstone that accretes in the bowels of Blight City, and the prophetic glimmerings traded in Excelsis, for instance. Regardless, those who tamper with realmstone usually find that disaster lurks close behind.

AZYR, REALM OF HEAVENS

The Realm of Heavens is ruled by Sigmar and Sigmar alone. Life in celestial Azyr was once a glorious existence, endless days of wonder and possibility shared by deities, demigods and mortals. Though the realm still remains sacrosanct, since the Battle of Burning Skies it has turned to the business of war.

The God-King has always had a deep connection to the Realm of Heavens. It was there that he first entered the Mortal Realms, borne upon the core of the world-that-was and given new life by the breath of the celestial Great Drake, Dracothion. Over the course of the Age of Myth, the God-King explored the reaches of Azyr. He strode the lands high and low, each kingdom lit by nearby Hysh during the day and the High Star Sigendil at night. He discovered mortal tribes there, and fanned the conflagration of civilisation among them. Long ago, he had raised a mighty empire from barbarian tribes, so he had mastered the art of nourishing new societies – and he knew well the secrets of men's hearts. His influence over the inhabitants of Azyr was so profound and positive that he vowed to bring his light to

the other Mortal Realms, and spread humanity throughout them. These would be his kingdoms, and Azyr would be the jewel in their crown.

In his wanderings through the new realms shown to him by Dracothion, Sigmar won the awe and allegiance of the scattered peoples who lived there. He led the strongest of them in the Great Founding of Azyr. Legend tells that Azyrheim's first foundation stones were laid at the place where Sigmar initially arrived in the realm, in a wide valley encircled by mountains. Slowly, incredibly, the city of Azyrheim was raised upon that mountainous domain, bathed in the strange light of Mallus – the orb-like core of the World Before Time. The city's grandeur was such it made the settlements of the world-that-was look humble. The golden spires

and citadels reached ever higher, glinting in the benign starlight. Every iota of the mortal races' artifice was bent to its creation, their ambitions and ancestral skills combining to form a domain fit for the God-King's chosen. Over long millennia, Azyrheim became the stellar metropolis that now shines brightly at the heart of the Celestial Realm. It was known by many names – amongst them the Eternal City, the First City and the City of the Lost, for to Azyrheim fled the refugees that Sigmar mustered after the critical Battle of Burning Skies and the Nexus Wars. It was the last of its kind, for even the greatest cities of the Mortal Realms crumbled before the Chaos onslaught. As generations came and went, Azyr became the fortress of the lost, the stronghold of the dispossessed, the pride of Sigmar's vengeful sons.

A new history was stitched like a tapestry across the fabric of space, with entire civilisations rising and falling throughout the fantastical realms that Dracothion had revealed to Sigmar. Wars were fought against the living and the dead, the monstrous and the cunning. Before Sigmar ordered the Gates of Azyr shut, at the height of the Age of Chaos, people from every realm had sought sanctuary there, swelling the numbers of the city from what was already a vast and diverse population to a cauldron of civilisations – some new, some of which could trace their ancestry back to the oldest of humanity's great nations. There they coexisted, united by their common hatred of Chaos and their dreams of one day reclaiming their lost lands. The echo of that which had gone before grew not softer, but ever louder and more strident, until the clamour of warlike souls filled the heavens. Though some had been

driven from their homelands, and others cast adrift on the tides of time, every one of those displaced peoples dreamed of taking their revenge upon the forces of Chaos.

THE SIGMARABULUM

The God-King found that he was irrevocably drawn to the dark sphere of Mallus, core of the world-that-was. Where Dracothion had set that burning, tortured orb in the skies of Azyr, Sigmar felt his connection to the past most strongly of all.

So it was there that he bent the divine power of his pantheon to the creation of a structure like no other – the Sigmarabulum.

Through Grungni's artifice, Lord Tyrion's mastery of the metaphysical arts and Dracothion's power over the heavens, a ring was built around the Broken World so vast it could house the population of Azyrheim three times over. There was founded the Vault Celestial, home of the pantheon in times of crisis. There too shone Sigendil all the brighter, its light illuminating the dark moon of Dharroth below. The forges of the Six Smiths were created there – the very Anvil of the Apotheosis whereupon the Stormcast Eternals were created, and from whence they were sent to reclaim the Mortal Realms. Since its construction, the Sigmarabulum has rung to the hammers of a legion of warsmiths, those who create not only the sigmarite weapons and armour with which to wage war against Chaos, but the warriors to wield them.

CRIME AND PUNISHMENT

Sigmar's tolerance for lawbreakers is famously low. Through lawlessness comes disorder, and that way lies Chaos. It was not always this way, for Sigmar originally hailed from a tribe of barbarians who fought, loved and lived as they pleased. But with uncounted billions of souls looking to him for salvation, his methods have become ever more extreme. Long ago, in allowing peoples from every realm to seek safe haven in Azyr, he also allowed an influx of hidden agents of Chaos to infect his city. Matters came to a head, and he descended in wrath, not only slaying every citizen who bore the mark of Chaos, but destroying all those who harboured hatred in their hearts. It was a statement of intent that few could ignore.

THE REALM OF CHAOS

The Realm of Chaos is not truly a Mortal Realm at all, but a vile and nightmarish reality only tangentially linked to the rest of creation. It is the home of the Dark Gods and the legions of hellspawn that are formed from their power, each cursed daemon – from the most spiteful imp to the fiercest monster – created from dark emotion.

The Chaos Gods and their dominions are one, for they are formed of the same aetheric energy. As a Chaos God's influence over other worlds and realities expands in power, its corresponding influence upon the Realm of Chaos broadens, and its territory grows. As extensions of the gods, the appearances of these domains are shaped by the same emotions that created their masters: Khorne's realm is founded on anger and bloodletting, Tzeentch's lands are constructs of change and pure magic, Nurgle's territory is a haven of death and regeneration, and Slaanesh's dominion is a paradise of damning temptations. Though realm and god are one, the Chaos Gods each have a form that embodies their personalities and dwells at the heart of their territories. Surrounded by their attendant daemons, the Chaos Gods watch over their vast and sprawling domains, whilst also seeking any opportunity to invade the Mortal Realms.

Much of the Realm of Chaos is random, constantly churning and reforming; rivers of burned souls flow through petrified woodlands under crimson skies, great stairways lead up to the sky only to bend back impossibly to join themselves below in an everlasting loop, castles made of bones and fortresses of hardened ichor stand amidst tangled forests of limbs that clutch and grasp at those passing by. Every dream and nightmare, every lunatic vision and deranged fancy, finds its home somewhere in the Realm of Chaos, but those of the Dark Gods are the most powerful and abiding of all.

The domain of Khorne is a land of fury and violence. It is built upon foundations of murder and conflict, and is home to every form of battle. This blood-soaked dominion echoes with Khorne's bellowing anger and the clash of weapons, the cracking of whips and the clarion calls of innumerable brass war horns. At its

heart is the Brass Citadel, the fortress of Khorne himself. Decorated with red-veined marble, the metal walls of the unholy fortress are broken by jagged outcrops, encrusted with blood and armoured with serrated spurs of burnished brass. Outside, hideous gargoyles leer from every parapet, ready to spew scalding streams of fiery metal across those foolish enough to besiege the fortress. The moat of the Brass Citadel is filled not with water, but with the boiling blood of those who have lost their lives to war.

Of all the outlandish landscapes of the Realm of Chaos, Tzeentch's domain is the most bizarre and incomprehensible. His realm is woven from the raw fabric of magic. The Crystal Labyrinth, as it is known, sits upon an immense iridescent plateau, and its presence is felt across all the daemonic realms. Shifting avenues made from realmstone of every kind criss-cross Tzeentch's domain as it contorts through nine realities at once. Hidden pathways built from lies and schemes infiltrate the territories of Tzeentch's rivals and the Mortal Realms themselves, binding the lands of men to the insanely complex plans of the Great Conspirator.

The domain of Nurgle is not a barren wasteland, but a macabre paradise, a near-infinite jungle of life, death and grotesque rebirth. Tended by the Lord of Decay, this unwholesome realm is home to every pox and affliction imaginable. Twisted, rotten boughs entangled with grasping vines cover the mouldering ground, entwining like broken fingers. Spectacular fungi break through the squelching mulch, puffing out clouds of choking spores. Jutting from amidst this primordial mire is Nurgle's Manse. Decrepit and ancient, yet eternally strong at its foundations, the mansion is an eclectic structure of rotten timbers and broken walls.

Beneath its mildewed and sagging beams, Nurgle works eternally at a huge rusted cauldron, a receptacle large enough to contain all the oceans of the realms. Chuckling and murmuring to himself, Nurgle labours hard to create contagions and pestilence, ladling them out to rain into the Mortal Realms so those lands too might rejoice in plague and putrescence.

The Palace of Slaanesh was once a six-fold realm of uninhibited glories and unbound pleasure – though beneath its glamorous facade, doom and vileness have long lurked. Since Slaanesh's capture by Tyrion and Teclis, this realm has fallen into faded glory, its once-dazzling palaces now derelict and crumbling. None truly know whether this realm will dwindle to nothing or flourish once more should Slaanesh's followers succeed in their long and rapturous quest – all that is known is that Slaanesh's minions, his daemons and his worshippers will never rest until the Dark Prince sits on his rightful throne once more.

Valan Swordseer squeezed the young prince's heart, the blood offering filling his scryer-bowl. He incanted the words of his forefather, smearing hot crimson liquid across his eyes with a brush tipped with silky human hair. 'Blood-lord, King of Carnage, show unto me the place of my soul's fate.' For a while, the bowl remained flat, its coppery stink filling his nostrils. Then something shimmered – a vision of a citadel, hard to discern at first, but growing clearer. The figures marching from that fell fortress' gates were daemons all. Valan screamed as he was drawn into their midst. Then he was gone, and the brush of human hair clattered to the flagstones.

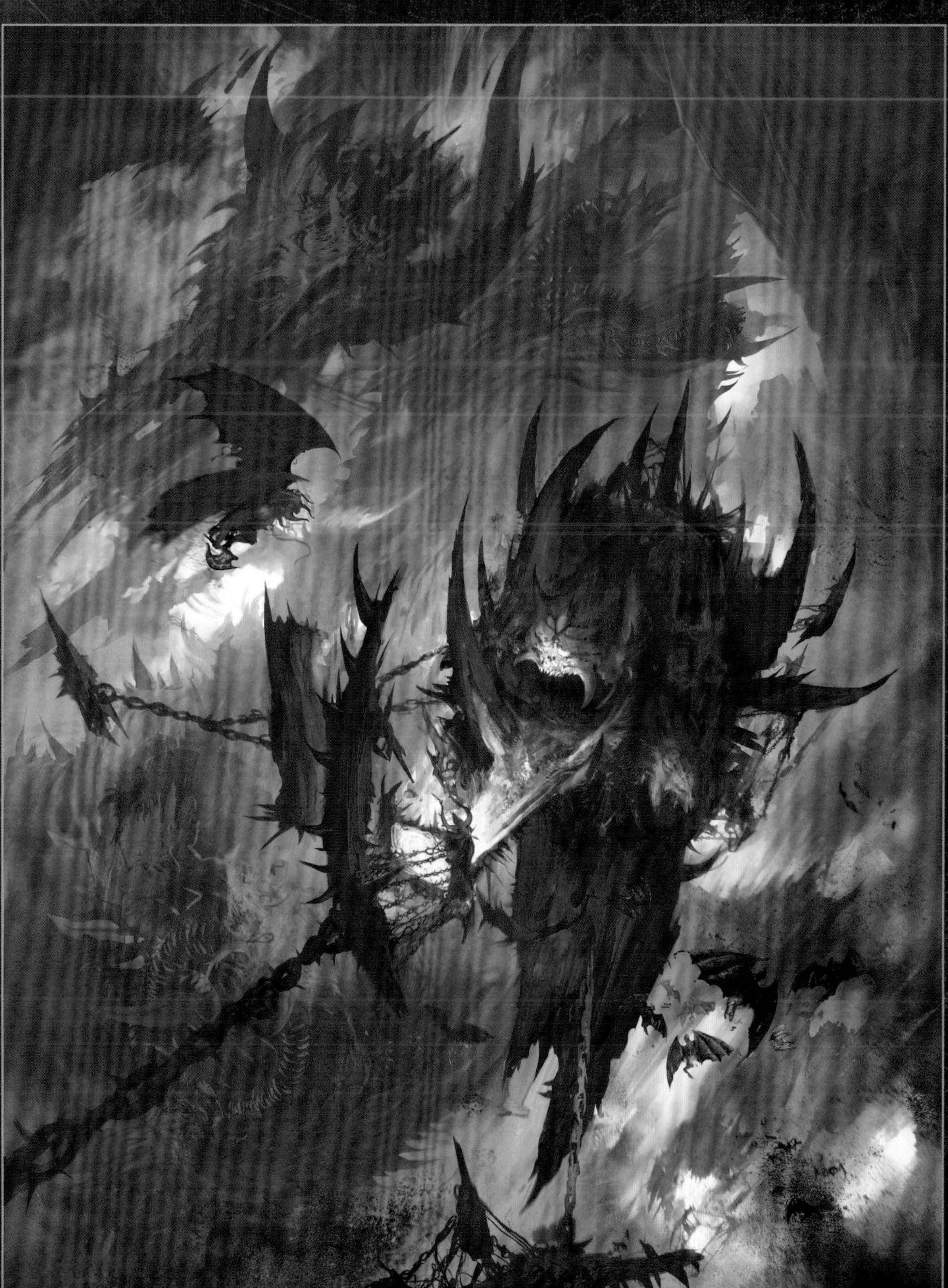

FACTIONS OF THE MORTAL REALMS

THE FORCES OF ORDER

In the eternal battle, the forces of Order will always stand against the darkness of Chaos. They are a shield wall protecting that which is still whole and sound, a bulwark against madness and misrule. Law and stricture govern them, duty and oath guide their blades. They guard the civilians of their cultures and man the walls of their cities against whatever horrors the Dark Gods unleash, no matter the cost. In such times, compassion and morality are often seen as dangerous luxuries; Order is not synonymous with good. Yet these enclaves advance the cause of civilisation, and in doing so, bring harmony.

Once, these forces formed an alliance so strong they brought illumination to the far corners of the Mortal Realms. But the many weaknesses of man, duardin and aelf were cracks through which Chaos filtered its corruption, widening the divisions between allies, friends and brothers until ambition and resolve became blind pride and hateful stubbornness. The worlds of Order were shattered, their works torn down. Only now, as the God-King Sigmar casts his lightning across the firmament, do the disparate races of Order come together as one in the hope of defending the fabric of reality once more.

The hosts of the celestial tempest; the Free People of Sigmar; the aelves of forest, shadow and deep water; the duardin of the mountains and of the sky; the Seraphon from beyond the stars – they fight together for the first time in aeons. In doing so, they may yet break the stranglehold that Chaos has maintained over the Mortal Realms for blood-soaked centuries. But the dominion of the Dark Gods is endless, and victory will not be won without terrible sacrifice…

STORMCAST ETERNALS

From troubled skies blast the shining warriors of the Stormcast Eternals. Born of celestial Azyr, these indomitable warhosts blaze into the Mortal Realms as twin-tailed thunderbolts hurled by the God-King Sigmar himself. Theirs is a fighting force without equal, for they are created to destroy Chaos in all its forms.

With the power of the Realm of Heavens crackling in their veins, the Stormcast Eternals are demigods in comparison to the kin they once called their own. Long has Sigmar Heldenhammer waited to unleash these exemplars of battle upon his ancient foes, summoning his power as a tempest gathers on the horizon.

Now, as the Chaos-blighted realms crumble away and reality itself teeters on the edge of catastrophe, uncounted thousands of these elite paragons stand ready to answer the call to war. The Age of Sigmar has come, and vengeance will be meted out on a colossal scale.

Though they stride the realms with the surety of living legends, each Stormcast Eternal began as a mere mortal. Throughout the realms there are those who fight valiantly against the Chaos brutes who grind their nations and cultures under the iron heel of tyranny. Whether by guiding their people from corruption in the face of anarchy, undoing the works of their oppressors, or taking up arms against those who force them into servitude, these heroes come to the notice of Sigmar. Just as it seems they will be slain for their defiance against the Dark Gods, their souls vanish, plucked from battle in a flash of aetheric energy.

All Stormcast Eternals wear armour of blessed sigmarite, a formidable magical metal that can transmute into lightning along with its wearer.

To High Azyr such souls are taken. Three days of feasting in the Heldenhall follow, a riotous welcome to the afterlife where the claimed ones build their strength for the ordeals to come. Then the mystical process of transformation begins in earnest. These warriors make their way to the Chamber of the Broken World, where they are blasted apart by unknowable powers. In this way, their spirits are purified, ready to receive Sigmar's ultimate gift. Those that endure this ordeal are reforged, an agonising process by which every mote of their body and soul is imbued with celestial magic. After being visited by the violent blessings of the World Hammer, they become powerful indeed, forged into beings as much of magic as of flesh.

These living embodiments of Sigmar's will are far stronger, faster and more resilient than the warriors they once were. But still their transformation is not complete. Over the course of a gruelling initiation in the Gladitorium, these novitiates learn battle arts that temper their deadly skills still further. There they strike down those that will be their brothers, and are struck down in turn, only to rise again unharmed at the end of each day's fighting. They learn of their own enhanced abilities from each painful experience, but also how to watch each other's backs. To fight united is far better than to fight alone.

Each Stormcast Eternal is girded with sigmarite, an arcane metal drawn from Mallus, the preserved core of the world-that-was. Armour fashioned from this metal is proof against the sharpest blade or the heaviest axe; when burnished to a high sheen, it affords protection not only to the body, but also the soul. No less remarkable are the hammers, swords and glaives wielded by the Stormcast Eternals. They too are made from sigmarite, and to feel their touch is to meet a swift end.

Each Stormcast Eternal is one aspect of a far greater war machine. A successful initiate will soon become part of a wider organisation known as a chamber, of which the Strike Chambers are the most numerous. Together with the Tempest Chambers – most notable of which are the Vanguard Chambers, who roam the worlds of men at will, and the Extremis Chambers, who are one with the celestial children of Dracothion – these are formed into indomitable Stormhosts.

Stormhosts are gatherings of well-trained and like-minded souls with the military strength to conquer entire nations. Not only are each Stormhost's retinues and conclaves schooled in battlefield tactics and manoeuvres, they also learn how to bind the power of the storm, bolstering and augmenting each other's prowess so that every assault hits home in a hurricane of force.

Because of their bond to the celestial tempest, the Stormcast Eternals can blaze as living lightning from Azyr to any one of the Mortal Realms. It was Grungni, creator-god of the duardin, that gave Sigmar this thunder-gift, and the God-King has used it well. When Sigmar wishes to smite his foes, he hurls bolts of meteoric light, pure and incandescent, down from the Realm of Heavens. Shining champions stand in their afterglow where none had stood before.

The journey back to Sigmar's halls is far more gruelling. Once a Stormcast Eternal has taken form upon mortal soil, they cannot ascend once more without either passing through a Realmgate portal to Azyr, or dying in battle. When such a warrior is killed, in all but the most extreme circumstances, he is not truly lost. His body discorporates in a heartbeat, transmuting into a crackling cloud that flashes upwards in a blur of mystical force. When this soul-stuff reaches Azyr, it is drawn back to Sigmar's vaults, where it is painfully reforged into the Stormcast Eternal that was slain. Though this process is imperfect and never easy, the sight of a fallen Stormcast is rare indeed.

This process has spawned rumours that Sigmar's supernatural warriors walk in the shadow as well as the light. There is not always time for the reforging to run smoothly, for the forces of Chaos are potent beyond sane limits, and the domains of the realms numerous beyond measure. For many, this transformation causes them to lose a part of themselves, and each time they return to Sigmar's forge, there is a higher chance they will emerge altered in mind as well as in body. This is troubling in the extreme for the Stormcast Eternals, for under their shining battle armour, they are still in part human, with all the hopes, fears and ambitions that come with that birthright. Many feel the duty of their new lives weighing heavily on their shoulders, and are unable to prevent their mortal flaws rising to the surface.

THE FORGING OF HEROES

In the midst of battle, the mightiest of mankind's warriors were transported away, for they were needed for a greater cause. With rolling thunder and a blinding flash, each of these aspirants was taken to Sigmaron amongst the stars. It was there, in the Celestial Realm, that their true trials were to begin.

In Heldenhall, the great Hall of Heroes, can be found the endless feast. For three days and three nights each warrior must build up strength for the trials ahead.

In the Chamber of the Broken World, barbarians and technocratic nomads alike are blasted apart by lightnings. They are reforged anew – an agonising process that can last anywhere between a few heartbeats to long centuries. Even time turns molten in the Forge Eternal. Not all survive the process.

Seven times seven are the Cairns of Tempering, where body and soul are blended with the Gifts of the Gods. Those that endure these ordeals awaken for the final test.

Upon the Anvil of the Apotheosis are the Stormcast Eternals finally wrought. If they endure the shock waves from the last blessings of the World Hammer, they awaken imbued with the energies of the Realm of Heavens, bequeathed a portion of the God-King Sigmar's own divine powers.

Some Stormhosts, such as the Blackhammers, suffer from sudden and profoundly powerful destructive impulses, while others, like the Hammers of Sigmar, are unable to accept anything other than unalloyed success, striving no matter the cost for total victory. Many Stormhosts, the Celestial Vindicators foremost amongst them, are single-mindedly driven by an unquenchable need to wreak bloody revenge upon those who butcher and enslave the innocent people of the Mortal Realms. Others find lightning crackling from their gaze when their ire is raised, or thunder rumbling under their every word. Some amongst these troubled individuals whisper that to be reforged too many times is to relinquish one's former existence altogether, becoming something that is both less than human and far more at the same time.

The future of the Stormcast Eternals is as unpredictable as the rage of the tempest that forges them. Perhaps they will rise ascendant to usher in a new era, returning notions of justice, honour and freedom to the shattered peoples who have cast aside such luxuries in the simple struggle for survival. Perhaps they will be found wanting in the direst test of all – the battle to drive back the forces of Chaos. One thing is certain: the Stormcast Eternals strike with unstoppable vigour, and by their hammers and blades, the Mortal Realms will be changed forever.

Stormcast Eternals strive to keep their former cultures alive. Though they are united by the heraldry of their Stormhost, and though they are renamed after their reforging, few wish to relinquish their former identity entirely.

HAMMERS OF SIGMAR
First to be Forged, Never to Fail

The first of the Stormhosts to be hurled into the Mortal Realms, the Hammers of Sigmar bear the responsibility of that honour with strength and nobility. They of all the Stormhosts have been reforged time and time again, for they are ever at the forefront of war. Some amongst them, the vision-plagued leader Vandus Hammerhand included, have begun to pay the price. As one of the largest of the Stormhosts, the Hammers of Sigmar can call upon almost all of the breeds of warrior Sigmar has entrusted with leading his crusade. As the first to be forged, they fear nothing except their own failure. Every man, woman and child across the realms looks to them for salvation, and they cannot be found wanting.

THE CELESTIAL VINDICATORS
Steeled by Hatred, Bound by Revenge

The Celestial Vindicators are vengeance incarnate. Stern and unforgiving, their hearts burn with an enmity for Chaos which knows no bounds. While soaked in the blood of the enemy, as mortals these warriors had prayed to Sigmar – not to be saved, avenged or transported to the safety of Azyr, but for strength enough to smite those who had wronged them. They were granted that wish. During their reforging they have to pass through the Sturmdrang Gate, and many do not return. Those who survive are given a measure of holy rage. Only by the chanting of grim war songs are the Celestial Vindicators able to channel and focus their fury, but in the heat of combat that hate becomes a wildfire that cannot be extinguished.

THE HALLOWED KNIGHTS
Only the Faithful

Zealous beyond measure, loyal beyond question, the Hallowed Knights are driven to fight with unrelenting fervour. They consider the war against Chaos to be a sacred crusade for which no sacrifice is too great. They go to battle clad in burnished silver armour and the royal blue of Azyr, and those who have been reforged many times in Sigmar's service – of which Lord-Celestant Gardus is unquestionably the most holy – emit a lambent celestial light. They fear no evil and welcome a martyr's death, for their trust in the God-King is absolute. Hence they are armoured spiritually as much as physically, often able to shrug off the baleful sorceries of evil-hearted warriors.

ANVILS OF THE HELDENHAMMER
We are the Hammer, We are the Anvil

Reforged as the Broken World span sinister beneath a fell aspect, the Anvils of the Heldenhammer are the dark and brooding heroes of an elder age. Ominous and archaic, they fight like spectres out of legend, preserving practices and battle rites long lost to mortal memory, yet all the more potent for it. They know well that Nagash would shatter the realms to reclaim their souls, and make them his servants for all eternity. The Stormhost's Lord-Relictors brood long on the subject of how best to escape that deathly destiny, creating weapons that can capture errant souls and fighting to the darkest corners of the realms to claim vital knowledge on Sigmar's behalf.

The Whispering Gate was shunned by the hillfolk as a place of great evil. Darksome idols were raised before it, and ravager warbands enacted debased rites in its shadow. Then came the thunder – and with it the Stormcast Eternals, wreathed in lightning. Hundreds were slain, mauled by claw, melted by daemonfire, or hewn by hellish axe – yet they won victory nonetheless.

FYRESLAYERS

Fyreslayers are ferocious duardin that go to war armoured in fiery conviction. Known for their incandescent temper and stubborn refusal to die even when mortally wounded, the Fyreslayers make extremely valuable allies – provided the would-be employer has the right amount of gold, of course.

To some, the legendary duardin Fyreslayer is a war-hardened mercenary who fights with the passion of an enraged bear and honours his word above all things. To others he is a muscle-bound maniac who skirts the edge of a dangerous madness, so obsessed with gold he will stop even mid-battle should a glinting auric bounty be scattered before him. There is truth in both of these suppositions. In every land that harbours smoking volcano chains and fire-bellied mountains, the Fyreslayers are respected by warlords and kings alike. Their tenacity and fury in combat are legendary – and as with all duardin, they take oaths and honour very seriously indeed.

Fyreslayers are single-minded and volatile, for their way of life has endured since the times when the wrath-god Grimnir walked

the lands. Since the duel between Grimnir and the godbeast Vulcatrix saw both god and titanic salamander slain, the Fyreslayers have been engaged in a desperate quest – to locate and claim the fragments of their god that glitter across creation as the priceless metal ur-gold.

Only the Runemasters of the Fyreslayer lodges – elders steeped in the sacred lore and metallurgic knowledge of their kin – can tell ur-gold from its terrestrial equivalent. Because of this, the Fyreslayers covet all forms of gold, mining it, trading for it and even taking it by force so their Runemasters may sift the priceless from the mundane. They do not let their treasure lie inert once it has been found, but instead use it to empower themselves. The ur-gold is smelted into its purest form, cast into sacred runes of strength and endurance, and then

– in a process that is every bit as agonising as it sounds – fused into the Fyreslayers' muscular frames. When the battle-rage is upon a Fyreslayer, he can channel the godly magic of these runes into his own body, increasing his physical might to supernatural levels.

Though gold can be looted from ruined empires and carved from the seams of the earth, the biggest hauls by far come from the spoils and profits of war. As such, Fyreslayers readily wade into the thick of the fight, led by Runefathers riding vast fire-tongued volcano-beasts known as Magmadroths, shattering the enemy battle line in a storm of claws, fyresteel and blazing embers. Even the gold of High Azyr has been expended to secure the services of these consummate mercenaries; over the course of the Realmgate Wars, many hosts of Stormcast Eternals fought alongside armies of Fyreslayers bought with coin more than with common cause.

When the Fyreslayers go to war their presence is an assault upon the senses, even to those who also hail from the sulphurous lands of Aqshy, where the duardin's lodges are the most numerous. Each throng marches from great volcanic strongholds or burrows up from the parched earth in explosions of lava, bodies shimmering with golden flame, steam wreathing their limbs and cinders venting with each breath. Even savage blows glance off their glowing skin without leaving a mark – but should a foe succeed in hacking a wound in the corded flesh, the insult drives the Fyreslayer to the heights of apoplectic, killing fury. Their own weapons, master-crafted by talented artisans and warsmiths in the belly of sacred volcanoes, strike with the force of flaming meteors. These are the warriors of the forge and the crucible, and they bring the scorching heat of their homelands to burn away their foes.

Vulkite Berzerkers wield fyresteel axes that smoulder with the flames of the braziers in their hafts. The stubbornness and fury of these duardin is legendary.

'But that's just ridiculous,' said Vandersnitch, the magister's voice high in disbelief. 'How much gold have you stupid ashfeet given away in this manner? How many walls and war engines could have been built with that money?'

The villagers cowered back, eyes wide in soot-stained faces. It seemed to the eldest of them, a gaunt man with a crown of curling firegoat horns, that the finely robed Azyrite wore enough gold upon his mantle to see a whole village fed throughout the winter.

'The volcano people,' he replied, 'they are vengeful. My grandsire told me of the winter-oath. It must be honoured!'

'Nonsense. The outdated babblings of senile old fools are not evidence enough to waste a king's ransom in gold from so rich a seam. In Sigmar's name, this behaviour stops, now.'

The tribespeople of the Cinder Bleak muttered and shuffled their feet unhappily, yet the elder said nothing. The newcomer had claimed to be the architect of their salvation, and bore the same celestial symbols as the Lightning Gods wore upon their shields. The elder had witnessed the breaking of the Bloodied Hand, and did not wish to share their fate. The snow-swept plains in the valley below were still littered with split skulls.

'Run!' shouted the horn-crowned elder. 'Flee, for the love of Sigmar!'

His tribesmen scattered from their midsummer ritual, coughing in the choking black smoke. Storming through the ceremonial yurts was a bellowing mob of orruks daubed with bright war paint, roaring in a guttural tongue as they set fire to buildings and laid into tribesmen too slow to escape. The bodies of greenskins lay strewn across the volcano's flanks, pierced by the flint arrows of the elder's warriors, but their deaths had not even slowed the horde.

To the west of the encampment was a gaping sinkhole, its insides glowing with molten rock. The rancid smell of roasting greenskin was drifting from the hole. The elder looked around for the last of his tribe, but he saw only the ruddy flesh and tall head-crests of the volcano people. Gold and silver glowed bright as axe and flail bit deep into painted orruk flesh. Sheets of fire billowed left and right as salamander-like riding beasts burst from the smoke to incinerate swathes of bone-pierced brutes. Blood flew as several of the volcano people were smashed to the floor by stone axes but, to the elder's amazement, two got back to their feet, laying into the orruks with berserker frenzy. Within a few minutes, the orruks were dead.

A thick-set duardin, covered crest-to-toe in blood, strode from the inferno to stare hard at the elder.

'Right then, you,' he said, flames crackling as he levelled his axe. 'Where's last winter's gold?'

KHARADRON OVERLORDS

Driving down from aether-lit storm clouds, the Kharadron Overlords are masters of technology and the deadly machineries of war. Endlessly inventive and with a keen eye for a deal, these duardin live by a stringent Code – though they are not above bending its rules in the name of profit.

The Kharadron Overlords have only recently revealed their skyborne society to the peoples of the Mortal Realms, but they have already made their mark. So majestic are their airborne fleets that they fill the mind with wonder – to witness them is to be dazzled by the spectacle, and even brutish orruks and haughty aelves talk in awed tones of the sight. To see them make war is another thing entirely – such devastating pyrotechnics erupt from each army of the Kharadron Overlords that their adversaries are not so much conquered as blasted apart.

A Kharadron fleet is a free-flying armada of metallic vessels, each bristling with guns and crewed by die-hard duardin warriors. These miraculous craft are held aloft by metal spheres, each filled with the lighter-than-air substance known as aether-gold. This bizarre material – sometimes called sky-gold, or

the Breath of Grungni – is rich in Chamonic energy, but invisible to the naked eye. Only one skilled in the aethermantic arts can detect it, let alone turn it to the purpose of war. Yet it is the very substance that keeps the Kharadron cities afloat – to the Overlords it is vital, and even a wisp of it is worth more than a chest of the finest diamonds.

Long ago, the Kharadron Overlords were as other duardin. They lived in mountainous holds, mining the earth for precious substances and perfecting their metallurgic arts. But the scourge of Chaos bit deep. They had thought to join forces with their allies, but found them absent, and though they prayed for aid from their ancestral gods, no help was forthcoming. With the lands consumed by a tide of violence, and with the anarchy threatening to reach even the highest peaks, the duardin were forced to seek the

relative safety of the sky – an act once inimical to their traditionally down-to-earth mindset. In that great leap of faith and technology, however, the forefathers of the Kharadron went from the ever-faithful refugees of an ancient empire to the founders of a secular new era.

For long centuries, the Kharadron Overlords traded only amongst themselves, for the embattled remnants of mankind were more concerned with survival than with claim-barter or haggling over mineral resources. With the resurgence of civilisation across the Mortal Realms, however, the skyborne duardin see worthy trade partners in humanity's teeming cities once more. Lasting alliances have been struck, for where there is profit to be made, the Kharadron Overlords will protect their interests. The sacred Code is quite

Jorvek's Grundstok Thunderers opened fire. The ratmen swarming up the mountain path erupted into flame, furry bodies hurled in all directions. On came the rest, while yet more scaled the cliff directly behind the duardin.
'Another volley, then fall back!' boomed Jorvek. His crew obliged, their aethershot tearing another dozen skaven apart. Then Grungni's Brow hove into view from around the side of the mountain, its escort of Skyriggers pulling the Thunderers to the safety of the Ironclad's deck. Mere feet away was the scurrying tide, its momentum bearing hundreds of mangy bodies over the cliff – and straight into the climbing rats nearing the cliff's edge. Jorvek smiled wide. Life in the Grundcorps was never dull.

The armour and equipment of the Kharadron Overlords protect them from the transmutative aetheric energies they harness to fuel their impossible craft.

explicit that a duardin must often speculate to accumulate, and if that means delivering a thrashing to a rampaging orruk horde from on high, or blasting a clutch of Deadwalkers from a mountainside before it can reach a human fortress, they will waste no time in restoring order to their trade routes. Though an unkind observer might conclude that the Kharadron act only in the interests of their own material gain, they have proved stalwart allies to the Stormcast Eternals, and have

even been seen fighting alongside aelves – though when pressed on the matter, they soon change the subject.

As the Age of Sigmar establishes hope across the realms, these sky-mining duardin unleash their fantastical weaponry once more. Though it is designed to defeat floating harkraken, sky-urchin shoals and Chimera flocks, it is just as effective against the enemies of Order. With the arcane power of aether-gold driving their guns, the

Kharadron do not fire lead shot or cannonballs, but blasts of blinding energy that annihilate anything they touch. None know whether their lust for favourable trade deals will see the Kharadron thrive at the expense of the God-King's people, or usher in a new age of cooperation between the two races. As far as mankind is concerned, when the spectre of Chaos looms long, survival comes first, and profit later – but to the Kharadron Overlords, they are one and the same.

SYLVANETH

The Sylvaneth are the vengeful spirit-kin of Alarielle the Everqueen. Sprouted from soulpods that Alarielle and her most favoured spirits planted in places rich with life magic, they grow tall and strong, taking up sword and bow to defend the lands against those who would defile and despoil them.

The Wargroves of the Sylvaneth advance with fluid grace. Forest spirits of fierce joy and vengeful anger, they come to life from amongst the tangled woodland, the air around them buzzing with verdant energies. The rustle of leaves and creak of branches mingles with the melody of ancient war-songs as they slip and stalk through the shadows of tall trees, the smell of amber sap filling the air. Some of these miraculous creatures appear like the spirits of legend clad in bark and knotted heartwood, others as towering lords of the forest so massive they can peer over castle walls – and tear them down with their gnarled hands. All Sylvaneth

are creatures of tough plant matter as well as hard flesh. Within them is the strength to rend armour and split stone, just as the green shoots of a forest can break through the metal and masonry of the civilised world. These are creatures of nature first and foremost, and they destroy those who would threaten the cycles of life with choking briar, ripping thorn, and piercing spear. Left alone, the Sylvaneth would have been content to exist in seclusion for long aeons – but war has come to their realm, and they have answered its call with devastating force.

The Sylvaneth are not true mortals at all, but rather creatures of magic.

Their connection to the aligned energies of Ghyran is innate, and they are strongest when in the Realm of Life from which they originally hail. But they are invigorated in body and soul by wild places wherever they go, and their sacred groves can be found in the life-rich places of all the realms. The Sylvaneth are deadly to trespassers, no matter their allegiance, and are death to those who bear ill will into their domain – these creatures are elemental beings first and foremost, and do not lightly compromise. Given that only the Sylvaneth truly know the borders between their demesnes and the unclaimed lands nearby, it is easy to see them as fickle destroyers rather

Branchwraiths are strange arboreal spirit-creatures that have a natural affinity with the burgeoning energies of life magic.

'*Thy shirker-beasts be in the wood, say I.*' Emurghan the Foul took off his horned helm and secured it to his bicep to save from getting entangled. '*I can sniff them, all a-feared.*'

'*Lead on then,*' slurred Ghougth, a stooped toad of a man with too many teeth. '*Or is it your own reticence that perfumes the air?*'

The Maggotkin lord stuck out his ulcerated tongue in response before taking his greataxe to the tangled foliage and barging into the clearing shoulder-first. He was greeted by the sight of a hundred beastman corpses held in a writhing net of thorned briars, fluids drizzling from their broken legs.

Then the foliage twisted and came alive. The bark-clad pillars around them were not tree trunks, but the legs of arboreal giants, the branches cruelly clawed hands.

'*Oh bloggorbs,*' said Emurghan, raising his axe. A wooden fist batted it aside just as another staved in his skull.

than stalwart defenders of their own way of life. Yet in their hearts the majority of the Sylvaneth are good and noble beings, staunch enemies of Chaos one and all.

During the Age of Myth the Sylvaneth became a thriving society, growing to colonise vast swathes of the natural world. Some believe their origins lie in another time, another place – that their goddess, Alarielle the Everqueen, survived the destruction of the world-that-was, and that some amongst the Sylvaneth embody the spirits she once called kin. Those spirits were planted as soulpods in the most fertile places she could find. Since those early days their numbers have blossomed,

burgeoned and spread – just as the tree becomes the copse, then the wood, then the forest. But, as with all things, they have begun to dwindle away, the reaping of the Age of Chaos taking its toll on their numbers.

The Sylvaneth's animosity towards Chaos is intense. Having become one with the places they settled, they fought and died for their sacred regions when the invasions of Chaos sought to tear that power away for the Dark Gods. Ghyran in particular was assailed by countless plague-ridden hosts as the maggoty hordes of Nurgle invaded through places abandoned and corrupt. The Father of Plagues saw the fecundity of Ghyran's endless cycles as the

ultimate prize, and as his diseases took hold across swathes of Ghyran, Nurgle's power increased, and the Sylvaneth found themselves fighting a losing battle. But the coming of Sigmar's Tempest gave the Sylvaneth chance to regroup. Though the Everqueen had been all but consumed by bitterness and despondency during the Age of Chaos, becoming little more than a seed of potential futures, she was able to regather her strength and flourish into full godhood once more. Now she goes to battle as a vengeful deity of nature resurgent, the spirit-song trilling loud in every Sylvaneth heart as they strike back with terrible fury against their oppressors.

DAUGHTERS OF KHAINE

Lithe, cruel and swift of blade, the Daughters of Khaine are a religious order of matriarchal aelves hailing from Ulgu. Though they have enclaves within civilised Azyrite society, in truth they live for the thrill of open war and spilt blood. Their altar is the cut and thrust of the battlefield and their wine the hot blood of their victims.

The Daughters of Khaine have their power base deep in the mists of Ulgu, where duplicity and misdirection are commonplace and, for some, a way of life. These warrior women are the inheritors of a long-standing tradition built on blood sacrifice and gory battle rites – though this is a heritage they cannot openly claim, lest they incur Sigmar's wrath and be cast out from civilisation entirely. Instead, they operate behind an elaborate series of masks, lies and schemes – and none more so than their doyenne and ruler, the dark-hearted demigoddess Morathi.

These Khainites – as the worshippers of the gore-handed aelf god call themselves – are sustained and given vigour by the act of spilling blood. Though an echo of the ancient blood cults, this life-stealing practice is just as effective today as it has ever been. The priestesses of this strange religion have all but perfected their art, and some have lived thousands of years on the stolen essence of others. By bathing in hot gore or drinking in the energies of their enchanted cauldrons full of blood, they can transform from stooped and wrinkled crones to lissom maidens without so much as a blemish on their alabaster skin. They count among their number some of the very first aelves to be freed from Slaanesh's dominion – those

who sought refuge not by hiding from their nemesis, but by offering their hearts and souls to another god so they would have a measure of protection. These are the high priestesses of their cult, those who have sought succour in slaughter and the rich red lifeblood of the realms. Yet some suspect even Khaine himself is a lie, another mask worn by she who would take his place.

Morathi has fashioned a society in her own likeness, forming a dynasty of Witch Aelves that obey her every whim. She claims to be the high oracle of Khaine, using his image and bloody creed to fuel her followers' devotion, leading elaborate

The Daughters of Khaine are lithe, acrobatic killers that make even seasoned duellists seem clumsy and slow.

Vellen Candlemar hefted his halberd and did his best to look fierce. The aelves were fighting the first orruks only a dozen feet away. The Daughters. They had haunted his dreams ever since the gambler's arena – visions of loveliness, all alabaster skin, lithe limbs and flowing hair, wearing coy smiles beneath flashing eyes that promised illicit pleasures. Here on the field they were hellish banshees.

Lashings of orruk blood whipped from their blades, splattering across Vellen's heraldic tunic as he advanced. The greenskins were roaring fiercely, but each time one raised its arm to swing, a Daughter would cut off its hand at the wrist. The orruks fell back as the she-aelves redoubled their assault. One of the Daughters caught a backhand blow and flew through the air, landing close by. Vellen instinctively rushed to her aid. She smiled through a mask of blood before stabbing him in the heart.

rituals and chants, and even raising menacing enchanted statues to his glory. With her new-found Daughters of Khaine keen to seek refuge in the arms of an aelven god, few gainsay her – and those that do soon see the light as they are reborn in the form of blood-maddened Medusae. In truth, however, Khaine remains silent. Morathi, though claiming to be nothing more than a humble and devout mouthpiece for a greater power, has become the despot of a new civilisation moulded to suit her needs.

In forging an alliance with the forces of Order, Morathi has engineered another level of deception with which to shroud her secret agenda. The Daughters of Khaine have found a niche in the free cities as gladiatorial performers, putting on such dazzling spectacles of athleticism and titillating bloodsports that their coffers quickly fill with gold. They occupy a half-legal status, performing in subterranean vaults, empty warehouses and abandoned libraries as often as they do in sanctioned arenas and amphitheatres, but the frisson of criminal activity only adds to their appeal. The truly rich can buy their way into the more exotic spectacles that follow the main event – the impromptu arenas of the Witch Aelves are home to more than battle-hungry aelf maidens and those warriors foolish enough to answer their challenges, for in the shadows, unnatural creatures slither and hiss.

The true reason why Sigmar tolerates this shadowy organisation and the cities it has raised across the Mortal Realms is clear enough. When the spectre of Chaos falls over the lands, or should a great push be needed to claim more ground for resettlement, the Daughters of Khaine come into their own, and prove their value to the forces of Order. They attack in a wave of razored blades, possessed of a bloodthirsty frenzy that sees them fight with blurring speed and dexterity. To watch the Daughters of Khaine at their bloody art is a privilege for which rich men pay a king's ransom – though to see them in battle is a truly eye-opening experience, a visceral nightmare that will be carried to the graves of any who witness it.

IDONETH DEEPKIN

The Idoneth Deepkin are otherworldly aelf raiders that attack in a wave of aggression before receding into mist. They dwell in the stygian profundity of the Mortal Realms' deepest oceans and seas. When they venture onto dry land they do so in a tide of magic to capture the souls of the unwary for their own mysterious wars.

The Idoneth Deepkin do not see themselves as evil. If anything, they are champions of Order, devoted to the overthrow of the Dark Gods. Tracing their origins to the world-that-was, they were once consumed body and soul by Slaanesh, but have been freed by the greatest miracle ever worked by a member of their kind. Now they raid the coasts of the Mortal Realms, leaving nothing behind but the tang of salt and a profound sense of loss. The Idoneth are so adept at seclusion they can commit acts of spirit-theft without their victims ever realising the truth – that their kin have been snatched away into the depths, and that they will not return in that lifetime. Wherever there are tales of a village's populace disappearing, a city plunged into a permanent sleep, or an area of the ocean where stray vessels enter but never come back, the Idoneth will likely be the cause.

It was Teclis the Illuminator that first taught the Idoneth's ancestors of their former lives, of the island home they had loved so dearly and the aelven pantheon they had once revered. He underestimated the depths of their trauma, however, for even when touched by the healing light of Hysh they were still the same beings that had been swallowed by the Dark Prince, and remembered their ordeal. Upon their release into the Mortal Realms the rescued aelves did not rebuild, but fled as far and as fast as they were able from anything resembling Chaos worship. They plunged as deep as they could into the incalculably massive oceans of the Mortal Realms. There was no better place to hide from the god of sensory excess than in the crushing, inky blackness of the lightless depths – for there sight, smell and taste were useless, and to find a soul, let alone touch one, was nigh impossible.

In cold abysses did the Idoneth languish for long centuries, becoming ever more attuned to their aquatic environment with each passing generation. They communicated through ripples, keening songs beyond the hearing of men, and eddies in the water, remaining hidden entirely from the wider world. The most powerful amongst them raised great underwater strongholds somewhere between pearlescent citadels and coral reefs, and learned how to charm the sightless creatures of the deep to become their servants and guardians. A culture without new blood will die, however, and the Idoneth knew they would one day fade completely in their isolation.

Despite being imbued with long life, the Idoneth generations came ever slower, for they were troubled souls indeed, and only one in a hundred were born wholly sentient. As their populations dwindled, they pioneered a way of expanding their numbers by capturing the essence of others – not their souls, personality or memories, but their life force. The Idoneth royal echelons, those most adept at seeing the spirits of others, bound these essences within the empty shells of their offspring. These husks, when inhabited by a captive animus, became a new breed – the warrior caste known as the Namarti.

Over their long years spent in the dark, the Idoneth mystics known as Tidecasters learned how to help their kin forget their torment-haunted past with mind-numbing magic that faded the memories of those around them. This sorcery they now turned upon the mortal races that opposed them, as well as the victims of their raids. They would pull the fabric of a memory away so that reality was forgotten just as a waking sleeper forgets a dream, then bring the recollections crashing back in a bewildering, terrifying tide that completely overwhelmed their prey.

The Akhelian Kings have hearts as cold as the depths over which they rule. To see such a lethal rider in the flesh is to court death – or worse, enslavement.

As the Age of Chaos reached its zenith, the existence of the Idoneth was uncovered. Some say that pre-eminent Seekers punished their Slaaneshi rivals by sending them to the bottom of the ocean where they could experience no more – and in doing so, inadvertently sent them against the Idoneth. It is said that one of that cursed warband somehow made it to dry land and brought the message of the aelves' existence to Archaon himself. Others believe the skaven's incessant burrowing through the fabric of the Mortal Realms led them to these hidden regions, or that the shadowy agents of the Clans Eshin passed through the Gates of Utter Blackness and found an Idoneth enclave beyond.

Whatever the cause, these disturbing aelves are more active in the Mortal Realms than ever before, striking hard before disappearing like the retreating tide. With each raid they take more souls, bolstering their armies as they take the fight to Chaos with the wrath of a sudden tsunami.

'Ho. Slow-brains. You smell that?' Vossak Thrice-Blooded turned to his fellows, motioning them to stop their advance upon the snow-covered ridge. The Bloodbound sniffed the air, turning to one another in confusion. The tang of salt and fresh sea breeze was unmistakeable, but they were nowhere near the coast. There was a soft whisper of waves crashing onto dry land, receding for a few moments, then coming back all the stronger. Plaintive cries haunted the cusp of Vossak's hearing.

The Bloodsecrator shook his head and resumed his march. Yet now his steps were slowed, and it was getting worse. It was as if he waded through an invisible stream. A few steps more, and it felt like he was pushing through a waist-deep river, then fighting against a sucking, pulling riptide. Pushing down a rising sense of panic, Vossak drew his axe and ran a finger to blood it, awakening the daemon within. It was slow to respond, for the enemy was still nowhere to be seen.

Vossak was on the verge of shouting out a challenge when a wave of sleek bodies, ethereal and terrifying, came over the ridge – surging, boiling, spilling across the land towards him. At their fore were slender knights, riding not horses but strange, darting sea serpents that undulated through the air as if underwater. He swung his axe at the nearest eel-steed, but it writhed out of reach even as its tall-helmed rider impaled Blask the Sinner through the mouth. Behind the slender knights were more creatures mounted on larger sea-beasts, shark-like and vicious. A living wave rose up behind them, taking form to become an ancient sea god given terrible life. Vossak opened his mouth to cry out, only for a wave of invisible force to slam into his throat and fill his lungs. Then a jagged spear punctured his chest, and all was black.

SERAPHON

Creatures of Order and celestial light, the Seraphon are anathema to the armies of Chaos. The skies blaze with glittering constellations as these reptilian killers descend from the firmament, summoned by the slann who evacuated them from the world-that-was. They are the wrath of the cold stars made manifest.

Sometimes, when all seems lost and the agents of darkness stand upon the cusp of victory, a strange, squat figure will appear in the middle distance. He is borne aloft on a floating palanquin, protected by a magical aegis from the weapons and spells hurled his way. He raises his spindly arms, and emits a rattling croak – a feeble sound, but one that has heralded the doom of empires.

In a strobing flash of light, the Starmaster's armies appear, summoned from the fleet of stars that spins high above. Hulking saurian monsters charge headlong from nothing more than light, the tang of ozone filling the air. On they come, roaring and shaking the earth, weapons of black celestite and strange relics of arcane power raised high. Reptilian jaws snap and tails thrash as the Seraphon leap forth, ripping flesh and breaking bone even as their heavy clubs and spiked maces smash armoured fiends into the dirt. Where resistance musters heavy, towering Kroxigor line-breakers shatter shield walls and crush blood-maddened knights with each powerful swing of their mauls. Nimble skink skirmishers harry the flanks, cutting off the enemy's escape as winged predators swoop from the crackling aether, biting and tearing at those skulking behind the front line. Even a dread fortress offers little protection against the thunderous stampede of Stegadons and the pulverising mace-tails of Bastiladons.

Storming through the fray come the veteran war leaders of the Seraphon upon terrifying Carnosaurs, the roars of rider and steed mingling as they bear down upon their prey. Those daemonic hosts and monsters formed from the raw stuff of Chaos are seared, burned and ultimately blasted to nothingness by the celestial energies of the slann, for the sorceries of these ancient Starmasters are potent indeed. In this shocking onslaught of violence, the battlefield is soon slicked with gore, the Chaos host ripped from supremacy and cast to doom-filled defeat. Once victory is assured, the Seraphon vanish once more in blurs of shimmering light, a sudden wind racing across a field of broken armour and fang-scored bone.

Gokko da Fist, foremost Skullnob of the Bovva Boyz, felt a sharp sting in his neck. He wheeled, his meaty palm slapping back to pull a feathered dart from his weather-beaten green skin. He roared in anger, his lads doing the same. Atop the ridge were strange blue lizards standing upright, hissing as they lobbed javelins into the orruk mob. A dragon-thing spat a gobbet of liquid fire, setting Drokkit ablaze. Gokko felt a surge of war-strength, bellowing as he charged forward. A dozen orruks went with him, then a hundred. When Gokko crested the ridge, his entire tribe was close behind.

Down in the valley were two battle lines, the large one red, the small one blue. Gokko saw the lizard creatures down there in the rocks and charged toward them. The orruks were running full pelt when the lizards just disappeared in a flash of light.

And the orruks hit the red battle line like an avalanche.

The Saurus Sunblood is a creature of iron-hard scales, dagger teeth and clawed, muscular limbs – every bit the equal of the Chaos Warriors it fights.

The constellation empires of the Seraphon exist in the highest parts of Azyr, thriving far from the light of Sigendil. Philosophers of the God-King's realms posit that the Seraphon are the children of Dracothion, awakened by his celestial breath, or summoned by his tears after he witnessed a vision of the race's tragic past. The aelves believe them to be from another time, the slann that command them but motes of light in the darkness, yet powerful enough to keep the memory of the Seraphon and their war gods alive. Some say they have vessels that can sail between worlds, and that they have fought their arch-enemies the Dark Gods in a dozen other realities. There are even theories that the Seraphon, somewhat like the daemons of Chaos, are conjured from raw emotion – not those of the mortal races, but of beasts, or the primordial races of an unknowable order that existed before humans first crawled from the caves.

The Seraphon can descend to the Mortal Realms as shooting stars, shimmering sky-lights and meteor strikes. Whole starhosts emerge from the fires of their descent. Their targets are not always the armies of Chaos, but each action they take is part of the slann's greater work against the Dark Gods. No unthinking warriors are these – each has a savage animus, and echoes the fierce personality of the heavenly constellation from which it came. A skilled astromancer could parse the glittering skies to divine when and where a Seraphon host might strike, but only the slann know the truth – they move their cohorts and warrior hosts across the Mortal Realms as a grand master moves the pieces of an elaborate game, always striving to stay three steps ahead of their nemeses. Though their numbers are few, their skill in the ways of strategy is such that they have thwarted the designs of a thousand warlords, their deeds glittering points of order

that preserve the tapestry of life against the forces of entropy and despair. Since the Age of Sigmar's dawn, the Seraphon have watched the Stormhosts hurl back the armies of Chaos, and even fought alongside them on more than one occasion. Though formal alliances have yet to occur, many a warrior salute has been raised from one faction to the other, for both fight for hope, order, and the downfall of the Dark Gods.

'They care for neither gold nor glory, and they fight for neither realm nor king. They are the wrath of the slann given form, and theirs is a war without mercy and without end. As long as the Chaos Gods exist, the Seraphon will seek their destruction.'

- Olwyn of Stratosi, The Saurians of High Azyr

THE FREE PEOPLES

Where Sigmar and his allies have struck hardest, the lands have been claimed in the name of Order and progress. Generations have gone by since the first Stormcast Eternals descended from the Tempest, and an alliance of humanity, aelves and duardin has thrived, united in the face of their common enemy.

The sites of Sigmar's first strike against the forces of Chaos were carefully chosen. By attacking the Realmgates known as the Gates of Azyr, and in flinging open the routes of reinforcement from the Realm of Heavens, Sigmar ensured he had hundreds of beachheads from which to wage his new crusade. At first it was the Stormhosts themselves that guarded these sites, their Lord-Castellants mounting stalwart defences against any great beast or savage horde that sought to take these vital inter-realm portals. Then came the next wave, sent by Sigmar via his most trusted seconds, the Council of Azyr. Stalwart humans and duardin joined the Stormcast Eternals in consolidation and defence of each Realmgate site – and in doing so, created a new beginning with the sweat of their brows and the blood of their calloused hands.

THE DISPOSSESSED

Those gateways that proved stable allowed large numbers of the people of Azyrheim to re-enter the Mortal Realms. Amongst them were the duardin known as the Dispossessed, hard-bitten warriors and masons who built new keeps and strongholds on these sites with expert skill and tireless efficiency. They are the spiritual descendants of the long-dead Khazalid empire – the original worshippers of the smith-god Grungni and his fearsome brother Grimnir – and by their hands much of Azyrheim was built. Their Warden Kings have proved faithful allies to humanity, and though their armoured throngs are relatively few in number, the grudges they hold against the Chaos destroyers who brought low their ancestral homes lend them great strength.

The vicious counter-attacks of the Chaos hosts at first dictated the building of defensible structures made for war, but the Stormcast Eternals proved equal to the task of fending their enemies off whilst civilian constructions were raised ever higher by the Dispossessed. With the adaptable skills of mortal men at their beck and call, and with a scattering of aelven artisans to complement their rugged constructions with slender works of art, the Lord-Castellants, their requisitioned work teams and their Azyrite duardin allies raised fortified villages, then townships, then cities in those areas claimed in Sigmar's name. Each phase of construction saw the walls built over again in a series of concentric rings, with the Realmgate right at their heart. Watching over the portal, or even constructed right around it in some cases, would be the Stormkeep of the chamber that had claimed it – with the Dispossessed working in concert with the Lord-Castellants, these structures became mighty indeed, capable of repelling a daemonic invasion. Still, even the most redoubtable fortress or towering Stormcast citadel cannot survive without food, nor can it be built without access to raw materials. Here the faithful of Sigmar come into their own.

DEVOTED OF SIGMAR

Sigmar has always inspired faith and fanaticism in his followers, both through his natural charisma and his stubborn refusal to let the forces of darkness overwhelm the realms. Countless thousands devote their lives, body and soul, to his cause. During the terrible times of the Age of Chaos, the beleaguered populace prayed to him for salvation. Despite their devotion, for decades those entreaties went unheard, for Sigmar had withdrawn from the Mortal Realms and turned a deaf ear to their pleas. Some mortals lost their faith, but many others – those who refused to give in to doubt – finally saw those prayers spectacularly rewarded as Sigmar's Tempest struck hard at the dark heart of Chaos. Now they join with the jubilant worshippers of Azyr in cleansing their ancestral lands.

Wherever new settlements spring up, the Devoted of Sigmar march out in great numbers to reconsecrate the soil polluted by the taint of Chaos. Led by the Warrior Priests of Sigmar and Arch Lectors that ride impressive war altars at the heart of each gathering, they sing rousing hymns in unison. Most of these ardent faithful are clad in no more than rags, for they maintain that no worldly possession can rival the value of their creed. Wild-haired and manic of gaze, they lash themselves with spiked whips, barbed chains and iron flails, so that their blood might be strewn across the lands – throngs of Flagellants and war priests blessing the ground with each bleeding footstep and heartfelt prayer. Such is their faith that the lifeblood actually cleanses corruption from the soil. Wherever the Devoted display such acts of martyrdom, the earth is spiritually cleansed – it can harbour crops once more, and farmers can ply their trade without fear of their harvest bearing noisome fruit.

Should the Devoted encounter the worshippers of the Dark Gods, or the beasts of Chaos that roam the wilderness, they will turn their flails and chains against them, charging pell-mell in a maniacal throng that tears apart the enemy no matter the cost. It is well that Sigmar inspires such faith, for the attrition rate of these Devoted processions is daunting indeed.

The value of the Devoted is not confined to the reclamation crusades and the cleansing of the realms. Alongside them stand the zealous ranks of the Witch Hunters, more properly known as the Order of Azyr. Held in awe and fear alike by those that have seen their red work, they root out the taint of Chaos in Sigmar's new kingdoms. Like vengeful shadows they move through the cities, whispering in the ears of their fellow Devoted and those lords they deem to be worthy of trust, gathering knowledge of hidden heretical cults. When they have tracked their prey to their lairs, they will burn out the infection, or else slay the corrupted with stake, fire and greatsword – even should that traitor be of the highest office in the land. All must fear the Order of Azyr, for it answers only to Sigmar himself.

THE FREEGUILDS

Over time, the settlements of Sigmar have become the nexus points of entire nations. Though it took decades of back-breaking labour and no small amount of creation magic to achieve it, the rise of these cities has heralded a new era, and each has grown to earn its own proud heraldry and military history.

The roving well-criers, minstrels and skalds of Sigmar's realm claim the cities prospered due to their Azyrite benefactors, but the truth is more complex – the new settlements have drawn on local resources wherever they can. In some places the ruins of ancient cities have been reclaimed and built anew, those structures still sound used as foundations or inspirational monuments whilst those unsafe regions are broken down into raw materials and repurposed. In other areas, the scattered tribes that could be saved from the hordes of Chaos have been brought, filthy and starving, into the city limits to found shanty towns, in places doubling the population even before they start their families anew.

The Freeguilds recruit from every stratum of society – when the city is under attack, military aristocrats from the inner districts and low-born officers command stalwart professional soldiers, ex-criminals and even armed militia, their common humanity uniting them against the horrors they must face. Over time, these melanges of races and creeds have intermingled, forming new alliances and factions thirsty to prove themselves or to avenge their predecessors. An army or garrison from a Sigmarite city may include a dozen different kinds of footsoldiers, knightly orders, beast riders, proven militia and city guard, all with their own uniforms, traditions and rivalries. Some go to war in resplendent plate armour, others have not even a pair of boots to call their own, but they are rich in spirit one and all. When their hard-won way of life is threatened, they put aside their differences, fighting as one under the steely gaze of a Freeguild general.

THE IRONWELD ARSENAL

Acting in concert with the Freeguilds come the gunners, artillerists and engineers of the Ironweld Arsenals. The finest scientific duardin and human minds have combined forces to create the most potent weapons of destruction they can devise, for the people of Sigmar's new world order face a profusion of monsters, daemons and mutated barbarians that cannot not be defeated by sword and spear alone. This is a brotherhood united not by faith, but by ingenuity, capability, and science – the industrialisation and innovation of mankind twinned with the artifice and expertise of the duardin makes for a potent combination. The Ironweld artillerists man the walls of the largest of the free cities, their great cannons, mortars, volley guns and rocket batteries seeking out the largest of foes whenever dark hordes muster beyond the city limits. Each of their machineries of destruction is made to be man-portable, or at the least towable by beasts of burden. The famed artillery trains of the Ironweld regularly take the field in support of the Freeguilds to blast apart daemon and monstrous predator alike.

THE COLLEGIATE ARCANE

High above the city streets dwell the wizards, mages and sorcerers of Sigmar's people. The Collegiate Arcane is mostly comprised of human mages that follow the old ways of manipulating magic, each dedicating himself to the understanding of one type of magic above all others. These form the ruling elite of the Collegiate, the most skilled of their number creating wondrous devices to channel the innate magic of the Mortal Realms. Where once these men of learning poured their efforts into the furtherance of knowledge, of progress and of the blending of magic with technology, the last few generations have been obsessed with the turning of magic to the business of war. Most mortals are unable to channel aetheric power at will without risking the most disastrous side-effects, and so instead make use of arcane foci and sorcerous machines with which to wield magic. Using celestial orreries, aetheric lenses and enchanted objects such as masks, orbs, staves and hourglasses, the Battlemages of the Collegiate Arcane work devastating spells that can incinerate foes, turn them to stone or transmute them to scattering sand.

142

THE ELDRITCH COUNCIL

More learned still are those of the Eldritch Council. Comprised of Azyrite aelves that have been brought together by Lord Tyrion, tutored by his brother Teclis, and given a solemn duty to keep the hermetic traditions of the ancestors alive, the Council represents millennia of arcane knowledge distilled into a living body of adepts. Each studies not just one type of magic, but all the traditional elemental forces of the aelves to hurl forth flame, frost and gale. Some of the Council go to war accompanied by Swordmaster escorts – aelven scholars of the blade so skilled they can cut enemy arrows from the sky. Others, usually the most charismatic and hot-blooded of their kin, form lasting bonds with the draconic denizens of Azyr. These brave Drakeseers ride to war on serpentine dragons, the white flame of their elemental spells mingling with the red heat of their mount's breath with each deadly pass.

Those sites that are so corrupted by Chaos that even the spilt blood of the Devoted cannot heal them are visited by the Eldritch Council. Their master elementalists wield such intense and searing flame that most sites bearing daemonic taint can be burned clean, the cratered earth rendered sterile enough to be reconsecrated once it has finally cooled. Yet even then there are places so supernaturally twisted that only the flames of resurrection can hope to heal them.

THE PHOENIX TEMPLE

The Phoenix is a potent symbol for the aelves, for it symbolises rebirth from the fires of tragedy – and the ability to emerge all the stronger. The temple that bears its image is a warrior conclave dedicated to the godbeast known as the Ur-Phoenix. These monastic aelven warriors have been through the fiercest fires of war and survived. They have been borne, scarred and traumatised, by silent guardians to the shrouded top of the temple. There, should they prove themselves worthy, each will be chosen by one of the giant, supernatural Phoenixes that make that towering spire their home. Burned body and spirit by

a Flamespyre Phoenix or frozen to inert crystal by a Frostheart Phoenix, he will rise again after his days-long trial. From that point on this warrior is Phoenix Guard, claimed by the magic of his resurrection to serve the cause of his temple – to eradicate the filth of Chaos from the realms – until his final death. In complete and unnerving silence, the ranks of the Phoenix Guard march forth across befouled lands to cut down the champions of Chaos with shimmering halberds, the magic of the Ur-Phoenix protecting them from the return blows of their enemies. Overhead, the skies are scored by the glowing flights of Phoenix riders, blazing orange and brilliant blue, burning and freezing all that fall under their shadows.

LION RANGERS

A warrior brotherhood that can be traced to the rangers that hunted the mountains around Azyrheim during the Age of Myth, the Lion Rangers are masters of close-quarters battle. Whilst the Azyrite cities rose high, these aelves sought the sanctuaries of their monasteries, retreating to wooded islands and mountain peaks far from the din and confusion of civilisation. But even there they were not beyond the reach of Chaos. Their order held out until the very last against the tides of disorder that battered their once-peaceful domains, and when the Gates of Azyr closed, only the barest handful made it back to the safety of Azyrheim. Now, with their order bolstered by the rise of Sigmar's people, they bring skills long-honed to the war once more. They do not linger long in the free cities – walls

and fortresses failed them utterly in the past – and so they prefer to roam the natural places of the realms. The Lion Rangers carry huge war axes so sharp they can cleave an armoured enemy in two, and their cloaks – the pelts of celestial lions – can turn aside crossbow bolts as if they were little more than pine needles. Led by veteran commanders in chariots pulled by graceful leonine beasts, the Lion Rangers have turned the tide in many a battle thought lost – for though these expert warriors often arrive unbidden, their presence always makes an impact.

THE ORDER DRACONIS

Some of those aelves that were united under Sigmar's rule in Azyrheim found solace not in men, nor in their fellows, but in the noble beasts of the realms. Forming powerful kinships with pure-blooded stallions and wise drakes, they became the forefathers of an order of warriors known as the Order Draconis. Dozens of generations have passed since the first aelf knights of the order took up their lances and hunted the scourge of Chaos, but though they were deadly warriors indeed, the task they undertook was all but impossible. Ultimately they were forced to rely on their sheer speed and bravery more than their skill at arms to survive. Now, as a new era breaks across the land, they are able to take the offensive once more. They follow the roiling thunderstorms that signify the presence of Sigmar's elite hosts, knowing that to strike alongside such allies is to give themselves the best chance of securing a lasting victory at the least possible cost in blood.

SWIFTHAWK AGENTS

The Swifthawk Agents spread messages between the armies of Azyrheim to help coordinate their grand assaults, whilst cutting the web of information that binds the armies of their foes. They are the fastest and most nimble of Sigmar's rare aelven hosts, and they are fearless in their duty. They are capable and independent, able to outrun those foes they cannot slay. Amongst their number are cloaked

Shadow Warriors that swathe themselves in darkness, and chariots pulled by fleet-footed Purebreed steeds and giant Swiftfeather Hawks. They are the messengers of Order, and as the light of Azyr reaches all the Mortal Realms, so too do their warriors roam to every corner of civilisation and beyond.

SCOURGE PRIVATEERS

Raiders and pirates, the Scourge Privateers are not merely expert mariners, but also amongst the finest beast hunters in the Mortal Realms. They are descended from those aelves who sought the solace of the open seas – not becoming one with them, as did the Idoneth Deepkin, but learning to sail and master them. They still hone their skills of navigation and reaving, their majestic vessels cutting through even the most stormy seas to fall upon their quarry without warning.

While once the Scourge Privateers might have raided indiscriminately, since Sigmar united the civilised races, they work alongside the nations of human, duardin and aelf rather than preying upon them. It is their habit to hunt down misshapen monsters and deadly creatures to capture, whether at sea – in the case of their favoured warbeast, the Kharibdyss – or on land, where their chariots and corsairs work together to run to ground even the fiercest prey. These beasts they train for their own menageries and prized collections, to sell to the arenas of the free cities, or to barter with wizards and warlords of an unscrupulous nature. Their Fleetmasters are steel-willed and determined, feared both aboard their armadas and across the ports in which they ply their trade, for every one is an expert swordsman, and each has a ruthless streak as wide as a shark's smile.

DARKLING COVENS

There is something deeply sinister about the aelven subcultures known as the Darkling Covens. They exist in the most remote and shadowy districts of the free cities, allied to the hosts of Azyrheim through necessity rather than design, and none truly knows what manner of malfeasance might happen behind their high walls. The rank-and-file of each Darkling Coven acts in uncanny synchronicity, almost as if they are bound to a single will in the manner of an undead horde – and that is not too far from the truth. Each coven has at its heart a Sorceress of such charisma she can enthral hundreds of her own kin; the mightiest of their kind can even bind dragons to their service. Whether this is done through means fair or foul none can say – certainly the lesser footsoldiers of the Darkling Covens are utterly devoted to their mistresses, and will fight to the last drop of blood to earn her favour. It is whispered in the free cities that it is not only aelves that are in thrall to these darkly beautiful Sorceresses – yet they fight against Chaos and, for now, that is enough.

SHADOWBLADES

The path of the Assassin has a long and proud history amongst the aelf nations. Though the Free Peoples look down on the profession as the remit of thugs and murderers, the aelves see grace and beauty in the art of taking a life swiftly and silently. A skilled aelf Assassin is thought given form, appearing but for the barest flicker of an eye before receding into darkness once more, their target breathing their last in a pool of their own blood.

Shadowblades are the true masters of murder. Some say they can change their faces, the better to move through cities whilst hidden in plain sight. Others believe they are beings native to Ulgu, the servants of some ancient tenebrous god that can move from one shadow to another as easily as passing through a door. Still more claim they are a gift from Malerion to Sigmar, for they turn their blades against the tyrants of Chaos and those city-dwelling traitors that do their bidding more often than any other foe. All that is known for sure is that when a sorcerous black mark in the shape of a curved blade appears on a target's flesh, it will not be long before a Shadowblade's dagger is at his throat.

ORDER SERPENTIS

Like a dark reflection of their Order Draconis kin, the Order Serpentis tame the cruel-hearted and savage beasts of the realms. They are not so much trusted allies of the Azyrite hosts as they are living weapons, pointed and loosed at the enemy as an archer might fire an arrow. Once, they were an order of Black Dragon riders – but now, with such majestic steeds dwindling in number, only their leaders can uphold this tradition. The majority ride the saurian predators known as Drakespawn, or else steer chariots pulled by a pair of the scaled and cold-blooded beasts. They are relentless in battle, ripping apart their enemies in a storm of dark steel and wicked lances. Those that are harried by the Order Serpentis will be struck anew each night until there is nothing left but terror, confusion and corpses torn by fang, claw and blade.

THE WANDERERS

Noble but fierce, the Wanderers are the aelven nomads that once called the wild places their home. Expert archers and talented bladesmen, they have always fought for the sanctity of the natural world, opposing the chaotic forces that would tear apart the order of life and replace it with anarchy. During the Age of Chaos, that battle was all but lost. The magical ley lines that link the sacred places of each Mortal Realm are shimmering cords cast by the light of Sigendil that can only be seen by witch-sight. In the Age of Chaos they were shattered by spilt blood and dark magic. Now, the Wanderers trace their paths to hidden lands, laying waystones to amplify and restore their power. They have a symbiotic relationship with the free cities, the sharp-eyed aelves acting as scouts and guerrilla strike forces when necessary, in exchange for occasional shelter and succour. One day the Wanderers hope to redeem themselves for their betrayal during the Age of Chaos – in abandoning Ghyran to the infestations of Nurgle and hence leaving the people of the Everqueen to their plight, they have broken a long-standing alliance that will take lifetimes to rebuild.

The Hammers of Sigmar lead the forces of Order to claim the Greater Viarshan Portal. Amongst them is the Celestant-Prime, descending like a comet to smite the Bloodbound from on high.

Stormcast Eternals
Knight-Incantor

Stormcast Eternals
Evocator-Prime

Stormcast Eternals
Sacristan Engineer

Stormcast Eternals
Castigator-Prime

Sylvaneth
Kurnoth Huntmaster

Sylvaneth
Tree-Revenant with Glade Banner

Together with her Stormcast Eternal allies, the Hallowed Knights, the ▶
Everqueen Alarielle unleashes a tempest of violence upon the warriors of
Nurgle that dare intrude upon her sacred Ghyranite havens.

The Kharadron Overlords are masters of aetheric science and cut-throat deals. They ply the aerial trade routes of the Mortal Realms in flying vessels bristling with arcane cannons, harpoons and drill-tipped bombs.

Fyreslayers
Auric Runemaster

Fyreslayers
Battlesmith

Fyreslayers
Auric Runesmiter

Fyreslayers
Vulkite Berzerker

Seraphon
Saurus Oldblood

Seraphon
Skink Starpriest

Seraphon
Skink

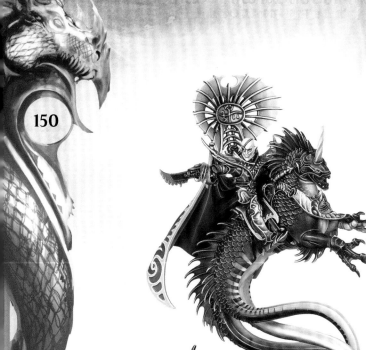

Idoneth Deepkin
Volturnos, High King of the Deep

The Daughters of Khaine are a sisterhood of fierce killers so agile and athletic they can flow around the clumsy blows of their enemies like smoke. They make offerings of spilt blood, punctured flesh and still-beating hearts to their god.

The Idoneth Deepkin surge from magical mist-shrouded seas to slay, steal and capture the souls of their victims before ebbing away once more, the memory of their attack already fading like a forgotten dream.

Daughters of Khaine
Morathi, High Oracle of Khaine

THE FORCES OF CHAOS

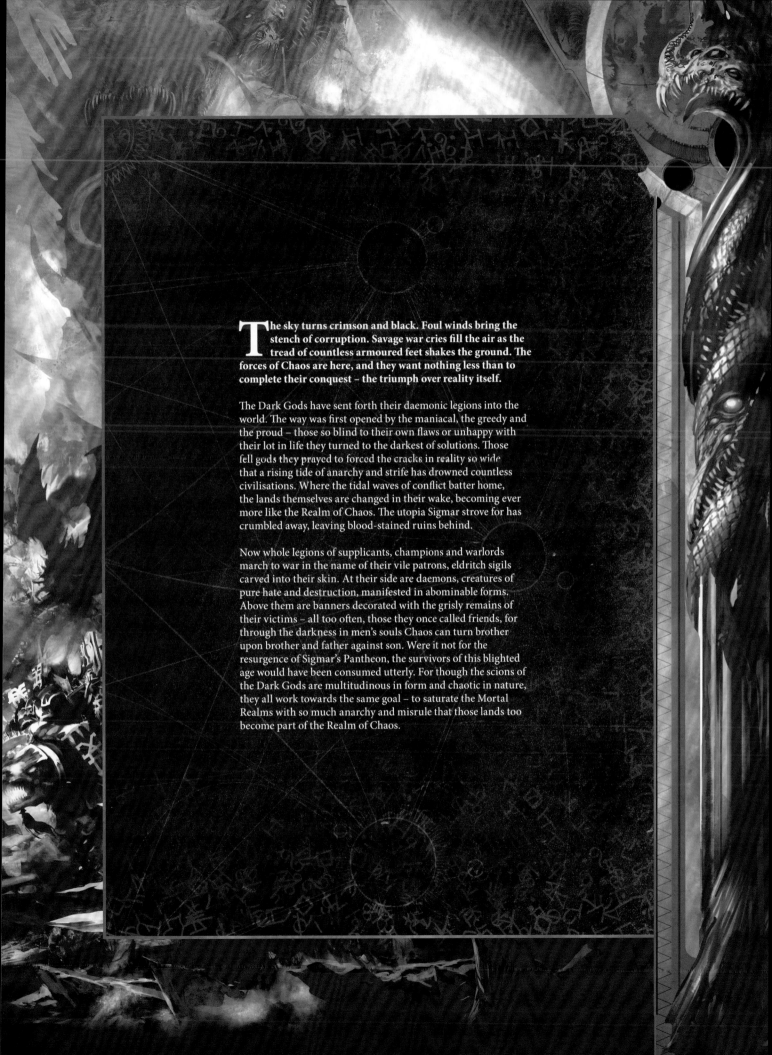

The sky turns crimson and black. Foul winds bring the stench of corruption. Savage war cries fill the air as the tread of countless armoured feet shakes the ground. The forces of Chaos are here, and they want nothing less than to complete their conquest – the triumph over reality itself.

The Dark Gods have sent forth their daemonic legions into the world. The way was first opened by the maniacal, the greedy and the proud – those so blind to their own flaws or unhappy with their lot in life they turned to the darkest of solutions. Those fell gods they prayed to forced the cracks in reality so wide that a rising tide of anarchy and strife has drowned countless civilisations. Where the tidal waves of conflict batter home, the lands themselves are changed in their wake, becoming ever more like the Realm of Chaos. The utopia Sigmar strove for has crumbled away, leaving blood-stained ruins behind.

Now whole legions of supplicants, champions and warlords march to war in the name of their vile patrons, eldritch sigils carved into their skin. At their side are daemons, creatures of pure hate and destruction, manifested in abominable forms. Above them are banners decorated with the grisly remains of their victims – all too often, those they once called friends, for through the darkness in men's souls Chaos can turn brother upon brother and father against son. Were it not for the resurgence of Sigmar's Pantheon, the survivors of this blighted age would have been consumed utterly. For though the scions of the Dark Gods are multitudinous in form and chaotic in nature, they all work towards the same goal – to saturate the Mortal Realms with so much anarchy and misrule that those lands too become part of the Realm of Chaos.

THE EVERCHOSEN

Archaon is the Exalted Grand Marshal of the Apocalypse. He is the will of the Dark Gods writ large, and the lord of every mortal and daemonic warrior of Chaos that marches to battle across the Mortal Realms. All fear Archaon, for he is the Ruinous Powers given terrible physical form.

There is no mortal champion of Chaos more powerful than Archaon. He is known as the Destroyer of Worlds, and for good reason – it was Archaon that brought about the demise of the world-that-was, and as the supreme leader of the Chaos hosts, he has conquered many other realities since. Now the Three-Eyed King turns his gaze to the Mortal Realms, his sole intention to conquer every one of them in the name of anarchy and misrule. Sitting astride his vast daemonic mount Dorghar, wielding the Slayer of Kings to scythe down his foes, Archaon is death to all who face him. He unleashes armies beyond number, mortals and daemons of every description marching at his command. The shadow of Archaon stretches long and dark across the Mortal Realms, blotting out hope and life and ushering in the end of days.

The Gods of Chaos cannot lead their legions in person, no more than fire or starlight can command the multitudes of the realms. Neither can their daemonic generals take physical form over the long term, for they are creatures of magic, and their connection to the material plane can wax and wane depending on place and circumstance. Because of this the Chaos Gods need mortal intermediaries and – if they are to bind the fractious hosts that worship them to one overriding goal – a true king of conquest whose masterful command over his legions cannot be denied. Archaon is such a man.

The Everchosen is the ultimate champion of the Chaos Gods, marked with the favour of each, yet beholden to no single deity. Others have borne this title in the past, but none have excelled in the role more than Archaon. Inhumanly cunning, unutterably evil, and possessing his own labyrinthine plans for glory, he has made great strides towards supremacy in the Mortal Realms.

So powerful has the Everchosen become that the Gods of Chaos themselves have tried to kill him more than once, sending their greatest champions to cast him down for fear that he might devote himself solely to the glory of one of their hated rivals. Archaon has killed every challenger, fighting the greater war against the Mortal Realms even when the gods themselves lost sight of their goals. Thus far he has even resisted the gift of daemonhood, no matter how many times it is offered, for he sets his sights higher still and will not submit to being the puppet of any godly master. The Everchosen remains the greatest nemesis of Sigmar and the tattered remnants of his Pantheon of Order. Some say that in a former life Archaon bent the knee to Sigmar, but that he learned a terrible truth about the God-King, and has striven to destroy him ever since. Now the Everchosen will not consider his victory complete until all lies broken at his feet.

Though he stands at the very apex of power, Archaon is not alone in his endless war. Every Chaos warlord and daemonic general must bow to him, or else pay the bloody price. Over and above these agents, Archaon has his impressive lieutenants in the Varanguard and the Gaunt Summoners.

The Varanguard rise from amongst the greatest mortal champions of Chaos, and must complete many trials to prove their worthiness. Those who survive these punishing ordeals become Archaon's personal heralds, enforcers and destroyers. Mounted upon towering steeds of Chaos, armed and armoured with the most nightmarish wargear the forges of the Everchosen can provide, the Varanguard are Archaon's ultimate weapon against the forces of civilisation. These monstrously powerful shock cavalry are organised into eight distinct circles, each great in number and possessed of its own broad remit. Some are assassins who strike down key enemy heroes, while others serve as the punishers who make examples of those who fail the Everchosen. Whatever their role, they are a nigh-unstoppable force, and on the charge they sweep all before them.

The Gaunt Summoners are potent daemonic sorcerers of Tzeentch, and are amongst Archaon's greatest servants. It is said that he outwitted these beings long ago, binding them to his will through the power of their true names. He uses them as spies and seers, prophets of what will come to pass. These magical messengers manipulate the very fabric of reality to ensure that Archaon's will is enacted across the endless battlefields in every region of the Mortal Realms.

Archaon's fortress is the Varanspire, a hellish fastness that dominates the fabled Eightpoints. Built to ensure its master's control over that most vital of sites, the Varanspire is not a single tower, but a collection of citadels so tall their tips claw at the void. Archaon has not set foot within them for many centuries, however – his methods of conquest are those of a warrior king rather than a politician. He has vowed not to rest upon his throne of darkness until his final victory is won.

SLAVES TO DARKNESS

The Age of Chaos has lasted for long and terrible centuries, drowning the Mortal Realms in endless war. Though many mortals have fought to their last breath against the invaders, many more have instead chosen to worship the Chaos Gods as their masters, and to follow the perilous path to glory.

When the Slaves to Darkness march to war, they bring with them all the cruelty and power of the rapacious Gods of Chaos. Barbaric marauder tribesmen and armour-clad warriors pour across the lands, ragged banners waving above them emblazoned with hellish runes that burn with inner power. Cruel horsemen and thundering chariots crash into battle at their fore. From amidst the marching hordes rise twisted shrines dedicated to the Dark Gods, and monstrous beasts drawn from the worst nightmares of mortals. Leading each of these fearsome armies stride the champions of Chaos, warriors elevated to levels of inhuman power as a reward for their service to the gods. The lords of Chaos wield their armies like vast and terrible weapons, using them to hack and smash at the surviving bastions of Order across the Mortal Realms. They lay waste to all who oppose them, and for their brutal efforts they are rewarded richly.

To join the ranks of the Slaves to Darkness, a warrior need only dedicate himself to one or all of the Gods of Chaos. Some go freely into such damnation – the mad, the heartless, the damaged and the deranged all willingly trade away their souls in exchange for the promise of otherworldly power. But many more, whole tribes, cities and nations, fall to the worship of the Chaos Gods through a desperate

A Chaos Warrior is a merciless butcher clad head to toe in heavy plate. His long and bloody quest for power will end in glory, death or damnation.

*K*nodd the Bear pushed his spined thumbs deeper into the giant orruk's eye sockets, roaring as he brought his armoured knee up under its jaw over and over again. The beast's cabled neck was becoming weak, stringy. 'Die!' roared Knodd, spattered in a crimson baptism as he wrenched the Ironjaw's head from his neck and offered it to the skies. He felt power surge through him. His head hurt fit to burst, but he laughed in triumph. Finally, he would ascend to godhood.

A ripping, tearing sound came from below. Knodd looked down eagerly, watching his muscular body ripple and bulge. Horror took him, for strange limbs writhed under his skin like worms in a rotting stomach. They burst free in a shower of nameless fluids even as his head split in half, jaw flapping as he moaned in terror and pain. The Knodd-thing fell upon the orruks once more, razored tentacles flailing. This day, his path was complete.

need to survive. As the dominion of Chaos spread ever further across the Mortal Realms, life became darker and more horrific for those beneath its shadow. For many, the choice was simple: submit to the will of Chaos or be slain by those who did. The Dark Gods are no saviours, however. Those who swore to serve Chaos soon found themselves tearing down that which they held dear – often the very things they had made their devil's bargain to protect. Lost to the corruption and madness of the path to glory, most no longer cared.

So have the ranks of the Slaves to Darkness swollen until their blight covers all the lands. One who begins their journey as a tribal chieftain, or even a humble warrior of the rank-and-file, kills and conquers their way swiftly to a position of power. As word spreads about their glorious exploits, bands of tribesmen, charioteers and heavily armoured knights hasten to swear themselves to this champion's cause.

Little by little the horde grows, further warbands joining the first as the tales of glorious slaughter spread further afield. Soon enough, what began as a mere raiding party has swollen into a massive army, led by a singularly powerful warlord.

The obsession of all such chaotic overlords is the same. They wish to please their chosen deity, and in so doing, prove themselves worthy of his gifts. This is the Path to Glory, the lonely and selfish road that all aspiring champions of Chaos must walk if they wish to earn the ultimate reward. To proceed along this metaphysical path, a champion must destroy all who stand in their way, and make such offerings of carnage and corruption that, for the briefest of moments, they succeed in catching the eye of a god. Even

should a champion earn the boons of their chosen patron, these rewards can themselves spell their doom. For every Chaos champion who rises, burning with dark might, to claim immortality as a Daemon Prince, there are countless others whose bodies twist and buckle under a bombardment of freakish mutation. Muscles bulge through tearing skin and skeletons sprout hideous nests of spines until their bodies are reduced to crawling nightmares. Finally, the minds of the former champions snap altogether and they become gibbering Chaos Spawn.

No matter the terrible dangers they face, countless warriors swell the ranks of Dark Gods' armies with every passing day. In such dire times as these, they reason that it is better to wear the iron-shod boot of the oppressor than to be the weak and terrified victim ground beneath its tread.

KHORNE

Khorne is the mightiest of all the Chaos Gods, for he is rage incarnate. The savage hosts of mortal, daemon and barbarian that worship him, known collectively as the Blades of Khorne, are frenzied killers one and all – for those who do not add to the skull-pile through daily slaughter may find their own heads adorning it at day's end.

Known as Kharneth, Khorghar, Kashorin the Skysplitter and a hundred other names, the Blood God is worshipped in almost every corner of the Mortal Realms. He is always portrayed as an angry, roaring being of infinite strength and supreme battle prowess that rewards bravery, might at arms and conquest. The gore-maddened followers of Khorne range far and wide in search of skulls to offer him – they will hunt and kill even to the daemon-haunted borders of the Mortal Realms, delighting in slaughter whether under the baking sun or by the light of a Chaos moon. Khorne hungrily watches the carnage wrought in his name, and his bellows of bloodlust can be heard echoing across the void between worlds.

In the woodcuts and scrimshaw images that depict him, Khorne appears as an overly muscled, dog-headed giant in baroque plate mail. He sits brooding upon a vast and ornately carved brass throne, which in turn sits atop a great mountain of blood-stained skulls. These are the remains of not only his faithful champions, but also those worthy foes that his devotees have slain in his name. Their number is beyond counting, for every minute of every day, yet more decapitations are offered unto this most violent of gods. Khorne's daemonic Flesh Hounds gnaw upon each new offering, ever ready to hunt those cravens who will not fight in open battle. There can never be enough skulls laid at the foot of Khorne's throne, for though they feed his glory, they can never quench his eternal thirst for blood.

The tribes of Aqshy have claimed much of that fiery realm in Khorne's name, but they are far from alone in his worship. Many civilisations revere aspects of Khorne under a different name – even the ancient aelven god of murder, Khaine, is thought by some to be an aspect of the Blood God. There are few temples built to Khorne, though, for conflict is his only ceremony. The God of War is worshipped on the battlefield with blades and axes, not in halls with solemn words. The indiscriminate bloodletting is accompanied by little ritual other than the chilling battle cry that has become infamous throughout the Mortal Realms: 'Blood for the Blood God! Skulls for the Skull Throne!'

The Bloodsecrator is steeped in Khorne's favour – through his mighty icon he can summon the power of the Brass Citadel itself.

THE BLOODBOUND

The warrior code of Khorne's mortal followers is simple: let the blood flow, regardless of the source – though some methods are favoured over others. Khorne is drawn to duels and lethal contests of skill, though he despises spellcasting in general, seeing it as the refuge of weaklings. There are no wizards devoted to Khorne – their role is instead taken by Slaughterpriests that can boil the blood of the enemy in their veins – though magical weapons that aid the business of killing are much favoured by his warriors.

The warriors of the Bloodbound are single-minded in their battle lust, for a day that passes without slaughter in Khorne's name is a day wasted. At the end of each day's killing, those of the enemy who have fought well enough to survive are given a stark choice – join the Bloodbound in the dark cannibal feast that cements their victory, or die. In this way the ranks of the Bloodbound are constantly replenished, though even this crude ecosystem has its limits.

Khorne looks well upon those who sacrifice their friends or allies in the name of indiscriminate bloodletting, and he will punish a worshipper who fails in his duty as executioner. As his followers often say, Khorne cares not from whence the blood flows. For this reason, those high in his favour are feared and hated even by other Chaos worshippers.

The Bloodbound armies that march to war in the name of Khorne are a terrifying sight. The elite warriors march tirelessly, menace in their every step. The brass-bound banners of their Bloodsecrators drip with gore, decorated with disembodied heads and slicked with arterial blood. Around them, the air seems to crackle with tension, for the longer each warrior keeps his blade sheathed, the more violent the outburst when he releases his rage. When a Mighty Lord of Khorne reaches the field and battle lines are drawn, his warriors transform into a roaring, charging mass of steel and sinew that slams into the enemy line like the fist of the Blood God himself.

DAEMONS OF KHORNE

The air shimmers and writhes as if in pain as the daemons of Khorne stalk the lands of men. Summoned by extensive displays of butchery, the cohorts of the Blood God delight in taking their blades to mortal flesh. They are not natural creatures, but projections of their lord's infinite rage, given life and animus for the singular purpose of murder, and unleashed to prove the might of their divine creator. The most numerous are the Bloodletters, lithe and long-limbed killers who wield greatswords so sharp they can carve stone pillars in twain. The most favoured of their number sit astride the massive, brass-bodied daemon steeds known as Juggernauts, or else ride upon strange chariots and living cannons, the earth shaking as they charge into the fray. But the most monstrous of all are the Bloodthirsters – the greater daemons that epitomise everything violent, bloodthirsty and hateful in the cosmos. Against these giant winged monstrosities, even Stormcast Eternals cannot stand for long – for they are ruin incarnate.

The Black Years, the Reaving Time, the Great Slaughter. The Age of Chaos was called many things. It was an era of long defeat, an epoch of brutality. Seven of the eight realms were overrun, and spike-walled fortresses raised to the glory of the Dark Gods. Each drained the land's essence and spilled forth baleful energies. Yet in the Age of Sigmar, that dominion has been fiercely contested

TZEENTCH

The skies above a Tzeentchian warhost writhe and blaze with untrammelled power. The blades of these eldritch warriors glow with balefire, and their sorcerous leaders rain curses and spells of transmutation upon their foes until only hideous ruin is left behind. Such spectacles are pleasing to the Disciples of Tzeentch.

Tzeentch is the Changer of Ways, and he is flux embodied. He has a masterly comprehension of magic, but also destiny, intrigue, history, tricks and subterfuge. As change is inherent in the essence of Chaos itself, Tzeentch has a strong claim to ultimate power over all who worship Chaos. Without change, a warrior cannot ascend to greatness, the gods cannot bestow their gifts, and the living cannot die.

The entity that men worship as Tzeentch has a thousand names and faces. The only constant is Tzeentch's inconstancy. He is a subtle manipulator with all-encompassing knowledge – Tzeentch knows each

trivial seed of hate in a man's heart, just as he knows the ultimate fate of every star in the cosmos. His plans are inevitably convoluted and vast, spanning across untold aeons, inexplicable and contradictory to mortal minds. He is the ultimate puppetmaster, pulling the strings of fate and controlling the destiny of his followers and enemies alike. He does not always guide the lives of men towards a specific end, at least not for long; for Tzeentch, the very act of manipulation is an end unto itself.

Tzeentch does not have a single form, often manifesting as a cloud of magical light that constantly changes

colour. When he does take shape, his skin crawls with changing faces that leer and mock the onlooker. As he speaks, these faces repeat what he says with subtle but important differences. His head is a puckered and frowning thing in his chest, and his horns seem to spring from his shoulders rather than his brow. The firmament around Tzeentch is heavy with brooding magic that winds like liquid smoke around him, forming bewildering and interweaving patterns that are impossible to follow. To look upon him is to offer up one's sanity – mortal minds are not meant to glimpse infinity, and Tzeentch sits at the nexus of all possible futures.

TZEENTCH ARCANITES

As well as being lord of flux, Tzeentch is also master of aetheric energy, and all of his mortal servants bear his mark. Known as the Great Sorcerer and the Architect of Fate, Tzeentch gifts those who honour him with superior magical powers that they use to bend fate to their will. The slighted, the desperate and the sly all embrace his creed, asking for predominance over their rivals and the favour of fate itself.

Though they may be horribly mutated in form, many Arcanites can change their appearance, for Tzeentch is synonymous with physical transformation. The mutant beastmen known as Tzaangors are amongst the most otherworldly of all his mortal servants. They are blessed with both exceptional warrior skills and the arcane powers of the Lord of Magic. This deadly combination makes them cunning leaders and lethal fighters, and their Shamans command Kairic Acolytes and Tzaangor armies with uncanny prescience. When the Great Schemer is in the ascendant, his warriors are gifted with a preternatural ability to react to a dozen different futures. They draw yet more eldritch power into the ranks of the faithful even

as they unleash bolts of magical fire that immolate everything they touch.

DAEMONS OF TZEENTCH

The daemonic manifestations of Tzeentch are damaging to mortal sanity. They are gangling creatures frequently gifted with eerie bird-like beaks, claws and multicoloured feathers. Their skin and armour is in constant flow, changing shape and texture, forming grotesque cackling faces and kaleidoscopes of blazing colour that confuse and disorient those who look upon them. From their eyes and maws flickers deadly warpfire – these energies do not burn their targets in the manner of natural flame, but instead change them drastically into shapes even more disturbing than a scorched corpse. Yet their most mind-bending aspect is their ability to defy death

– should a Horror of Tzeentch be slain, it will not return to the Realm of Chaos, but split into two smaller daemons bent on revenge.

The capering Horrors form the multitudinous host of the Daemons of Tzeentch. Only the most capricious and steeped in mischief become the Heralds trusted with their command. Above them, the avian Lords of Change rule the daemon throng, sending forth fire-spewing Flamers and swooping Screamers to assail the foe. All the while they work their spells of destruction, sorceries so powerful they can topple empires.

The appearance of a host of Tzeentch often heralds some drastic change in the ebb and flow of battle – an all-conquering hero finds himself reduced to a mewling idiot, a safe haven is transformed into a death trap, or a courageous last stand becomes a panicked rout. Such are the spectacles that amuse and occupy the Great Schemer, for he thrives on irony and cruel twists of fate. If the changes that entertain him can be wrought in flesh and blood, then so much the better, for the transformation from life to death is the most profound of all.

163

'Down with the gilded tyrants!' shouted Iyago Farr, ripping away his worker's smock to reveal the symbol his fellow street scourers had carved into his chest. 'Order kills freedom! None shall suffer the privileged men of gold!' He donned his moon mask, brushing its emerald feathers to stand proud as a vulcharc's crest. Venta Smaine handed him one of the shields she had pulled out from under their rubble cart, sharing her secret smile as she donned her own buckler. Iyago found his heart thumping hard as he and his fellow Changemen drew their swords and clashed them together in the Congress of Sparks. Perhaps this would be the day of his dreams after all.

'The Sky Tyrants!' shouted Iyago, 'They are coming!' He pointed his curved blade at the glowing figures winging through skies. His fellow Acolytes were fighting hard, cantrips and firedarts burning overhead as they pushed back against armoured duardin. Their initial attack on the Archimandrite's Palace, with its spell-steel gates flung wide by sympathisers within, had started exceptionally well. The corpses of the Freeguild still dotted the courtyard, the garrison betrayed by carefully planned ambushes

and misdirections. But even Iyago's mentor, the Lord Transmuter, had not expected a contingent of fully armoured duardin to rise up from hidden tunnels beneath the flagstones. Someone had to have tipped the beard-scum off; that vile slumlord Valastein, no doubt. Too late to do anything about it now.

Mayhem reigned in the courtyard. Iyago desperately fought to keep his calm, but he could not see a single one of the Changemen still fighting. Now he stood shoulder to shoulder with weird avian monsters – the fabled Tzaangors, not in contraband woodcuts this time, but in real life. The Lord Transmuter had called them to him and they fought like wild lions, strange runic weapons leaving traces of pink energy in the air. There came a booming voice from behind him, and Iyago felt heat on the back of his neck. A shadow fell long. He turned for a moment, eyes widening at the sight of a massive, bull-horned giant plucking a Sky Tyrant from the air before incinerating it with an arcane curse. Iyago felt a massive impact in his knees, spinning back to see a duardin hammer loom high. A moment later, the last of the Changemen had his brains splattered across the cobbles.

NURGLE

The devotees of Nurgle are horrific to look upon, more so even than other warriors favoured of Chaos. Their peeling flesh, stomachs bloated with corpse-gas and charnel stench are a reminder of the eventual fate that awaits all creatures. None can escape them forever, for these hosts are entropy incarnate.

Nurgle is the Lord of Decay. It is he who unleashes famines and pestilence upon the world, and so it is to Nurgle that mortals turn when they wish protection from the ravages of disease and the inevitable decline brought by the passing years. Sooner or later every mortal feels Nurgle's debilitating touch. When the crops are spoilt, when a child falls feverish, and when wounds begin to fester on the field of battle, supplications are offered to Nurgle for him to stay his hand. These prayers are often successful, but Nurgle's favour is bought at a terrible cost.

Known also as Nurglitch, Onogal, Neiglen and many other titles, Nurgle is an ancient and well-established god. He has claim to the title Lord of All Things, for no matter how solid and permanent something seems, it is always liable to physical corruption. The palace of today is tomorrow's ruin, the maiden of the morning is the crone of the night, and the hope of a moment is but the foundation stone of everlasting regret.

A darker counterpart to ancient deities of fertility and nature, Nurgle is portrayed as a kindly, almost jovial god, known as Father or Grandfather Nurgle to his blighted acolytes. Though he is the Lord of Decay, whose body is wracked with disease, he is full of ebullient energy and a desire to enlighten. Nurgle cherishes all life, be it mewling babe or bubonic pox. While non-believers may moan in anguish when crippling plague sweeps the lands, those dedicated to Nurgle laugh and dance to see the great works of their master unfold. They have accepted the futility of defying Nurgle and the inescapable dilapidation that he brings, embracing the fruitful delights of decay, disease and ruin. For what use is it to rail against the onset of entropy, as implacable as the passage of time itself?

ROTBRINGERS

Nurgle's mortal warriors, largely known as Rotbringers, are toughened by their patron's favour to such an extent that they are nigh impossible to kill with mortal weapons. Although ravaged by disease, they are themselves protected from such plagues, and have become immune to pain and discomfort. While their bodies may corrupt and split open, the spirit of Nurgle sustains them. Thus the warriors of Nurgle can endure wounds and afflictions that would cripple others and still fight on in his name.

Nurgle's armies are repulsive indeed. Clouds of fat-bodied flies surround them, bathing in exposed sores and pustules and clustering into the eyes, nostrils and ears of any who look upon them. A miasma of pestilence hangs around the decomposing legions like a grey-green cloud, all but suffocating any who come within range of their plagueswords and pock-marked blades. But not all is grimness and squalor amongst the footsoldiers of Nurgle, for the favoured openly rejoice in their deity's approval. So it is that the hosts of the Plague God stride to battle with the exuberance of a carnival, phlegm-choked laughter ringing out as they bring their deadly gifts closer to the foe.

DAEMONS OF NURGLE

The Plague God's daemons echo their patron in form, though they are but insects next to his mountainous massiveness. Great Unclean Ones appear as hugely bloated creatures, festering with boils, poxes and suppurating sores. They are surrounded by dark clouds of tiny daemonic insects, each of which carries the symbol of the Plague God upon its back. Their skin is rent and torn, and indescribable organs, rank with decay, spill through their ruptured skin and hang like drapes about their girth. From their exposed guts spill Nurglings, the spiteful mites giggling and cackling amidst the filth. Around them march the Plaguebearers, droll tallymen whose duty it is to count the diseases that course across the battlefield. Their task is all but endless; for all his hideousness, Father Nurgle has a generous spirit. He is never mean or thrifty with the contagions he brews, and within his putrescent cauldron he has gifts enough for all.

165

*F*addrox Muckspreader
let a guffaw burst from
his ravaged lungs. After
thirty years of smoking harsh
Aqshian fireweed, laughing
was painful, even with Nurgle's
blessings – but battle always
put him in a good mood, and
the antics of the Bilepiper
daemon got him every time.
Right now the capering fool was
using a dead aelf's disembodied
torso as a puppet, making its
mouth flap and its limp hand
stroke its hair.

Faddrox shook his head and
strode back to the front line.
There his fellow Rotbringers
were hacking rusted blades into
the frenzied aelves that fought
in nothing more than scraps of
armour. He hefted his blade.
There was hard graft to be
done – he had been a struggling
farmer once, and even though
his body had turned to rot,
his work ethic was fine and
well. He chortled as his blade
took an aelf head from its
slender neck. It bounced in the
furrowed soil. To reap a good
harvest, he thought, the seeds
must be sown well.

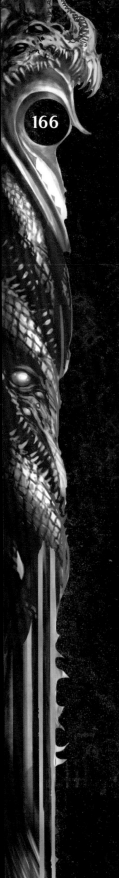

SLAANESH

No one is safe from the Dark Prince, even whilst his power lingers in obscurity. He is not some foe that can be avoided or met with blade and shield, but the embodiment of the hidden lusts and desires that nestle in every being's soul. Those who follow his dark creed are cunning and quick, the demise of proud empires given form.

Slaanesh, the Dark Prince of Chaos, is the youngest of the four greater Chaos Gods – and though he has fallen captive to Sigmar's Pantheon of Order, he is worshipped still throughout the Mortal Realms. The Lord of Pleasure is the patron of excess in all things. Master of luxury and creative power, his spheres of influence include music, art and passion, but also sadism, perversion and cruelty. He is the embodiment of indulgence in all its forms, and can be found wherever discipline bows to temptation and virtue falls to vice.

Divinely beautiful and alluring, Slaanesh exudes a palpable and irresistible charm that can leave a mortal smitten for eternity. Slaanesh is depicted in the artwork and verse of the depraved as a radiant and slender colossus, male on the left side and female on the right, with a subtly disturbing voice that can bind a man as a spider binds a fly. He loves to tease the souls of his enemies from their bodies even as they gaze with adoration and longing into his lustrous eyes.

THE ABSENT GOD
Being the embodiment of utmost obsession and greed unbound, Slaanesh could not resist feasting on millions of aelf souls during the cataclysmic end of the world-that-was. Many such spirits have since been freed from his near-comatose form by Tyrion, Teclis, Malerion and Morathi – but like a surgeon teasing a splinter of glass from a wound, they run the risk of aggravating that which they intend to heal. Though Slaanesh remains trapped in the Gloaming, every aelf soul taken from his essence brings him closer to wakefulness – and the dread revenge that will likely follow.

Since his incarceration in the Gloaming, Slaanesh has been missing from the pantheon of the Dark Gods. The devotees that worship Slaanesh seek him not purely for pleasure and the thrill of the hunt, but also for personal gain. The Dark Prince of Chaos has it within his power to instil in his followers a portion of his radiant glory. Slaanesh is worshipped in secret in many of the free cities – Hammerhal Aqsha amongst them – where his principles of indulgence in every whim and vice enjoy a clandestine following. His allure is highly addictive, and those who follow him are quickly overcome by the temptations of pride, arrogance and excess.

Slaanesh hungrily preys upon these mortal weaknesses, watching greedily through half-shut eyes as his playthings fall from grace. How many have inadvertently slipped into his tender embrace as they succumb to the sins of self-indulgence? How many lords and leaders have turned to the Dark Prince to secure their position, or to gain the support and respect of their fellows?

THE DECADENT HOSTS
The lords of the nomadic hosts that seek Slaanesh are majestic, charismatic leaders who are adored by their followers and attract ever more armies to their side. As each champion becomes more self-absorbed, he begins to lose that which once made him human. The favoured one becomes more distant from his followers, his otherworldly persona only furthering the devotion of his acolytes. As the favoured of Slaanesh slide ever deeper into the depths of depravity, a little more of their humanity drips away with every unnatural act, until they are reborn as beautiful but cruel tyrants, All other creatures become subservient to the will of the champion, there merely to give adulation or be destroyed.

The glittering warhosts of Slaanesh are marvellous to behold. Long, elegant banners proclaim the glory of the lord of the warhost and pledge undying devotion to the Dark Prince. Each warrior is tattooed and pierced with obscene sigils and runes that hurt the naked eye, and fine silks and carefully flayed skins are draped across polished and bladed armour. The warriors of Slaanesh stalk and glide across the battlefield with a languid and unhurried grace, long tongues flickering as they taste the tang of fear in the air. For although the minions of the Dark Prince indulge themselves in every vice, their favourite excess is on the field of battle, where they can bathe in the hot blood of their victims and rejoice in the screams of the dying.

Vaela Angelica sat in the window of her father's tower, using her fan to guide the scent of incense into the cool night air. The Ulgu-shade swathed Granid City, keeping it safe from the reavers. How she hated its stifling embrace. Yet she could already hear sounds of excitement rising from the city below.

And there they were, coming through the breadman's quarter – the Seekers. A riot of colour in the gloom, forcing their way through the streets in a carnival of blood and violence. She could make out fabulous knights charging atop serpentine bipeds, bladed chariots of gold cutting down the Grey Guard, and silk-clad courtesans dancing through the carnage, each wearing what seemed to be hideous masks and mock claws. She wafted more incense from her brazier, filled to the brim with the sugared tongues and fingers of lovers. They would follow the scent, and life would begin anew.

SKAVEN

Scurrying, vicious and entirely malevolent, the multitudinous skaven gnaw at the roots of reality. They are hunched, mangy rat-things little stronger than men, though they almost always attack in swarms, and their maniacal inventiveness and cunning make them a threat to the Mortal Realms like no other.

The skaven are a race apart. They are creatures of Chaos, and will gladly side with the victors in any conflict, but they would turn against their allies in a heartbeat if it benefited them. Treachery is a way of life for these vile rat-things. Short-lived and prone to fits of aggression due to their fierce metabolism, they do everything they can to climb the twisted and rickety ladder of their society before another aspirant can tear them down and scramble to victory over their twitching corpse. They have a jerky agitation to their every movement, tails thrashing

and claws scrabbling with the need to make their mark upon reality. Yet their ambition far outweighs their reach. Only through trickery and deception can they overcome the strong. As such, the skaven have found a hundred different ways to tip the scales in their favour – foremost amongst them is to attack in a thousands-strong swarm of furry bodies more akin to a crashing wave than an ordered military advance. Though the greater clans all specialise in different ways of destroying their foes, they are all underhand and scurrilous.

The barefaced lie is a time-honoured way of securing status in skaven society. Should a skaven work his way up to the position of leader, he will claim every shred of success for himself, whilst quickly placing the blame elsewhere if he presides over a failure, or somehow turning the situation around to his benefit. A Warlord or Grey Seer who loses thousands of lives in a costly attack to no discernible gain will claim he was betrayed by incompetent underlings, sabotaged by the other clans, or did it on purpose to cunningly rid his clan of traitors.

The skaven are a dire menace that infest and despoil every Mortal Realm, craven and opportunistic ratmen whose frantic ambition has spelled ruin for entire civilisations.

'*Again! Quick-quick!*' Reequeak pushed at his human minion, and the ancient bell was struck for a tenth time. The barbarian turned sharply, yellow teeth bared, but Reequeak showed his warpstone amulet, and the human went back to his work. The tribal warriors swung the battering ram once more, and it boomed against the giant bell. Eleven, now. Reequeak felt his lips curl as the resounding boom shivered dust from the ancient temple walls. The city above would fall this night, and he would claim the spoils. The bell's twelfth toll boomed.
'*Again!*' said Reequeak, '*for the Horned Rat!*'
The ram crashed home and the bell cracked with an ear-splitting detonation, tearing the walls of reality with it. Pouring through came a swarm of brown bodies so thick that Reequeak and his humans were buried in an instant, then ripped apart by the chisel teeth of a thousand starving vermin. On and on they came in a tide of filth. The way was finally open, and the doom of New Kasvar had arrived.

Whatever the excuse, he will do all he can to avoid censure. Whether anyone truly believes him is academic, for truth is a rare commodity. Similarly, the skaven will backstab one another if they believe they can get away with it – their society is a tyranny moderated by assassination. So numerous is the ramshackle, duplicitous civilisation that scurries and swarms in the dark corners of the Mortal Realms, breeding hundreds of thousands of cut-throat ratmen with every passing moon, that it survives – even thrives – nonetheless.

The greater clans of the skaven are present in every realm to some degree. They include the Clans Skryre, twisted alchemists and masters of warpstone magic; the Clans Moulder, who breed experimental war-creatures of terrible genius; the Clans Pestilens, devout bringers of disease that seek the Thirteen Great Plagues; the Clans Verminus, whose teeming hordes are without number; and the Clans Eshin, stealthiest of their kind. Overseeing them all is the Masterclan – the white-furred, horned mage-caste known as the Grey Seers and the daemonic Verminlords they summon to guide them. Together they are joined in worshipping the hateful deity known as the Great Horned Rat. The newest addition to the pantheon of the Dark Gods since Chaos' victory over the world-that-was, he is a god of pestilence, blight and encroaching doom. Whereas Father Nurgle lavishes his fecund entropy in order to grow vile new forms of life, the Great Horned Rat wishes to bring only desolation and ruin. Where his verminous children grow strong, they leave barren fields, empty storehouses and starvation behind them. In half-mad desperation does the Horned Rat find his strength. His forte is panic and mania, paranoia and disaster wrought on an epic scale.

The skaven and their cruel god have grown strong indeed over the course of the Age of Chaos. With sorcerous poxes and strange alchemical devices, they burrow tunnels from their half-real metropolis of Blight

City into the Mortal Realms, these gnawholes so labyrinthine and numerous they can strike anywhere, at any time. There are rumours that the skaven have even managed to penetrate the wards of Sigmar's palace in Azyr. It is said that wherever a person stands in the realms, they are never more than a spear's throw from a hungry skaven waiting to pounce. In that is a kernel of truth, but so uncomfortable is the notion that civilised folk prefer to denounce the rat-creatures' existence as a myth dreamed up by fevered minds to scare the credulous. In denying the skaven's existence, however, they are lending them great power, for it is in the shadows of civilisation that the skaven thrive most of all…

'There are no giant vermin men, laddy-o-mine. Not in either Hammerhal nor in the wilds beyond. Who told you these wild tales? The baker's boy, was it? Obsessed with rats, those Vendessens. Any excuse for poor merchandise! I tell you now, boy, there's more chance of you dying to a loaf of their commoner's bread than by some filthy rodent burrowing up from below.'

– Nenso de Vinst,
Duke of the Merchant Hills

CREATURES OF CHAOS

If a visionary knew of even a fraction of the hideous creatures bound to the cause of Chaos he would lose his mind in an instant. Tainted beasts and freakish daemons roam the Mortal Realms, and the champions of Chaos are quick to exploit their strength and savagery whenever they can.

The coming of Chaos has done terrible things to the Mortal Realms. Nature has been perverted out of true by insidious energies wherever the lands have felt the touch of the Dark Gods. The further the dominion of Chaos spreads, the more corrupted a realm becomes, and the more its denizens suffer the same fate. Predatory beasts that were once part of the natural cycle grow into rapacious horrors, swollen and writhing with the stigmata of chaotic transmutation. Once-noble beasts are twisted into aberrant shapes, their minds broken or filled with an insatiable bloodlust. Worse still are the cruel creatures that spill from tainted Realmgates to infest the realms. From wild and sadistic tribes of drunken Centigors to rampaging Chaos gargants, these unnatural monsters have claimed great swathes of the realms as their hunting grounds. Woe betide those who stray near their lairs, for many of these horrors will do worse than merely kill their prey. The Cockatrice can turn a man to a cursed statue with its petrifying gaze, whilst the Mutalith Vortex Beast's very presence brings terrible mutation, reducing those nearby to gibbering heaps of writhing flesh and flailing tentacles.

The monsters of the Mortal Realms would be dangerous enough were they but mindless beasts roving the wilderness, but a warlord with sufficient willpower and favour in the eyes of the Dark Gods can yoke them to his will. Enlisting such beasts is a perilous game, for they often possess unnatural powers that make them deadly to their masters as well as their foes, but such is the carnage they wreak in times of war the risk is seen as worthwhile. Packs of wolfish Chaos Warhounds bay wildly as they flood around the enemy's flanks to rip and tear. Centigors, drunk on blood-mead and the scent of carnage, stampede wild-eyed into the foe to trample and gouge. Razorgors plough headlong through enemy phalanxes, tossing broken corpses left and right as their mad charge reaches its bloody end. Shrieking Harpies swoop down from bruised skies to snatch up the unwary and carry them screaming into the clouds. In the thick of the fray, smashing the enemy battle line to bloody ruin, are the Slaughterbrutes – massive claw-beasts bound to a Chaos champion by flesh-ritual and the magical blades that protrude from their spines.

When a whole army of such terrifying beasts gathers, perhaps driven by the will of a sorcerer or demigod, they are a force unstoppable. Falling upon armies on the march or springing from cavern networks and overgrown ruins, they thrash and stamp and gore, warriors dying beneath their ripping claws and piercing fangs until the battlefield is littered with torn and broken corpses scattered as if by the most violent hurricane.

DAEMONS UNBOUND

Even then, there are worse things than monsters abroad in the realms. Those daemons that have entered the material world and not yet been banished – perhaps via a catastrophic magical event or summoning that has yet to be reversed – usually dwell close to the Realm's Edge that they might prey on creatures of flesh and blood whilst subsisting on the chaotic energies that tear at the foundation of reality. Those not aligned to a particular god may escape the summons of their chaotic masters for weeks, months, even years. The sight of a rampaging Soul Grinder or flock of gargoyle-like Furies near the shimmering periphery of a realm is not uncommon; it is said that even Daemon Princes roam the edges of each world, glorying in their power whilst secretly dreading their eventual return to the dimension of pure Chaos – and taking that angst out on anything foolish enough to get close.

THUNDERSCORN DRAGON OGORS

From high mountain peaks wreathed in magical storms come the Thunderscorn, strange centaur-like beasts that are as much drake as they are ogor. These looming monsters are ancient beyond human reckoning. It is said they entered into a pact with the Dark Gods before mankind even ventured forth into the light – eternal life for everlasting servitude. That dark bargain has lasted aeons, and is still not fulfilled. Fuelled by the electric ravages of the storm, they roar and bark in their ancient tongue as they stomp towards the foe with bestial faces set in grim scowls. The hulking Shaggoths that lead them, each massive enough to crush a fortified building under its scaled bulk, are living wrecking balls sent against the hardiest of the Chaos host's prey. With their strange cold-blooded metabolisms invigorated and even healed by the lightning that plays around their mountainous homes, the Dragon Ogors make for a potent weapon against the Stormhosts that seek to challenge the rule of Chaos – even a Lord-Celestant must respect the raw power of the Thunderscorn in battle.

BRAYHERDS & WARHERDS

Wild and bestial, Brayherds worship the Gods of Chaos by sacrificing enemies, raiding settlements and ambushing marching armies. All beastmen are twisted monsters that dwell in the dark and dangerous corners of the realms, but the Warherds are truly terrifying – stampeding half-bull mutants that live to gorge on hot flesh.

The first sign of an attacking Brayherd is a discordant rallying cry that spreads fear and confusion through the enemy ranks. Warriors cower in fear, eyes wild as they look for their attackers amidst gnarled woodlands or shadowed crags. Steeds rear and shriek as the stink of monsters fills their nostrils. When the Brayherd finally attacks, it does so from every side, closing with the sudden savagery of a beast's jaws.

Some believe that the gor-kin of the Brayherds are mutant creatures, barbarian tribesmen transformed into twisted monsters by the pervading powers of Chaos. Others claim that they are creatures native to the Realm of Chaos, who have spilled into the Mortal Realms along with the invading daemon armies. Whatever the truth of their origins, these bestial hordes are present across every Mortal Realm in great number, and their constant raids are a threat to those who stand against the forces of Chaos. The Brayherds are primitive and territorial, claiming wild areas and incessantly attacking all who stray close. When a Chaos champion rises, Brayherds may be drawn to his banner, abandoning their monolithic herdstones to rampage in search of bloodshed.

The gor-kin are crude and base creatures in thrall to their own brutish desires. They have little skill at the crafting of anything other than war and woe. Whether cowardly ungor or iron-thewed Beastlord, all such warriors live to kill, to feast, to rut, and to tear down all signs of ordered society. They are creatures of Chaos by nature, and their revulsion for the trappings of civilisation goes beyond mere instinct. Culture and civilisation of any kind evokes a disgust and contempt in the gor-kin that is all consuming. To the Brayherds, such things are signs of revolting weakness, and must be smashed asunder.

These primitive creatures hate and fear the Gods of Chaos as much as they worship and adore them. Their Bray-Shamans read the gods' desires in spilled innards and crude runes, omens and signs, and they are invariably violent. The Brayherds seek worthy victims to be brought before the herdstones and forced onto the altars in their shadows. There the luckless have their throats slit, their hearts torn out, and their corpses strung up so that the gods might be appeased for another day.

The weak and feeble in gor-kin society are swiftly devoured. Their way of life is utterly without mercy, and no gor-kin long survives that is not a capable warrior of some description. Thus while the hunched ungors are used as slinking scouts and vicious bowmen, the gors and Bestigors make up the massed herds of the Brayherd battle line. Led by monstrous Beastlords and sorcerous Bray-Shamans, and with rumbling chariots sweeping around their flanks, the Brayherds charge into battle bellowing their hatred for all living things. Their attacks are anarchic and brutal in the extreme, stampedes of wild animals tearing at their victims and bludgeoning them into the gore-stained mud. Soon enough, the beleaguered defenders are left as gristle, crushed beneath the gor-kin's cloven hooves.

WARHERDS

Huge and hulking, the monstrous warriors of the Warherds are driven by animal fury. Nomadic and supremely destructive, the Warherds rampage across the Mortal Realms, annihilating everything in their path. As their Doombull leaders bellow in a mindless, frothing frenzy, the Warherd redoubles its assault. Towers are toppled and villages ripped apart like matchwood. Warriors courageous enough to stand against them are not just slain, but rent to shreds and gobbled down like sweetmeats to satisfy the endless bloodthirst of the bullgors.

Warherds care nothing for possessions beyond their weapons and perhaps a few scraps of battered armour. Their savage hunger drives them on to kill and kill, gulping down blood gushing straight from the artery and swallowing chunks of still-twitching meat as they hack their way into the next rank of the foe. It is truly horrifying for those battling a Warherd when they realise they are fighting not just to defeat a powerful enemy, but to avoid being torn apart and devoured. Many hideous creatures gather at the battle-feast of the Warherds, most commonly the magic-eating Cygors and monstrous Ghorgons that follow the ragged banners of the bullgors. These bestial horrors exult in the pounding beat of the bullgors' flesh-drums and the bellowing war cries of the Bloodkine.

To face the onslaught of a Warherd is to face a charging mass of muscle, bone, metal and rock that is all but unstoppable. As the Warherd drop their heads and charge, the ground shudders beneath their pounding hooves. Their foe will break rank and flee rather than face the stampede, but this will not save them – once the Warherd has smashed headlong through the weakened enemy lines, they run down those who have fled without mercy.

Archaon, Exalted Grand Marshal of the Apocalypse, leads the forces of the Varanspire to war. With him come not only his Varanguard but countless Slaves to Darkness and daemon minions.

Khorne Bloodbound
Korghos Khul, Mighty Lord of Khorne

Khorne Bloodbound
Chaos Champion

Khorne Bloodbound
Blood Warrior

Woe to those who witness the daemons of the Blood God! With axe, blade and whip, Bloodthirsters reap a mighty harvest of skulls in Khorne's name, whilst the Bloodletters that advance alongside them add more heads to the tally.

The avian sorcerers known as Lords of Change command a motley horde of Tzeentchian daemons, their warpfires setting reality ablaze. Cackling with glee, they wreak horrific change upon those brave enough to stand against them.

Daemons of Tzeentch
The Changeling

Tzeentch Arcanites
Tzaangor Shaman

Tzeentch Arcanites
Gaunt Summoner

Daemons of Nurgle
Horticulous Slimux

Nurgle Rotbringers
Gutrot Spume

Daemons of Nurgle
Spoilpox Scrivener, Herald of Nurgle

Daemons of Nurgle
Sloppity Bilepiper, Herald of Nurgle

Daemons of Nurgle
Beast of Nurgle

The immensity that is Rotigus, Rainfather of the Maggotkin, brings with him ▶ the Deluge of Nurgle. Only the faithful can hope to survive his unclean curse.

Daemons of Slaanesh
Herald of Slaanesh

Daemons of Slaanesh
Heartseeker

Daemons of Slaanesh
Alluress

The fiendish warbands that worship Slaanesh number lithe Daemonettes, serpentine Seekers and scythe-wheeled chariots.

The skaven, verminous servants of the Great Horned Rat, create ever more arcane engines and beasts of war.

The call of the Brayherd is the doom of civilisations, for these beastmen are savage and hateful in equal measure.

The Clans Pestilens are skaven devoted to plague and ruin, who search for the perfect diseases to infect all living things.

THE FORCES OF DEATH

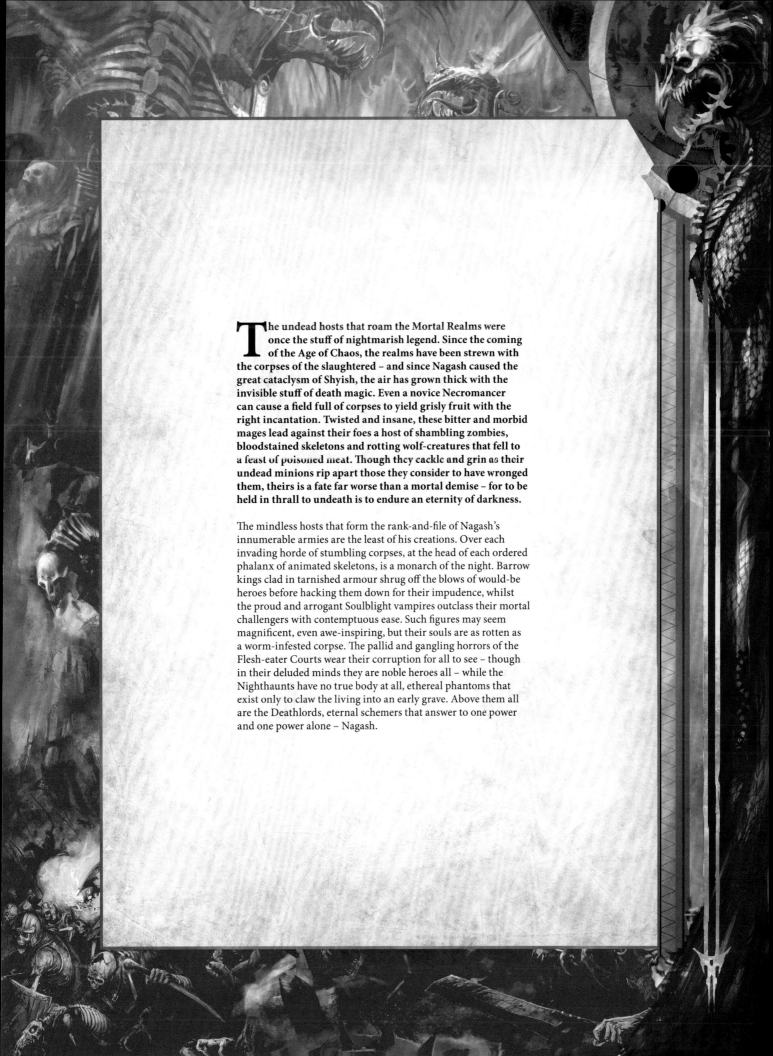

The undead hosts that roam the Mortal Realms were once the stuff of nightmarish legend. Since the coming of the Age of Chaos, the realms have been strewn with the corpses of the slaughtered – and since Nagash caused the great cataclysm of Shyish, the air has grown thick with the invisible stuff of death magic. Even a novice Necromancer can cause a field full of corpses to yield grisly fruit with the right incantation. Twisted and insane, these bitter and morbid mages lead against their foes a host of shambling zombies, bloodstained skeletons and rotting wolf-creatures that fell to a feast of poisoned meat. Though they cackle and grin as their undead minions rip apart those they consider to have wronged them, theirs is a fate far worse than a mortal demise – for to be held in thrall to undeath is to endure an eternity of darkness.

The mindless hosts that form the rank-and-file of Nagash's innumerable armies are the least of his creations. Over each invading horde of stumbling corpses, at the head of each ordered phalanx of animated skeletons, is a monarch of the night. Barrow kings clad in tarnished armour shrug off the blows of would-be heroes before hacking them down for their impudence, whilst the proud and arrogant Soulblight vampires outclass their mortal challengers with contemptuous ease. Such figures may seem magnificent, even awe-inspiring, but their souls are as rotten as a worm-infested corpse. The pallid and gangling horrors of the Flesh-eater Courts wear their corruption for all to see – though in their deluded minds they are noble heroes all – while the Nighthaunts have no true body at all, ethereal phantoms that exist only to claw the living into an early grave. Above them all are the Deathlords, eternal schemers that answer to one power and one power alone – Nagash.

THE DEATHLORDS

Nagash, the Great Necromancer, has the power of a god. He is revered as such by the morbid tribes that worship him. He seeks to bind all of the Mortal Realms in a web of grave-cold order and mindless obedience. At his side march vampiric generals and deadly Morghasts magically created from the remains of worthy foes.

The self-proclaimed God of All Shyish, Nagash's ambition is to rule over all creation. He has long sought to bind humanity to his rule, ever since his mortal life as a priest of the Mortuary Cult in the long-gone desert realm of Nehekhara. Then, his ambitions were vaunting and uncompromising, but still those of a man. As he rose to kingship over the cooling corpse of the brother he murdered, as he became ever more powerful and corrupt on a diet of stolen dark magic and precious wyrdstone, Nagash began to exist more on the supernatural plane. Fascinated with the energies of death, he became saturated with morbid power as his works became ever darker and more disturbing. In feasting long on the raw stuff of magic, he grew taller and more skeletal. By the time he met his first death at the hands of the skaven that sought his warpstone hoard, he was long beyond the notion of a mortal demise. Slowly, agonisingly, he reformed, though the only physical remains left to him after the skaven attack was a giant skeletal hand. Though it took a thousand years, he enacted a spectacular revenge.

Since that ancient time, Nagash has died and been resurrected by his own fell magic over and over again. Each time he is slain, whether by the hand of Sigmar, the malevolence of the skaven or the grand entropy of Chaos, Nagash's spirit flees to a sarcophagus deep in his most formidable stronghold. There his body reforms around the seed of his essence as a black pearl forms around a speck of grit. Decades, centuries, even millennia pass before he is whole once more, but Nagash has time on his side. Once he has been restored he soon goes in search of vengeance, hosts of bone-winged Morghast constructs at his side. What is death to one who consumes gods and breathes raw magic? What is physical harm to one saturated in the energies of resurrection?

Nagash's initial forays into the pioneering of new forms of necromancy saw the curse of vampirism spread through the ancient civilisations of his birthlands. Some of those first infected serve him even now, the bond between the servant and the master so potent it lasts across the aeons. It was Neferata, the prideful Queen of Ancient Lahmia, that initially stole the rarest and most eldritch of Nagash's treasured tomes, and she who distilled an elixir of immortality from its teachings. In drinking the crimson liquid Neferata became the first vampire, the central figure of a coven of fellow Lahmians that spread their blood-curse amongst a hidden network of nobles. In doing so, they became the rulers of several powerful vampiric dynasties, each claiming independence despite the fact that every sire and scion was bound inextricably to Nagash's will.

Neferata still serves Nagash to this day as one of his Mortarchs – kings and queens of the night that rule over vast empires of their own. Resurrected after the demise of her initial empire, Neferata has founded an echo of the city she ruled over as a mortal. Accustomed to luxury as she is, Neferata prefers to act through proxies, for she is an expert seductress, the mistress of an extensive network of spies both living and dead. She rarely stoops to physical violence, but when she does, her quicksilver speed is lethal.

Neferata's principal rival is Mannfred, last of the von Carstein dynasty. Cunning as an old wolf and serpent-fast in a duel, Mannfred's scheming has diverted the course of entire epochs. He has long worked to ensure his own pre-eminence. He rose above the rest of his vampiric kin in the arts of treachery, usurping his father in darkness and claiming their homeland Sylvania for his own – even having the temerity to raise Nagash from his slumbers in the hope of binding the arch-necromancer to his will. Though Mannfred survived the cataclysm that followed, Nagash ensured his punishment was long and excruciating. Now Mannfred vies with Neferata for the position of Nagash's foremost lieutenant, but in truth that position already belongs to another – Arkhan the Black.

Arkhan is a liche lord, a sorcerer and necromancer of unparalleled ability save for Nagash himself. Though skeletal and ancient, Arkhan is a giant of a man, clad in the finest of kingly robes, his staff of office able to channel the subtle energies of Shyish and his arcane gestures able to turn flesh to dust. Like his fellow Mortarchs, Arkhan rides to war upon a dread abyssal, a leonine construct of bone, spirit and predatory intent.

To a mortal, these lords of undeath are primal forces given form, dark and terrifying entities from the Realm Below. For a man even to witness them is to find himself unable to sleep, to rest, to gain succour from home and hearth. These are the masters of undead legions beyond counting, and where they cast their dead-eyed gaze, the chill of the grave is never far behind.

NIGHTHAUNTS

The Nighthaunts that roam the fell places of the realms are truly terrifying, manifesting as ethereal phantasms that soar to battle on cold winds. Shaped by the magic of Nagash into forms that echo the sins of their mortal lives, the Nighthaunts are driven by the darkest emotions to inflict horror and death upon the living.

In a hundred thousand graveyards across the Mortal Realms, a bone-numbing chill seeps out from opened tombs and exhumed mass graves. With it comes a deathly mist, and within that strange miasma are the Nighthaunt hosts. These are not corporeal foes, creatures that can be slain with blade or shot, but ethereal entities all but immune to blows from mundane weapons. Imbued with the resurgent energies of Shyish, their power comes from an immortal rage, spite and bitterness that gives them the power to tear flesh and rend the soul. They are able to drift through walls and reach through the flesh of men with their cold talons to still the hearts within.

The Nighthaunts hail from the Realm of Death, especially near the Shyish Nadir and the Innerlands around its sloping rim. These are not normal gheists, spirits of mortal men that have found rest only to be called to another's service, but truly evil undead apparitions, spectres so twisted by Nagash and his undead acolytes that they become ghostly killers fixated on visiting horror upon the living.

Like an ill wind that howls up from the darkest pits of creation, the Nighthaunts attack as an onrushing host of dark spirits. They are sustained by a fathomless hatred for the living. These wraiths fight

to send fresh souls screaming down into the Shyishan underworlds, taking cruel pleasure in knowing the torments that await them as they too suffer the reign of Nagash.

The Nighthaunt armies form the vanguard of Nagash's legions, rising from the corpse-strewn ground or pouring through Realmgates to fall upon their prey. As these spectral hosts howl across the battlefield, damned spirits break away to bring death to their chosen quarries. Even a rag-tag horde of Chainrasps can prove the demise of a phalanx of armoured warriors, for unless a blow is levelled against them with powerful intent and unstinting

Goodmother Devendra looked out once more, anxious to see signs of the warrior host returning. Three days ago they had marched out to battle, all the fine young men desperate to impress in the wake of the storm-comers. She had known even then – feared, she told herself, only feared – that her sons were going to their doom.

There was a plaintive cry, calling her from outside. The voice of her youngest son. For a moment, she dared to hope he had returned. But something was wrong. Frost crept across the glass before her. She felt the air move behind her, and turned.

Three heads rose out of the floorboards, distorted skulls bald and grinning. They reached their claws towards her as they drifted higher, their hands impossibly long, each talon still dripping with spilt blood.

She smiled, and made the sign of Almighty Nagash. Her sons had come home.

Nighthaunts are creatures of tortured spirit and undying hatred. They are feared across the Mortal Realms, for they are evil incarnate.

courage, it will find little purchase upon them. Only those attacks with the driving force of intense emotion behind them can tear through the ectoplasmic body of the Nighthaunt. The fear and confusion that bleeds from each of these unholy gheists is a weapon in itself, for by robbing the mind of conviction, they also rob the body of strength.

Amongst the tattered spirits that form the main body of a Nighthaunt host come those so steeped in evil they have become the de facto leaders of their kind. These wraith-like beings are the shades of murderers, evil sorcerers and executioners, risen from crude graves to take their long-bladed scythes to the souls of the living.

As with most of their kind, the form they take is a vile reflection of their former sins and the manner of their death, for the Great Necromancer has a twisted sense of justice for those he sees as criminals. Those who died in chains, hoping to be finally free in death, find themselves shackled for eternity. Those who turned away in horror from the necromantic arts find undead flocking towards them forever more. Those who took great care to do their murder in secret are remade as screaming, frenzied killers. Knights who rebelled against their masters are forced to betray life itself, leaving hoofprints of cold fire in the air as they ride; those struck by their blades can have their very soul severed from their body.

Wraithly hosts are comprised of many types of strange apparitions, from Lord Executioners and Glaivewraith Stalkers sent to execute those who have earned Nagash's ire, to burning Hexwraith riders and the legendary Black Coaches, infernal carriages which contain coffins that house the regenerating body of an undead monarch. Amongst the throng can be seen magic-eating crones and shrieking banshees that float as if underwater, each the departed spirits of a black-hearted murderess. When these haggard she-gheists let fly their howls of spite and bitterness, the deathly shriek can turn a stalwart soldier to a milk-white corpse. Even an armoured king or hulking orruk will collapse, dead as stone, at the Banshee's wail.

FLESH-EATER COURTS

Afflicted by a morbid supernatural curse, the Flesh-eater Courts believe themselves to be heraldic warriors of good breeding and noble intent. In truth they are vile, pallid troglodytes possessed of a horrifying hunger – a need that can only be sated with acts of barbaric predation and chilling, blood-fuelled feasts.

In every corner of the realms, when the night draws in and the fires burn low, bone-chilling tales are told of the Flesh-eater Courts. These creatures are caught within a hellish existence, cursed by a moment of weakness to a slide into depravity. The only cure for their madness is fire and sword – though few indeed have encountered these ghoulish figures and lived. In the altered minds of the Flesh-eaters, it is they that are the saviours, and the people of the realms the fiends to be slain.

When war and famine ravage a land, its most desperate and determined people survive in any way they can. Giving in to hunger, they turn upon the fallen, the weak, and even each other in their quest for sustenance. Retreating into the shadowed ruins of their towns and cities, these cannibal cults often devolve into hideous parodies of society, kept alive on a diet of rancid flesh and bone. Even then these creatures are worthy of pity, for their transformation is not yet complete. Only once a cannibal partakes of an abhorrant king's feast do they become what is known as a mordant.

The clammy and stinking ghouls of the Flesh-eater Courts garb themselves in bone and blood, but think they are clad in courtly finery.

The deathly kings themselves are bestial vampires who rule over swathes of the Mortal Realms by the strength of their ragged courts. Completely delusional, they have become known as abhorrants by the rest of their bloodsucking kin. Abhorrant Ghoul Kings are so lost in their madness that they believe themselves to be mortal monarchs. When they come to a place infested with cannibals, they see not monsters, but starving peasants and soldiers eager for the hand of a beneficent master. Yet this supernatural curse runs deep, for each abhorrant king brings with him more than just dark rulership – he also spreads a contagious madness. Weak minds are quickly turned, but even the strong-willed soon see the visiting king as he sees himself. Before long, those that once hid in shame from the light stand tall, armoured in delusion. In a mockery of Sigmar's newly founded cities and civilisations, the king brings them into his court, dubbing the pale horrors that bow and scrape before him his mordants.

By the will of the abhorrants do the Flesh-eater Courts congregate in the realms. Gathering up feasts from the remains of the living and the dead, they rend apart their enemies and prepare the fallen's flesh for their lord's culinary pleasure. Some among the mordants might even be blessed to sup the king's blood – in their minds, they are drinking wine from their master's table. However, the thick crimson draught brings with it a terrifying transformation. These creatures arise as drooling horrors, slaved utterly to their new master, and bereft of what remained of their sanity.

In time, a few of these 'blessed' ones might even ascend from mordants to join the vampiric ranks of the abhorrants. If fortune favours them, they will in turn found their own courts, thus disseminating the

Flesh-eaters' madness even further. Like a virus, the delusion spreads across the lands, often running unchecked as those caught in its madness venture forth on their gory crusades. There are entire continents in Aqshy and Shyish overrun by ghoulish terrors. Where the endless assault of Chaos conquest renders the lands ruined in their wake, there spring up the Flesh-eater Courts, for amongst starvation, deathly wastelands and cloying despair their foul phenomenon takes root. In dark mockery of the civilisations that have come before, the ruins of mankind's domain become home to a new citizenry. The abhorrant king, attracted to the plaintive cries of the starving and deranged, takes a shattered throne amidst the ruin. Ragged skin banners flap wetly above crumbling castles, the caw of carrion birds fills the air. Amongst the tumbled stone stalk hulking, pale monsters, thinking themselves knights and men-at-arms standing proudly atop the ramparts of a glorious edifice. In their talons they carry sharpened thigh bones and

broken ribs, fondly imagining them to be fine swords and bejewelled daggers. Scouting parties of crypt-haunting troglodytes range across the land in search of fresh meat. In the remains of cities, nests of ghouls take up residence, stockpiling bones and heaping offal piles that ripen in the sun. The winged mutants of the king's court roam ever further in search of trespassers in their master's realm. At the heart of these filthy strongholds can be found dark shrines to the godly master that presides over king and ghoul alike – Nagash, the Great Necromancer.

Though the Flesh-eater curse brings delusions of nobility, it is they who are the scourge upon the civilised lands, they who are the monsters. When away from their masters, such creatures become feral and fierce, but now and then the veil of madness will lift, and these hideous creatures will take stock of their devolution in a moment of terrible clarity. Only then does the terrible nature of their fate sink in – and the cycle of madness begin anew.

Lord Pergrin drove his sword up to its hilt into the monster's stomach. It hissed and spat, filthy claws scrabbling on silver armour.

'You are a curse upon creation!' growled Pergrin, feeling nothing but disgust. With a boot, he heaved the dying beast off his blade, causing an arc of gore to spray out. Nearby, Pergrin's men-at-arms battled with cannibal beasts, his soldiers' tabards spattered with rancid blood.

'Show no mercy, men!' he screamed, charging once more. Somehow he had lost his blade, but it mattered not. He seized another creature. This close, he could see the naked terror in the thing's eyes as he wrapped his fingers around its neck.

'Please…' it gasped, but he was hardly listening. Not even the reflection of red eyes and fangs in his victim's gaze was enough to stop what came next.

Listen well to the tale of the Rot-skinned King and his darksome court. From the weft and weave of war he came, claws a-scrabbling. Alongside the king his lordly courtiers did prance, sniffing the air for morbid smells. What blade and axe had planted, hungry talons harvested for their king and his subjects. Reason, like a setting sun, faded from their eyes, replaced with endless madness.

THE SOULBLIGHT CURSE

The generals and kings of the undead nations are usually afflicted with the Soulblight curse. Having become vampires through the fell magic of the blood kiss, they are powerful beyond the dreams of men – yet though they consider themselves free to work their own agendas, they are in truth bound irredeemably to Nagash's plans.

The Soulblight vampires are the direct descendants of the first undead to bear the curse of eternal thirst. In their veins runs the taint of aeons long lost, the echo of an elixir that gave immortality, but at a terrible cost. The legacy of a civilisation that has long turned to dust, that curse lends eternal life to those that bear it, sustaining them far beyond their mortal span. It brings with it an unnatural resilience, an impossible strength, and a mind so sharp it can endure the aeons without being dimmed by madness or decrepitude. But the cost is high indeed – an insatiable thirst for blood that sees each Soulblight vampire become a ravening beast should he be starved of mortal vitae for too long.

Since those who bear it first walked the Mortal Realms the curse of vampirism has been spread to a hundred lineages and more. The Soulblight vampires, considering themselves something of an aristocracy, prefer to prey upon those they deem to have rich or even royal blood – they count a great many kings, queens and nobles amongst their ranks. To feed their unnatural appetites, they raise entire armies of undead, siring more vampires at need and marching to war so their kingdoms might forever run red with rivers of blood. Some keep their regal appearance, bedecked in the fine lacquered plate armour of the Blood Knights, or framed in the finery of a courtly coven. A Soulblight queen may go to war in an elaborate coiffure and ruffled dress, her handmaidens lounging around her as her throne is held aloft by flying spirits.

Other Soulblight vampires devolve over time until their appearance echoes the bestial nature of their soul, for their ancient curse, if improperly transferred, can warp bodies and minds alike. Those known as Vargheists are vampires who have lost the last shreds of their humanity and been reborn with the monstrous physiologies of bat-winged horrors. Regarded as brutish cousins by the vampiric nobility, they are tolerated for their sheer ferocity and hunting prowess. The Soulblight curse has an affinity with chiropteran forms; those bat-like beasts that have sampled the blood of a vampire are forever bound to his command – much as a prized falcon pecks grain from its master's hand. When the Soulblight vampires go to war en masse they are accompanied by Fell Bats – each with a wingspan yards across and eyes that can be seen glowing red as they prowl the darkness – and swarms of lesser creatures that flit and swarm in clouds thick enough to obscure the sun. A cloud of predatory shadows, the bats engulf their prey, bringing men and women down with a thousand tiny bites before the red feast begins in earnest.

Though the leaders of these vampiric hosts pretend to a rare refinement and prefer to sup from noble blood, they too have an animalistic savagery lurking beneath their fine appearances. When the red thirst overtakes them, they too will fall upon even the most filthy peon to slake their need for the hot, pulsing fluid that runs within his veins.

BEASTS OF THE GRAVE

Some vampires deliberately prey upon the great beasts of the realms, or resurrect their remains with dark magic, the unnatural power that runs in their blood binding the monstrous cadavers to their will. With skeletal limbs and talons the size of scimitars, these creatures kill remorselessly, catching their master's prey in their great jaws and gulping them down, only for their remains to spill from opened throats and vermin-infested stomachs.

No creature of flesh, bone and blood is beyond the power of necromancy. The most physically powerful of the creatures that answer the call of the Soulblight vampire is the Zombie Dragon, a towering monstrosity able to breathe a pestilent cloud so acrid it can strip flesh from bone. These creatures serve as attack beasts capable of bowling over an entire phalanx of armoured knights, but some amongst them are used as mounts for their vampiric masters, soaring high above the battlefield.

The Zombie Dragon's only true rival in terms of might is the Terrorgheist, an undead hell-bat of colossal size. The remnants of an ancient chiropteran race returned to a semblance of life, the Terrorgheists once fed on the gargantuan beasts of the realms, sucking their rich blood from their veins. Now this same hunger is magnified by the dark magic that animates their corpses. This beast is infamous for its chilling, deathly scream; once used to stun its prey as it swooped down to latch its maw onto neck or flank, it has become so supernaturally intense that the Terrorgheist can cause a man's heart to explode in his chest from the sonic onslaught. Even should this vile creature be slain by the blade of a true hero, its infested corpse collapses in on itself to disgorge hundreds of blood-sucking bats that cluster in close to eat their host's assailant alive.

THE NECROMANTIC HOSTS

For every lordly vampire or legendary Mortarch there are a hundred lesser Necromancers, ranging from corpse-pale sycophants of the undead court to the bitter hermits that skulk on the outskirts of society, banished by right-thinking folk for their repellent practices.

The outcast dabblers in morbid magic known as Necromancers all have their own reasons for taking the first steps on the path to damnation. Some seek revenge for some real or imagined slight, others strive for eternal life, but many simply wish to seize riches and wealth by raising armies of shambling cadavers and hurling them against their rivals until nothing but the spoils of war are left. Such individuals either sign their own death warrants – many of the flourishing civilisations of the Age of Sigmar hunt down and burn any who openly exhibit necromantic power – or instead damn themselves to an even worse fate as they come to the notice of those with the true power of undeath. The dark fate they walk towards holds them back not at all, for Necromancers usually skirt the edge of madness, little caring that the means they employ will ultimately lead them to eternal torment.

The energies of undeath weigh heavily on each student of the necromantic arts, rendering him a stooped and twisted figure with tattered rags draped across his bony frame. Sometimes the magic of death infects them completely and they cease to be truly living. Many ride grotesque carriages to war, drawn not by beasts of burden but reanimated cadavers. The most vaunted of their kind stand proud atop the strange mobile reliquaries known as Mortis Engines – borne aloft by a host of bound and howling spirits, these grim ancient artefacts have locked at their heart the bones of a once-powerful Necromancer whose material remains are still redolent with dark power. The Corpsemaster that rides this morbid and baroque construction can unlock the reliquary in times of need, allowing waves of baleful energy to bleed out to invigorate nearby undead even as they sap the life force from the still-living warriors nearby.

THE DEADWALKERS

To the Necromancer, no cost is too high in the pursuit of power, no act too base. The very idea they may have made a horrible mistake is buried as they delve ever deeper into the secrets of the grave. On the day of reckoning, they go to war at the head of whole armies of rotten, stinking corpses they have exhumed with the dark arts.

The most common of undead servants are the Deadwalkers, for every land in every realm has corpses buried in its soil. Each staggering cadaver is a cobbled-together nightmare of dead flesh, mouldering bone, rope, cloth, nesting vermin and rusted metal, all clad in the motley of the grave. These fell creatures are the least of all undead, with barely enough sentience to stagger moaning towards their prey. Without a nearby Necromancer or vampire to sustain them, they will likely fall apart. Conversely, because of their lowly status they are the easiest to raise from the grave – no energy need be expended to bind a stubborn spirit or empower an iron-hard frame. The strength of the Deadwalkers lies in their numbers, for even the most valorous knight can be brought low if enough black-fingered, splinter-nailed hands grab for his limbs and dig into the vital organs hidden beneath.

DEATHRATTLE ARMIES

The Deathrattle kingdoms are regions and sub-realms that have fallen to dust over the relentless march of passing millennia, yet have hung onto a grisly mockery of life. Skeletal and strange, they are animated by an undying malevolence that binds bone and fills marrow. Their rulers are hollow-eyed Wight Kings that stand tall and proud at the head of their tattered legions, despite the fact their flesh long ago rotted from their bones. These armoured lords wield great iron blades limed with witchfire – such ensorcelled weapons can take a hero's head from his neck with disturbing ease, for they are enchanted to deliver an executioner's blow with each well-aimed swing.

Unlike the shambling hordes of the Deadwalkers, or the mad frenzy of the Flesh-eater Courts, the Deathrattle armies fight in neatly ordered ranks with a discipline that few mortal armies can match. At the barrow king's side ride the long-decayed cavaliers known as Black Knights – once the princes, dukes and nobles of their kingdom, they still bear the faded remnants of fine mesh armour, sculpted plate and heraldic sigils that once spoke of untarnished nobility. Now they ride to war at the behest of undead fiends bent on bringing death to as many as possible. About the pitted armour of the Black Knight an icy wind howls, for the heart of each knight forever holds the frigid darkness of death.

The skeletal populations of the Deathrattle kingdoms are more than just warriors, for they are truly indefatigable in times of preparation as well as times of war. By their fleshless hands were the first and greatest cities of the Mortal Realms built – and by those same hands was the Great Black Pyramid raised, that edifice through which Nagash has brought a deathly apocalypse to the lands of men, duardin and aelf.

The lord of undeath, Nagash, is attended by his Mortarch lieutenants, his Soulblight vampire vassals, and the Nighthaunt hosts bound to his will. Together they are an unstoppable force.

195

Deathlords
Morghast Archai

Deathlords
Morghast Harbinger

◄ The barrows and dolmens of Shyish are stalked by the unquiet dead – the skeletal Deathrattle legions are led to battle by chilling Deathlord masters.

Arkhan the Black has iron-willed control over the numberless ranks of undead that form his master's legions.

The thunder of hooves shakes the parched earth as the Blood Knights drive their charge into the ranks of the living.

Deathlords
Mannfred, Mortarch of Night

Nighthaunt
Guardian of Souls

Nighthaunt
Grimghast Reaper

Nighthaunt
Chainrasp

Nighthaunt
Spirit Torment

Flesh-eater Courts
Crypt Flayer

Flesh-eater Courts
Crypt Infernal

The troglodytic Flesh-eater Courts are accompanied to war by massive Terrorgheists, bat-winged nightmares whose wretched shriek can cause an orruk to die of sheer fright.

Flesh-eater Courts
Crypt Horror

Flesh-eater Courts
Crypt Haunter

Flesh-eater Courts
Abhorrant Ghoul King

THE
FORCES OF
DESTRUCTION

The rampaging hordes of Destruction plunge headlong into battle at the slightest provocation. No subtlety or grand strategy lies behind their massed invasions – they are driven only by the primal need for violence. For them, the desire to crush, stamp, thump axe into flesh and tear the refined works of the civilised races into rubble and dust is all but overwhelming.

The forces of the orruks are nigh elemental in their aggression, whilst their grot, ogor and troggoth allies easily get caught up in the carnage and follow their green-skinned leaders into wars that will never end. Though they range in size and strength, from snotlings no bigger than a weasel to towering gargants that wield fallen oaks as weapons, they all feel the call of the brutal two-headed god Gorkamorka, and are all bound up in the same instinct – to batter at civilisation until no stone is left atop another.

The creatures of Destruction gladly take up their axes, maces and clubs against the scions of Chaos, for the armoured hosts of the Dark Gods have mercilessly and efficiently repressed the bestial tribes with centuries of carefully planned war. But as the Chaos hordes are driven back, and the God-King's pantheon unites once more to rebuild in the Age of Sigmar, it is all too likely that the forces of Destruction will attack the free cities just as often as they do the spined, corpse-adorned Dreadholds of Chaos. All they want is to crush, and when united under a powerful war leader, they have might and momentum enough to topple even Azyrheim itself.

IRONJAWZ

Crashing, clanking steel and guttural bellows announce the arrival of the Ironjaw warclans. These brutish orruks are the biggest and fiercest of all their kind. In a savage society where 'might makes right' is the only rule, their size and strength makes them the leaders of city-wrecking invasions in every realm.

For all their savagery, the Ironjawz are not stupid. They favour thick iron plates adorned with spikes and other 'urty bits, not only to protect them from the blades of the enemy when they crash into the midst of the foe, but also to ensure every kick, knee, shoulder barge and stomp hits home with flesh-mangling force. They usually command their grot lackeys to paint their armour the bright colours of their tribe, for there is nothing worse than committing a spectacular display of carnage that no one can see. Should the massacre be impressive enough, they may even earn a rumble of approval from Gorkamorka himself as he looks down from the tempestuous skies.

The largest portion of the Ironjaw tribes are known as Ardboys, marching to war in great throngs that are literally armed to the teeth with a variety of bashas and choppas. The larger Ironjawz are called Brutes. Keen to get to the front line as fast as possible, some will bully beasts into bearing them into battle, adding to their killing power. A common tactic is to batter a boar-like grunta into submission so often that it ceases its attempts to disembowel its would-be rider for a few moments. By jumping fully-armed atop these hideous boar creatures and steering them with jabs from their jagged knee plates, the Ironjawz force the foul-tempered monsters to become their steeds. A rampaging herd of pig-headed Gore-grunta cavalry can storm through even a shield wall of Stormcast Liberators. Their sheer mass in muscle and beaten iron means that, with sufficient run-up, they hit home with the force of an avalanche.

The fiercest of orruk war leaders are known as Megabosses, for the title of 'boss' hardly does them justice. Ten-foot tall killing machines that wield pig-iron axes heavy enough to fell a Ghorgon, these green-skinned terrors are famous for their explosions of apoplectic fury.

Each weighs a ton in his armour, and would likely break the back of a grunta should he try to ride one. Instead Megabosses go one step further and make the hulking beasts known as Maw-krushas their steeds, chaining themselves to the iron-hard scales of these thuggish half-drakes so they can ride to war upon their back and still have both hands free for when the killing starts. The combination proves all but unstoppable, for a Maw-krusha is so massive it considers even the ten-foot ogors of Ghur a light snack. The Megaboss rider roars in fierce elation as his steed bowls across the battlefield with a loping, gorilla-like charge – nothing is safe when a Maw-krusha is on the rampage. Capable of short bursts of flight when its prey tries to evade, the beast's giant fists can pound flat even the cavalry of Chaos, slamming down with the force of falling boulders as their crocodilian jaws gnash and bite. Small wonder that whole hosts of Ironjawz will follow a war leader powerful enough to bind such a creature to his service.

Ironjawz are more military-minded than other orruks, and their leaders will often exploit their race's tendency for tribal groupings in times of war. Each gathering of orruk Brutes is known as a mob – and rightly so, given their unruly and destructive behaviour. These mobs are gathered into groups of five around a particularly strong leader, each grouping known as a fist. There are many kinds of these groupings.

A Weirdfist, for example, will gather around one of the tribe's Weirdnob Shamans, the better to be near the rampant energies of Destruction he channels, whereas an Ardfist gathers around a Warchanter, the better to revel in the fierce greenskin battle songs and the invigorating energies of the Waaagh!. When any five fists gather together, the Ironjawz call the armoured throng a brawl.

This simple terminology, based around the notion of punching each other in the face, appeals to Ironjawz across the Mortal Realms – not least because many of them find counting higher than the fingers on their hands a rather confusing concept. Some say the largest Waaaghs! are so huge they need another set of numbers entirely. The fabled Megaboss Gordrakk, known as the Fist of Gork, has a Waaagh! so large he makes use of all the numbers up to ten – a formidable feat, for according to Ghur legend, 'seven ate nine'. In truth, the greenskins do not worry about counting as soon as their armoured throng reaches a critical mass of violence. When they have enough axes and mauls at their disposal to hack down an entire Sylvaneth Wargrove or smash apart a Dispossessed fortress through sheer brute force, the only thing the Ironjawz truly care about is the crashing tumult of violence itself.

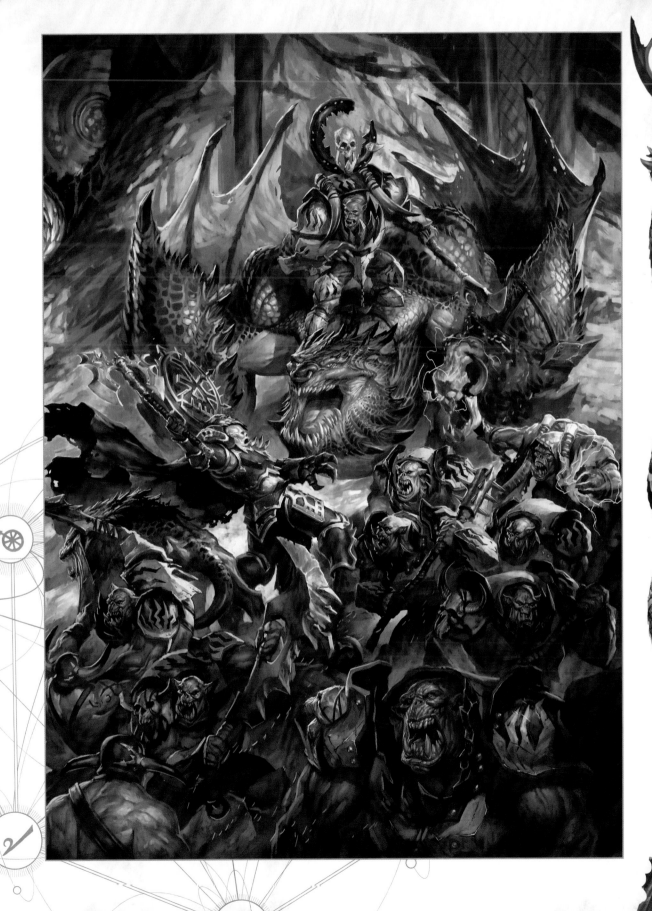

When orruks gather, the ground shakes, simmering violence boils over and the skies scream out in bestial rage. This is the power of the Waaagh! ready to unleash its brutal force upon the Mortal Realms. The stronger an orruk army is, the mightier this energy becomes – and none are stronger than the Ironjawz.

BONESPLITTERZ

Bonesplitterz are the most savage and unhinged of all orruk-kind. They are barbaric, going to war in little more than loincloths and warpaint, and using weapons of bone and flint. They believe their faith in Gorkamorka protects them – and, somehow, they are usually right.

In the heartlands of Ghur, the Bonesplitter tribes roam at will. They are orruks who have at some point been caught up in a bow wave of Waaagh! energy – and rather than feeling it disperse after the battle is done, they have instead taken it into themselves on a permanent basis. Now it rattles around their thick skulls, colouring every sensation and experience, and making them hopelessly addicted to the frenzied thrill of life-or-death combat.

The Bonesplitter tribes number in the thousands, each with their own variant creeds and totems, but all are united under the Great Green God they worship. They are not all

born into the brutish and simple lifestyle that occupies their every waking hour. Some, when visited by Waaagh! power, become consumed by it, and are soon banished from their tribe for talking to themselves or hitting other orruks in the face with rocks they claim to be blessed by Gork. They wander the Ghurish Hinterlands, following odd portents and signs until they eventually find one of the strange masked figures known as Wurrgog Prophets. These shamans oversee the aspirant's transformation into a Bonesplitter, a sacred warrior of the greenskin race whose mind is permanently aflame with the joyous violence of his two-headed god.

The Bonesplitterz are hunters of the giant beasts that stride across the lands, and will swarm like soldier ants around mountainous creatures that could squash any one of them with a single stray footstep. Yet it is the tribe that is to be feared more than the beast. Long ago, the Bonesplitterz perfected the method of driving their massive prey into a place of ambush, using flint arrows to take its eyes, and spears – which are so heavy they take two burly orruks to carry – to penetrate its leathery hide. When enough blows have been landed to bleed the beast to death, they hack the fallen creature apart, gorging on its remains – but their conquest does

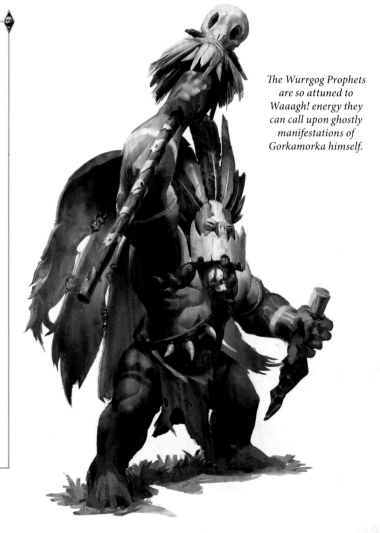

The Wurrgog Prophets are so attuned to Waaagh! energy they can call upon ghostly manifestations of Gorkamorka himself.

'*Gork's guts, Bogginz,*' said Slobba, chewing a salted gob-squig. '*Look at 'im go. What's he up to?*'
The cloaked shaman ahead, his heartwood mask fringed with brightly coloured feathers, stomped and twirled and howled with war-lust. Around him was a whole tribe of Bonesplitterz, all hooting and roaring like beasts on the hunt.
A loud whirring came from the south as a trio of duardin sky-ships crested the ridge, cannons blazing yellow-white. A triple boom, and Bonesplitter bodies flew high in explosions of blood and sand. The shaman pointed his wavin' stick, and a bolt of green lightning shot from his eyes to smash into the first of the duardin ships. The vessel trailed black smoke as it arced down to crash into the dunes, spilling armoured stunties left and right.
'*Ha,*' said Slobba, picking up his axe as the Bonesplitterz charged over the dunes. '*Better get moving, or there'll be none left for us!*'

not end there. They then strip the beast to its component parts, most of which they eat.

After gorging themselves on raw meat and drinking still-warm, frothing blood, they take great pride in adorning themselves with the creature's fangs, claws, jawbones and tusks. The piercing of a Bonesplitter's flesh is seen as a sacred act through which they inherit the bestial energy that once gave the creature strength, and in some cases they will enact that ritual in the midst of battle, delving into the chests of slain beasts so as to be the first to snap off its ribs and push them into their own muscular flesh.

In addition to the bones they harvest, the Bonesplitterz mark their bodies with crude tattoos depicting the creatures they have killed, the elemental forces they have overcome and the nature of the spirits they have consumed. As the spirit of the Waaagh! overcomes them, these tattoos seem to shift and thrash about with a life of their own – an unnerving sight even to a fellow greenskin. But for the Bonesplitterz, this is the power of Gorkamorka at work, granting them a measure of the god's belligerent might with which to defeat their enemies. They see omens in the strangest places; an oddly shaped cloud, for instance, might be interpreted by

a Wurrgog Prophet as a charging boar, instigating a war dance that sets a fire of aggression in his whole tribe. Countless battles have taken place, cities toppled, even empires brought low and continents crumbled into the sea because a Bonesplitter prophet witnessed one of these omens.

'Lads, Gorkamorka wants us ta smash up them shiny humies over there. No one orders us orruks around. Let's get em!'

BEASTCLAW RAIDERS

The freezing cold of the Everwinter follows the Beastclaw ogors wherever they roam. These massive, nomadic thugs are one with the blizzard – only the hardiest souls can survive the unnatural winter's coming, let alone the stampede of monster-riding gluttons that follows.

Some ogors ride to battle atop a beast known as a Mournfang – a thick-skulled, bad-tempered monster. Rider and steed have much in common.

A natural cycle of the seasons comes to every realm other than Aqshy, just as the false sun of Hysh glides into the sky each day. Some lapse into long and hostile winters, but even the most bitingly cold seasons are nothing next to the phenomenon that follows the Beastclaw Raiders. The Everwinter, as it is called, is a supernatural blizzard that roams the lands much in the manner of a vast hurricane, freezing the ground to ice-hard permafrost and turning those caught in its grip to icicle-encrusted statues. Legend has it that the great blizzard is drawn to the Beastclaw ogors due to a terrible curse laid upon them by Gorkamorka himself, and that they are driven before it as much as they bring it with them. The Beastclaw Raiders may hold the occasional feast in caves or chasms after a successful hunt or beast-cull, but they can never truly rest, never call a place their home. If they stay in one location too long even they will become frozen and inert as statues, consumed by the Everwinter's arctic wrath.

Each Beastclaw ogor is a looming mountain of hunger and ill temper. Such is their strength that they can crush an orruk's skull with one meaty hand, and their stocky but muscular physiques are so doughty they wear little in the way of armour for protection. Inured to winter, they can ride out the coldest weather in nothing more than scraps of fur. Their sheer hardiness makes them formidable opponents, but it is the bestial monsters they ride that make them an all but unstoppable force. With battering clubs and bloody displays of dominance, the Beastclaw Raiders bully the creatures of the Everwinter into their service as steeds, beasts of burden, hunting packs and savage allies that feast alongside them when the meat-harvest is done.

Beastclaw tribes are known as Alfrostuns. These are wandering

209

armies led by the oldest and most powerful ogor of each nomadic tribe, known as the Frostlord. Under the command of this hunter chieftain are the packs of hulking Mournfang riders that form his heavy cavalry, each mounted atop an aggressive beast of muscle and hair with tusks as long as a horse. At the fore of each tribe are the cunning Icebrow Hunters, expert trackers that make use of Frost Sabres, stealthy leonine cave-beasts with jutting teeth that can open a man's torso from belly to throat. Icebrow Hunters and Frost Sabres range ahead of the tribe in hunting packs known as Skals, seeking out their prey and guiding the Alfrostun to its next gory feast. During times of war, they scout the battlefield undetected, attacking from the least expected quarter when battle is joined.

While the Skals roam ahead of the Alfrostun, the white-furred beasts known as Icefall Yhetees lope in its wake. Drawn to the Alfrostun's supernatural cold and the promise of prey, the Yhetees are completely

at home in the slate-grey gloom of the storm. They are a degenerate race of loping, simian snow-fiends that wear the skulls of their prey in their matted hair; so attuned to the Everwinter have they become that they are surrounded by an aura of crippling cold.

Most fearsome of all the Alfrostun's beasts are the steeds of the Frostlords and their Huskard lieutenants, sometimes also ridden by ogors high in their favour. Thundertusks, elephantine creatures that exude cold, are able to belch forth spheres of ice that slam into the enemy in a burst of magic, freezing the foe to death even before their riders have brought their giant, beast-killing spears and jagged harpoons to bear. More terrifying still are the Stonehorns, massive creatures of rage and raw bestial power whose supernatural skeletons are not made of bone, but rock. To face the charge of such a beast is to stand before a living battering ram that can pulverise the wall of a Dreadhold in a single thunderous charge.

'*I'd like to see the bastards try!' laughed Mannis, sending another crossbow bolt winging over the moat. 'There's a reason they call this place the Keep Impregnable.'*

Far below, a trail of nomadic ogors approached. From this high up, they were not so bad.

'I got one!' shouted Vaskia, pointing at an arrow sticking from the blubbery chest of an ogor beast rider. The ogor plucked it out and used it as a toothpick as his riding beast breathed out an icy cloud that rolled over the moat. Mannis snorted as it dissipated harmlessly, but his smug smile fell when the trio of horned monstrosities charged headlong across the now-frozen moat.

With a tremendous crash, the wall came tumbling down. The screams of the wounded grew louder as the ogors burst through, roaring in triumph.

Mannis turned and ran.

THE SAVAGE TRIBES

The tribes of Destruction that infest the Mortal Realms are without number. Though they too suffered under the iron dominion of Chaos, they have gathered their strength once more, amassing under the promise of a Waaagh! without end that will sweep all before it.

GREENSKINZ

The greenskin mentality is so simple even a brain-dead squig can understand it. Bigger is better – and the biggest of the lot gets to be the boss. This simple truth underlines every aspect of orruk society. Those who challenge it usually have the concept beaten into them so thoroughly they do not forget again. If one of their number is sufficiently large and ferocious, thousands, if not millions, of his fellows will flock to his banner. Such a Warboss is capable of great feats of strength, such as beating the living daylights out of a mighty Wyvern to make the monster fall in and behave for a bit. This beast he will ride into battle, the greenskins that follow him in no doubt of his 'ardness. Whether slogging it on foot, clinging to the backs of ferocious boars or gripping the rails of crude chariots, they charge forward in his wake, waving their choppas and roaring their battle-lust. All greenskins like a good scrap, and will seek out a worthy foe purely for the pleasure of fighting. Their crusades are so fierce the greenskin word that describes them can only be pronounced at deafening volume – *Waaagh!*. The Great Shamans of the orruk tribes channel the magically charged Waaagh! energy as the greenskins go to war, unleashing it upon their foes with devastating effect.

Although they love nothing more than a brawl, greenskins know how to direct their aggression strategically when they need to. Gorkamorka, the psychopathic deity worshipped by the greenskins and their savage kin, is a two-fold god. One side is that of Gork, brutal but cunning, whereas the other – his brother Mork – is cunning but brutal. Underhand sneakiness, or *finkin'* as it is sometimes known, plays a significant part in greenskin society. No matter how big and brutal he may be, an orruk will not get far without a little cunning.

GITMOB GROTS

It is quite possible that a greenskin who displays enough cruelty and vicious intelligence will bind others to his side, no matter his stature. Even a common grot can rise to rulership over an entire Waaagh! if he is stabby enough. Though they would have to stand on tiptoe to come level with a man's shoulder, their talent for skulduggery and fighting dirty can set their reputation in stone. Gitmobs are full of the most unscrupulous and mean-spirited goblinoids in all the Mortal Realms, fond of playing lethal practical jokes and kicking their mates when they are down, just for the spite of it. They devise primitive but effective ways of bringing down larger foes from afar, their favourites being the ramshackle war machines they construct. They'll use anything for ammunition in these madcap creations, from gigantic spears to massive boulders, even loading their fellow grots into catapults to propel them across the battlefield.

MOONCLAN GROTS

Moonclan grots are subterranean creatures even smaller than the common grot, but with a deadly cunning. Worshipping Gorkamorka in the form of a celestial body they call the Bad Moon, they hate the bright light of day more than anything. They venture forth at night, and even then wear long black robes to cover their skin, usually complemented by tall pointy hats to give the illusion of size. They breed like fungus in the dark; to see an entire clan boiling up from its subterranean lairs is to witness stream upon stream of black-robed bodies converging until the land turns dark. Their fondness for dank underground lairs is not all they have in common with their skaven rivals – though individually weak as pig sweat, they find a kind of rebellious courage in numbers, and can be very dangerous en masse. They typically bring with them demented, ball-and-chain-wielding Fanatics and mushroom-addled Shamans, the better to spring nasty surprises on their enemies. The strangest, yet arguably most effective, of all their practices is their use of the subterranean creatures known as squigs – ravenous balls of muscle, claw and tooth that are little more than mouths on legs, with a voracious appetite to match.

SPIDERFANG GROTS

Some grot tribes have made their homes in the sweltering jungles and forests of the realms, those places so overgrown and poisonous that larger humanoids cannot pass through. Sharing their cobweb-strewn arboreal homes with innumerable insects and arachnids, they worship Gorkamorka in the form of a many-eyed spider god. By partaking in the poisons of their spider allies and becoming one with them on a spiritual level, they have slowly been changed by the magic that thrums through their tangled domains. Some boast multiple sets of eyes, extra limbs, or poisonous bites as a result of their devotion – others ride to war atop scuttling spiders the size of ponies. The most favoured worship at a living altar – a colossal creature known as an Arachnarok Spider. Should the massive arachnid neglect to kill them for long enough, they may even build a cobwebby howdah upon its back and cling onto it as it thunders into battle.

Much like their more common cousins, that which the Spiderfang grots lack in physical strength they more than make up for in numbers. When they attack, it is in a scuttling host that crawls up and over terrain as easily as flat ground, the grot riders hollering and hooting as they surge towards their next meal.

GUTBUSTERS

Ogors are a hardy species, half again as tall as orruks and with strength enough to batter them to a pulp if angered. Gutbuster ogors are obsessed with two things – eating and fighting, and all too often the first follows directly after the second. Unlike their allies they are not green of skin, but their coarse and savage lifestyle has many similarities, making them natural allies of the orruk and grot races. They harness some of the fiercest native creatures ever to roam Ghur's Hinterlands as beasts of burden and steeds alike. Driven by an insatiable gluttony, ultimately they answer to their stomachs alone. Even their selection of weapons is influenced by their desperate need to eat. Clubs and maces are preferred for their ability to tenderise and bludgeon to death the meal-to-be without spilling too much of its juicy vital fluids in the process; even those scimitars and swords used by the Gutbusters are carefully blunted to a dull edge the night before each battle. An ogor trusts his club, and will eat it only in the direst circumstances.

It is well that these creatures are so strong, for their tribes are nomadic, and they take with them everything they own. Those in their path will not only be stomped flat and greedily devoured, but their corpses eagerly robbed to boot. Though ogors are far happier destroying things than creating them, they have a certain flair for repurposing the smashed remnants of the settlements they crush. They may be thick as two short planks, but they have enough nous to nail them together and beat their prey to death with the result. The grots that follow the Gutbusters around are even better at improvisation, creating shonky artillery pieces strapped to Rhinox beasts to support the Gutbusters in battle. Scavenging from the ruins of each ogor attack and running errands in return, they have a symbiotic relationship with the hulking ogors that protect them, and are hardly ever eaten as a result.

MANEATERS

Ogors are possessed of a great wanderlust. This is an evolutionary need as much as anything, for a tribe of ogors is so ravenous that if it stays in one place for too long it will devour every living thing within a hundred miles. The most enterprising and independent will take off on their own, travelling far and wide and plying their trade as mercenaries. These Maneaters, as they are known, do not have cultural artefacts of their own, beyond the tools of their primitive tribal lifestyle, but they willingly adopt those of the civilisations around them, collecting the trophies and trappings of those that hire them until they settle on a new identity. Often taking important-sounding names such as Garodd Greathammer, the Meat Man of New Midasheim and Thragg the Kingiest, veteran Maneaters take every opportunity to boast at length about how amazing they are, telling inflated stories of their own prowess to any who will listen.

FIREBELLIES

Firebellies are priests of the volcano. Primitive yet filled with fiery conviction, they believe that long ago Gorkamorka ate the sun, but it gave him such bad heartburn that he later vomited it back up again – and hence the cycle of day and night was born. They echo this divine miracle by consuming the hottest substances they can find, starting as youngsters with the sometimes-lethal firegheist chilli and working through the fiercest of Aqshian curries cooked to red-hot, scalding temperatures before finally consuming lava from the volcano itself. If they survive this, they take the fire into themselves, able to breath gouts of flame and swathe themselves with raging firestorms at will.

TROGGOTHS

Destruction armies of all stripes often have dim-witted but powerful troggoths along with them. Found in the dank and forsaken places of the realms, these creatures have a number of variant offshoots, but as yet no scholar has been foolish enough to try to catalogue them all. Each troggoth is a comically ugly specimen able to regenerate the most hideous of wounds, and being possessed of strength enough to rip a warhorse into chunks with its bare hands, makes for a valuable beast of war if it manages to shamble in the right direction. Some can vomit the acidic contents of their stomachs over great distances, whilst others exude stinking grease, can breathe underwater, or produce exhalations foul enough to stun a man into a comatose state.

ALEGUZZLER GARGANTS

The towering oafs known as gargants are present in every realm. Some myths claim them to be the descendants of the World Titan, Behemat, having crawled out of his mouth after he was knocked unconscious by a blow from Sigmar's hammer. Others say gargants are the remnants of the first races to have lived in the Mortal Realms; that long ago they had fine minds as well as strong bodies, and by their hands were the monolithic wonders of the realms hewn from bare rock. Whatever the truth, they are little more than ale-sodden gluttons in the present day. They raid and pillage at will, stamping flat any who try to stop them. Although they can be bargained with if offered enough livestock and barrels of ale, it will not be long before they are back on the drunken rampage once more. The best a prospective employer can hope for is to guide them in the right direction and hope they do more harm to the enemy than to their allies – but when a gargant's clubbing, stamping attack gets into full swing, it is easy enough to see why so many take the risk.

Gordrakk, the Fist of Gork, leads a horde of Destruction across the Hinterlands of Ghur. With him come not only Ironjawz but Beastclaw ogors and even a clan of Aleguzzler gargants.

Beastclaw Raiders
Frost Sabre

Beastclaw Raiders
Icebrow Hunter

Beastclaw Raiders
Icefall Yhetee

*An Alfrostun of Beastclaw Raiders attacks as a devastating avalanche of iron-hard muscle, thick hair and bad temper –
when joined in battle by their Ironjawz allies, they fight all the harder to show that the biggest fighter is still the best.*

Ironjawz
Weirdnob Shaman

Ironjawz
Warchanter

Ironjawz
Brute

Bonesplitterz
Wurrgog Prophet

Bonesplitterz
Savage Big Boss

Bonesplitterz
Savage Boarboy Maniak

Bonesplitterz
Savage Orruk

Bonesplitterz
Savage Big Stabbas

The primal spirit of the Waaagh! drives the greenskin hordes deep into the heartlands of Nagash. Even the dead must fear their wrath.

Aleguzzler Gargant

The Arachnarok Spider is worshipped as a god by the mad-eyed greenskins that ride on its cobwebbed howdah.

From the forsaken forests of the Mortal Realms come savage tribes of Spiderfang grots.

Moonclan Grots swarm from their dank caves at night, squigs, troggoths and gargants amongst their maniac hordes.

Troggoths are repulsive creatures, able to vomit acid, regenerate wounds and crush armour with devastating blows.

FIRE & THUNDER

BATTLES IN THE
MORTAL REALMS

Welcome to Fire & Thunder, a guide to playing games in the Mortal Realms and the key to a treasure chest of different ways to enjoy Warhammer Age of Sigmar. Packed with inspiration and brimming with battles, this section of the book is an essential resource for gaming and glory.

Fire & Thunder provides the core game rules for Warhammer Age of Sigmar. These rules explain how you can use your collection of Citadel Miniatures to fight exciting battles set in the Mortal Realms. They show you how to organise an army, set up a game, move and fight with the warriors under your command, and what you need to do to lead your army to ultimate victory!

After the core rules, you will find other sections that expand upon them to support an array of gaming styles for all hobbyists, from casual collectors who play occasional games with their friends to veteran warriors who spend years honing their forces for competitive tournaments.

Everyone enjoys the Games Workshop hobby in different ways. Some hobbyists are avid painters who collect stunning centrepiece models, and others spend their hobby time reading the background and learning the lore. For some, though, using their collections to play games against like-minded opponents across the tabletop is at the very heart of their hobby. If you fall into this latter category, then this section of the book is for you, as it focuses on that aspect of the hobby where the miniatures meet the battlefield.

It is important to note that all of the rules presented in this book are optional; they can be used, or not, in any combination that you and your tabletop adversaries find enjoyable. To this end, Fire & Thunder has been designed to work as a gaming toolbox, providing many options to get the dice rolling and play games with your collection of Citadel Miniatures. For instance, there are allegiance abilities for armies of models that all have the same keyword, instructions for several different types of campaign, plenty of battleplans, battle reports for example games and much, much more.

INTRODUCTION

This section is about exploring the fantastical, battle-filled Mortal Realms in your tabletop games. You'll find a number of battleplans to try out and ideas to inspire you, including a desperate siege, a stealthy raid and an epic Chaos incursion, as well as the core rules you need to get started.

Whether you are simply trying to beat your friend's army or aiming to recreate the many challenges that Vandus Hammerhand had to overcome to retrieve Ghal Maraz, you are playing a Warhammer Age of Sigmar battle. From small skirmishes to clashes between massive invading armies, battles range in size as well as complexity. You can play a one-off game that lasts for an hour, or several interconnected battles in an ongoing campaign involving dozens of players, or anything in between. Tabletop commanders can test their tactical skills, fight a series of linked games or recreate some of the epic conflicts from the Mortal Realms' long and storied history.

This section of the book is split into different chapters, each one dealing with an aspect of setting up and playing your own battles. There are many examples of the different ways to play, and plenty of battleplans to try out. As you read through the section you'll quickly realise that there are few hard and fast rules that you have to follow to fight a Warhammer Age of Sigmar battle.

The creative freedom this offers is one of Warhammer Age of Sigmar's greatest strengths. This section only begins to scratch the surface of the options available to you when fighting battles in the Mortal Realms.

THE CORE RULES

Whatever type of game you want to play, you'll need the core rules, which form the foundation of playing games of Warhammer Age of Sigmar. These rules show you how your models move, use magic spells, shoot their ranged weapons, charge into battle, and fight with their close-range weapons – basically everything you need to start waging miniature war! They provide you with the key mechanics for everything from battle-hardened infantry to gigantic monsters, allowing you to

quickly build up from your first few simple games to grand spectacles of large-scale conflict.

The core rules also provide plenty of helpful clarifications, hints and tips, along with a starting battleplan (the suitably titled 'First Blood'), which serves as a perfect introduction to gaming in the Mortal Realms.

Wherever you go with your games, the core rules will provide the basics you need to get started, and will be your constant gaming companion. Before trying out too many of the diverse options offered by Warhammer Age of Sigmar, it's recommended that you fight a few battles using just these rules. This will act as a great grounding for what comes afterwards.

THREE WAYS TO PLAY

At its heart, Warhammer Age of Sigmar is a game that pits one army of warriors against another in a tabletop conflict to the death. Beyond that core premise, it is a hobby of vast and thrilling variation that allows you to depict everything from lightning-fast assaults to continent-spanning wars of conquest. These different ways of playing are covered in more depth in the three sections that follow the core rules: Open Play (pg 264), Narrative Play (pg 278) and Matched Play (pg 306).

Open play is the least restrictive type of gaming because it can be as simple or as complex as you like. Just pick any Citadel Miniatures in your collection and start playing. Narrative play is based around the stories of the Mortal Realms, either those you can read in our books or those you write yourself. Narrative play can involve one-off games fought between mighty heroes, or multiple games linked in a campaign. Matched play allows for armies to be tested against each other under conditions that give no particular advantage to either side, to see which army is strongest and which general is canniest.

You can choose to introduce any of the rules from these sections to your games, or even combine several different aspects in a single game. All of these optional mechanics build upon the core rules – they add to or provide variation on these rules, rather than requiring you to learn a whole new game system! From huge multiplayer battles and sprawling sieges, to campaigns fought over strange magical landscapes, these sections will provide you with exciting new gaming experiences to suit whatever type of game you want to play.

If all the involved players agree, you can take your games in any direction you like. If you and your gaming group want to run a weekend-long tournament with balanced forces using some Realm of Battle rules that you have made up yourselves based on a region of the Mortal Realms that inspires you, do that! If you want to tell a story of epic conquest with your games, where your progress is recorded on a map, and each location you control grants your army special magical abilities, then that's the way to go – you can use any of the maps published in Warhammer Age of Sigmar books, or you can draw your own. Whether you've just picked up your first

Start Collecting! box or are dusting off a vintage collection from days long past, the open, narrative and matched play sections are here to help you find your favourite way of playing, and give you the tools to bring the Mortal Realms to life on the tabletop.

The different ways to combine the rules in this book are practically endless, and this flexible system ensures that, whether you are just getting started or have decades of experience, you can find a style of play that suits you. These styles are fluid, and their component parts can often be used together depending on what you are trying to achieve. There is no right or wrong way to

play Warhammer Age of Sigmar, so long as everyone adheres to the Most Important Rule. We're all here to have fun, after all!

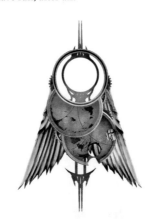

THE MOST IMPORTANT RULE
In a game as detailed and wide-ranging as Warhammer Age of Sigmar, there may be times when you are not sure exactly how to resolve a situation that has come up during play. When this happens, have a quick chat with your opponent and apply the solution that makes the most sense to you both (or seems the most fun!). If no single solution presents itself, both of you should roll a dice, and whoever rolls higher gets to choose what happens. Then you can get on with the fighting!

Each game of Warhammer Age of Sigmar is a chance to field your Citadel Miniatures on a fantastical battlefield, whether to tell a rousing story, to pit your wits against one another, or purely for the fun and spectacle of the experience.

THE CORE RULES

Prepare to enter a world of war and death, of violence, nobility and madness. You will take command of a force of mighty warriors, monsters and siege engines and do battle in strange and sorcerous realms, unleashing powerful magic, darkening the skies with arrows, and crushing your enemies in bloody combat.

The following rules explain how to play a game of Warhammer Age of Sigmar. First, you must prepare the battlefield and muster an army of Citadel Miniatures. The battle is then fought in a series of battle rounds, where each player takes a turn to move and fight with their army.

BATTLEPLANS

Before fighting a battle, you must pick a battleplan to use. The battleplan will tell you how to set up the battlefield, where each army will be set up, any special rules that apply to the battle, and (most importantly!) what you need to do in order to win. You can find more about battleplans on page 236.

WARSCROLLS

The Citadel Miniatures in Warhammer Age of Sigmar are referred to as 'models'. Each model has a warscroll, which provides all of the information needed for using the model in a game. You can find more about how to use warscrolls on pages 238-239. Some models can be included in formations known as warscroll battalions, which provide additional rules. You can find more about warscroll battalions on page 240.

THE ARMIES

Each player in a game of Warhammer Age of Sigmar commands an army. Armies can be as big as you like, and you can use as many models from your collection as you wish. The more models you decide to use, the longer the game will last and the more exciting it will be. Typically, a game with around a hundred miniatures per side will last for about an evening.

Models from your army are referred to as friendly models, and models from the opposing army are referred to as enemy models. If a rule states

that it affects 'models' or 'units' without specifying that they are friendly or enemy, then it affects all models, friend or foe.

UNITS

Models fight in units. A unit can have one or more models, but cannot include models that use different warscrolls. A unit must be set up and finish any sort of move as a single group, with all models within 1" horizontally, and 6" vertically, of at least one other model from their unit.

If a unit is split up at the end of a turn, models must be removed from the unit until only a single group of models remains in play (see Split Units on page 230).

Sometimes there will not be enough room to set up all of the models from a unit. When this is the case, any models that cannot be set up are considered to have been slain.

TOOLS OF WAR

In order to fight a battle you will require a ruler or tape measure (to measure distances) and some dice. Warhammer Age of Sigmar uses six-sided dice (sometimes abbreviated to D6). Some rules refer to 2D6, 3D6 and so on – in such cases, roll that many dice and add the results together. If a rule requires you to roll a D3, roll a dice and halve the total, rounding up. If a rule requires a dice roll of, for example, 3 or more, this is often abbreviated to 3+.

RE-ROLLS

Some rules allow you to re-roll a dice roll, which means you get to roll some or all of the dice again. If a rule allows you to re-roll a result that was made by adding several dice together (e.g. 2D6, 3D6 etc.) then, unless otherwise stated, you must roll all of those dice again. You can never re-roll a dice more than once, and re-rolls happen before modifiers to the roll (if any) are applied. Rules that refer to the result of an 'unmodified' dice roll are referring to the result after any re-rolls but before any modifiers are applied.

ROLL-OFFS

Sometimes a rule may require the players to make a roll-off. When this is the case, each of the players rolls a dice, and whoever rolls highest wins the roll-off. If there is a tie for the highest roll, make the roll-off again. Neither player is allowed to re-roll or modify any of the dice when making a roll-off.

MEASURING DISTANCES

Distances in Warhammer Age of Sigmar are measured in inches ("), between the closest points of the bases of the models you're measuring to and from. If a model does not have a base, measure to and from the closest point of that model instead.

When measuring the distance between units, always use the closest model from each unit to measure how far apart the units are. So, for example, a unit is within 12" of another unit as long as any model from one unit is 12" or less from any model from the other unit. You can measure distances whenever you wish.

THE BATTLEFIELD

All games of Warhammer Age of Sigmar are fought upon a battlefield. This can be any flat surface upon which the models can stand – for example a dining table or the floor – and can be any size or shape provided it's at least 2-foot square.

The scenery found on a battlefield is represented by models from the Warhammer Age of Sigmar range. These models are called terrain features to differentiate them from the models that make up an army. Terrain features are set up on the battlefield before the battle begins and the armies deploy.

It doesn't really matter how many terrain features you use in your battles. A good guide is to have at least one terrain feature for every 2-foot square area of the battlefield. The more terrain features your armies have to navigate around, the more interesting and dynamic your battles will be.

THE BATTLE BEGINS

With the battleplan chosen and the battlefield prepared, you are now ready to deploy your armies ready for the coming conflict. Before the battle begins you must set up your army, choose your general, and use any pre-battle abilities.

SET UP ARMIES

Details of how the armies should be set up can be found in the battleplan you are using.

Sometimes an ability will allow a unit to be set up in a location other than the battlefield; when this is the case, tell your opponent where the unit is set up and keep it to one side rather than placing it directly on the battlefield. It will arrive later as a reserve unit as described on the right.

CHOOSE GENERAL

Once you have finished setting up all of your units, nominate one of the models you set up to be your general. If your general is slain, pick another model from your army to become your new general.

RESERVES

Reserves are units that are part of your army, but which have an ability that allows you to set them up in a location other than on the battlefield and deploy them later once the battle has begun. Setting up a reserve unit is not considered a move for the unit, but it may restrict a unit's ability to move in the same turn. Any reserves that have not been set up when the battle ends are treated as if they had been slain when you are working out which side won the battle.

KEYWORDS

Every warscroll includes a list of keywords that apply to the model the warscroll describes. Keywords appear in **KEYWORD BOLD** in the rules.

Keywords are sometimes linked to (or 'tagged' by) a rule. For example, a rule might say that it applies to 'all **ORDER** models'. This means that it would apply to models that have the **ORDER** keyword on their warscroll.

All models from the same unit must be within 1" of at least one other model from their unit. The leader of this unit of Stormcast Eternals could not be placed in the position shown above, as he would be more than 1" away from any other model from his unit.

BATTLE ROUNDS

The maelstrom of battle begins! Units of bellowing warriors charge and counter-charge, hacking at the foe with axe and sword. The ground trembles under the hooves of galloping cavalry. Archers unleash barrages of bolts at the foe, and monstrous creatures crush their enemies with mighty blows from their taloned fists.

A Warhammer Age of Sigmar battle is fought in a series of battle rounds, each of which is split into two turns – one for each player. Once the first player has finished their turn, the second player takes theirs. Once the second player has also finished, the battle round is over and a new one begins.

At the start of each battle round, the players must roll off, and the winner decides who takes the first turn. If the roll-off is a tie, then the player who went first in the last battle round can choose who goes first in this one, but if it is the first battle round, the player that finished setting up their army first chooses who has the first turn.

TURN SEQUENCE

1 Hero Phase
Cast spells and use heroic abilities.

2 Movement Phase
Move units across the battlefield.

3 Shooting Phase
Attack with missile weapons.

4 Charge Phase
Charge units into combat.

5 Combat Phase
Pile in and attack with melee weapons.

6 Battleshock Phase
Test the resolve of depleted units.

1 HERO PHASE

Many of the abilities found on warscrolls are used in your hero phase. In addition, **WIZARDS** in your army can cast spells in this phase (pg 233).

COMMAND ABILITIES

If you have any **HEROES** in your army, you can use command abilities. Some command abilities are available to all armies, like the three on the right, while others are specific to certain models and appear on their warscroll. Some of these command abilities can only be used if that model is your general; when this is the case, it will be noted in the rules for the command ability.

In order to use any command ability you must spend 1 command point. You start the battle with 1 command point for each warscroll battalion you have in your army. In addition, you receive 1 command point at the start of each of your hero phases. You can use the same command ability several times in the same phase as long as you have enough command points to do so. Any command points you do not use can be used in a future turn. A command ability will usually specify when it is used; if it does not, it is used in your hero phase.

At the Double: You can use this command ability after you make a run roll for a friendly unit that is within 6" of a friendly **HERO**, or 12" of a friendly **HERO** that is a general. If you do so, the run roll is treated as being a 6.

Forward to Victory: You can use this command ability after you make a charge roll for a friendly unit that is within 6" of a friendly **HERO**, or 12" of a friendly **HERO** that is a general. If you do so, re-roll the charge roll.

Inspiring Presence: You can use this command ability at the start of the battleshock phase. If you do so, pick a friendly unit that is within 6" of friendly **HERO**, or 12" of a friendly **HERO** that is a general. That unit does not have to take battleshock tests in that phase.

② MOVEMENT PHASE

Start your movement phase by picking one of your units and moving each model in that unit until you've moved all the models you want to. You can then pick another unit to move, until you have moved as many of your units as you wish. No unit can be moved more than once in each movement phase.

MOVEMENT

You can change the position of a model on the battlefield by making a move with the model. Models can be moved in the movement phase, the charge phase and the combat phase, and some abilities may allow a model to make a move in other phases too.

Whenever you move a model, it can be moved in any direction or combination of directions, but cannot be moved across other models or their bases, nor can it cross the edge of the battlefield. You can pivot the model at the end of the move so that it is facing in any direction. The distance a model moves is measured using the part of the model's base that moves furthest from its starting position (including pivoting). If the model has no base, measure the move using whichever part of the model moves furthest from its starting position.

Remember that a unit must finish any type of move as a single group, with all models within 1" horizontally, and 6" vertically, of at least one other model from their unit. If this is impossible, then the move cannot be made.

MOVING OVER TERRAIN

Unless stated otherwise, a model can be moved over a terrain feature but not through it (so models can't move through a wall, or pass through a tree, but can climb up or over them).

A model can be moved vertically in order to climb or cross a terrain feature, counting the vertical distance up and/or down as part of its move.

NORMAL MOVES

Moves made in the movement phase are referred to as normal moves, to differentiate them from charge moves (made in the charge phase) and pile-in moves (made in the combat phase). A model making a normal move can move a distance in inches equal to or less than the Move characteristic shown on its warscroll.

ENEMY UNITS AND RETREATS

When you make a normal move for a model, no part of the move can be within 3" of an enemy unit.

Units starting a normal move within 3" of an enemy unit can either remain stationary or retreat. If a unit retreats, it can move within 3" of an enemy, but must end the move more than 3" from all enemy units. Models in a unit that retreats can't shoot or charge later in the same turn.

RUNNING

When you pick a unit to make a normal move, you can declare that it will run. Make a run roll for the unit by rolling a dice. Add the result of the run roll to the Move characteristic of all models in the unit for that movement phase. The unit can then move up to that distance in inches. Models in a unit that runs can't shoot or charge later in the same turn.

FLYING

If the warscroll for a model says that the model can fly, it can pass across models and terrain features as if they were not there when it makes any type of move. Any vertical distance up and/or down is ignored when measuring a flying model's move. It cannot finish the move on top of another model.

The Lord-Arcanum has a Move characteristic of 12". It moves 4" to reach a low wall that is 2" high. It will need 4" of movement to cross the wall (2" up and 2" down), leaving it with a maximum of 4" of movement on the other side.

3 SHOOTING PHASE

In your shooting phase, you can shoot with models armed with missile weapons. Pick one of your units. Each model in the unit attacks with all of the missile weapons it is armed with (see Attacking, opposite). Remember that models that have run or retreated cannot shoot in the same turn. After all models in the unit have shot, you can choose another unit to shoot with, until all units that you want to shoot with have done so.

ENEMY UNITS

A unit can shoot when it is within 3" of the enemy, but if it does so it can only target enemy units that are within 3" of it with its shooting attacks. A unit can shoot at an enemy unit that is within 3" of another friendly unit without penalty.

LOOK OUT, SIR!

You must subtract 1 from hit rolls made for missile weapons if the target of the attack is an enemy **HERO** that is within 3" of an enemy unit that has 3 or more models. The Look Out, Sir! rule does not apply if the target **HERO** is a **MONSTER**.

4 CHARGE PHASE

Any of your units within 12" of the enemy in your charge phase can attempt to make a charge move. Pick an eligible unit and make a charge roll for it by rolling 2D6. Each model in the unit can move a number of inches equal to the charge roll. You cannot make a charge move with a unit that has run or retreated earlier in the turn, or with a unit that is within 3" of an enemy unit.

The first model you move from a unit making a charge move must finish the move within ½" of an enemy model (you do not have to pick the target for the charge before making the charge roll). If that's impossible, or you decide not to make the charge move, the charge fails and no models in the unit can move in this phase.

Once all models in one unit have made their charge moves, you can pick another eligible unit to make a charge attempt, until all units that you want to make charge attempts have done so.

5 COMBAT PHASE

In the combat phase, the players take it in turn to pick units to fight with, starting with the player whose turn is taking place.

When it is your turn, you must either pick an eligible unit to fight with, or pass (note that you cannot pass if there is an eligible unit from your army that can fight). A unit is eligible to fight if it is within 3" of an enemy unit, or if it made a charge move in the same turn. No unit can fight more than once in each combat phase.

If you pick a unit to fight, it first piles in, and then the models in the unit must attack.

If you pass, you do nothing, and the option to fight or pass goes back to your opponent. If both players pass in succession, the combat phase ends.

PILING IN

A unit can make a pile-in move if it is within 3" of an enemy unit or has made a charge move in the same turn. If this is the case, you can move each model in the unit up to 3". Each model must finish its pile-in move at least as close to the nearest enemy model as it was at the start of the move.

FIGHTING

Each model in the unit must attack with all of the melee weapons it is armed with (see Attacking).

6 BATTLESHOCK PHASE

In the battleshock phase, both players must take battleshock tests for units from their army that have had models slain during the turn. The player whose turn it is tests first.

You must make a battleshock roll for each unit that has to take a battleshock test. To make a battleshock roll, roll a dice. Add the number of models from the unit that have been slain this turn to the dice roll, and add 1 to the unit's Bravery characteristic for every 10 models that are in the unit when the test is taken.

If the modified battleshock roll is greater than the unit's modified Bravery characteristic, the battleshock test has been failed. If the test is failed, for each point by which the modified roll exceeds the unit's modified Bravery characteristic, one model in that unit must flee. You decide which of the models from your units flee – remove them from play and count them as having been slain.

SPLIT UNITS

At the end of each turn, you must remove models from any of the units in your army that are split up into two or more groups, until only one group of models from the unit remains in play. The models you remove count as having been slain.

A unit of Castigators prepares to open fire on a Chainrasp Horde.

ATTACKING

Battles are decided by the spilling of blood. Arrows fall like rain, war machines hurl their deadly payloads at the foe, and warriors cut and stab at each other with blade and claw. Soldiers fall from grievous wounds and fortifications burn as carnage engulfs the battlefield.

When a unit shoots or fights, it makes attacks with the weapons it is armed with. A unit attacks with all the weapons it is armed with, including any used by its mount.

The weapon options a model has are listed on its warscroll. Missile weapons can only be used in the shooting phase, and melee weapons can only be used in the combat phase.

PICKING TARGETS

When a unit shoots or fights, you must first pick the target unit(s) for all of the weapons it is using, before any of the attacks with the weapons are resolved. Only enemy units can be chosen as the target for an attack.

If a unit can use two or more different weapons in the same phase, the unit can use the weapons in any order you wish after targets have been picked, but you must resolve all of the attacks for one type of weapon before using the next type of weapon.

MISSILE WEAPONS

In order to attack with a missile weapon, the model using the weapon must be in range of the target unit (i.e. within the maximum distance, in inches, of the Range listed for the weapon making the attack), and the target unit must be visible to the model with the weapon (if unsure, stoop down and look from behind the shooting model to see if a model from the target unit is visible). For the purposes of determining visibility, a model can see through other models in its unit.

Some missile weapons have a Range characteristic with a minimum range, for example 6"-48". Such weapons cannot attack units that are wholly within the shorter range.

MELEE WEAPONS

In order to make an attack with a melee weapon, a model must be in range of the target unit.

ATTACKS CHARACTERISTIC

The maximum number of attacks that can be made by a weapon is equal to its Attacks characteristic. Make the attacks one at a time, unless you are using the rules for Multiple Attacks (pg 232).

If a weapon has an Attacks characteristic of more than one, you can split the attacks between any eligible target units you wish. When you split the attacks made by a weapon between two or more enemy units, you must resolve all of the attacks against one unit before moving on to the next one.

Some models are armed with two identical weapons. When attacking with these weapons, do not double the number of attacks that the weapons make; either the Attacks characteristic for the weapon will already take the extra weapon into account, or the model will get an ability on its warscroll that represents the effect of the additional weapon.

A Chainrasp Horde charges in to attack a unit of Sequitors.

MAKING ATTACKS

Attacks are resolved one at a time using the following attack sequence. In some cases, you can resolve all of the attacks made by the same type of weapon at the same time (see Multiple Attacks, below).

1. **Hit Roll:** Roll a dice. If the roll equals or beats the attacking weapon's To Hit characteristic, then it scores a hit and you must make a wound roll. If not, the attack fails and the attack sequence ends. A hit roll of 1 before modification always fails to hit the target, and a hit roll of 6 before modification always hits the target.

2. **Wound Roll:** Roll a dice. If the roll equals or beats the attacking weapon's To Wound characteristic, then it is successful and the opposing player must make a save roll. If not, then the attack fails and the attack sequence ends. A wound roll of 1 before modification always fails, and a wound roll of 6 before modification is always successful.

3. **Save Roll:** The opposing player rolls a dice, modifying the roll by the attacking weapon's Rend characteristic. For example, if a weapon has a -1 Rend characteristic, then 1 is subtracted from the save roll. If the result equals or beats the Save characteristic of the models in the target unit, the save succeeds and the attack sequence ends without causing any damage. If not, the save fails and the attack is successful, and you must determine damage on the target unit. A save roll of 1 before modification always fails.

4. **Determine Damage:** Each successful attack inflicts damage on the target unit equal to the Damage characteristic of the weapon making the attack. Most weapons have a Damage characteristic of 1, but some have a Damage characteristic of 2 or more.

MULTIPLE ATTACKS

In order to resolve several attacks at once, all of the attacks must be made by models from the same unit, with the same type of weapon, and against the same target unit. If this is the case, make all of the hit rolls at the same time, then all of the wound rolls, and finally all of the save rolls.

MULTIPLE HITS

Sometimes a single successful hit roll will score 2 or more hits. If this is the case, make all of the wound rolls for those hits at the same time, and then all of the save rolls.

ALLOCATING WOUNDS

Once all of a unit's attacks have been resolved, add up the damage that was inflicted. The player commanding the target unit must then allocate a number of wounds to the target unit equal to the damage that was inflicted.

Wounds are allocated one at a time to models in the target unit. You can allocate the wounds inflicted on your units as you see fit (the models do not have to be within range or visible to the attacking unit). However, if you allocate a wound to a model, you must keep on allocating wounds to that model until it is slain – a unit can never have more than one wounded model.

Some abilities allow you to make a roll to negate a wound or mortal wound allocated to a model; in this case the roll is made for each individual wound or mortal wound as it is allocated to the model in question. If the wound or mortal wound is negated it has no effect on the model.

COVER

Add 1 to save rolls for a unit if all of its models are wholly on or within a terrain feature when the rolls are made. This modifier does not apply in the combat phase if the unit you are making save rolls for made a charge move in the same turn, and never applies to units containing models with the **Monster** or **War Machine** keyword that have a Wounds characteristic of 8 or more.

MORTAL WOUNDS

Some attacks, spells and abilities inflict mortal wounds. Do not make hit, wound or save rolls for mortal wounds. Instead, the damage inflicted on the target is equal to the number of mortal wounds that were suffered. Allocate any mortal wounds that are caused while a unit is attacking at the same time as any other wounds caused by the unit's attacks, after all of the unit's attacks have been completed. Mortal wounds caused at other times are allocated to models in the target unit as soon as they occur, in the same manner as wounds caused by damage from an attack.

After they have been allocated, a mortal wound is treated in the same manner as any other wound for all rules purposes.

SLAIN MODELS

Once the number of wounds allocated to a model during the battle equals its Wounds characteristic, the model is slain. Place a slain model to one side – it is removed from play.

HEALING WOUNDS

Some abilities allow wounds that have been allocated to a model to be healed. For each wound that is healed, remove one of the wounds that have been allocated to the model. You can't heal wounds on a model that has been slain.

WIZARDS

The realms are saturated with magic, a seething source of power for those with the wit to wield it. In battle, magic is a force as real and potent as a sword blade. It can be used to infuse allies with strength and valour, and enemies with frailty and dread. More commonly, wizards unshackle the raw power of magic to smite their foes with bolts of eldritch power.

Some units have the **WIZARD** keyword on their warscroll. You can use a wizard to cast spells in your hero phase, or to unbind spells in your opponent's hero phase.

Sometimes an ability will allow a model that is not a wizard to attempt to cast or unbind spells. They do so using the rules below and are affected by abilities that modify casting or unbinding rolls, but they are not a wizard for any other rules purposes.

CASTING SPELLS

A **WIZARD** can attempt to cast spells in its own hero phase. You cannot attempt to cast the same spell more than once in the same turn (even with a different wizard).

In order to cast a spell, first say which spell the wizard is going to attempt to use (it must be one they know). To cast the spell, roll 2D6. If the total is equal to or greater than

the casting value of the spell, the spell is successfully cast.

If a spell is cast, the opposing player can choose one of their **WIZARDS** that is within 30" of the caster to attempt to unbind the spell before its effects are applied. To unbind a spell, roll 2D6. If the roll beats the roll used to cast the spell, then the spell is not successfully cast. Only one attempt can be made to unbind a spell.

LORES OF MAGIC

The spells a **WIZARD** knows, and the number of spells it can attempt to cast or unbind in a hero phase, are detailed on the wizard's warscroll. Most wizards know the following Arcane Bolt and Mystic Shield spells.

Arcane Bolt: Arcane Bolt has a casting value of 5. If successfully cast, pick an enemy unit within 18" of the caster that is visible to them. That unit suffers 1 mortal

wound. If the casting roll was 10 or more, the unit suffers D3 mortal wounds instead.

Mystic Shield: Mystic Shield has a casting value of 6. If successfully cast, pick a friendly unit within 18" of the caster that is visible to them. Re-roll save rolls of 1 for that unit until your next hero phase.

UNITS OF WIZARDS
Wizards are usually fielded as a unit consisting of just one model. If a unit with the **WIZARD** keyword has more than one model, it counts as a single wizard for all rules purposes, and you must pick a model from the unit to cast or unbind a spell before you attempt to cast or unbind it; measure the distance and check visibility using the model you picked.

TRIUMPHS

Victory in battle can inspire warriors to even greater feats of valour when they fight again. Confident in their ability to defeat the foe, they may be inspired to redouble their efforts when they attack, or hack at the foe with bloodthirsty fury, or to carry on fighting with an indomitable spirit even if they have grievous wounds.

TRIUMPHS
If your army won a **major victory** in its previous battle, roll a dice when you pick your general and look up the result on the table below.

D6	Triumph
1-2	**Inspired:** Once per battle, when a friendly unit is selected to shoot or fight, you can say that it is inspired. If you do so, re-roll failed hit rolls for that unit until the end of the phase.
3-4	**Bloodthirsty:** Once per battle, when a friendly unit is selected to shoot or fight, you can say that it is bloodthirsty. If you do so, re-roll failed wound rolls for that unit until the end of the phase.
5-6	**Indomitable:** Once per battle, when a friendly unit has to make a save roll, you can say that it is indomitable. If you do so, re-roll failed save rolls for that unit until the end of the phase.

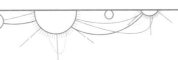

A Knight-Incantor casts Arcane Bolt at a unit of Grimghast Reapers, mortally wounding two of them.

A host of Nighthaunt units led by a Guardian of Souls advances towards a Celestar Ballista.

TERRAIN

Be they pillars of flame, altars of brass or haunted ruins, the realms are filled with strange sights and deadly obstacles. Mighty skull-studded fortresses rise from plains littered with bones, while other, older ruins mark the scarred and smoking landscapes of the Mortal Realms. These are the sites of battlefields and massacres, ruled over by power-hungry warlords.

The rules for movement and cover explain how models can cross or take cover on terrain features. Terrain features are considered to be friendly to both sides and cannot be chosen as the target of an attack.

When you set up the terrain for a battle, you and your opponent can agree to give each terrain feature one of the scenery rules from the Scenery table on the right if you wish. Either pick a scenery rule for each terrain feature, or roll a dice for each terrain feature to randomly determine a rule. If a warscroll is available for a terrain feature, you can use the rules on the warscroll instead of using a rule from the Scenery table.

SCENERY TABLE

D6   Scenery Rule

1   **Damned:** At the start of your hero phase, you can pick one friendly unit within 1" of a Damned terrain feature to make a sacrifice. If you do so, that unit suffers D3 mortal wounds, but you can re-roll hit rolls of 1 for it until your next hero phase.

2   **Arcane:** Add 1 to casting or unbinding rolls for **WIZARDS** while they are within 1" of any Arcane terrain features.

3   **Inspiring:** Add 1 to the Bravery characteristic of units while they are within 1" of any Inspiring terrain features.

4   **Deadly:** Roll a dice for each unit that finishes a normal move or charge move within 1" of any Deadly terrain features. On a 1, that unit suffers D3 mortal wounds.

5   **Mystical:** Roll a dice each time you allocate a wound or mortal wound to a model within 1" of any Mystical terrain features. On a 6+ the wound or mortal wound is negated.

6   **Sinister:** Subtract 1 from the Bravery characteristic of units while they are within 1" of any Sinister terrain features.

OBSTACLES
Some terrain features are obstacles that block attacks to targets that lie beyond them. When this is the case, it will be noted on the warscroll for the terrain feature.

When a missile weapon targets an enemy unit that has all of its models within 1" of an obstacle, then the target unit receives the benefit of cover if the attacking model is closer to the obstacle than it is to the target unit.

GARRISONS
Some terrain features can be garrisoned by units. When this is the case, it will be noted on the warscroll for the terrain feature.

A unit can be set up as a garrison at the start of a battle if the terrain feature is wholly within the unit's territory. Alternatively, a unit can garrison a terrain feature instead of making a normal move if all of its models are within 6" of the terrain feature, and there are no enemy models within 3" of the terrain feature or already garrisoning it.

Units that garrison a terrain feature are removed from the battlefield and are assumed to be 'inside' the terrain feature. Units must treat a terrain feature garrisoned by the enemy as if it were an enemy model.

The range and visibility to or from the garrisoning unit is determined to or from the terrain feature instead. A garrisoning model can attack and be attacked, cast or unbind spells, and use abilities, but cannot move. A garrisoning unit counts as being in cover if it is attacked.

In addition, subtract 1 from the hit rolls of attacks made against a garrisoning unit.

A garrisoning unit can leave in your movement phase. When it does, set it up so that all models from the unit are within 6" of the terrain feature and more than 3" from any enemy units. This counts as their move for that movement phase.

Many terrain features that can be garrisoned include flat areas upon which models can stand. Only garrisoning models can be placed or moved onto the flat areas (other models that can fly can move over flat areas but cannot finish a move or be placed on that area unless they are part of the garrison). Doing so is purely decorative; these models are still treated as garrisoning the terrain feature for rules purposes.

BATTLEPLANS

Before you can wage war in a game of Warhammer Age of Sigmar, you must select a battleplan.

We have included a battleplan here – First Blood – which is ideal to get the action started quickly. Other battleplans can be found in the books we publish for Warhammer Age of Sigmar, or you can use a battleplan of your own creation. If you and your opponent can't agree on which battleplan to use, roll off, and the winner decides which battleplan is used.

BATTLEPLAN INSTRUCTIONS

All battleplans include a set of instructions that describe how a battle is fought.

1 TITLE

The name of the battleplan and a short description of the circumstances of the battle, to give you an understanding of what it is about and what you will need to do in order to be victorious.

2 SET-UP

Each battleplan includes a map that shows where each side can set up the models in their army (called the army's territory), and will list any restrictions that apply to setting up.

The maps we include with our battleplans assume that the battlefield is a 6' by 4' rectangle. If you are using a battlefield that is a different size or shape, you will need to adjust distances, and the location of territories, objectives and terrain features, in a way that is appropriate for the size and shape of the battlefield you are using.

3 SPECIAL RULES

Many battleplans include one or more special rules. These cover unique situations, tactics or abilities which can be used during the battle, or which affect how you pick your army or set up terrain on the battlefield. The 'First Blood' rule in the First Blood battleplan, opposite, is an example of a special rule.

4 GLORIOUS VICTORY

Most battleplans will tell you when the battle ends and what you need to do in order to win the game. If neither player manages to achieve a victory then the game is considered to be a draw.

If the battleplan does not explain how to win the battle, you must slay all of the models in the opposing army to win a **major victory**. If neither player has done this by the end of the fifth battle round, the player that has slain a higher percentage of models in the opposing army than they have lost from their own army wins a **minor victory**.

OBJECTIVES

Battles are sometimes fought to gain control of one or more vitally important locations. In Warhammer Age of Sigmar, these locations are called objectives, and use the following rules.

If a battle has any objectives, then the battleplan will say where they are located upon the battlefield. Objectives need to be represented by a suitable marker, such as a coin. Even better, if you have components available, you can model your own objective markers using parts from Citadel Miniatures kits.

When measuring distances to and from objectives, always measure to and from the centre of the marker.

At the end of each player's turn, you must check to see if either player has gained control of any objectives. To do so, you and your opponent must count up the number of models you have within 6" of the centre of each objective; you gain control of an objective where your count is higher than your opponent's count. Once you gain control of an objective, it remains under your control until the enemy is able to gain control of it.

A model can only be counted towards gaining control of one objective per turn. If one of your models could be counted towards gaining more than one objective, you must pick which one they are counted towards that turn.

BATTLEPLAN
FIRST BLOOD

Two armies meet upon an open battlefield. Each must strive to destroy as many of the enemy as possible – whoever first spills the blood of their foe will be inspired to fight all the harder!

Designer's Note: *In the Mortal Realms, battles are brutal and uncompromising. They are often fought to the bitter end, the victorious side having destroyed its foe entirely.*

However, as all wise generals know, wiping out the opposing army does not in and of itself guarantee success. If one side slaughters the other but suffers massive casualties in doing so, then their victory is pyrrhic indeed.

In this battle, the annihilation of the foe must be achieved without allowing the enemy to inflict more damage on the conquering army than was suffered in return. The victor will therefore be the side that causes the most bloodshed, rather than the side that is simply left standing once the battle is over.

SET-UP

The players roll off, and the winner decides which territory each side will use. The territories are shown on the map below.

The players then alternate setting up units one at a time, starting with the player that won the roll-off to determine territories. Units must be set up wholly within their own territory, more than 12" from enemy territory.

Continue to set up units until both players have set up their armies. If one player finishes first, the opposing player sets up the rest of the units in their army, one after another.

FIRST BLOOD

The player in command of the army that first slays an enemy model receives 1 extra command point.

GLORIOUS VICTORY

The battle continues until one player has no units left on the battlefield, or at the end of the fifth battle round should this occur sooner.

When the battle ends, each player calculates a victory score by adding up the Wounds characteristics of all the models from the opposing army that were slain during the battle. If one player beats their opponent's score by 50% or more, they win a **major victory**. Otherwise the player with the higher score wins a **minor victory**.

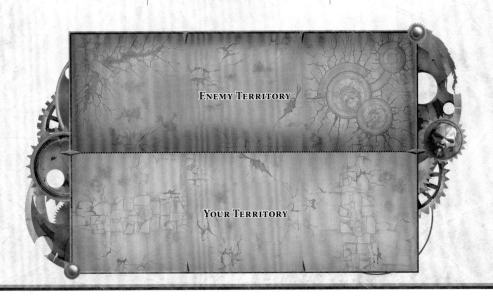

ENEMY TERRITORY

YOUR TERRITORY

WARSCROLLS

Every Citadel Miniature in the Warhammer range has its own warscroll, which provides you with all of the information needed to use that model in a game of Warhammer Age of Sigmar. The key below explains what you will find on a warscroll.

WARSCROLL RULES

All warscrolls include rules that tell you how the model described by the warscroll is used in a battle.

1 CHARACTERISTICS
Warscrolls include a set of characteristics that are referred to in the core game rules and which determine how the model can be used in the game. For example, a model's Save characteristic determines what you must roll in order to make a save roll, a weapon's Attacks characteristic determines how many hit rolls are made for it, and so on.

Save of '-'
Some models have a Save of '-'. A Save of '-' means that you must roll a 7 or more. In most cases this will be impossible, so no roll need be made, but sometimes modifiers will allow you to modify a save roll so that a result of 7 or higher is possible, in which case you can attempt to make the save roll.

Random Values
Sometimes, one or more characteristics on a warscroll will have random values. For example, a Move characteristic might be 2D6, or an Attacks characteristic might be D6.

When a unit with a random Move characteristic is selected to move in the movement phase, roll the indicated number of dice. The total of the dice rolled is the Move characteristic for all models in the unit for the duration of that movement phase.

Generate any random values for a weapon (apart from Damage) each time it is used by a model.

The result applies to that model's weapon for the rest of that phase. When determining random damage in step four of the attack sequence, make a separate roll to generate the value for each successful attack the weapon makes.

2 DESCRIPTION
All warscrolls include a description. This will tell you how to organise the models into a unit, and what weapons the models in the unit can use.

Unit Size
If a model is fielded as part of a unit of two or more models, then the description will say how many models the unit should have. If you don't have enough models to field a unit, you can field one unit of that type with as many models as you have available. This is known as an understrength unit.

Command Models
Some units can include uniquely named champions, standard bearers and/or musicians. These are known collectively as 'command models', and will have abilities that apply only to them. Command models must be represented by appropriate Citadel Miniatures if they are included in a unit. Command models are assumed to carry the same weapons as any other model in the unit unless noted otherwise, even if they are not shown on the model itself.

Mounts
Sometimes the description for a model will include information about the model having a mount, such as a battle steed, a powerful monster that they can ride, or a massive war machine that they can stand upon. Note that when the model is slain both the rider and their mount are removed.

3 ABILITIES
Most warscrolls include one or more abilities that can be used by the warscroll's models during a game of Warhammer Age of Sigmar. Abilities take precedence over the core rules.

Many abilities are triggered by something that happens during the phase. For example, an ability may allow you to re-roll a failed hit roll. In this case the ability is used immediately after the event that triggered it.

Other abilities can be used during a phase if a player wants to use them. For example, you can use most command abilities in the hero phase. Abilities that must be used at the start of a phase are carried out before any other actions. By the same token, abilities used at the end of the phase are carried out after all normal activities for the phase have been completed. Other abilities can be used over the course of the phase, in any order and whenever you desire. If both players want to use abilities at the same time, the player whose turn is taking place uses their abilities first, followed by their opponent.

Note that abilities can only be used in the phase specified in their rules; for example, an ability that says it can be used in 'the movement phase' cannot be used to affect a unit making a move in the hero phase, while an ability that says it can be used in 'your movement phase' cannot be used in the opponent's movement phase.

If a unit has an ability that affects friendly units that are within a certain distance of it, then the ability will also affect the unit itself.

Lastly, any extra attacks, hit rolls or wound rolls gained by the use of an ability cannot themselves generate extra attacks, hit rolls or wound rolls. For example, if a hit roll of 6 or more allows you to make 1 extra attack, this extra attack could not generate further attacks should you roll another 6+.

Modifiers

Sometimes modifiers apply to characteristics or abilities. For example, a rule might add 1 to a hit roll or the Move characteristic of a model. Modifiers are cumulative. Modifiers can never reduce a dice roll to less than 1.

If a modifier applies to a random value, work out the random value first and then apply the modifier(s) to it. For example, if an ability adds 1 to a Damage characteristic of

D3, the result would be worked out by rolling the D3 and adding 1 to the roll.

4 DAMAGE TABLES
Some models have a damage table that is used to determine one or more of the model's characteristics. Look up the number of wounds the model has suffered (i.e. that are currently allocated to the model and have not been healed) to find the value in question.

5 KEYWORDS
Every warscroll includes a list of keywords that apply to the model the warscroll describes. Keywords appear in KEYWORD BOLD when they appear in the rules.

Keywords are sometimes linked to (or 'tagged') by a rule. For example, a rule might say that it applies to 'all KHORNE models'. This means that it would apply to models that have the KHORNE keyword on their warscroll.

Sometimes you will be allowed to assign or add a keyword to a unit for a battle. If you do so, treat the unit as having the assigned keyword on its warscroll for the duration of the battle.

PRE-BATTLE ABILITIES

Some warscrolls allow you to use an ability 'after set-up is complete' or 'before the battle begins'. These abilities are used before the first battle round. If both armies have abilities like this, roll off, and the winner can choose which player must use all of their pre-battle abilities first.

After any pre-battle abilities have been used, the battle begins with the first battle round.

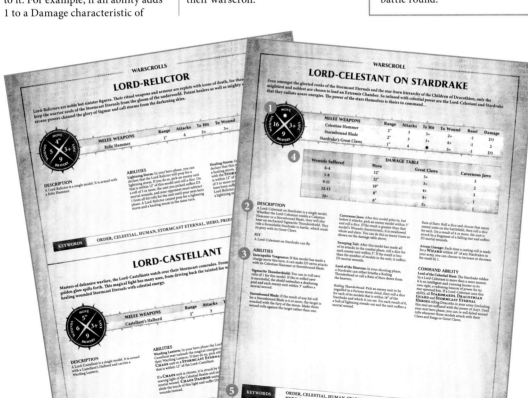

WARSCROLL BATTALIONS

If you wish, you can organise the units in your army into a special type of formation by using a warscroll battalion. Doing so will give you access to additional abilities that can be used by the units in the battalion.

The following rules apply to a warscroll battalion, in addition to the rules that apply to a warscroll.

① BATTALION ORGANISATION

A warscroll battalion is made up of two or more units. You must decide which warscroll battalions you want to use and which units are in each one when you pick your army. Reinforcements cannot be part of a warscroll battalion.

The organisation section of a battalion lists the titles or keywords for the units it can or must include. If an entry is the title of a unit, any unit with that title can be used (you can ignore sub-headers under the title unless they are included in the entry for the unit). Understrength units (pg 238) cannot be used as part of a warscroll battalion.

If the entry for a unit is a **Keyword**, then any unit with that keyword can be used (including any units that you assign a keyword to).

During set-up, you can set up some or all of the units from a warscroll battalion at the same time rather than setting up each unit individually.

② BATTALION ABILITIES

The abilities listed for a warscroll battalion only apply to the units that make it up (even if there are other units of the same type in your army), and they are in addition to the abilities listed on the units' warscrolls.

Usually, a unit can only belong to one battalion, and so can only benefit from a single set of battalion abilities. However, some very large battalions include other, smaller battalions, and in this case it is possible for a unit to benefit from the abilities of two different battalions at the same time.

BATTALION BONUSES

Including a warscroll battalion in an army confers two additional bonuses:

- You receive 1 command point at the start of the battle for each warscroll battalion included in your army.

- If you are using the rules for allegiance abilities (pg 242-243), you can take 1 extra artefact of power for each warscroll battalion included in your army.

REALM OF BATTLE

After picking a battleplan to use, you can pick a Mortal Realm for the battle to take place in. If you do so, the Mortal Realm that you pick will determine which Realm of Battle rules you can use for your game. If you can't agree on the Mortal Realm to use, roll off and the winner decides.

REALM OF BATTLE RULES

The Mortal Realm you have chosen determines which (if any) of the Realm of Battle rules apply to the battle that is taking place there.

Sets of Realm of Battle rules are included in many of the books published for Warhammer Age of Sigmar, and new ones are being added all the time. On pages 254-260 you will find Realm of Battle rules for each of the Mortal Realms.

1 REALMSPHERE MAGIC
WIZARDS can know additional spells that are aligned with the energies of the Mortal Realm in which they are located.

Any such spells are in addition to the spells that the wizard already knows.

2 REALMSCAPE FEATURES
The geography of each realm, its climate, and the flora and fauna that inhabit it are hugely varied and diverse, and can have a major impact on battles that are fought there.

3 REALM COMMANDS
Each realm has a set of unique command abilities that can be used by the **HEROES** that are fighting there.

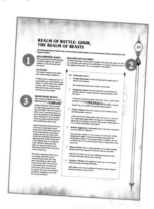

REGIONS OF WAR

Each Mortal Realm is truly vast, and contains myriad incredible regions. Sometimes, a Realm of Battle will include details of one or more of these regions. If this is the case, the player that picked the realm can also say that the battle is taking place in one of the regions, allowing the Realm of Battle rules that are specific to the region to be used.

THE MORTAL REALMS

The Mortal Realms you can choose from are:

- Aqshy, Realm of Fire
- Shyish, Realm of Death
- Ghyran, Realm of Life
- Hysh, Realm of Light
- Ghur, Realm of Beasts
- Chamon, Realm of Metal
- Ulgu, Realm of Shadow

This game is set in arid, Chaos-tainted Aqshy. Introducing Realm of Battle rules to your game adds a new and characterful angle.

ALLEGIANCE ABILITIES

If your army has an allegiance, you can use a set of allegiance abilities for it in your games of Warhammer Age of Sigmar. Allegiance abilities allow your army to use additional abilities and spells.

Sets of allegiance abilities are included in many of the books published for Warhammer Age of Sigmar, and new ones are being added all the time. The rules in this section explain how to use allegiance abilities in your games.

ARMY ALLEGIANCE

When you choose your army, you can also choose an allegiance for it. If you do so, you can use the allegiance abilities that correspond to the allegiance you have chosen. If an army can have more than one allegiance, you must pick one to apply to it during the game.

GRAND ALLIANCES

Units in Warhammer Age of Sigmar owe allegiance to one of the Grand Alliances – either Order, Chaos, Death or Destruction. The Grand Alliance a unit belongs to is determined by the keywords on its warscroll. For example, a unit with the **DEATH** keyword is part of the Death Grand Alliance.

An army has allegiance to a Grand Alliance if all the units in the army are part of that Grand Alliance (including any units that you assign a keyword to during set-up). For example, if all of the units in an army have the **ORDER** keyword, then the army can have allegiance to the Order Grand Alliance, and would be referred to as an Order army.

FACTIONS

Many units also owe allegiance to a faction that is part of one of the Grand Alliances. For example, Stormcast Eternals are a faction of the Order Grand Alliance.

An army can have allegiance to a faction instead of a Grand Alliance if all the units in the army have the keyword for that faction, including any units that you assign a keyword to during set-up. For example, if all of the units in an army have the **STORMCAST ETERNAL** keyword, then the army can have allegiance to the Stormcast Eternals faction, and would be referred to as a Stormcast Eternal army.

ALLIES

One out of every four units included in an army can be an allied unit.

Allied units are treated as part of your army, except that they are not included when working out your army's allegiance, and can therefore be part of a different Grand Alliance or faction. In addition, an allied model cannot be the army's general, and cannot use or benefit from your army's allegiance abilities.

The factions that an army can ally with can be found in its battletome, or with its Pitched Battle Profiles in the current edition of the *General's Handbook*. For example, a Stormcast Eternal army can have allies from any other **ORDER** faction.

REINFORCEMENTS

Units that are added to your army once a battle is under way can be allies. They do not count against the limit on the number of allied units you can include in the army.

WARSCROLL BATTALIONS

A warscroll battalion can include allies. They do not count against the limit on the number of allied units you can include in the army.

TYPES OF ABILITY

Most allegiance abilities include sets of battle traits, command traits, artefacts of power and spell lores. These are sometimes presented on a table – you can either roll on that table to randomly generate an ability or you can choose one. Remember that allegiance abilities cannot be used by allied units in your army.

NAMED CHARACTERS

Named characters such as Nagash, Archaon and Alarielle are singular and mighty warriors, with their own personalities and artefacts of power. As such, these models cannot have a command trait or artefact of power.

BATTLE TRAITS

An army that shares common goals and ideals is much deadlier than a ragtag force of unlikely allies. To represent this, armies that share the same allegiance often benefit from powerful additional abilities called battle traits.

COMMAND TRAITS

Whether cunning strategist or berserk butcher, every general has a unique style of command. If your general is a **HERO** and the allegiance abilities for your army include any command traits, you can choose or roll for one for your general. If, for any reason, you must select a new general during a battle, immediately choose or roll for a trait for them. Command traits have no effect on attacks made by a general's mount unless noted otherwise.

ARTEFACTS OF POWER

These treasures are borne to war by mighty heroes. If the allegiance abilities for your army include any artefacts of power, you can choose or roll for one to be carried by a **HERO** from your army. You may choose one additional **HERO** to have an artefact for each warscroll battalion you include in your army. A **HERO** cannot have more than one artefact of power, and an army may not include duplicates of the same artefact of power. Artefacts of power have no effect on attacks made by a hero's mount unless noted otherwise.

*This Nurgle army is comprised not only of Rotbringers from the Maggotkin of Nurgle battletome, but also skaven from the Skaven Pestilens battletome. All of its units have the **Nurgle** keyword, and hence it uses Nurgle allegiance abilities.*

SPELL LORES

Wizards may know additional spells drawn from lores of magic that are only used by the faction or Grand Alliance they are part of. If the allegiance abilities for your army include any spell lores, each **Wizard** in your army knows one of the spells from the lore, in addition to any other spells they know.

UNIQUE ABILITIES

Some sets of allegiance abilities will include other types of unique ability. When this is the case, the set of allegiance abilities will explain how and when they are used.

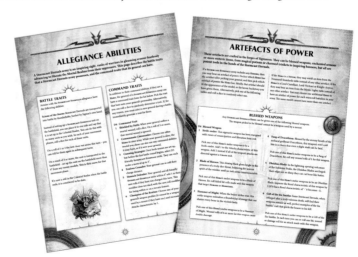

CONQUEST
UNBOUND

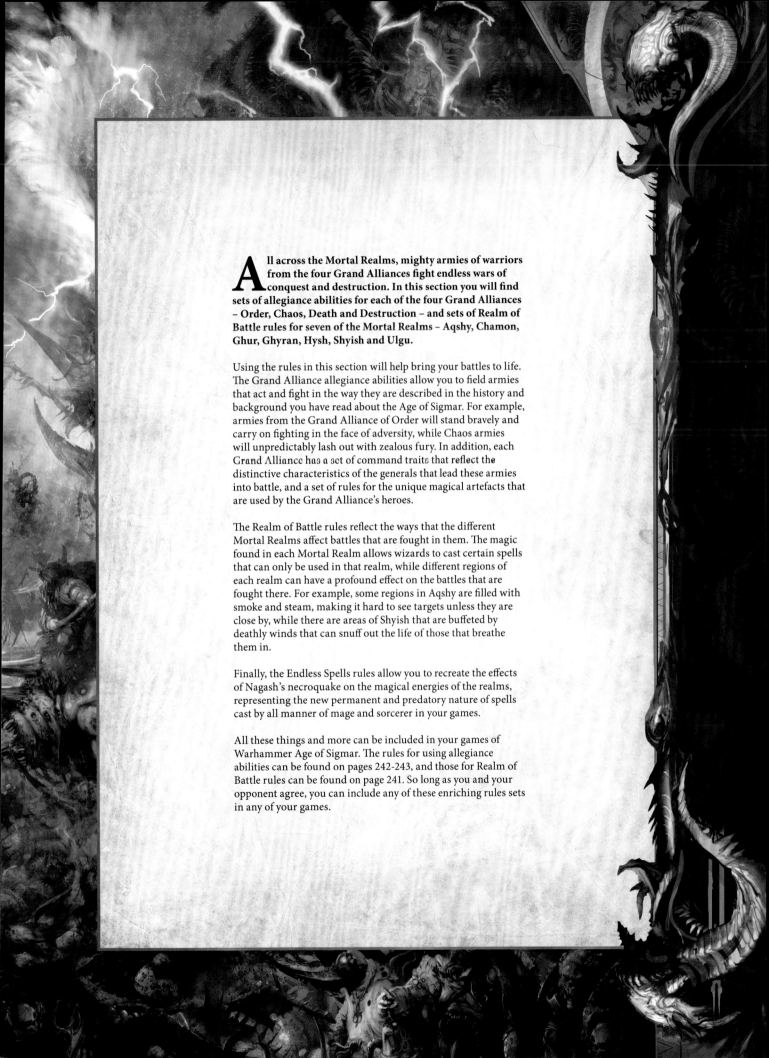

All across the Mortal Realms, mighty armies of warriors from the four Grand Alliances fight endless wars of conquest and destruction. In this section you will find sets of allegiance abilities for each of the four Grand Alliances – Order, Chaos, Death and Destruction – and sets of Realm of Battle rules for seven of the Mortal Realms – Aqshy, Chamon, Ghur, Ghyran, Hysh, Shyish and Ulgu.

Using the rules in this section will help bring your battles to life. The Grand Alliance allegiance abilities allow you to field armies that act and fight in the way they are described in the history and background you have read about the Age of Sigmar. For example, armies from the Grand Alliance of Order will stand bravely and carry on fighting in the face of adversity, while Chaos armies will unpredictably lash out with zealous fury. In addition, each Grand Alliance has a set of command traits that reflect the distinctive characteristics of the generals that lead these armies into battle, and a set of rules for the unique magical artefacts that are used by the Grand Alliance's heroes.

The Realm of Battle rules reflect the ways that the different Mortal Realms affect battles that are fought in them. The magic found in each Mortal Realm allows wizards to cast certain spells that can only be used in that realm, while different regions of each realm can have a profound effect on the battles that are fought there. For example, some regions in Aqshy are filled with smoke and steam, making it hard to see targets unless they are close by, while there are areas of Shyish that are buffeted by deathly winds that can snuff out the life of those that breathe them in.

Finally, the Endless Spells rules allow you to recreate the effects of Nagash's necroquake on the magical energies of the realms, representing the new permanent and predatory nature of spells cast by all manner of mage and sorcerer in your games.

All these things and more can be included in your games of Warhammer Age of Sigmar. The rules for using allegiance abilities can be found on pages 242-243, and those for Realm of Battle rules can be found on page 241. So long as you and your opponent agree, you can include any of these enriching rules sets in any of your games.

ALLEGIANCE ABILITIES

ALLEGIANCE ABILITIES: ORDER

This section describes the allegiance abilities available to an Order army, including battle traits for the army, command traits for its general and the artefacts of power available to its heroes.

BATTLE TRAIT

Defiant Avengers: *The forces of Order are confident of their abilities and are determined to drive the minions of Chaos from the Mortal Realms.*

In the battleshock phase, you can re-roll battleshock tests for friendly **ORDER** units.

Stormcast Eternals
Lord-Castellant

COMMAND TRAITS

D6	Command Trait
1	**Strategic Genius:** *This mighty battle leader is a master of the art of war, a keen strategist capable of turning the tide of battle with a single action.* At the start of the first battle round, you receive 1 extra command point.
2	**Inspiring:** *This renowned hero is so celebrated in legend that his mere presence on the battlefield inspires his followers to feats of incredible valour.* Friendly **ORDER** units do not have to take battleshock tests while they are within 6" of this general.
3	**Dauntless:** *With a mighty bellow the general hurls himself at his enemies, heedless of any obstacle or peril that might come before him.* You can re-roll charge rolls for this general.
4	**Tenacious:** *Tough and robust, this warrior is incredibly hard to kill, fighting on long past injuries which would have felled a normal man.* Add 1 to this general's Wounds characteristic.
5	**Legendary Fighter:** *The general moves in a blur of speed, his weapon an extension of his arm. With a flurry of blows he forces his foe into submission.* When this general is selected to fight, add 1 to the Attacks characteristic of one of their melee weapons for that fight.
6	**Master of Defence:** *This wise warrior has studied the art of defensive warfare and is almost impossible to hit, parrying and feinting to evade his foe's attacks.* Each time you allocate a wound or mortal wound to this general, roll a dice. On a 6+ the wound is negated.

ARTEFACTS OF ORDER

D6   Artefact

1   Quicksilver Potion: *This potion is brewed from the liquid metal found in the lakes of Viscid Flux. When drunk before battle commences, it imbues the user with lightning-fast reflexes.*

Once per battle, at the start of the combat phase, you can use this potion. If you do so, in that combat phase, the bearer (and its mount, if it has one) fights immediately, instead of fighting later in that combat phase.

2   Obstinate Blade: *This enchanted blade is a symbol of supremacy that cleaves through even daemonsteel as if it were gossamer.*

Pick one of the bearer's melee weapons. Improve the Rend characteristic of the weapon by 1.

3   Relic Blade: *Some say the Relic Blade is a remnant of the World Before Time. Whether this is true or not, it can part heads from necks with a single swing.*

Pick one of the bearer's melee weapons. Increase the Damage characteristic of that weapon by 1.

4   Hoarfrost: *Hoarfrost is all that remains of the enchanted glacier Fjoerdos. Those struck by it find their blood freezing solid in their veins.*

Pick one of the bearer's melee weapons. If an enemy model is allocated any wounds from this weapon and is not slain, subtract 1 from that model's hit rolls for the rest of the battle.

5   Talisman of Blinding Light: *The runes on this amulet's multifaceted surfaces blaze with the light of Hysh. It emits dazzling arcs of white light that blind those who look upon it.*

Once per battle, at the start of the combat phase, you can use this amulet. If you do so, in that combat phase, subtract 1 from hit rolls made for attacks that target the bearer.

6   Phoenix Stone: *Phoenix Stones are incredibly rare gems that can be found buried within the blackened granite rock formations of the Brimstone Peninsula. Wearing such a stone against the skin can heal injuries and ward off any disease.*

In each hero phase, you can heal 1 wound that has been allocated to the bearer.

ALLEGIANCE ABILITIES: CHAOS

This section describes the allegiance abilities available to a Chaos army, including battle traits for the army, command traits for its general and the artefacts of power available to its heroes.

BATTLE TRAIT

Unbridled Malice: *The servants of the Chaos Gods are bloody defilers that corrupt anything in their path. Occasionally, their devotion to the Ruinous Powers will drive them to even greater acts of wanton murder.*

When a friendly **Chaos** unit is picked to fight, roll a dice if it is within 12" of your general or 3" of a friendly **Hero**. On a 6+, add 1 to hit rolls for the unit for that fight.

Nurgle Rotbringers
Lord of Blights

COMMAND TRAITS

D6	Command Trait
1	**Dark Avenger:** *This mighty Chaos battle leader loathes the followers of Order and has vowed to destroy any foolish enough to meet him in battle.* Add 1 to hit rolls for this general's melee weapons if the target unit has the **Order** keyword.
2	**Spiteful Duellist:** *The enemy's defences mean nothing to this unrelenting leader, each of his vicious attacks fuelled by the hatred that drives him.* Each time this general is picked to fight, you can re-roll one wound roll for one of their attacks in that fight.
3	**Cunning Deceiver:** *Myriad are the stratagems and ruses known by this corrupt trickster, who weaves the threads of fate to better his own chances of victory.* Roll a dice at the start of each of your hero phases as long as this general has not been slain. On a 5+ you receive 1 extra command point.
4	**Lord of War:** *This warlord is so feared by those under his command that he can incite them to ever greater acts of barbarism with but a glance.* In your hero phase, pick a friendly **Chaos** unit within 3" of this general and roll a dice. On a 4+ you can add 1 to hit rolls for the unit you picked until your next hero phase.
5	**Terrifying Presence:** *Warped and corrupted by Chaos, this foul warrior is horrible to behold, his presence casting a pall of terror over any who venture near.* Subtract 1 from the Bravery characteristic of enemy units while they are within 3" of this general.
6	**Malicious Conqueror:** *This grim warlord inspires his followers to perform acts of terrible mayhem – woe betide the brave and foolish who stand before him in battle.* Add 1 to Unbridled Malice dice rolls (see battle trait) for units while they are within 12" of this general.

ARTEFACTS OF CHAOS

D6   Artefact

1   Daemon Weapon: *This weapon is possessed by the spirit of a bound daemon. Furious at its imprisonment, the daemon lashes out with magical fury.*

Pick one of the bearer's melee weapons. Each time you roll a wound roll of 6+ for that weapon, that attack inflicts 1 mortal wound in addition to its normal damage.

2   Chaos Runeblade: *The blade of this weapon is marked with Chaos runes of damnation that allow the bearer to strike again and again.*

Pick one of the bearer's melee weapons. Increase the Attacks characteristic of that weapon by 1.

3   Beguiling Gem: *This rough-hewn gemstone glows with an unnatural light, drawing the attention of those nearby, dulling their wits and mesmerizing them into immobility.*

Once per battle, at the start of the combat phase, you can pick one enemy model within 3" of the bearer. Subtract 1 from hit rolls made for that model in that phase.

4   Chaos Talisman: *Every Chaos Talisman is marked with the icon of the bearer's patron god, and carries some of their dark power. Depending on the whim of the gods, the talisman may occasionally protect its wearer from harm.*

Roll a dice each time you allocate a wound or mortal wound to the bearer. On a 6+, the wound is negated. Add 1 to the roll if the wound was inflicted by a model with the **ORDER** keyword.

5   Favour of the Gods: *The Chaos Gods bestow their blessings upon favoured followers, gifting them with some mark or mutation, and strengthening them with the raw energy of Chaos.*

Add 1 to the Wounds characteristic of the bearer.

6   Crown of Conquest: *This eight-pointed crown is a mark of the wearer's total devotion to the Dark Gods. The mere sight of a champion wearing this crown fills the followers of Chaos with frenzied bravado.*

Friendly **CHAOS** units do not have to take battleshock tests while they are within 6" of the bearer.

ALLEGIANCE ABILITIES: DESTRUCTION

This section describes the allegiance abilities available to a Destruction army, including battle traits for the army, command traits for its general and the artefacts of power available to its heroes.

BATTLE TRAIT

Rampaging Destroyers: *Those that owe allegiance to Destruction are always eager to get to grips with their enemies.*

In your hero phase, roll a dice for your general and each friendly **DESTRUCTION HERO** on the battlefield. Add 2 to the roll for the general. On a 6+, pick a friendly **DESTRUCTION** unit within 6" of the general or **HERO** being rolled for. That unit can immediately move 6" if it is more than 12" from the enemy, can immediately pile in if it is within 3" of the enemy, or can immediately declare a charge in any other circumstances. It cannot run when it makes the move, but can move, charge or pile in again later in the same turn.

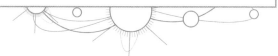

Ironjawz
Orruk Megaboss

COMMAND TRAITS

D6   Command Trait

1   **Nothing Left Standing:** *This tyrant tears down walls and turns forests to splinters in his endless rage. Only ruins and ashes are left in the wake of his rampages.*

In your hero phase, pick a terrain feature that is within 6" of this general and at least 5 other friendly **DESTRUCTION** models. For the rest of the battle, that terrain feature no longer gives cover to models that are in or on it.

2   **Might is Right:** *This commander is renowned for the contemptuous ease with which he cuts down his foes, and will not allow any opponent to damage that reputation.*

Add 1 to wound rolls made for this general's melee weapons.

3   **Wild Fury:** *Attacking this berserk warrior only increases the fury with which he responds, like a baited animal lashing out with unbridled ferocity.*

When this general is picked to fight, pick one of their melee weapons. Add 1 to the Attacks characteristic of that melee weapon for that fight. While 3 or more wounds are allocated to this general, instead add 2 to the Attacks characteristic of that melee weapon for that fight.

4   **Bellowing Tyrant:** *Disobeying the orders of this murderous psychopath is simply not an option. His warriors will overcome any fear they have of the foe to ensure his will is carried out.*

In your hero phase, pick a friendly **DESTRUCTION** unit within 6" of this general. Until your next hero phase, add 1 to charge and run rolls for the unit you picked, and use this general's Bravery characteristic for the unit instead of its own.

5   **Big and Brutish:** *By any standard, this warlord is a muscle-bound brute, his skin thick like animal hide and his nature so stubborn that any blade capable of piercing it slows him not an iota.*

Add 1 to this general's Wounds characteristic.

6   **Ravager:** *The followers of this maniacal overlord are always eager to attack the foe, needing little or no provocation to charge into battle with weapons brandished.*

Add 3 to the Rampaging Destroyers dice roll (see battle trait) for this general instead of 2.

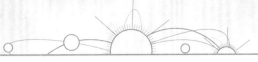

ARTEFACTS OF DESTRUCTION

D6 Artefact

1 Hammerblade: *The Hammerblade is moulded from a massive lump of compressed meteoric iron. When swung down to smash into the ground, devastating energies explode outwards from the point of impact.*

Pick one of the bearer's melee weapons. Instead of attacking normally with that weapon, you can roll a dice for each model within 3" of the bearer (apart from the bearer). On a 5 or 6, 1 mortal wound is inflicted on that model's unit.

2 Battered Talisman: *This once finely wrought jewel is now a dirt-encrusted, chipped remnant of its former glory, but its defensive powers still ward against powerful attacks.*

Roll a dice each time you allocate a mortal wound to the bearer. On a 5+, the mortal wound is negated.

3 Rockeye: *The bearer of a Rockeye has plucked out one of their own eyes and replaced it with this rough gemstone, which gives them the power of second sight.*

In your hero phase, pick an enemy unit within 12" of the bearer. Until your next hero phase, add 1 to hit rolls made for the bearer when they target the unit you picked.

4 Bellowing Blade: *This blade seems to empower the wielder in proportion to the volume of insults he shouts at the leaders of the opposing army.*

When the bearer is picked to fight, you can re-roll one wound roll for the bearer's attacks in that fight for each enemy **Hero** that was within 12" of the bearer when they were picked to fight.

5 Collar of Domination: *This studded collar is inscribed with ancient glyphs that have the power to subdue the fiercest monstrous creatures.*

At the start of your opponent's movement phase, pick an enemy **Monster** within 3" of the bearer and roll 2D6. If the roll is equal to or greater than the enemy monster's Bravery characteristic, it must retreat in that movement phase.

6 Battle Brew: *This pungent liquid can rouse the drinker to prodigious feats. If too much is drunk, though, it will quickly rot his innards.*

Once per battle, in your hero phase, you can declare that the bearer will take either one or two swigs of Battle Brew. If the bearer takes one swig, add 1 to hit and wound rolls made for the bearer until your next hero phase. If the bearer takes two swigs, add 2 to hit and wound rolls made for the bearer until your next hero phase, but you must allocate D6 mortal wounds to the bearer at the end of the turn in which they drank the brew.

ALLEGIANCE ABILITIES: DEATH

This section describes the allegiance abilities available to a Death army, including battle traits for the army, command traits for its general and the artefacts of power available to its heroes.

BATTLE TRAITS

Deathless Minions: *The servants of the rulers of the dead are all but immune to pain, shrugging off wounds that would slay a living creature. This unnatural resilience is bolstered if their lord and master is nearby, making them even more difficult to kill.*

Each time you allocate a wound or mortal wound to a friendly **DEATH** model within 6" of your general or a friendly **DEATH HERO**, roll a dice. On a 6+ the wound is negated.

COMMAND TRAITS

D6	Command Trait

1   **Ruler of the Night:** *The presence of this dark lord invigorates any minions of Nagash that are nearby, ghostly forms allowing blades to pass right through them and necrotic flesh reknitting in seconds.*

Friendly **DEATH** units are affected by the Deathless Minions battle trait if they are within 12" of this general rather than only 6".

2   **Predator of the Shadows:** *This creature of darkness summons the shadows to conceal him, vanishing into a pool of gloom on even the brightest day.*

Add 1 to hit and wound rolls for this general if they are in cover.

3   **Death Incarnate:** *An avatar of death made flesh, this blighted creature is so terrifying to look upon that it drains the life force from its foes.*

In your hero phase, pick an enemy unit within 3" of this general and roll 2D6. If the roll equals or exceeds the enemy unit's Bravery characteristic, inflict D3 mortal wounds on the unit.

4   **Master of the Black Arts:** *This dark-souled necromancer has studied the arcane arts for millennia and wields the magical energies of the realms with ease.*

This general is a **WIZARD** who knows the Arcane Bolt and Mystic Shield spells. If this general is already a wizard, add 1 to all of their casting and unbinding rolls instead.

5   **Red Fury:** *After this general gets a taste of blood, he is overcome with the thirst for more, pursuing his prey relentlessly until the fatal blow is struck.*

The first time this general is picked to fight in each combat phase, roll a dice at the end of that fight. On a 5+ they can immediately fight again.

6   **Supernatural Horror:** *It is almost impossible to remain in the presence of this scalp-tingling creature of horror, even the most stalwart warriors dropping their weapons and running in abject fear when it draws close.*

In the battleshock phase, double the number of models that flee from enemy units while they are within 12" of this general.

Nighthaunt
Lord Executioner

ARTEFACTS OF DEATH

D6 Artefact

1 Cursed Book: *Every Cursed Book is filled with the writings of depraved practitioners of the necromantic arts. They radiate an aura of pure evil, which has an enervating effect on living creatures that are nearby.*

You and your opponent must subtract 1 from hit rolls made for units within 3" of the bearer, unless the unit has the **DEATH** keyword.

2 Cloak of Mists and Shadows: *At a word of command, the wearer of this cloak can transform their body into a cloud of dark mist that swirls swiftly across the battlefield.*

At the start of any combat phase, the bearer can use this cloak. If it does so, remove the bearer from the battlefield, and then set it up anywhere on the battlefield within 12" of its original location and more than 3" from any enemy models. If this is impossible, this model remains in its current location

3 Blade of Dark Summons: *This blade pulses and glows with sinister magic. Its wielder can draw upon this power to summon the minions of Death to the battlefield to fight at their side.*

Once per battle, in your hero phase, you can set up a **SUMMONABLE DEATH** unit wholly within 12" of the bearer and more than 3" from any enemy models, and add it to your army. The models in the unit must have a combined Wounds characteristic of no more than a 2D6 roll.

4 Black Amulet: *This maleficent ebony jewel can store necromantic magic and then unleash it on the foe.*

Once per battle, in your hero phase, the bearer can use this amulet. If it does so, pick an enemy unit within 12" of the bearer. Inflict a number of mortal wounds equal to the number of the current battle round on the unit you picked.

5 Tomb Blade: *This evil weapon steals the life energy of those it slays and uses it to vitalise the undead.*

Pick one of the bearer's melee weapons. For each wound roll of 6+ you make for this weapon, you can heal 1 wound that has been allocated to a friendly **DEATH** model within 6" of the bearer.

6 Ring of Immortality: *If the bearer of this ring is struck down, the ring transports them from danger and restores some of their vitality – but after its power has been spent it becomes little more than a decorative trinket.*

The first time the bearer is slain, before removing them from the battlefield, roll a dice. On a 3+ the bearer is not slain and D3 wounds allocated to them are healed (any excess damage is negated). Then, remove the bearer from the battlefield and set them up again within 18" of their original location and more than 3" from any enemy models.

REALMS OF BATTLE

REALM OF BATTLE: SHYISH, THE REALM OF DEATH

The following Realm of Battle rules can be used for battles fought in the Mortal Realm of Shyish, also known as the Realm of Death.

REALMSPHERE MAGIC

WIZARDS know the following spell in battles fought in this realm, in addition to any other spells that they know.

PALL OF DOOM

A cloud of terrifying darkness pours forth and engulfs the wizard's foes.

Pall of Doom has a casting value of 6. If successfully cast, pick an enemy unit within 18" of the caster that is visible to them. Subtract 2 from the Bravery characteristic of the unit you picked until your next hero phase.

REALM COMMANDS

You can use the following command abilities in battles fought in this realm, in addition to the command abilities that you are normally allowed to use.

HONOUR THE DEAD

The dead are honoured by the living ending the lives of their remaining foes.

You can use this command ability at the start of any combat phase. If you do so, pick a friendly unit that is within 3" of a friendly HERO or 12" of your general, and roll a dice. If the dice roll is less than the number of models that have been slain from the unit you picked, you can add 1 to the Attacks characteristic of weapons used by that unit in that combat phase.

SOUL-FORCE SACRIFICE

Your general can siphon soul-force from their minions to extend their life.

You can use this command ability at the start of your hero phase. If you do so, pick a friendly unit that is within 3" of your general. Allocate

REALMSCAPE FEATURES

If a battle takes place in this realm, the player that picked the realm can roll a dice and look up the result on the table below to see which realmscape feature rule applies for the battle. The result applies to both players.

D6	Realmscape Feature
1	**Barren Moorland:** *Wastelands of bone and dust stretch as far as the eye can see.* This realmscape feature has no effect on the battle.
2	**Life Leeching:** *The land here can drain the life force from a living being, causing them to suddenly drop dead in their tracks.* At the start of your hero phase, roll a dice. On a 6+, pick an enemy unit. That unit suffers D3 mortal wounds.
3	**The Winds of Death:** *Swirling zephyrs of deathly energy skitter across this realm, snuffing out the life-force of those whose path it crosses.* At the start of your hero phase, roll a dice. On a 6+, pick an enemy unit, and then roll a dice for each model in it. For each 5+, that unit suffers 1 mortal wound.
4	**Haunted Realm:** *The buildings and features of these lands are haunted by the restless spirits of those that have died here.* Terrain features have the Sinister scenery rule (pg 235), in addition to any other scenery rules that they have.
5	**Eternal War:** *Those that fight and die in these lands will be reborn at the next day's dawn if they acquit themselves with valour.* Add 1 to the Bravery characteristic of all units.
6	**Aetherquake Aftershock:** *As the battle begins, a thunderous aftershock of aetheric energy rolls across this land, filling sorcerers with deathly magical energy.* Add 1 to casting rolls.

any number of wounds to that unit that you wish – you can heal 1 wound that has been allocated to your general for each wound that you allocate.

REALM OF BATTLE: AQSHY, THE REALM OF FIRE

The following Realm of Battle rules can be used for battles fought in the Mortal Realm of Aqshy, also known as the Realm of Fire.

REALMSPHERE MAGIC

WIZARDS know the following spell in battles fought in this realm, in addition to any other spells that they know.

FIREBALL

The wizard claps their hands, conjuring a small orb of flame that they hurl at the foe. As the flame travels through the air it grows in size until it becomes a blazing ball of fire that explodes amongst the ranks of the enemy.

Fireball has a casting value of 5. If successfully cast, pick an enemy unit within 18" of the caster that is visible to them. If the enemy unit consists of one model it suffers 1 mortal wound, if it has two to nine models it suffers D3 mortal wounds, and if it has ten or more models it suffers D6 mortal wounds.

REALM COMMANDS

You can use the following command ability in battles fought in this realm, in addition to the command abilities that you are normally allowed to use.

FIRESTARTER

The parched kindling surrounding a piece of terrain is set alight. In moments, the area is engulfed in flames.

You can use this command ability at the start of your movement phase. If you do so, pick a terrain feature that is within 12" of a friendly **HERO** and within 3" of another friendly unit, and roll a dice. On a 4+ the terrain feature is set alight. If a terrain feature is set alight, for the rest of the battle, any unit with models in or on it at the end of their movement phase suffers D3 mortal wounds. In addition, a model cannot see another model if a straight line drawn from the centre of its base to the centre of the other model's base passes across this terrain feature.

REALMSCAPE FEATURES

If a battle takes place in this realm, the player that picked the realm can roll a dice and look up the result on the table below to see which realmscape feature rule applies for the battle. The result applies to both players.

D6	Realmscape Feature
1	**Scorched Landscape:** *The region is parched and arid, but there are no obvious hazards in view.* This realmscape feature has no effect on the battle.
2	**Flaming Missiles:** *As missiles hurtle through the air they suddenly ignite, burning with magical flames which inflict terrible searing wounds.* Improve the Rend characteristic of missile weapons by 1 while the range from the attacking unit to the target unit is more than 12".
3	**Clouds of Smoke and Steam:** *The battlefield in this region is wreathed in smoke and steam.* A model cannot see another model if a straight line drawn from the centre of its base to the centre of the other model's base passes across a terrain feature other than open ground and/or hills.
4	**Every Step a League:** *The very moisture in one's body seems to drain away, and every step taken feels like a league marched in full battle-gear.* If a run roll is 6+, or a charge roll is 10+, then you can either say that the unit will not run or charge after all, or you can move the unit but it suffers D3 mortal wounds immediately after the move is completed.
5	**Burning Skies:** *The skies are wreathed in flames that will burn those that approach too closely.* In the movement phase, if an enemy unit can fly and moves more than 6", roll a dice. On a 4+ the enemy unit suffers 1 mortal wound. On a 6+ it suffers D3 mortal wounds instead.
6	**Geysers of Boiling Blood:** *Scattered across the battlefield are bubbling pools of boiling blood that can erupt into geysers of sanguinary death.* At the start of each of your hero phases, roll a dice. On a 6+, a geyser explodes. If it does so, pick a point on the battlefield and roll a dice for each unit within 6" of that point; on a 4+ that unit suffers D3 mortal wounds. On a 6+ the unit suffers D6 mortal wounds instead.

REALM OF BATTLE: CHAMON, THE REALM OF METAL

The following Realm of Battle rules can be used for battles fought in the Mortal Realm of Chamon, also known as the Realm of Metal.

REALMSPHERE MAGIC

WIZARDS know the following spell in battles fought in this realm, in addition to any other spells that they know.

TRANSMUTATION OF LEAD

As the wizard gestures at his foes, their weapons and armour become significantly heavier and more cumbersome – twice the burden they were but moments before – making them an easy target for an attack.

Transmutation of Lead has a casting value of 7. If successfully cast, pick an enemy unit within 18" of the caster that is visible to them. Until your next hero phase, halve the Move characteristic of the unit you picked, rounding up. In addition, if the unit has a Save characteristic of 2+, 3+ or 4+, then until your next hero phase you can re-roll hit rolls of 1 for attacks that target that unit.

REALM COMMANDS

You can use the following command ability in battles fought in this realm, in addition to the command abilities that you are normally allowed to use.

ADAPT OR DIE

Warriors in the Realm of Metal quickly learn to adapt and evolve as the lands shift and meld. A wise general knows to harness this resilience and use it to ensure victory.

You can use this command ability at the start of your hero phase. If you do so, pick a friendly unit within 3" of a friendly **HERO** or 12" of your general. Until your next hero phase, roll a dice each time you allocate a wound or mortal wound to a model in the unit you picked. On a 6+ the wound is negated.

REALMSCAPE FEATURES

If a battle takes place in this realm, the player that picked the realm can roll a dice and look up the result on the table below to see which realmscape feature rule applies for the battle. The result applies to both players.

D6	Realmscape Feature
1	**Metallic Hinterlands:** *The land ahead is as smooth and featureless as brushed steel.* This realmscape feature has no effect on the battle.
2	**Iron Trees:** *The bark on the trees in this region is made of metal rather than wood.* Worsen the Rend characteristic of a weapon by 1 (to a minimum of '-') if the target has cover from a Citadel Wood or Sylvaneth Wyldwood.
3	**Rust Plague:** *The terrain of this land has been infected with a plague that can cause armour to turn to rust in mere moments.* At the start of your hero phase, roll a dice. On a 6+, pick an enemy unit that is in cover. Subtract 1 from save rolls made for that unit for the rest of the battle.
4	**Steel Rain:** *The cold-grey clouds in the skies above the battlefield can suddenly unleash a hail of steel rain.* At the start of your hero phase, roll a dice. On a 6+, pick an enemy unit that is not in cover. Roll a dice for each model in that unit. Inflict 1 mortal wound for each roll that is less than the unit's Save characteristic. A Save characteristic of '-' counts as a 6 for the purposes of this rule.
5	**Brittle Isles:** *This region is so cold that weapons may shatter when they strike a target's armour, making well-protected opponents much more difficult to harm.* Ignore the Rend characteristic of all weapons for the duration of the battle.
6	**Irresistible Force:** *Tzeentch covets the Realm of Metal, and his interference sometimes makes spellcasting more effective, but also more dangerous.* If a casting roll is a double, after re-rolls but before modifiers are applied, it is successful (even if the roll is less than the casting value of the spell being attempted) and the spell cannot be unbound. After the effects of the spell have been carried out, each unit within 3" of the caster suffers 1 mortal wound.

REALM OF BATTLE: GHUR, THE REALM OF BEASTS

The following Realm of Battle rules can be used for battles fought in the Mortal Realm of Ghur, also known as the Realm of Beasts.

REALMSPHERE MAGIC

WIZARDS know the following spell in battles fought in this realm, in addition to any other spells that they know.

WILDFORM

The wizard transforms their allies into swift-moving bestial forms.

Wildform has a casting value of 5. If successfully cast, pick a friendly unit within 12" of the caster that is visible to them. Add 2 to charge and run rolls made for the unit you picked until your next hero phase.

MONSTROUS BEASTS

After set-up, each player can set up a **MONSTER** that is not a **HERO**, starting with the player that finished setting up their army first. These monsters are called 'monstrous beasts' in the rules that follow. They are not part of either army. A monstrous beast can be set up anywhere on the battlefield that is more than 9" from any other monstrous beasts and more than 9" from models from either army.

Monstrous beasts choose their prey at the start of each battle round. Their prey for that battle round will be the army that has a unit closest to them. For the rest of that battle round, the monstrous beast joins the opposing army. If both armies have a unit equally close to a monstrous beast, roll off to determine who picks the monstrous beast's prey. Monstrous beasts will not pick each other as their prey.

Note that a monstrous beast's prey can change each battle round, and monstrous beasts will 'swap sides' depending on which army has the closest unit. Also note that a monstrous beast can attack any unit in their prey's army, not just the closest unit, and cannot itself be attacked or charged by units from the army it has joined.

REALMSCAPE FEATURES

If a battle takes place in this realm, the player that picked the realm can roll a dice and look up the result on the table below to see which realmscape feature rule applies for the battle. The result applies to both players.

D6	Realmscape Feature
1	**Savage Hinterlands:** *It seems the lands of this region pose no threat, at the moment.* This realmscape feature has no effect on the battle.
2	**Hungering Animus:** *Even the landscapes are possessed of a predatory instinct, using avalanches or ground-quakes to kill their prey.* At the start of your hero phase, roll a dice. On a 6+, pick a point anywhere on the battlefield. Roll a dice for each unit within 6" of that point. On a 4+ the unit being rolled for suffers 1 mortal wound. On a 6+ it suffers D3 mortal wounds instead.
3	**Primal Violence:** *Here every creature is red in tooth and claw, and both predator and prey.* At the end of each combat phase, roll a dice. On a 6+, carry out the combat phase again before moving on to the battleshock phase (do not roll again at the end of the second combat phase to see if a third combat phase takes place).
4	**Reckless Aggression:** *A philosophy of eat or be eaten is needed to survive amidst the wilderness.* Any unit that is within 12" of an enemy unit at the start of their charge phase suffers 1 mortal wound unless they finish that charge phase within 3" of an enemy model. In addition, you can re-roll hit rolls of 1 for units that have made a charge move in the same turn.
5	**Beasts of Ghur:** *This is a realm of predators, an endless hunting ground where the strong survive and the weak are consumed.* Roll off. The winner can set up an additional monstrous beast using the Monstrous Beasts rule on the left.
6	**Territory of Beasts:** *Great migratory trails criss-cross the lands, made by groups of hunting behemoths.* Both players can set up an additional monstrous beast using the Monstrous Beasts rule on the left.

REALM OF BATTLE: GHYRAN, THE REALM OF LIFE

The following Realm of Battle rules can be used for battles fought in the Mortal Realm of Ghyran, also known as the Realm of Life.

REALMSPHERE MAGIC

WIZARDS know the following spell in battles fought in this realm, in addition to any other spells that they know.

SHIELD OF THORNS

At the wizard's command, crawling brambles burst from the ground, forming a living barrier around his allies.

Shield of Thorns has a casting value of 5. If successfully cast, pick a friendly unit within 18" of the caster that is visible to them. Until your next hero phase, any enemy unit that finishes a charge move within 3" of the unit you picked suffers D3 mortal wounds.

REALM COMMANDS

You can use the following command ability in battles fought in this realm, in addition to the command abilities that you are normally allowed to use.

COMMAND THE LAND

In the Realm of Life even the landscape can be bent to your will.

You can use this command ability at the end of your hero phase. If you do so, a friendly **HERO** can attempt to cast the Shield of Thorns spell (above), even if they are not a **WIZARD**, and even if the spell has already been attempted in the same hero phase.

If the **HERO** is a **WIZARD**, using this command ability allows them to attempt to cast the Shield of Thorns spell in addition to any other spells they have already attempted to cast, and even if the spell has been attempted by either themselves or another **WIZARD** in the same hero phase.

REALMSCAPE FEATURES

If a battle takes place in this realm, the player that picked the realm can roll a dice and look up the result on the table below to see which realmscape feature rule applies for the battle. The result applies to both players.

D6	Realmscape Feature
1	**Verdant Landscape:** *The region is lush and vibrant, and appears to conceal no lurking dangers.* This realmscape feature has no effect on the battle.
2	**Spontaneous Growth:** *The lands of Ghyran burgeon with all forms of life, waiting below the surface to suddenly bloom forth.* At the start of your hero phase, roll a dice. On a 6+, you can set up a Sylvaneth Wyldwood terrain feature anywhere on the battlefield that is more than 1" from any other models or terrain features.
3	**Lifesprings:** *It is said that bathing in the lifesprings of Ghyran can cure disease and increase vitality.* Before the battle begins, each player picks a **HERO** from their army. Add 1 to the Wounds characteristic of the heroes that are picked.
4	**Hidden Festering Corruption:** *Once, the varied kingdoms of Ghyran were beautiful to look upon, but Nurgle's invading legions have turned many into twisted, blighted places.* At the start of your hero phase, roll a dice. Add 1 to the dice roll if your army has allegiance to **NURGLE**. On a 5+ pick an enemy unit that is within 1" of a terrain feature. The unit you picked suffers 1 mortal wound.
5	**Fecund Quagmire:** *Hasty progress is all but impossible for those attempting to cross the cloying battlefield of this region.* Models cannot run unless they are able to fly.
6	**Seeds of Hope:** *Even though much of the Realm of Life has been overrun by Nurgle's legions, new hope and new life is always ready to emerge.* If a battleshock roll is an unmodified 1, then no models from the unit will flee. In addition, heal all wounds that are currently allocated to that unit.

REALM OF BATTLE: HYSH, THE REALM OF LIGHT

The following Realm of Battle rules can be used for battles fought in the Mortal Realm of Hysh, also known as the Realm of Light.

REALMSPHERE MAGIC

WIZARDS know the following spell in battles fought in this realm, in addition to any other spells that they know.

PHA'S PROTECTION

The wizard calls upon the beneficent Guardians of Light to protect his allies from harm.

Pha's Protection has a casting value of 5. If successfully cast, select a friendly unit within 18" of the caster that is visible to them. Subtract 1 from hit rolls made for attacks that target the unit you picked until your next hero phase.

REALM COMMANDS

You can use the following command ability in battles fought in this realm, in addition to the command abilities that you are normally allowed to use.

STRIKE QUICKLY

The aetheric particles in this realm enhance the speed and reactions of those that live here. It is possible to harness this power and strike before an opponent is ready to strike back.

You can use this command ability at the start of the combat phase. If you do so, pick a friendly unit within 3" of a friendly **HERO** or 12" of your general, and within 3" of the enemy. That unit fights immediately, instead of fighting later in that combat phase.

REALMSCAPE FEATURES

If a battle takes place in this realm, the player that picked the realm can roll a dice and look up the result on the table below to see which realmscape feature rule applies for the battle. The result applies to both players.

D6	Realmscape Feature
1	**Gleaming Vista:** *The plain ahead is clear and illuminated by a radiant light.*
	This realmscape feature has no effect on the battle.
2	**Dazzling Glow:** *The structures and plant-life of this realm often pulsate with glowing light.*
	Subtract 1 from hit rolls made for attacks that target units that are in cover.
3	**Speed of Light:** *The light in this land knows no burden of flesh, and nor do those that receive its blessing.*
	At the start of your movement phase, roll a dice. On a 6+, you can pick a friendly unit. Remove that unit from the battlefield, and then set up it anywhere on the battlefield that is more than 9" from any enemy models. This counts as that unit's move for that movement phase.
4	**Domain of Symmetry and Purity:** *This region is suffused with the purest light, unsettling anything created from the raw stuff of Chaos, darkness and disorder.*
	Subtract 1 from the Bravery characteristic of **CHAOS**, **DESTRUCTION** and **DEATH** units.
5	**Wilderness of Broken Dreams:** *Some regions in Hysh have been cast down by the subtle curse of Chaos or broken by the violence of open war.*
	Subtract 1 from the Bravery characteristic of **ORDER** units.
6	**Aetheric Beams of Light:** *The magical energy of Hysh travels the lands and skies as beams of pure yellow-white illumination. Wizards can tap into this energy to create aetherquartz prisms, which will enhance their powers.*
	In your hero phase, one friendly **WIZARD** can craft an aetherquartz prism instead of attempting to cast any spells in that phase. If they do so, they can attempt to cast one extra spell in each of their future hero phases, and attempt to unbind one extra spell in each future enemy hero phase. A **WIZARD** cannot craft more than one aetherquartz prism per battle (though your other wizards can do so in future hero phases).

REALM OF BATTLE: ULGU, THE REALM OF SHADOW

The following Realm of Battle rules can be used for battles fought in the Mortal Realm of Ulgu, also known as the Realm of Shadow.

REALMSPHERE MAGIC

WIZARDS know the following spell in battles fought in this realm, in addition to any other spells that they know.

MYSTIFYING MIASMA

The wizard creates a numbing fog that causes their foolish foes to listlessly stagger and stumble.

Mystifying Miasma has a casting value of 4. If successfully cast, select a enemy unit within 18" of the caster that is visible to them. That unit cannot run until your next hero phase. In addition, subtract 2 from charge rolls for that unit until your next hero phase.

REALM COMMANDS

You can use the following command ability in battles fought in this realm, in addition to the command abilities that you are normally allowed to use.

LORD OF THE SHADOW REALM

The hidden pathways of this realm offer great strategic opportunities to those who can master them.

You can use this command ability at the start of your hero phase. If you do so, you can use either the Shadowed Mansions or Shadow Realm realmscape feature on the right. In addition, after transferring or setting up the unit in its new location, you do not have to roll to see if any models from the unit become lost in the shadow realms.

Note that if the Shadowed Mansions or Shadow Realm realmscape features apply in your battle, you can use them normally as well as using them with this command ability.

REALMSCAPE FEATURES

If a battle takes place in this realm, the player that chose the realm can roll a dice and look up the result on the table below to see which realmscape feature rule applies for the battle. The result applies to both players.

D6	Realmscape Feature
1	**Shrouded Lands:** *A veil of gloom hangs over this region, but no dangers are apparent.* This realmscape feature has no effect on the battle.
2	**Impenetrable Gloom:** *The lands of Ulgu have neither night nor day, but range from gloom to pitch black depending on region rather than time.* The maximum range of attacks or spells is 6".
3	**Perpetual Dusk:** *Many regions in this realm are places where half-light and half-truth are the best a traveller can wish for.* The maximum range of attacks or spells is 12".
4	**Darkly Shaded:** *In this place shadows stretch preternaturally across the landscape, covering all in shade.* The maximum range of attacks or spells is 18".
5	**Shadowed Mansions:** *This is the domain of secrets and lies, of twisted reason and mind-bending magic.* At the start of your hero phase, pick one friendly unit that is part of a garrison. You can immediately transfer that unit to a different terrain feature that can have a garrison. The unit cannot be transferred to a terrain feature that is garrisoned by an enemy unit, or if doing so would result in the number of models that can garrison the terrain feature being exceeded. Then roll a dice for each model you transfer; on a 1 the model being rolled for becomes lost in the shadows and is slain.
6	**Shadow Realm:** *The edges of the battlefield are shrouded in shadow and lead to a strange nether-world.* At the start of your hero phase, pick one friendly unit that has all of its models within 6" of any edge of the battlefield. You can remove that unit from the battlefield, and then set it up more than 9" from any enemy units, and with all models within 6" of a different edge of the battlefield. Then roll a dice for each model you moved; on a 1 the model being rolled for becomes lost in the shadows and is slain.

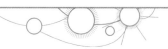

Games set in the Realm of Shadow are typified by misdirection and low visibility, with units suddenly shifting position in the mists, and ambushes being sprung from patches of living shade.

ENDLESS SPELLS

Endless spells are a special type of spell that wizards can use. Casting an endless spell creates a magical construct, represented by an endless spell model, that remains in play until it leaves the battlefield or is unbound. The rules in this section explain how to use endless spells in your games.

ENDLESS SPELLS

If you have an endless spell model and its warscroll, all **WIZARDS** in your army know that spell in addition to any other spells they know. We have included the warscroll for the Balewind Vortex endless spell opposite, which you can use if you have a Balewind Vortex model in your collection. Other endless spell models and the warscrolls for them are available in the *Malign Sorcery* supplement for Warhammer Age of Sigmar.

ENDLESS SPELL MODELS

Endless spell models are not set up on the battlefield at the start of a game. Instead, when an endless spell is successfully cast and not unbound, the model for the spell is set up on the battlefield. Where and how the endless spell model is set up will be described on its warscroll. If any restrictions make it impossible to set up the endless spell model, the attempt to cast it is unsuccessful. Endless spells have no effect on an army's allegiance.

Unless noted otherwise, an endless spell model cannot be attacked or affected by spells or abilities; it is treated as a friendly model by all armies for any other rules purposes. An endless spell model cannot be moved unless it is a predatory endless spell (see below).

In order to attempt to cast an endless spell, you must have a model for the spell available that is not already on the battlefield. For example, if you have two Balewind Vortex models in your collection, and both are on the battlefield, you cannot attempt to cast Summon Balewind Vortex again until at least one of them has been removed from the battlefield. A **WIZARD** cannot attempt to cast more than one endless spell in the same turn (even if they are different endless spells).

PREDATORY ENDLESS SPELLS

Many endless spells are immobile, and once cast remain in the same location. However, some can move across the battlefield in search of living prey: these are noted as being predatory endless spells. The following rules apply to predatory endless spells.

Predatory endless spells are moved at the start of each battle round, after the players determine who will have the first turn, but before the first turn begins. The players alternate picking a predatory endless spell to move, starting with the player who has the second turn. A player must pick a predatory endless spell to move if any are available, but only predatory endless spells that have not yet been moved can be chosen. Once all predatory endless spells have been moved, start the first turn of the battle round.

The distance a predatory endless spell can move will be noted on its warscroll. Some predatory endless spells can fly – this too will be noted on the warscroll.

Unlike other models, a predatory endless spell can cross the edge of the battlefield when it is moved. However, if it does so the spell is immediately dispelled (see Removing Endless Spells, below).

The effects and abilities of predatory endless spells are resolved by the player who moved that model for that battle round.

REMOVING ENDLESS SPELLS

An endless spell remains in play until it is removed from the battlefield. An endless spell can only be removed from play if:

a) A **WIZARD** dispels the endless spell as described below.

b) The endless spell crosses the edge of the battlefield when it is moved (see Predatory Endless Spells, above).

c) A method described on the model's warscroll is used to remove the spell from play.

UNBINDING AND DISPELLING

A **WIZARD** can attempt to unbind an endless spell when it is initially cast as normal. In addition, a **WIZARD** can attempt to dispel one endless spell at the start of each of their hero phases. If a wizard attempts to dispel an endless spell, they can attempt to cast one less spell than normal that phase.

In order to dispel an endless spell, first pick an endless spell model within 30" of the wizard and visible to them, and then roll 2D6. If the roll is greater than the casting value of the spell, the endless spell is dispelled. An endless spell model cannot be subjected to more than one dispel attempt per hero phase.

When an endless spell is dispelled its model is removed from play; the model can then be used again if the same endless spell is successfully cast later in the battle.

ENDLESS SPELL WARSCROLL
BALEWIND VORTEX

A Balewind Vortex is a terrifying sight to behold on the battlefield – a swirling, violently swaying cyclone of fell energies that can be summoned by a wizard and used as a platform from which to more effectively cast their spells.

Summon Balewind Vortex:
Summon Balewind Vortex has a casting value of 6. **WIZARDS** with a Wounds characteristic of 9 or more, that are part of a unit of two or more models, or that are already on a Balewind Vortex, cannot attempt to cast this spell. If successfully cast, set up a Balewind Vortex model within 1" of the caster and more than 3" from any enemy models, and then place the caster on the upper platform.

As long as the Balewind Vortex remains on the battlefield, the caster and the Balewind Vortex are treated as being a single model from the caster's army that uses the caster's warscroll as well as the Endless Spells rules. It is treated as an enemy model by the opposing player's army.

A **WIZARD** on a Balewind Vortex can attempt to cast an additional spell in each of their hero phases (including the turn in which the Summon Balewind Vortex spell was cast), and you can add 6" to the range of any spells that the wizard casts. A wizard on a Balewind Vortex cannot move. Add 1 to save rolls for a wizard on a Balewind Vortex.

If a **WIZARD** on a Balewind Vortex attempts to dispel it, the attempt is automatically successful (do not roll any dice). This uses up the additional spell that the wizard would have received in that hero phase, and still

counts as the single attempt they can make to dispel an endless spell this hero phase, but allows them to use any remaining spell casting attempts normally.

If the wizard on the Balewind Vortex is slain, then the Balewind Vortex is immediately dispelled and removed from play along with the slain wizard.

If a Balewind Vortex is dispelled and the wizard on it has not been slain, set up the wizard wholly within 6" of the Balewind Vortex and more than 3" from any enemy models, and then remove the Balewind Vortex model from play. If it is impossible to set up the wizard, then the wizard is slain.

| KEYWORDS | ENDLESS SPELL, BALEWIND VORTEX |

OPEN PLAY
GAMES

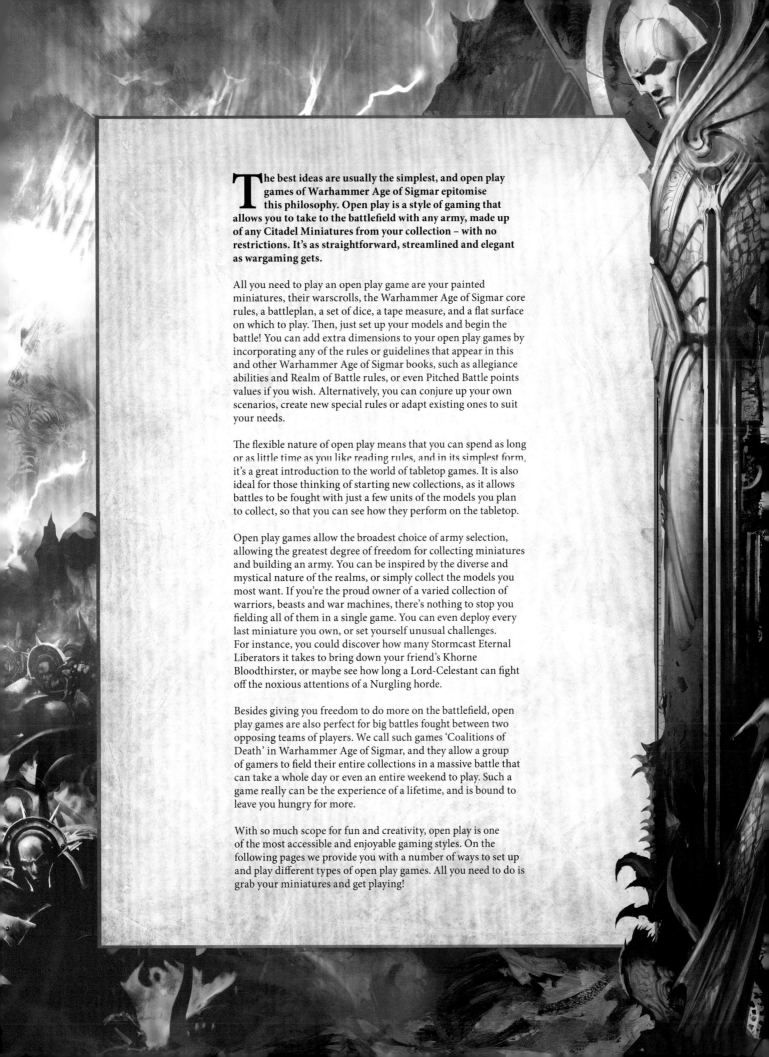

The best ideas are usually the simplest, and open play games of Warhammer Age of Sigmar epitomise this philosophy. Open play is a style of gaming that allows you to take to the battlefield with any army, made up of any Citadel Miniatures from your collection – with no restrictions. It's as straightforward, streamlined and elegant as wargaming gets.

All you need to play an open play game are your painted miniatures, their warscrolls, the Warhammer Age of Sigmar core rules, a battleplan, a set of dice, a tape measure, and a flat surface on which to play. Then, just set up your models and begin the battle! You can add extra dimensions to your open play games by incorporating any of the rules or guidelines that appear in this and other Warhammer Age of Sigmar books, such as allegiance abilities and Realm of Battle rules, or even Pitched Battle points values if you wish. Alternatively, you can conjure up your own scenarios, create new special rules or adapt existing ones to suit your needs.

The flexible nature of open play means that you can spend as long or as little time as you like reading rules, and in its simplest form, it's a great introduction to the world of tabletop games. It is also ideal for those thinking of starting new collections, as it allows battles to be fought with just a few units of the models you plan to collect, so that you can see how they perform on the tabletop.

Open play games allow the broadest choice of army selection, allowing the greatest degree of freedom for collecting miniatures and building an army. You can be inspired by the diverse and mystical nature of the realms, or simply collect the models you most want. If you're the proud owner of a varied collection of warriors, beasts and war machines, there's nothing to stop you fielding all of them in a single game. You can even deploy every last miniature you own, or set yourself unusual challenges. For instance, you could discover how many Stormcast Eternal Liberators it takes to bring down your friend's Khorne Bloodthirster, or maybe see how long a Lord-Celestant can fight off the noxious attentions of a Nurgling horde.

Besides giving you freedom to do more on the battlefield, open play games are also perfect for big battles fought between two opposing teams of players. We call such games 'Coalitions of Death' in Warhammer Age of Sigmar, and they allow a group of gamers to field their entire collections in a massive battle that can take a whole day or even an entire weekend to play. Such a game really can be the experience of a lifetime, and is bound to leave you hungry for more.

With so much scope for fun and creativity, open play is one of the most accessible and enjoyable gaming styles. On the following pages we provide you with a number of ways to set up and play different types of open play games. All you need to do is grab your miniatures and get playing!

INTRODUCING OPEN PLAY

Open play is the default setting for games of Warhammer Age of Sigmar. It allows you to set up and play a game with the minimum amount of fuss and preparation, while still providing you with almost limitless options and flexibility.

The easiest way to play an open play game is to select a battleplan from a Warhammer Age of Sigmar publication and then play that battleplan using whatever Citadel Miniatures you have in your collection. All you need to discuss with your opponent beforehand is which battleplan you want to play. There are no restrictions on how many models you include in your army, on what allegiance your army has, or what kind of models your army is made up of. For example, you can field an army consisting entirely of **Monsters**, or one that contains only **Heroes**. If your collection comprises Stormcast

Eternals and Ironjawz, you can field them all together. Your army can be as large or as small as you like, and take on any form you want – the main thing is to have fun!

While the essence of open play is as simple as that, there are things you can do to add an extra dimension to your games if you wish. Included in this section are tools you can use in your open play games, from the Open War battleplan generator that creates exciting games in an instant, to rules for multiplayer clashes in which teams of players go head-to-head for the glory of their coalition. You can organise a simple ladder

campaign to determine who in your gaming group is the ultimate champion, or even devise your own rules and scenarios to play.

The contents of this section are just the beginning. The beauty of open play is that it's a format limited only by your imagination. Using these tools as your inspiration, you can explore the near-infinite wonders of the Mortal Realms on the tabletop, and collect any of the amazing miniatures in the Warhammer Age of Sigmar range that you desire. Most importantly of all, you now have everything you need to start fighting battles right away.

OPEN PLAY BATTLEPLANS

One of the great advantages of open play is that you don't have to follow any particular rules other than those laid out in the core rules. While it's quick and easy to pick up a ready-made battleplan, it's great fun and highly rewarding to put together your own battleplans for your open play games. Here you will find some easy-to-follow instructions on how to do so.

Before you start writing your own battleplan, you will need to make sure your opponent is happy to play it. While many players are open to trying out homemade rules, it's always a good idea to check that what you have in mind will suit everyone involved. Discuss the rules you aim to include in the battleplan to make sure it appeals to all. You can even write a battleplan collaboratively with your opponent, so that you both have input on the rules that are included. You'll also need to ensure that your battleplan provides an equal opportunity for both sides to win, as fighting a losing battle is no fun at all!

We recommend that you take an existing battleplan, such as First Blood (pg 237), and use it as a template. To start with, try making small changes and seeing how they work. As you become more experienced at adapting battleplans, you will be able to customise them more and more.

Each battleplan should answer the following questions:

1. What, if any, restrictions are there on the models each player can include in their army?
2. What is each player's goal in the battle?
3. What does the battlefield look like?
4. What size and shape is each player's territory?
5. What, if any, special rules are in effect, and how do they work?
6. How are the armies set up at the start of the game?
7. Which player takes the first turn?
8. How long does the game last?
9. How is the winner decided?

Write down the answer to each of these questions and you will have a solid foundation for your battleplan.

ARMIES

In open play games, the default is that you can field any models you like. If a battleplan does not specify any restrictions on army composition, then simply follow the instructions in the core rules – essentially, your army can be made up of any units in your collection. However, for your own battleplan you might wish to impose certain limitations. You can tailor it to your and your opponent's collections; for example, if you have an army of Stormcast Eternals and they have an army of Ironjawz, you can make the battleplan specifically for those units.

Alternatively, you can incorporate a narrative element that calls for the presence of certain models on the battlefield; maybe Alarielle is leading an army of Sylvaneth against the Glottkin during the War of Life. You can even incorporate some matched play mechanics to balance out the armies; perhaps each player can take five units with a combined Wounds characteristic of no more than 100, or you can use Pitched Battle profiles to set a points limit for each army. Remember that the more units you include in each army, the longer the game is likely to last.

GOALS

The goals are what each side is trying to achieve in the battle. They help determine the tactics each player will use, and can also be used to help decide who wins (see Glorious Victory on the next page). The most common goal is simply to defeat the opposing army, but there are plenty of other options. For example, you might say the battle is being fought for control of an ancient monument, and whoever achieves this will be the winner. You can decide that achieving certain goals will award victory points, which is an easy way to keep track of how well each player is doing in a game. If you get stuck coming up with exciting goals, then the stories and scenarios we publish provide plenty of inspiration.

THE BATTLEFIELD

You don't need any terrain at all to play Warhammer Age of Sigmar, but every battlefield looks better if it includes at least some terrain features. The more time and effort you put into creating an attractive battlefield, the more interesting your battles will be.

Your battleplan can use the core rules for setting up terrain, or it can provide its own guidelines. A popular method is for one player to set up the terrain features and for the other to decide which side of the table they will claim as their territory (see Territories, next). This method ensures that the terrain is laid out in as even-handed a manner as possible, and it means that terrain can be set up in advance by the player hosting the game. An alternative is for players to collaborate on setting up the terrain features, and then roll off to see who will pick the territories.

A more competitive method of placing terrain features is for the players to first decide their territories, and then take it in turns to place terrain features upon the battlefield. The players keep on adding terrain features to the tabletop until a pre-determined total is reached – we've found that about six pieces is right for a 6' by 4' table. This method allows the players to create a battlefield where the terrain features help their own army or hinder their opponent's.

If you wish, you can set up the terrain so that it represents the battlefield from a famous fight. The tales of the Mortal Realms are often replete with descriptions of the local landscape, and Realm of Battle rules are ideal for recreating the various regions of the Mortal Realms.

267

TERRITORIES

Once the battlefield has been created, each player's territory must be established. For most games, we recommend you simply divide the table in half down its length, and set up the armies in the opposite halves of the table more than 12" from the dividing line. Alternatively, you can divide the table in half across its width, or diagonally, or by any other method you prefer.

Sometimes, however, the goals you have chosen will require a different or more elaborate deployment for the armies. For example, the goal might be for one side to ambush the other as it marches along a road, in which case one army will need to deploy along the road, and the other in hidden ambush positions. Once again, the background and scenarios published for Warhammer Age of Sigmar provide excellent examples of the different ways that armies can deploy.

SPECIAL RULES

Many battleplans don't have any special rules, allowing you to proceed with battle forthwith! At other times one or two special rules can do a lot to make a game unique and interesting.

Special rules cover certain situations, tactics or abilities that you feel need to be represented in your battle. For example, if you are fighting a battle set in frozen wastelands, you might want to include special rules for things like snowdrifts, blizzards and hazardous footing.

Sometimes the scenario might require that certain special rules are used; in the ambush game mentioned above, you could add a rule that allows the ambushing unit to remain hidden from the enemy until they start attacking, or until a specific battle round is reached. This helps to make the situation feel more realistic as you play.

SETTING UP ARMIES

The method players must use to set up their armies may well be dictated by the goals and territories decided upon earlier. Most commonly, one player will set up their entire army and then their opponent will set up theirs, or the players will alternate setting up units, one at a time. Some players like to place a screen across the centre of the table so that the two armies can deploy in secret, or have the side that will set up second draw a map showing where they plan to deploy their units, and so on. Sometimes you might want to make it so that several units are set up in reserve, arriving at a certain point during the battle to reinforce their allies or achieve a certain goal.

FIRST TURN

You can determine who takes the first turn in the first battle round based on whoever finishes setting up first, or the players can roll off. Maybe the scenario will require one player to take the first turn – for example, if one army is on the offensive.

GAME DURATION

There are a number of ways to determine when a battle will end. You can play until the main goal is achieved, when the battle ends immediately and the successful player is crowned the winner, or you can set an upper limit on the number of battle rounds you will play, at which point the player that has best achieved the goal of the battle is named the winner. Remember when setting a time limit that the larger the game the more time you will need to reach a satisfying conclusion.

GLORIOUS VICTORY

The player that has best achieved the goals of the battle is the winner. More often than not the winner will be obvious. Sometimes the game will be a draw, such as if both sides have accrued the same number of victory points. If you must finish a game before a natural conclusion is reached, then decide between you who has done the most to achieve the goals – that player is the winner.

EXAMPLE OF AN OPEN PLAY BATTLEPLAN

Robin and Stu are arranging to play their regular game of Warhammer Age of Sigmar. A couple of days beforehand, they meet up to discuss the format of the game, and agree to fight an open play battle using the following rules.

THE ARMIES

Stu will use all of the painted models he has ready for his Khorne Bloodbound army. Robin will use his Stormcast Eternals army – including the Celestant-Prime, which he's been working on for weeks. They know that their armies are reasonably well balanced against each other, though the Celestant-Prime may give Robin a slight edge.

THE GOAL

Robin and Stu decide that the goal for their game will be to capture the terrain feature closest to the centre of the table by controlling it for an entire battle round. The player with the most models on or touching the terrain feature at the end of each turn controls it – if a player controls it at the end of one battle round, and continues to control it until the end of the next round, then they capture it and win the battle.

THE BATTLEFIELD

Stu is hosting the game, so he will set up the terrain and Robin will choose which half of the table he wants to set up his army in. Stu will make sure that a suitably impressive terrain feature is set up at the centre of the battlefield for the two sides to fight over.

SET-UP & FIRST TURN

Armies will be set up in opposite halves of the table, more than 12" from the centre line.

Stu will set up first and take the first turn in the first battle round, which will allow him to have his army set up and everything ready by the time Robin arrives for the game. Robin will set up second and take the second turn in the first battle round.

SPECIAL RULES

A 'Reserves' special rule will be used. During set-up, each player will be allowed to keep up to D3 units in reserve (each player rolls their D3 separately). Reserve units enter play in their movement phase, measuring their first move from the battlefield edge. The unit may enter play from the long table edge of the player's territory starting from the second battle round, or from either of the short table edges in their territory starting from the third battle round.

GAME DURATION

Robin and Stu decide that battle will start at 7.30 pm, and last for two and a half hours, or until the goal is achieved. This will allow them to pack everything away after the game and discuss the outcome.

GLORIOUS VICTORY

The winner will be the player that captures the terrain feature. If neither player wins outright by capturing the terrain feature, each player adds up the Wounds characteristic of any enemy units that have been destroyed during the battle (excluding any new units that were added to the armies after the battle started). If one player has a higher total, they are the winner.

OPEN WAR BATTLEPLAN GENERATOR

The Open War battleplan generator tables are designed for players that like the ease and simplicity of open play games, and are looking for as much variety as possible. If you use them, no two games will ever be exactly the same.

Instead of picking a battleplan from a Warhammer Age of Sigmar publication, you can generate your own. This battleplan generator is made up of five tables, which are used to determine how the armies are set up (the Map table), what the players must do in order to win the battle (the Objective and Sudden Death tables), and if any special rules apply to the battle (the Ruse and Twist tables).

THE GENERATOR TABLES

Pick armies and set up terrain as described in the core rules. Then roll on the Map, Objective, Twist, Ruse and Sudden Death generator tables as described below.

MAP

One player rolls a dice and looks up the result on the Map table. This is the map for this battle.

OBJECTIVES

One player rolls a dice and looks up the result on the Objective table. This is the objective for this battle. Sometimes the Objective table will require the player to set up one or more objectives on the battlefield. If both players are required to set up objectives, roll off, and then alternate setting the objectives up starting with the player that won the roll-off.

TWIST

One player rolls a dice and looks up the result on the Twist table. The resulting special rule applies for the duration of the battle.

RUSES & SUDDEN DEATH VICTORY CONDITIONS

Each player must add up the Wounds characteristics of all of the models in their army. If one army has a total that is greater than the other, then the player with the lower total is allowed to roll on the Ruse table. That ruse can only be used by the player that rolled it. If one army has a total that is at least double the

other, then the player with the lower total is allowed to roll on the Sudden Death table as well. That victory condition applies only to the player that rolled it.

SET-UP

The players roll off and the winner decides which territory each side will use. After doing so, the players alternate setting up units wholly within their own territory, one at a time, starting with the player that won the roll-off to pick territories.

GLORIOUS VICTORY

In order to win a **major victory** a player must either achieve the victory conditions rolled on the Objective table, or the one they rolled on the Sudden Death table. Any other result is a draw.

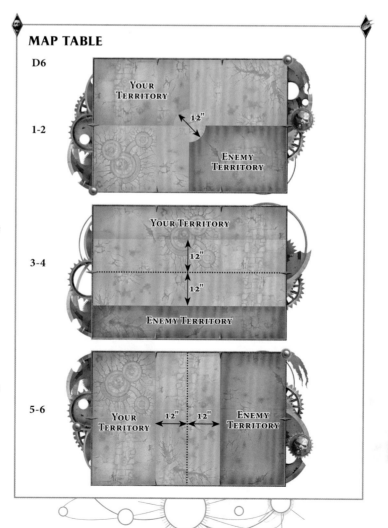

MAP TABLE

D6

1-2

3-4

5-6

OBJECTIVE TABLE

D6 Objective

1-2 Field of Glory: Place one objective in the centre of the battlefield, then the players roll off. Starting with the winner, each player sets up one objective in their territory, more than 6" from any battlefield edge. At the end of the fifth battle round, the player that controls the most objectives wins a **major victory**. You win a **major victory** immediately if you control all three objectives at the end of your turn.

3-4 War of Attrition: Add up the Wounds characteristics of all enemy models that your army slays. At the end of the fifth battle round the player with the highest total wins a **major victory** (even if their own army has been wiped out!).

5-6 Drawn & Quartered: The players roll off. Starting with the winner, take it in turns to set up two objectives each, more than 12" from the centre of the battlefield, more than 6" from any battlefield edge, and more than 18" from any other objectives. At the end of each of your turns, score 1 victory point for each objective you control. The player with the most victory points at the end of the fifth battle round wins a **major victory**.

TWIST TABLE

D6 Twist

1 No Twist: No special rules apply in the battle.

2 Dead of Night: The maximum range of any attack or spell is 12". Roll a dice at the start of each battle round after the first. Each time you roll a 4+, add 6" to the maximum range allowed for attacks and spells.

3 Lighting Strikes: Each player must roll 3 dice at the start of each of their hero phases. For each 6, they can pick a different enemy unit and inflict D3 mortal wounds upon it.

4 Eager for Battle: Add 2" to the Move characteristic of all models, and add 1 to all run and charge rolls.

5 Healing Winds: Each player can pick a friendly model at the start of each of their hero phases. Heal D3 wounds that have been allocated to that model.

6 Grudge Match: Players do not have to take battleshock tests in this battle.

RUSE TABLE

D6 Ruse

1-2 Ambush: During set-up, up to three of your units can be set up anywhere that is not in the enemy's territory and that is more than 9" from any enemy models.

3-4 Reinforcements: Once per battle, at the end of your movement phase, pick a friendly unit from which all of the models have been slain. You can set up the unit again, wholly within 9" of the edge of the battlefield and more than 9" from any enemy models. This counts as the unit's move for that movement phase.

5-6 Outflank: Pick a friendly unit. Instead of setting this unit up on the battlefield, you can place it to one side and say that it is outflanking. You must set it up at the end of either your first or second movement phase, wholly within 9" of the edge of the battlefield and more than 9" from any enemy models. This counts as the unit's move for that movement phase.

SUDDEN DEATH TABLE

D6 Sudden Death Victory Condition

1-2 Assassinate: You immediately win a **major victory** if you slay an enemy **Hero** or **Monster** that has a higher Wounds characteristic than any other enemy model that is currently on the battlefield.

3-4 Blunt: You immediately win a **major victory** if you have slain at least half of the models that your opponent had in their army at the start of the battle.

5-6 Endure: You immediately win a **major victory** if you have at least one model still on the battlefield at the end of the fifth battle round.

COALITION OF DEATH

The Mortal Realms are inhabited by myriad diverse races and factions, each with their own agendas, alliances and enmities. Multiplayer games help tap into this incredible variety and invite exciting, radically different styles of battle to boot.

Warhammer Age of Sigmar games are conventionally played between two people, but battling it out with several players lends the game a somewhat different dynamic, and requires only a few easy modifications to the core rules. Gathering around a tabletop in the thick of the action makes for a great shared experience, and including more players offers a host of practical benefits.

One of the quickest ways to arrange a multiplayer game is for two or more players to join up and fight as a team. The Age of Sigmar is, after all, an age of grand alliances, and the Coalition of Death rules in this section are a great representation of this. Every new alliance brings with it a host of fresh challenges, from making the most of army composition by selecting complementary forces, to seeing that the armies fight in a mutually supportive manner.

Coalition games can also be a boon for new players or those thinking about collecting a new army. Teaming up with a skilled veteran is a great way to learn the nuances of tabletop wargaming, while those dabbling with a new force can see how it might fare in a larger game.

COALITION OF DEATH RULES

A Coalition of Death battle is fought between two sides, each consisting of a team of players. All of the players in the same team combine their models and units into a single force, and must try to defeat the opposing team's combined army.

To play a Coalition of Death game, you must have three or more players. The battle can be fought using any of the battleplans for Warhammer Age of Sigmar – all you need to do is split the players into teams, with each team taking one side in the forthcoming battle. We have also included three battleplans on the following pages that are designed for use with these Coalition of Death rules.

THE ARMIES

Split the players into two teams, using any method you prefer. The two teams can be made up of different numbers of players. Each of the players then chooses an army as described in the core rules.

Each player commands the models they have provided to the coalition, and is allowed to decide what they do, how they move and so on, and they make all of the dice rolls for their own units. Any command abilities a player uses will only affect the units in their own army, not the rest of the coalition. Despite this, the armies belonging to the players on the same team are treated as a combined force during set-up and during the battle.

GENERALS AND WARLORDS

Each player picks a general for their army as normal. You must also pick one player from each coalition to be the warlord. This is often the player fielding the largest force. If, at any time during the game, the coalition cannot decide in what order to carry out actions, then the warlord has final say on the order of events.

In addition, if a dice needs to be rolled for the whole team, the warlord makes that dice roll. Finally, any victory conditions from a battleplan that apply to an army general only apply to the warlord's general unless specifically noted otherwise.

FIGHTING THE BATTLE

Instead of each player taking a turn during a Coalition of Death game, each team takes a turn. The teams' warlords roll off against each other to see which team has the first turn each round.

Where individual players would normally alternate taking actions, the teams alternate taking actions, with each player in the team being allowed to carry out their actions. For example, in the combat phase, each player on one team can attack with one of their units, then each player on the other team, and so on.

The same principle applies during set-up. For example, if you are fighting a battle where the players take it in turns to set up units, then in a Coalition of Death battle, the teams would take turns to set up, with each player in a coalition setting up a unit when it is their side's turn to do so.

Finally, it is worth noting that attempts to unbind a spell are limited to one attempt per team, rather than one attempt for each player on the team. There is only ever one chance to unbind a successfully cast spell!

Khorne Bloodbound
Skarr Bloodwrath

BATTLEPLAN
RACE TO DESTRUCTION

Two armies stumble across each other. The side able to organise an attack the fastest will be able to strike before their opponents are fully prepared.

COALITION OF DEATH

This is a battle for three or more players. Use the Coalition of Death rules from page 272.

SET-UP

Both warlords secretly bid (and write down) the amount of time they want to take setting up. Bids must be in whole minutes. The bids are then revealed, and the amount bid is the time that coalition will have to set up their armies. The side that bids lowest picks a territory and sets up first, within the time period they bid. Their warlord decides who has the first turn in the first battle round. Once the first coalition has been set up, the opposing side does likewise, within the time period they bid. In the case of a tied bid, the bids must be made again.

Units must be set up wholly within their territory more than 9" from enemy territory. Any units that are not set up within the time limit are placed in reserve instead of being set up on the battlefield. If a coalition's bid was twice as much or more than their opponent's bid, then the players from that coalition must roll a dice before they set up a unit on the battlefield; on a roll of 1 or 2 that unit must start in reserve (**HEROES** only have to be placed in reserve on a roll of 1).

Reserve units can enter play in any of their team's movement phases starting from the second battle round. All of the models in the unit must be set up in their coalition's starting territory, within 3" of the table edge, and more than 9" from any enemy units. This counts as their move for that movement phase.

OBJECTIVES

This battle is fought to control four objectives. The objectives are located at the centre of each quarter of the battlefield, as shown on the map.

GLORIOUS VICTORY

The coalition that has scored the most victory points (see below) at the end of the fifth battle round wins a **major victory**. In the case of a tie, both coalitions win a **minor victory**.

VICTORY POINTS

Victory points are scored as follows:

1 victory point is scored each time a coalition slays an enemy model that has a Wounds characteristic of 10 or more.

1 victory point is scored if a coalition slays an enemy general. 1 additional victory point is scored if the general was the enemy warlord's general.

Each objective is worth 1 victory point to the coalition that controls it at end of battle rounds one or two, 2 victory points to the coalition that controls it at the end of battle rounds three or four, and 3 victory points to the coalition that controls it at the end of battle round five.

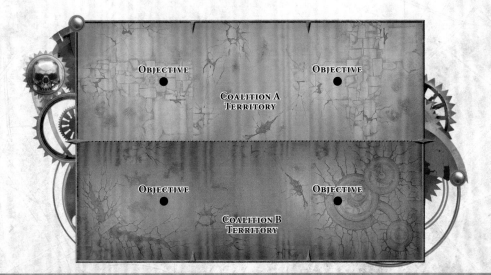

BATTLEPLAN
NIGHT MARCH

A battlefield is a confusing place at night, when it is not uncommon to be unsure of where other friendly forces are located, let alone the enemy.

COALITION OF DEATH

This is a battle for three or more players. Use the Coalition of Death rules from page 272.

SET-UP

Each coalition must be split into three contingents, each with roughly one-third of the units from the coalition. Contingents from the same side do not need to be exactly the same size, as long as none contains more than twice as many units as any other.

Both warlords roll off. The winning team sets up one contingent. All units from that contingent must be set up wholly within one of the six territories shown on the map below. The opposing team sets up one of their contingents in the same manner, and then the first team sets up a second contingent, and so on until all contingents have been set up.

Units must be set up more than 9" from any enemy units. Each contingent must be set up wholly within a different territory, which then counts as their coalition's territory for the rest of the battle.

If a player desires, they may place any of their units in reserve instead of setting them up on the battlefield. Reserve units can enter play in any of their team's movement phases starting from the second battle round. All of the models in the unit must be set up in the same territory as the rest of their contingent, within 3" of the table edge, and more than 9" from any enemy units. This counts as their move for that movement phase.

OBJECTIVES

This battle is fought to control six objectives. One objective is located at the centre of each territory (see map).

ILL MET BY MOONLIGHT

In the first battle round, the range of any missile weapons or spells is limited to 12". Roll a dice at the start of the second battle round. On a roll of 1-3 this rule ends immediately, and on a roll of 4 or more it continues until the end of the second battle round, and then ends.

GLORIOUS VICTORY

The coalition that has scored the most victory points (see below) at the end of the fifth battle round wins a **major victory**. In the case of a tie, both coalitions win a **minor victory**.

VICTORY POINTS

Victory points are scored as follows:

1 victory point is scored each time a coalition slays an enemy model that has a Wounds characteristic of 10 or more.

1 victory point is scored if a coalition slays an enemy general. 1 additional victory point is scored if the general was the enemy warlord's general.

Each objective is worth 1 victory point to the coalition that controls it at the end of their turn if it is located in their own territory, and D3 victory points if it is located in enemy territory.

BATTLEPLAN
CHANGING PRIORITIES

Often the goals for a battle will shift and change, forcing an army to first attack in one direction and then another, or to stubbornly defend an objective at one moment and launch an all-out assault the next.

COALITION OF DEATH
This is a battle for three or more players. Use the Coalition of Death rules from page 272.

SET-UP
Both warlords roll off, and the winning team must pick a territory and set up first. The opposing team then sets up their army in the remaining territory. Units must be set up wholly within their own territory more than 9" from enemy territory.

If a player desires, they may place any of their units in reserve instead of setting them up on the battlefield. Reserve units can enter play in any of their team's movement phases starting from the second battle round. All of the models in the unit must be set up in their coalition's starting territory, within 3" of the table edge, and more than 9" from any enemy units. This counts as their move for that movement phase.

OBJECTIVES
This battle is fought to control two objectives, one in each side's territory. However, the locations of the two objectives may change each battle round.

At the start of each battle round, each warlord rolls a dice. The objectives are located in each warlord's territory at the centre of the area shown on the map that corresponds to their dice roll.

GLORIOUS VICTORY
The coalition that has scored the most victory points (see below) at the end of the fifth battle round wins a **major victory**. In the case of a tie, both coalitions win a **minor victory**.

VICTORY POINTS
Victory points are scored as follows:

1 victory point is scored each time a coalition slays an enemy model that has a Wounds characteristic of 10 or more.

1 victory point is scored if a coalition slays an enemy general. 1 additional victory point is scored if the general was the enemy warlord's general.

Each objective is worth D3 victory points to the coalition that controls it at end of their turn if it is located in their own territory, and D6 victory points if it is located in enemy territory.

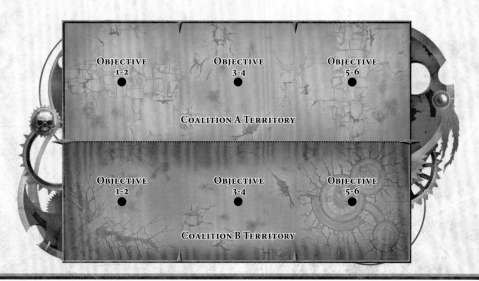

OBJECTIVE 1-2 OBJECTIVE 3-4 OBJECTIVE 5-6

COALITION A TERRITORY

OBJECTIVE 1-2 OBJECTIVE 3-4 OBJECTIVE 5-6

COALITION B TERRITORY

LADDER CAMPAIGN

Taking you beyond basic one-off battles, campaigns add a new dimension to your gaming. Essentially, they link the battles you fight together, so that the result of each battle will be affected by the one that went before and influence the one that comes after.

If battles are exciting short stories, then campaigns are epic novels, packed with plot twists and cliffhangers. In essence, a campaign is simply a series of battles that are linked together in some way. Ladder campaigns offer a simple, straightforward and highly enjoyable campaign structure, that will let you settle old rivalries and make brand new ones – all in the name of friendly competition, of course! Here you'll learn how to fight your way to the top, one rung at a time.

In its simplest form, a ladder campaign involves participants attempting to battle their way to the top of the 'ladder' by defeating their fellows. The more battles you win, the higher up the ladder you will climb.

The concept sounds simple, but there can be a great deal of strategy involved. Pick your opponents wisely, as your next battle might propel you into top position – or send you right to the bottom! The trickiest part about scaling the ladder's giddy heights is staying at the top. The champion's position is the most precarious, as every other player will be vying to depose them.

You can use any of the rules presented in this and other Warhammer Age of Sigmar publications when fighting your battles, but ladder campaigns are particularly well-suited to open play gaming. On the following page you will find an example ladder campaign that you can play – or use as inspiration for creating your own – as well as some hints and tips for making your campaigns even more exciting.

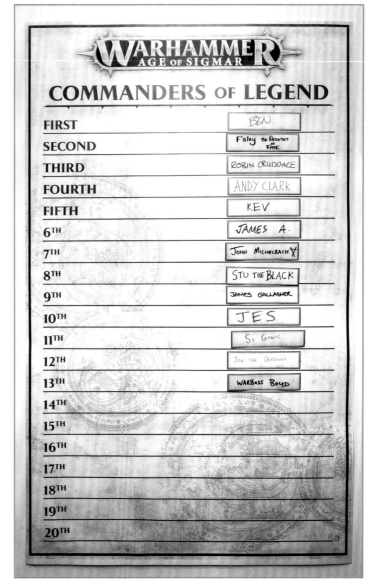

WARHAMMER AGE OF SIGMAR	
COMMANDERS OF LEGEND	
FIRST	BEN.
SECOND	F'oley THE ARCHITECT OF FATE
THIRD	ROBIN CRUDDACE
FOURTH	ANDY CLARK
FIFTH	KEV
6TH	JAMES A.
7TH	JOHN MICHELBACH
8TH	STU THE BLACK
9TH	JAMES GALLAGHER
10TH	JES
11TH	Si Grant
12TH	JON THE DESTROYER
13TH	WARBoss BOYD
14TH	
15TH	
16TH	
17TH	
18TH	
19TH	
20TH	

This is the ladder from our own Warhammer Age of Sigmar ladder campaign. Numerous battles have been fought as part of this campaign. At the time this picture was taken, Ben Johnson's Stormcast Eternals were in the top spot, Pete Foley's Disciples of Tzeentch were in second place, and Robin Cruddace's Stormcast Eternals were in third place but coming on strong. Some players have fought games almost every day, while others have only played now and then, but great fun is being had by all however frequently they take part in the campaign. This ability to dip in and out of a ladder campaign is one of its great strengths, and can give it incredible longevity – the campaign shown above has already been going on for several months, and continues to this day!

LADDER OF COMMAND

A Warhammer Age of Sigmar ladder campaign is a great way to organise a series of open play games. Players challenge each other in battle with the view of climbing the ladder, and whoever is at the top is considered the current reigning champion.

The concept of a ladder campaign is really very simple. A list of all of the players taking part is made, with the first player to join being number one, the second player to join number two and so on. As new players join the ladder, they add their name to the end of the list and take the next number.

So a ladder with six players would have a list of six names numbered from one to six. If two players later joined the ladder, they would be given positions seven and eight, and so on.

When players on the ladder fight a battle, the result will affect their position on the ladder as described in the rules that follow. To play a ladder game, all you need to do is choose a willing opponent from the ladder and arrange to fight a battle!

CLIMBING THE LADDER

If the winner of a battle is the lower of the two players on the ladder, they swap places with their opponent. If the winner is higher up the ladder, they swap places with the player that is directly above them, unless they are at the very top, in which case the loser drops a rung on the ladder. In the case of a tie, the players remain in their current positions.

For example, if player five defeats player three in battle, they swap places. But if player three is victorious over player five, player three swaps places with player two.

In addition to the above, anyone who doesn't play a game for a month drops to the bottom of the ladder, falling below any players who have played games in the last month.

The player at the top of the ladder is the current reigning champion!

HINTS & TIPS

Ladders are a great way to run a simple league, and are very easy to modify if you want to add more detail or complexity.

For example, you can stipulate that players use certain Realm of Battle rules in their games. Alternatively, you could say that they must use the Open War battleplan generator tables (pg 270-271) for the games they play.

Although ladder campaigns work really well with open play games, you can use them for any other format too. For example, you can get players to pick their armies using the Pitched Battle rules on pages 310-311.

Last, but far from least, you can tie in special games and events that take place at your club or gaming group to the ladder. Perhaps at the end of each month there is a special multiplayer battle fought between the top players (rules for this type of game can be found on pages 302-303). Or, at the end of the year, you could hand out trophies and certificates to players for their achievements, such as holding the top place for the longest period of time, fighting the most battles, advancing the most rungs in a single month, and so on.

NARRATIVE PLAY GAMES

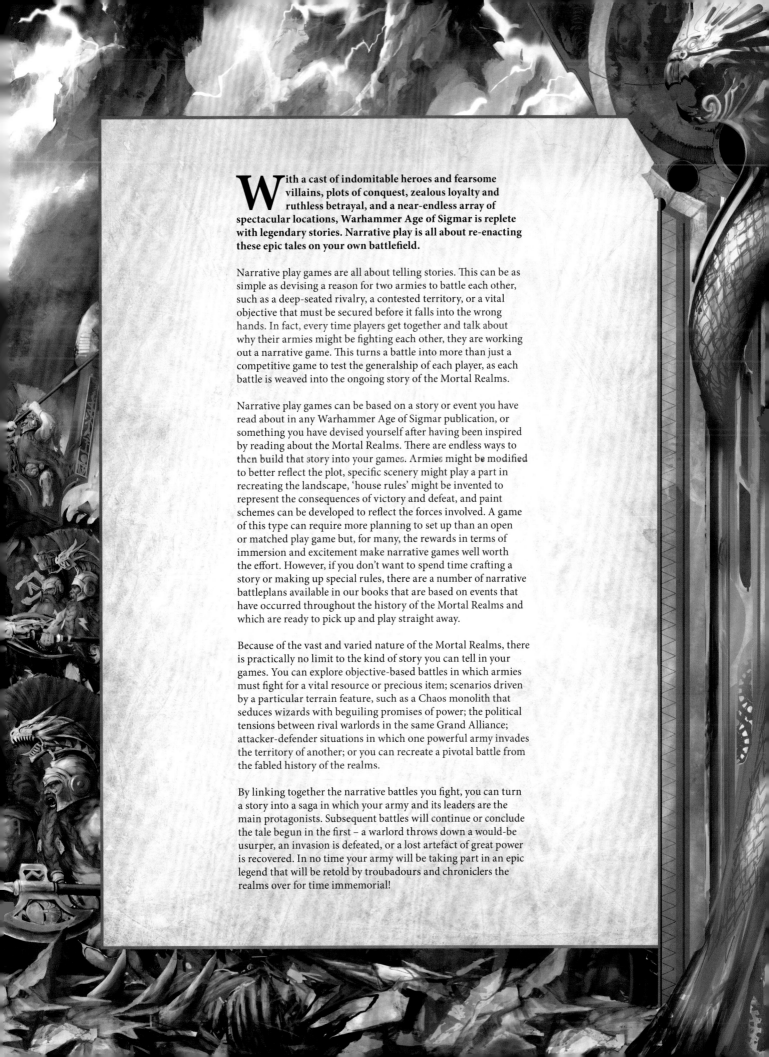

With a cast of indomitable heroes and fearsome villains, plots of conquest, zealous loyalty and ruthless betrayal, and a near-endless array of spectacular locations, Warhammer Age of Sigmar is replete with legendary stories. Narrative play is all about re-enacting these epic tales on your own battlefield.

Narrative play games are all about telling stories. This can be as simple as devising a reason for two armies to battle each other, such as a deep-seated rivalry, a contested territory, or a vital objective that must be secured before it falls into the wrong hands. In fact, every time players get together and talk about why their armies might be fighting each other, they are working out a narrative game. This turns a battle into more than just a competitive game to test the generalship of each player, as each battle is weaved into the ongoing story of the Mortal Realms.

Narrative play games can be based on a story or event you have read about in any Warhammer Age of Sigmar publication, or something you have devised yourself after having been inspired by reading about the Mortal Realms. There are endless ways to then build that story into your games. Armies might be modified to better reflect the plot, specific scenery might play a part in recreating the landscape, 'house rules' might be invented to represent the consequences of victory and defeat, and paint schemes can be developed to reflect the forces involved. A game of this type can require more planning to set up than an open or matched play game but, for many, the rewards in terms of immersion and excitement make narrative games well worth the effort. However, if you don't want to spend time crafting a story or making up special rules, there are a number of narrative battleplans available in our books that are based on events that have occurred throughout the history of the Mortal Realms and which are ready to pick up and play straight away.

Because of the vast and varied nature of the Mortal Realms, there is practically no limit to the kind of story you can tell in your games. You can explore objective-based battles in which armies must fight for a vital resource or precious item; scenarios driven by a particular terrain feature, such as a Chaos monolith that seduces wizards with beguiling promises of power; the political tensions between rival warlords in the same Grand Alliance; attacker-defender situations in which one powerful army invades the territory of another; or you can recreate a pivotal battle from the fabled history of the realms.

By linking together the narrative battles you fight, you can turn a story into a saga in which your army and its leaders are the main protagonists. Subsequent battles will continue or conclude the tale begun in the first – a warlord throws down a would-be usurper, an invasion is defeated, or a lost artefact of great power is recovered. In no time your army will be taking part in an epic legend that will be retold by troubadours and chroniclers the realms over for time immemorial!

INTRODUCING NARRATIVE PLAY

On the following pages, you will find advice that will help you create and fight exciting narrative battles. We will provide guidance on how to set up a narrative battle, and you will find examples of the rules and battleplans we have used in our own narrative games.

There are already many great resources for narrative play, and more are coming all the time. *The Realmgate Wars* series of books are a great example of this, and they provide a perfect jumping-off point for anyone interested in recreating events from that tumultuous period of the Age of Sigmar. The stories set out in the various Warhammer Age of Sigmar publications are there to provide more than just a setting for your collections of Citadel Miniatures. Some of these tales are about specific individuals, like the famous Vandus Hammerhand of the Hammers of Sigmar, while some tell the story of entire battles. All of them, however, can provide inspiration for games you might want to play.

These books often contain battleplans that allow you to play narrative games based on the tales you read there. Recreating a battle just as it happened in the narrative is great fun, and as we've already created many battleplans that do this, it's very easy as well. Simply choose a story you wish to recreate and play the battleplan associated with it.

With only a little effort, however, it is just as satisfying to use those battleplans as frameworks for making up your own stories, tailored particularly to your own model collections. You can even create entirely new battleplans to tell stories of your own.

PLANNING A NARRATIVE GAME
Planning a narrative game is often just as fun as playing the game itself, as it lets you really unleash your imagination. Maybe you're battling it out in the Realm of Beasts where the land itself is alive. Angered by the presence of strange armies, it shakes and ruptures, causing earthquakes, landslides and buildings to crash down upon those who venture across it. Once you've conjured up an idea for a battleplan, you can work out where your forces will fight and the aspects of that environment which could help or hinder the warring parties. The battleground could be a mountain range caught in a magic-draining blizzard or a barren plain blasted with scorching desert winds. Perhaps you wish to play out the story of an epic siege, recreating the daring actions of the invading force bringing down the battlements, or the stoic defenders standing strong against the onslaught. You can use any of the optional rules in this book and other Warhammer Age of Sigmar publications to give tactical significance to these story elements.

Whether you aspire to play a straightforward clash to destroy your opponent's army or you want to try out something more creative, such as casting down the arcane idols of your dark foes, there are some questions that should be addressed before you take to the field of battle. Existing battleplans routinely answer these questions for you, but if you want to invent your own battleplan you'll need to work them out for yourself. On pages 267-269 you will find a step-by-step guide to creating your own battleplan from scratch, and these same instructions can be used to write a battleplan that incorporates all the narrative elements you want. You can tailor each part of the battleplan to the story, from the armies included to the objectives being fought for, from the location of the battle to how the victory conditions are determined.

For example, you could recreate one of the battles fought on Decrepita in the Realm of Life, where Nagash sent his legions to steal the land from Alarielle's people. The armies could include Sylvaneth on one side, and Nighthaunt, Deathrattle and Deadwalker units on the other. You could use the Realm of Battle rules for Ghyran, and write a special rule to represent the seemingly endless hordes of undead that besieged the isle. Whatever story you want to tell, the rules to recreate it on the tabletop are at your fingertips.

Making your own battleplans, special rules and creatures is heady stuff, but be warned that it's not for everyone. Some players prefer to keep their games within the remit of the published rules, so it is vital to ensure that your opponent is happy to play with any bespoke rules you have created. While you may have built your own mighty monolith to the Dark Gods and come up with some great rules to go along with it, just as importantly you'll need to find an opponent that wants to fight a battle using your creation on the table. Springing such an invention onto an opponent expecting a matched play battle probably won't go down well. Setting up such a game as a special occasion will work better. In fact, clubs or gaming groups sometimes put on extravagant and highly themed games, on occasion even taking them to show off at major events such as Games Workshop's Warhammer Fest.

GAMES MASTERS

One of the best ways to introduce new rules or a bespoke battleplan into a game is with the help of a games master. A games master (or GM for short) is an optional figure who can preside over and run a particular battle. The GM helps the players by setting up the battleplan and interpreting – or even making up – the rules as needed.

Games masters offer fantastic opportunities for Warhammer Age of Sigmar players to vary their games. GMs are a neutral party who can coordinate any number of entertaining gaming options, such as an unexpected ambush. Just like real commanders, the players won't know where their enemy is (or in some cases, what their enemy is). Imagine a battle interrupted by a monster disturbed by fighting too close to its lair, or the sudden realisation that the ruined altars atop the hills still contain great power. Having a games master can put the players into the shoes of a 'real' general and offers great scope for creating battlefields where nothing can be taken for granted. Hidden objectives, secret agendas amongst players, and competitive rivalries between allies are all battleplan rules best coordinated by a GM.

A games master is not to be confused with a tournament umpire, who is there to act as an adjudicator in rules disputes. Being a games master should be more about incorporating creative ideas and elements into a game without upsetting the competitive balance of the rules than double-checking whether a unit is eligible to charge an opponent. The role of a GM is more to do with creating an immersive and interactive environment in which battles can take place, and ensuring the game runs smoothly.

If you are interested in coming up with new battleplan ideas, rules twists or ideas for new creature types then try making up a game for your gaming group. It is a good idea to stick to armies you or your friends have, and add a few creative touches, such as a new terrain feature, battleplan special rules or a specially created monster. Even rigid, by-the-book players are more comfortable with new rules mechanics when the game is presided over by a GM. Their presence should ensure balance, as the game won't be dominated by one player over-eager to try out their new modelling project. The key to being a great GM is to remain fair and impartial, while at the same time ensuring all the players have a fantastic time.

THE REALMGATE WARS

If you're looking for narrative games to play, *The Realmgate Wars* series is the perfect place to start. Replete with gripping stories and dynamic rules, these four books provide all you need to recreate the fateful battles of this era on the tabletop.

Each battleplan in these books represents a part of this epic narrative, but can also be adapted to suit similar scenarios in which different armies clash together. This means that whatever models you have in your collection, and whatever stories you'd like to tell, these battleplans can be easily modified to suit.

As well as battleplans, each of these books includes one or more sets of Time of War rules. These allow you to recreate some of the wondrous and terrifying environs discovered by the armies that fought in these battles. With rules representing many of the famed regions in which these conflicts took place, along with the incredible creatures and natural wonders of the realms that played their part in these encounters, these rules offer a plethora of tools for turning these and other stories into narrative games of Warhammer Age of Sigmar.

The combined content of these tomes provides narrative gamers with a wide range of inspirational ideas that you can use either straight from the pages, or adapt to create narrative battles of your own devising.

WAR IN THE GLYMMSFORGE CATACOMBS

The Hammers of Sigmar, led by the Celestant-Prime, have struck deep into Nagash's realm to combine forces with the Anvils of the Heldenhammer outside the city of Glymmsforge. They hope to recover an ossuary of sacred grave salt from the catacombs that have been claimed by Nagash's forces, and use it to restore the city's arcane defences.

We have created an example narrative battle using the amazing scenery and armies made and painted by the Games Workshop hobby team. It pits Nagash, the hobby team's Nighthaunt army, and several other Death models from the hobby team's collection, against a combined force of Hammers of Sigmar and Anvils of the Heldenhammer. The battle is shown in the photograph on this page, along with details of some of the special rules in effect for the battle.

1. Nagash: The Sentinel (see 4.) will quickly warn Nagash of any attempt to enter the catacombs, so that he can travel to the battlefield to deal with the intruders. At the start of each hero phase, the Death player rolls a dice, and if the roll is equal to or less than the current battle round, Nagash arrives and is set up at the top of Mount Sinister along with a bodyguard of two Morghasts.

2. Guardians of the Catacombs: The entrance to the catacombs is defended by two Morghast statues. The Sentinel can use an Animate Guardians spell with a casting value of 5 to bring a Morghast statue to (un)life.

3. The Lower Catacombs: The entrance to the lower catacombs is the objective of the Stormcast Eternals' attack. In order to win the battle, the Stormcast Eternals need to have a unit within 3" of the tunnel entrance at the start of their hero phase, and then roll a 4+ to find the hidden ossuary and win the battle. However, to complicate matters, starting from the first battle round, the Skeleton Warrior units in the Death army can use this entrance to move onto the battlefield.

4. The Sentinel: *A Necromancer known as the Sentinel stands eternal vigil over the entrance to the catacombs, his powers enhanced by a golden Numinous Occulum. The Sentinel is set up in the Occulum at the start of the battle. He can be used to animate the Guardians of the Catacombs (see 2.) and can use the Numinous Occulum rules (see games-workshop.com).*

5. Gate Sinister: *The Hammers of Sigmar are using a Realmgate called Gate Sinister to reach the battlefield. At the start of the battle, the Hammers of Sigmar units can be set up within 12" of the Realmgate. Any units set up in the Celestial Realm, using Scions of the Storm or a similar ability, can be set up within 12" of the Realmgate when they arrive on the battlefield instead of using the normal rule.*

6. The Sinister Underway: *The upper catacomb peaks are threaded with a network of magical tunnels called the Sinister Underway. With the exception of the entrance to the lower catacombs (see 3.), all of the tunnel entrances on the battlefield are treated as if they were Baleful Realmgates, using the rules from that warscroll (see games-workshop. com), with the exception of the Hazardous Journey rule. This allows units to move safely from one tunnel entrance to another, instead of making a normal move in their movement phase.*

9. The Celestant-Prime: *The Stormcast Eternals army is led by the Celestant-Prime.*

8. Sigmarite Mausoleums: *Nighthaunt units can be set up within 3" of a Sigmarite Mausoleum at the start of the battle. Any remaining Nighthaunt units can come into play using Sinister Underway entrances (see 6.) that are more than 6" from any enemy models.*

7. Anvils of the Heldenhammer: *These noble warriors have been fighting a prolonged campaign to defend the city of Glymmsforge, and march swiftly to aid their comrades. Anvils of the Heldenhammer units are not set up on the battlefield at the start of the battle, and instead arrive in the second and third battle rounds, on the old road at the corner of the battlefield.*

HISTORICAL BATTLES

Tales from the Age of Sigmar are filled with heroic deeds and legendary battles. With a little imagination you can recreate these battles with your armies on the tabletop and find out if history will repeat itself, or if your command can alter the course of fate.

The Mortal Realms are rich with legend, with events of great magnitude casting their shadows long over the aeons that follow, storied heroes rising at moments of strife to wrest power from the forces of Chaos, and figures of darkness manipulating fate to serve their own agendas. This vast and ever-unfolding tapestry of history is a mine of inspiration for your narrative games.

You can find exciting tales in any of our publications, from campaign books to Black Library novels. You might find a whole chapter dedicated to a battle you want to recreate in your games, or it might be just a brief mention in the pages of *White Dwarf* that grabs your attention. Crossed swords on maps mark the sites of past battles, their names receding into legend. Artwork provides a window into the Mortal Realms, offering astounding details that can be translated to tabletop games. The annals of the Age of Sigmar are filled with such material, a treasure trove of clashes between great armies, and the meeting of gods, heroes and monsters in battle.

Stormcast Eternals
Lord-Celestant
Thostos Bladestorm

Recreating the legendary battles from the history of the Mortal Realms is, for many, the pinnacle of narrative gaming. Fashioning rules that recreate the circumstances of such a monumental clash can be a truly satisfying exercise, and collecting and painting the fabled heroes and armies that fought in it is, for many, a hugely rewarding project.

Furthermore, the epic grandeur of these events makes for a really thrilling game, imbued with all the gravitas of these epoch-defining moments. However, in your games things might not unravel in the same way as history tells it – the hand of fate might intervene, reversing the fortunes of all involved, or your own strategic skills could turn the tide of battle at the last. Many players enjoy challenging history in this way, determining how they would fare in the shoes of the heroes and warlords that feature in these stories.

As was covered on the previous pages, there are a number of ways you can recreate a story from the Mortal Realms. Often there will be a battleplan that accompanies the story that you can play right away. Other times you may need to adapt a similar battleplan or create a new one. There is no right or wrong method for doing this, as long as all players agree beforehand. If you want to recreate an event accurately, this involves doing some research to learn the details of the battle, such as the size, disposition and appearance of the armies, which notable heroes were present, where the battle took place and how long it raged for. Special rules can be written to represent the unique situation of the battle you're fighting, and where such information is not available, you can use your imagination to fill in the blanks.

You can spend time tailoring your collection of Citadel Miniatures to represent a particular army at a

particular period in time, taking them through each of the milestone battles that moulded their fate. You can take pains to ensure the terrain matches the description of the region in which each battle took place, representing as best you can that fabled site. Ultimately, the more details you discover or create about the armies, terrain, strategies and special circumstances that were involved, the more enjoyable your historical battles will be. Designing rules, army lists and a modelled battlefield is all part of the fun.

On the following pages you will find an example of a historical battle that we have played, which you can use as inspiration for your own games. It recreates the events depicted in *The Realmgate Wars: Quest for Ghal Maraz*, in which Lord-Celestant Vandus Hammerhand of the Hammers of Sigmar at last seized the God-King's fabled hammer from the claws of Kairos Fateweaver and his coven of Tzeentchian sorcerers. Opposite, you can read the thrilling story of this crucial battle, and overleaf you can find out what happened when we took it to the tabletop!

To replay this pivotal moment, we assembled two armies, one of Stormcast Eternals, another of Lords of Change and their minions. Vandus Hammerhand and Kairos Fateweaver are each represented by their own models and warscrolls, while their armies are made up of models taken from the Stormcast Eternals and Disciples of Tzeentch ranges. Read on to see how we went about recreating this crucial battle…

THE QUEST FOR GHAL MARAZ

Having fought across the Great Crucible to the reach the Eldritch Fortress, the Heldenhammer Crusade neared its night-impossible goal. Warpflame lit the skies, and around the Stormcasts a hurricane of magical energy raged – the battle for Ghal Maraz was reaching its bloody conclusion…

Vandus and his warriors stood before the forbidding wall of skulls that formed the outer perimeter of the Eldritch Fortress, then plunged into the daemon gale, every step a new trial. The hurricane of magic pushed and plucked at them with ethereal claws, raining down daemons that hurled blasts of warpfire from the battlements or fell burning into their ranks from on high. By harnessing the storm magic that crackled above, the fortress had almost gathered enough aetheric energy to transport Ghal Maraz to the Realm of Chaos, where it would lie beyond the reach of the God-King forever.

The Stormcast Eternals fought on. With Ionus at Vandus' side and warrior brethren from a dozen Stormhosts at their command, they fought through gibbering daemons, walls of living crystal and raging Bloodbound warriors to reach the innermost keep. The layered walls of the Eldritch Fortress seemed endless, folding back on themselves like the most complex of mazes. Thostos alone had experience of them, and even then could claim only passing knowledge of their convolutions. Nonetheless, he led the crusade unerringly through the daemon gale. Vandus believed he was likely guided by vengeance itself. Soon enough, the Celestial Vindicators stood before the breach they had forced when the fortress had blighted Anvrok.

In the courtyard of the inner keep, the ground bubbled lazily around the cog-like workings of an Arcanabulum. The forbidden device plinked and pinged as it cooled in the ethereal winds raging around it, its magic spent in the titanic feat of wrenching the Alchemist's Moon backwards in the sky. Standing haggard by its side was a long-limbed, horned sorcerer – bent with age, yet still recognisably Ephryx, Ninth Disciple of Tzeentch. Thostos gave vent to a bellow of rage and charged, head lowered. Eyes lambent green, the sorcerer moved back inside the inner keep, waving for his army of halberd-wielding guardsmen to bar the Stormcast Eternals' path. In less than a minute, the broken cadavers of the Chaos Warriors were strewn across the courtyard, and eight hulking Retributors were taking their hammers to the wall of flame that formed its gate.

Cerulean shafts of light poured outward as widening holes appeared in the warpfire barrier. Thostos lifted his voice in thanks, and a thousand strident cheers echoed him – they saw the light of Ghal Maraz. All those struck by it found their tired limbs imbued with strength anew. The Retributors redoubled their efforts, their prize within reach. Fell chanting in the dark tongue drifted from within, a sign that the trickery of Tzeentch was not yet over. The curtain of flame finally vanished, revealing glory and horror alike. The Great Shatterer was found.

Held suspended by fetters of pure magic, the ancient relic was surrounded by a coven of nine greater daemons of Tzeentch. Each was chanting syllables so foul they made the ears of the Stormcast Eternals trickle with blood. The bird-like monstrosities turned to face the intruders, their wizened visages twisted with hatred. At the head of the ritual cabal was a two-headed Lord of Change clutching a tall staff, its elongated features leering cruelly.

Rippling and burning, the Shardgate descended through the domed roof of the keep. Time had almost run out. The Great Shatterer was finally within Sigmar's reach, though it was far from undefended: the cabal of nine Lords of Change stood between the Stormcast Eternals and their prize. The gods looked on, unable to tear their gazes away as the fate of Chamon was decided.

QUEST FOR GHAL MARAZ –
THE BATTLE FOR THE INNER KEEP

Inspired by the story of Vandus Hammerhand's quest to recover Ghal Maraz, we decided to begin our game at the point when he arrived at the inner keep of the Eldritch Fortress, at the very climax of the battle. We used the bulk of our collections of Hammers of Sigmar, Celestial Vindicators and Disciples of Tzeentch for the game, recreating the inner keep using our Chaos Dreadhold models and other pieces of scenery from our collection.

SET-UP

Even we were not able to rustle up all nine Lords of Change that were present at the final confrontation, so we decided to begin the battle at a point where their number had been whittled down to a rather more manageable four. This also allowed us to start with both sides very close together, which meant the fighting started almost straight away. The Tzeentch army was set up first, in or just beside the Chaos Dreadhold, and the Stormcast Eternals set up second just 12" away. We then rolled off to see who had the first turn…

ILLUSIONS AND MIRAGES

The Lords of Change created a magical maze of illusions and mirages to distract the Stormcast Eternals from their task. Only the Celestial Vindicators could forge a true path through this maze, their pure rage allowing them to see through the visions. To represent this, the Stormcast Eternals players had to subtract 1 from the Move characteristic of the Hammers of Sigmar units for each Lord of Change that was still alive (excluding Kairos Fateweaver). This modifier didn't apply to units that were within 6" of a Celestial Vindicator unit at the start of their move.

THE ARMIES

We split the Stormcast Eternals into a coalition with two contingents (each commanded by a different player), one consisting of a Hammers of Sigmar Warrior Chamber led by Vandus Hammerhand, and the other a Celestial Vindicators Warrior Chamber led by Thostos Bladestorm. The Disciples of Tzeentch army was a single combined force, led by an Omniscient Oracles warscroll battalion.

1. *Kairos Fateweaver:* General of the Tzeentch army.

2. *Ephryx the Ninth Disciple:* *This sorcerer was bewitched by Kairos Fateweaver in the story. To represent this, the Stormcast Eternals players rolled a dice in each of their hero phases. On a 6, Ephryx broke free from Kairos' control and was treated as part of the Stormcast Eternals army until the end of that turn, after which he vanished from the battle!*

3. *Vandus Hammerhand:* General of the Hammers of Sigmar contingent.

4. *Ionus Cryptborn:* *The Stormcast Eternals players were allowed to re-roll failed prayer rolls for Ionus, to reflect his prowess.*

5. *Thostos Bladestorm:* General of the Celestial Vindicators contingent.

ONWARDS REGARDLESS

The quest for Ghal Maraz was too important for any Stormcast Eternal to even think of turning back. Because of this, we said that Stormcast Eternals units didn't have to take battleshock tests in this battle.

GLORIOUS VICTORY

We decided that Ghal Maraz was hovering in the air just above the Skull Keep at the centre of the Chaos Dreadhold. In order to win, the Stormcast Eternals needed to get a **Hero** within 3" of the Skull Keep at the end of one of their turns, and then roll a 5+ to seize Ghal Maraz and win the game. 1 was added to the dice roll for each failed attempt there had been to seize the hammer (so a 5+ was needed the first time it was tried, then a 4+, and so on). If they failed to do this before the end of the battle, or if the Stormcast Eternals were wiped out, then the Disciples of Tzeentch would be the winners!

CAMPAIGNS IN THE MORTAL REALMS

Campaigns weave individual narrative play games together in an unfolding story. Each chapter of the story affects the one that follows, creating a truly immersive gaming saga. Providing scope to tell epic tales that involve numerous different battles, campaigns are ideal for expanding your narrative play experience.

If you feel like you want to take your narrative gaming to the next level, creating a campaign is a great way to start. By connecting games together, both with rules and with an over-arching narrative, you can engage in an even more immersive form of gaming. There are various mechanisms you can use to connect your games, some of which are explained here.

A campaign can be as extensive as you like, from a few battles between two players, to sprawling epic conflicts that involve your entire gaming group. For instance, you could pitch your army against that of a friend and spend a day playing a short campaign that encompasses a skirmish, an epic main battle and a desperate last stand. Alternatively, you can get a group of players involved in a campaign that lasts for weeks, or even months, before it comes to its epic conclusion. Campaigns like this are great motivators for developing an army, inspiring players to collect, build and paint new miniatures for each encounter.

If you're new to campaigning, it's best to start small. A set of connected battles with a manageable objective such as capturing a Realmgate is ideal. Once you have developed a taste for campaigning, you can make use of increasingly complex systems. Campaigns can develop into huge multiplayer battles where pacts are formed and armies expand as the sagas unfold. In fact, stories are at the heart of every successful narrative campaign, and when combined with a sound framework and organisation, they provide the excitement and interest that keeps everyone motivated to win.

LINKED BATTLE CAMPAIGNS

One of the simplest campaign formats, linked battle campaigns are literally just a string of battles connected together in a linear fashion. The outcome of each battle affects the scenario for the next, allowing you to create realistic plots that develop over time. It's only a short step from planning a story for one game to planning a story that extends across several. As the campaign goes on, a narrative arc will naturally form. Grudges will be established, vows of redemption will be sworn, heroic characters will show their worth.

For example, the objective of the first battle might be to secure a sacred relic. In the second battle, the losing army will challenge the victor to a rematch, but this time the army in possession of the relic benefits from its magical powers! Linking games together like this presents new and exciting tactical challenges. Players must consider the bigger picture in every decision they make, and remember that it is possible to lose a battle and still win the war.

The scope for linked battle campaigns is practically endless. Here's another example: Two regular gaming opponents agree to play a linked battle campaign. They decide the first game will be an ambush, with a Bloodbound pack surprising a Fyreslayers army on its way to a larger battle. Any models that survive this initial skirmish can take part in the second battle, a conflict between two larger armies, in which the survivors from game one arrive as reinforcements in the second battle round. If a ten-model strong unit of Vulkite Berzerkers suffers four casualties during the course of game one, then in the following game, the Fyreslayers player can add the unit of six surviving Vulkite Berzerkers to their army as reinforcements.

Even in this simple example, each battle presents interesting tactical decisions. A timely retreat in the first game might serve you well in the second when you will have more models with which to bolster your forces. Likewise, any enemies you let slip through your net will rally for the next encounter, so it's best to destroy them while you have the chance!

The boons offered to victorious players in the second and subsequent battles can vary enormously. Extra models to fight with, a deployment advantage, an opportunity to recruit a deadly monster, set up the terrain or even choose the next battleplan are all ideas you can try out. But ensure that these devices make the next battle more enjoyable, not less – both sides need to have a solid opportunity to win. If the odds are stacked too far in favour of one player, the game won't be much fun for either side.

Linked games provide even more opportunities when set up and run by a games master. A GM can add impromptu links and new rules as the battle rages. For instance, if a unit suffers grievous damage but boldly holds on, the GM might grant the survivors a special ability to reflect their hatred of their foes for the next battle. With all these possibilities, linked battle campaigns provide countless ways to enhance, expand and personalise your narrative games.

MAP CAMPAIGNS

Map campaigns provide a dynamic geographical setting for your battles, which you can explore and conquer as the campaign progresses.

Map campaigns are set within a particular collection of locations, with each battle allowing players to invade and capture the territories on the map. In any map campaign, the outcome of each battle determines who occupies a designated region. A battle is fought for each territory, using a battleplan that's appropriate for the area – or your own rules if you wish – with the winner planting their flag in that location.

The outcome of the campaign is determined by the number of territories that are controlled. The winner is usually whoever first wins control of a pre-agreed number of areas, or the player that controls the most after a set number of turns. Structuring your campaign around a map makes it even more immersive, as you are able to visualise where your army is fighting, where the campaign might take you and how rival armies are faring.

If you are inspired by a map you have found in a Warhammer Age of Sigmar book, you can adopt it for use in your own campaign. Equally, there's real joy to be had in drawing your own maps. A map can be a simple line drawing, a three dimensional gameboard, or anything in between. Collaborating on a design with other members of your group can be a rewarding experience in itself.

Raise the stakes by setting the players objectives that must be achieved in each location, or giving the armies accumulating benefits for winning territories. You can even create special rules for the various locations on the map that activate when an army arrives there. Realm of Battle rules really come into their own here, as they are great ways to represent different environments.

We've included an example of a campaign map here, which you can use as a framework for your own campaign.

TREE CAMPAIGNS

Tree campaigns add a compelling level of complexity to narrative games. Like linked battle campaigns, each game in a tree campaign affects the next, but rather than a linear series of engagements, battles are organised by a previously drawn flow diagram – the eponymous 'tree'. You will find an example of a tree campaign on the following two pages.

Each time a battle is fought in a tree campaign, the tree diagram will indicate which game should be played next based on the outcome. Usually, the winner will have some sort of advantage in the next game, but it all depends on how your gaming group designs the tree.

For example, the simplest tree campaign could consist of just two battles. In the first, one army must hold its ground (the defender), while the other must assault it (the attacker). If the attacker wins, the next battle might present a scenario in which the defender's depleted forces must fight a rearguard action while the rest of their army retreats. If the defender wins the first battle, the next might give the defender the opportunity to go on the offensive, forcing the attacker to fight a desperate last stand with a smaller force to account for the casualties suffered in the previous game.

There's no fixed limit to the number of battles a tree campaign is made up of, but the longer a campaign is, the larger and more complex the diagram will need to be.

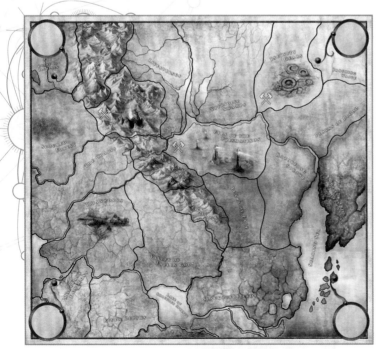

This map of the Flamescar Plateau is from the Season of War: Firestorm *supplement. It's a good example of the kind of map you can use in a campaign, and should serve as inspiration for maps of your own devising.*

BENEATH SKULL MOUNTAIN

Here you will find a tree campaign for two players. To fight the campaign, all you need to do is read the introduction below and gather two armies, then follow the instructions for Death in the Dark for your first battle.

INTRODUCTION

Two rival warlords have established their strongholds near to each other. Their domains are separated from each other by a mountain chain that is riddled with a network of tunnels. Each warlord is determined to crush their rival, but in order to do so they will need to fight their way through the tunnels and across the open plains that lie beyond, before they can finally besiege their opponent's stronghold.

THE ARMIES GATHER

Each player chooses an army using the Pitched Battle rules (pg 310-311). The armies must be recorded on a roster, and will remain the same throughout the campaign.

In addition, each player generates a Guile, Planning and Persuasion rating for their general, by dividing 6 points between the three ratings and recording the scores on their roster. No rating can have a value of less than 1 or more than 4. For example, you can give your general a rating of 2 Guile, 2 Planning, and 2 Persuasion, or 4 Guile, 1 Planning and 1 Persuasion, and so on.

DEATH IN THE DARK

Fight a battle using the Darkest Depths rules and Battleplan: Tunnels Wars (pg 298-300).

The Tunnel Wars battleplan requires the players to split their armies into three contingents and fight three battles in a row. Instead of receiving command points automatically at the start of their hero phase, in these battles the players must roll a dice, and only receive a command point that turn if the roll is equal to or less than one of their general's ratings. In the first of the battles, use your general's Planning rating, in the second of the battles use your general's Guile rating, and in the third of the battles use your general's Persuasion rating. Note that you use your general's rating even if your general is not present at the battle in person.

PITCHED BATTLE

The player that wins the Tunnel Wars battleplan can next invade their opponent's territory. That player is the invader. The loser must defend their territory; that player is the defender. Fight a Pitched Battle to decide the outcome.

After picking territories but before setting up any units from either army, each player must test their general's Guile, Persuasion and Planning by rolling a dice for each rating. The dice roll must be equal to or less than the rating being tested in order for the general to pass that test. You receive 1 extra command point to use during the battle for each of the tests that your general passes.

WHO WON THE PITCHED BATTLE?

If the invader won the Pitched Battle, go to Siege.

If the defender won the Pitched Battle, return to Death in the Dark.

SIEGE

Fight a battle using the Siege Warfare rules and Battleplan: The Relief Force (pg 294-296).

Before making any siege effect rolls, the players must compare the Guile, Persuasion and Planning of their generals.

A player whose general has a higher Planning rating can add 1 to or subtract 1 from the result of the Starve roll.

A player whose general has a higher Persuasion rating can add 1 to or subtract 1 from the result of the Batter roll.

A player whose general has a higher Guile rating can add 1 to or subtract 1 from the result of the Tunnel roll.

SIEGES IN THE AGE OF SIGMAR

The Mortal Realms are bristling with colossal fortresses, magically carved redoubts and naturally occurring places of power. Since the Age of Myth, countless bloody wars have been waged to conquer and defend these contested strongholds.

Some of the most exciting battles in the Mortal Realms take place along the walls of enormous castles and at the gaping mouths of cliff-side lairs. Playing narrative games centred around these epic sieges allows you to engage in different types of story-telling with your miniatures – stories of barbarous hordes scrabbling over crumbling walls, of ingenious ploys overcoming impenetrable defences, of flaming arrows raining down from battlements, of brutal assaults and desperate last stands.

There are no limits to the types of siege warfare that you can participate in, and no restrictions on which armies might be involved. Vast strongholds are maintained throughout the Mortal Realms by the forces of Order, Chaos, Death

The Disciples of Tzeentch assail an ancient Ghurish fortress defended by a brotherhood of Stormcast Eternals.

and Destruction, and these vary wildly in their appearance and purpose. All that matters is that you can envisage a scenario that fits the theme of your collection as well as that of your opponent. For example, an army of Stormcast Eternals may garrison one of their mighty Stormkeeps to defend the Realmgate housed within against an oncoming tide of Bloodbound savages determined to capture it in the name of the Blood God. Alternatively, the Bloodbound may erect a grisly palisade of skull and bone around one of their Khornate shrines so that the daemonic ritual they are performing can be protected from the Stormhost that is thundering across the horizon. The setting and stakes of these battles are entirely up to you.

A siege battle can also give you the opportunity to try out different miniatures in your collection, or to use your favourite models in new and inventive ways. You may be used to charging boldly into the fray with your Mournfang Pack, but you could also use this hard-hitting cavalry unit to hold the gate to an icy bridge as it is being overrun by a particularly bellicose band of Fyreslayers mercenaries. You could field every Terrorgheist and Zombie Dragon you own to stage a daring airborne assault against a fortified Kharadron Overlords sky-port. Or perhaps you are inspired to recreate one of the epic sieges depicted in *The Realmgate Wars* books or in Black Library novels and short stories.

Over the next few pages you will find the rules for playing siege games as well as two battleplans that you can use to create your own siege narratives. In Battleplan: The Relief Force, the defender must hold off the attacker long enough for reinforcements to arrive. This battleplan is perfect for staging sieges against smaller fortifications and battlefield redoubts. By placing a few Sylvaneth Wyldwoods, you can create a place of power that your Sylvaneth clan can defend against attacking Brayherd despoilers, or you can set up a ring of walls and fences to represent the hasty barricades built by Free Peoples to hold back ghastly columns of Deathrattle warriors that have been plaguing the Fellmarsh.

If you want to fight a battle along the ramparts of a mighty citadel or amongst the barbicans of a daemonic city, then Battleplan: The Great Wall is ideal. As the attacker in this scenario, your amassed forces must breach the foe's lines of defence before reinforcements can come to the aid of the standing garrison and drive you back. As the defender, you can use as much Warhammer Age of Sigmar scenery as you have available to create your impenetrable stronghold. This is the perfect opportunity to put your Fortress of Grim Corruption or Chaos Dreadhold Helfort at the centre of the action, or you can use whichever scenery suits the theme of your armies and the wars that they are waging.

SIEGE WARFARE

Strongholds of all different shapes and sizes stud the Mortal Realms. Only a sizeable and highly motivated force has any chance of capturing such an objective and the spoils that lie beyond its walls, and then only at a terrible cost in blood and lives!

Assaulting a fortress is no small matter. Many have tall, strong walls which are covered with protective devices designed to punish any intrusion, and within the walls stand garrisons of staunch defenders ready to rain death upon any attackers. Others are naturally occurring, such as an area of densely forested woodland or a series of ancient and long-abandoned caves, that can be used by a cunning or desperate defender to provide cover and stem an enemy assault.

The following rules allow you to fight a battle where one player must assault an enemy stronghold, and one must defend it. Also included are two siege warfare battleplans for you to use with them. Imaginative players will find it easy to modify the following rules to fight other types of siege games.

THE STRONGHOLD

All Warhammer Age of Sigmar sieges require a stronghold for the defender to occupy. As noted above, the exact nature of a stronghold varies a great deal; it may be a Direstone Redoubt, a Sylvaneth Wyldwood or a set of ancient ruins. Because of this, the defender is given free reign to make their stronghold from any terrain features that they have available.

The siege warfare battleplan you choose for your game will let you know how to pick the attacker and the defender, and which of the two territories that they occupy at the start of the battle. Set up the scenery in the attacker's territory and any neutral areas of the battlefield as normal, and then the defender can set up the scenery representing their stronghold in their territory.

The defender must set up at least five terrain features, and can set up any number more as long as all of the terrain features they set up fit fully

inside their territory. You can choose any terrain features you like in your own games, or use the examples shown on these pages as inspiration.

The players set up their armies once the stronghold has been set up, following the set-up instructions from the battleplan they have decided to use.

THE SIEGE PHASE

The following siege phase takes place after the stronghold has been built and the armies set up, but before the first battle round begins. It represents the siege tactics that the attackers have used before the assault to wear down the defenders, and the counter-tactics the defenders have used to ensure they can hold out as long as possible.

There are three main methods a besieging army can use to wear down the defenders before the battle starts, each of which has a corresponding counter-tactic the defender can use against it:

Starve/Gather Supplies: The attackers isolate the stronghold, so that the defenders starve to death once their supplies begin to run out. The defender can counter this by gathering as many supplies as possible either before or during the siege.

Batter/Re-build: The attacker batters away at the defender's

stronghold. With luck, one or more sections of the stronghold will be breached, making it easier to attack. The defender can counter this by organising working parties to repair as much of the damage as possible.

Tunnel/Counter-tunnel: The attacker builds underground tunnels that will allow at least part of their army to emerge inside the defender's stronghold. The defender can counter by building tunnels that intercept the attackers while they are still underground.

To determine what effect these tactics have, the players must each pick a siege tactic and then determine any siege effects, as described next.

SIEGE TACTICS

Both the attacker and defender must secretly pick one of the three siege tactics to concentrate their efforts on.

To decide what the attacker's main siege method will be, and the counter-tactic used by the defender, each player secretly picks a number by hiding a dice behind their hand. The attacker must pick a number from 1 to 3, and the defender a number from 4 to 6.

Once both players have chosen their numbers, the dice are revealed, and the numbers cross-referenced on the siege table opposite, which will tell you what modifiers (if any) apply to the effects of the siege.

For example, the attacker chooses to concentrate upon starving the defenders, while the defender chooses to counter-tunnel. This means that 1 is added to the dice rolls the attacker makes to see if any of the defending units starve, and that 2 is subtracted from the attacker's roll to see if they successfully dig a tunnel.

SIEGE EFFECTS

Next, the attacker makes rolls to determine the effect of their siege methods on the defenders. Make all of the Starve rolls first, then the Batter rolls, and finally the Tunnel rolls.

Starve: The attacker rolls a dice for each defending unit, subtracting 1 from the roll if the unit is a **Hero**, and applying any of the relevant modifiers from the siege table. On a 5+ the unit suffers D3 mortal wounds.

Batter: The attacker rolls a dice for each terrain feature in the defender's territory, applying any of the relevant modifiers from the siege table. On a 5+ the terrain feature has been breached, and none of its abilities can be used in the battle (it can still provide cover).

Tunnel: The attacker and the defender each roll a dice, the attacker applying any of the relevant modifiers from the siege table (the defender's dice roll is never modified). If the attacker's roll is higher, they have successfully completed their tunnel, and can pick one **Hero** and two other units (none of the units can contain models with the **Monster** or **War Machine** keyword that have a Wounds characteristic of 8 or more).

Any units sent into the tunnels are removed from the battlefield, and can emerge from the tunnels at the start of any of their movement phases. The attacker must first pick a point in the defender's territory where the tunnel emerges. The units using the tunnel must then be set up wholly within 6" of the tunnel exit, and more than 3" from any enemy units. This counts as their move for that movement phase.

THE ASSAULT

Once all of the siege effects have been rolled for, the attacker's assault begins. Start the first battle round of the game.

SIEGE TABLE

Defender's Counter-tactic	Attackers Main Siege Method		
	Starve (1)	Batter (2)	Tunnel (3)
Gather Supplies (4)	-1 Starve	+1 Batter -1 Starve	+2 Tunnel -1 Starve
Re-build (5)	+1 Starve -1 Batter	-1 Batter	+2 Tunnel -1 Batter
Counter-tunnel (6)	+1 Starve -2 Tunnel	+1 Batter -2 Tunnel	-2 Tunnel

SIEGE COMMAND ABILITIES

You can use the following command abilities in games that use the Siege rules. The attacker's command abilities can only be used by the attacking army, and the defender's command abilities can only be used by the defending army.

ATTACKER'S COMMAND ABILITIES

Cry Havoc!: *Warriors are ordered to attack no matter the cost.*

You can use this command ability in the combat phase. If you do so, pick a friendly unit within 6" of a friendly **Hero** or 12" of your general. For the rest of that combat phase, add 1 to hit rolls and subtract 1 from save rolls for that unit.

Demolition Charges: *Explosives are used to shatter enemy fortifications.*

You can use this command ability in your hero phase. If you do so, pick a terrain feature that is within 3" of a friendly unit, and within 6" of a friendly **Hero** or 12" of your general. Roll a dice for each enemy unit garrisoning that terrain feature. On a 4+ that enemy unit suffers D3 mortal wounds.

Reinforcements: *Fresh troops arrive to join the battle.*

You can use this command ability in your hero phase. If you do so, roll a dice. On a 4+, pick a friendly unit from which all the models have been slain. You can set up the unit again, wholly within 6" of the edge of the battlefield and more than 9" from any enemy models. This counts as the unit's move for the following movement phase.

DEFENDER'S COMMAND ABILITIES

Boiling Oil: *Sizzling hot oil is poured upon attacking troops.*

You can use this command ability in your hero phase. If you do so, pick a terrain feature that is garrisoned by a friendly **Hero** and at least five other friendly models. Roll a dice for each enemy unit within 3" of that terrain feature. On a 4+, that enemy unit suffers D3 mortal wounds.

Sally Forth: *A hidden gateway is opened, allowing the defenders to mount a counter-attack.*

You can use this command ability in your hero phase. If you do so, pick a terrain feature that is garrisoned by a friendly **Hero**. You can re-roll charge rolls in the following charge phase for any units that exit that terrain feature this turn.

Take Cover: *Troops are ordered to make the maximum use of any cover.*

You can use this command ability in the combat phase. If you do so, pick a friendly unit within 6" of a friendly **Hero** or 12" of your general. For the rest of that combat phase, add 1 to save rolls and subtract 1 from hit rolls for that unit.

BATTLEPLAN
THE RELIEF FORCE

A defending army has been under siege for a considerable time. A relief force has been despatched to aid them, but before it can arrive the attackers launch their final assault. Can the garrison hold out until reinforcements arrive?

SIEGE WARFARE

Use the Siege Warfare rules from pages 294-295.

SET-UP

The players roll off, and the winner decides who will be the attacker and who the defender. The territories for the attacking and defending armies are shown on the map below. The players then set up scenery as described on page 294.

Next, pick three different terrain features in the defender's territory to be the attacker's siege targets. The attacker picks the first terrain feature, the defender picks the second, and the attacker picks the third.

The armies can now be set up. The defender must set up their army first. The defending army is split into two contingents: the garrison and the relief force. There must be at least one unit in the relief force for each unit that is included in the garrison (the army general can be in either contingent). The defending player can only set up units from their garrison at the start of the battle – the relief force will arrive during the battle as described below. Defending units can be set up anywhere wholly within their territory.

The attacking army sets up second. Attacking units must be set up wholly within their territory, more than 6" from the defender's territory.

THE RELIEF FORCE

Roll 2D6 at the start of each of the defender's turns to see if the relief force arrives. Add the battle round number to the score. On a roll of 11 or more the entire relief force arrives. Roll a dice; on a roll of 1-2 it arrives on the narrow table edge to the right of the defender's territory; on a roll of 3-4 it arrives on the table edge opposite the defender's territory; and on a roll of 5-6 it arrives on the table edge to the left of the defender's territory (see map).

Units from the relief force can enter play in their player's movement phase. All of the models in the unit must be set up wholly within 6" of the table edge they arrive on, and more than 9" from any enemy units. This counts as their move for that movement phase.

SIEGE TARGETS

The siege targets in the defender's territory are controlled by the last player to have any models in or on the terrain feature. If both players have models in or on a siege target, it is controlled by the defender.

GLORIOUS VICTORY

The game ends at the end of fifth battle round. The attacker wins a **major victory** if they have captured all three siege targets, and the defender wins a **major victory** if the attacker has control of just one or none of the siege targets. If the attacker controls two siege targets, the battle is a draw.

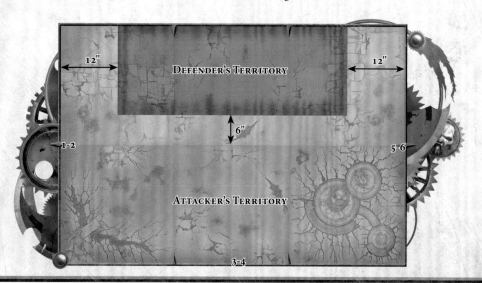

BATTLEPLAN
THE GREAT WALL

An attacking army finds its path blocked by a massive wall. The only option is to lay siege to the stronghold in an effort to break through the defensive line.

SIEGE WARFARE
Use the Siege Warfare rules from pages 294-295.

SET-UP
The players roll off, and the winner decides who will be the attacker and who the defender. The territories for the attacking and defending armies are shown on the map below. The players then set up scenery as described on page 294.

The armies can now be set up. The defender must set up their army first. The defending army is split into two contingents: the garrison and reinforcements. There must be at least one reinforcement unit for each unit that is included in the garrison (the army general can be in either contingent). The defending player can only set up units from their garrison at the start of the battle – reinforcements will arrive during the battle as described below. Defending units can be set up anywhere wholly within their territory.

The attacking army sets up second. Attacking units must be set up wholly within their territory, more than 6" from the defender's territory.

REINFORCEMENTS
Starting from the second battle round, the defender must roll a dice for each of their reinforcement units at the start of their movement phase. On a roll of 5 or 6, the unit arrives on the battlefield.

All of the models in a reinforcement unit that arrives must be set up within 6" of the table edge, wholly within the defender's reinforcement area as shown on the map, and more than 9" from any enemy units. This counts as their move for that movement phase. Set the unit up before rolling to see if the next reinforcement unit arrives.

GLORIOUS VICTORY
This battle is fought to control two objectives. One objective is located in the centre of the defender's territory, and the second in the centre of the defender's reinforcements area, as shown on the map below.

The battle ends at the end of the fifth battle round. The attacker wins a major victory if they control both objectives. The defender wins a **minor victory** if they control one of the objectives, and a major victory if they control both. Any other result is a draw.

18"	18"	
DEFENDER'S REINFORCEMENT AREA	DEFENDER'S TERRITORY	ATTACKER'S TERRITORY
● OBJECTIVE	● OBJECTIVE	

DARKEST DEPTHS

The landscapes of the Mortal Realms are often riddled with subterranean tunnels and caverns. Frantic battles are often fought to control these darkened passageways, turning the underground world into a battlefield that is just as bloody as any found on the surface.

Desperate battles are fought in gloom and darkness, the only light coming from flickering torches or the luminescent glow of subterranean fungus. Footing can be treacherous, with unexpected drops that can doom the unwary, while loose rocks or stalactites suddenly fall from the ceiling, crushing anyone unfortunate enough to be standing below. Last but far from least, underground realms are home to all manner of creatures, most of which are ferocious predators.

Commanding an army in such treacherous conditions calls for a special set of skills and stoic fortitude. It is very difficult to deploy an army in formation in any but the very largest caverns, and usually the battle will take place as a series of bloody skirmishes, each fought individually in scattered tunnels or caves. In such conditions it is hard to provide support for an embattled unit, and warriors will have to rely on their own strength of arm to defeat a foe, even if they are heavily overmatched.

A general must do their best to be at the right place at the right time, judging through intuition and experience where the fighting will be most desperate, and throwing themselves into the fray at this point in order to ensure victory.

DARKEST DEPTHS RULES

Darkest Depths introduces several new rules to help you fight battles below the surface of the Mortal Realms. These recreate the dark and dangerous underground environs, where cave-ins and pitfalls are ever-present dangers and where hungry monsters lurk in the gloom awaiting to attack the unwary.

The following rules can be used with the battleplans on pages 300-301, or in underground battles of your own devising.

GLOOM AND DARKNESS
The range of missile weapons and spells is limited to a maximum of 12".

LOW CEILINGS
Models cannot fly in battles that use the Darkest Depths rules, unless both players agree to designate certain areas of the battlefield as having ceilings that are high enough for them to do so.

WALLS OF SOLID ROCK

When you set up the battlefield you can nominate some of the terrain features to be walls of solid rock. These reach from the ground to the ceiling of the tunnel complex, and therefore cannot be moved across by any models.

MONSTROUS DENIZEN

Roll off after preparing the battlefield but before territories have been selected. The winner can choose to set up a **Monster**, if a suitable model that is not part of either army is available.

The monstrous denizen can be set up anywhere on the battlefield. Roll off to see which player controls the monstrous denizen at the start of each battle round. The winner of the roll-off treats the monstrous denizen as a unit from their army for that battle round. They can choose to attack the monster when it is part of their army if they wish to do so, but if they do, it joins the opposing army until the end of the battle round.

UNSTABLE SURROUNDINGS

Roll a dice at the start of each of your hero phases. On a roll of 6, the commotion of battle has either caused a cave-in or stalactites to fall from the ceiling (you can choose which).

Cave-in: Pick a point anywhere on the battlefield that is more than 3" from any models or terrain features. That point is where the cave-in took place. For the rest of the battle, no models can move or be set up within 3" of that point.

Falling Stalactites: Pick D3 different enemy units. Roll a dice for each unit you pick. On a roll of 4+ the unit suffers a mortal wound. On a roll of 6+ it suffers D3 mortal wounds instead.

COMMAND ABILITIES

You can use the following command abilities in games using the Darkest Depths rules in addition to the command abilities that you are normally allowed to use.

Hazardous Traps: *Sabotage is a common tactic used by those wishing to eradicate unwary opponents.*

You can use this command ability in your hero phase. If you do so, pick an enemy unit within 6" of a friendly **Hero** or 12" of your general. That unit is struck by falling stalactites, as described in the Unstable Surroundings rule. You can use this command ability in addition to the Unstable Surroundings rule.

Hidden Tunnel: *The depths reward those who study the ancient byways of the subterranean realms.*

You can use this command ability in your hero phase. If you do so, you can pick a friendly unit within 6" of a friendly **Hero** or 12" of your general. The unit you pick can move through walls of solid rock in your following movement phase, as long as no models in the unit finish the move in an area of solid rock.

Tame the Raging Beast: *Those who brave these nether-realms often earn the loyalty of the creatures that dwell there.*

You can use this command ability in your hero phase. If you do so, pick one monstrous denizen (see the Monstrous Denizens rule) within 3" of a friendly **Hero**. You control that monstrous denizen for the rest of the battle round. This can allow a monstrous denizen to take two turns in the same battle round.

TUNNEL WARS

Countless battles have been fought to control the tunnel networks that twist and turn below the surfaces of each Mortal Realm. Such conflicts are usually fought as a series of bitter encounters in near-total darkness, with no quarter either asked or given.

DARKEST DEPTHS

Use the Darkest Depths rules from pages 298-299.

Designer's Note: Tunnel Wars is rather different to most battleplans, in that instead of fighting a single battle, you will divide your army into three contingents, and fight three separate battles using one of your contingents in each one. The three battles represent the most important of the battles taking place to gain control of a maze-like series of corridors and caverns.

THE ARMIES

Each player picks an army as described in the core rules, but then each player must split their army into three contingents. A single contingent may not have less than a quarter of the units in the army, or more than half of the units in the army.

Having selected contingents, the players must fight three battles using the following instructions, one after the other. Before setting up the armies for each of the three battles, the players must write down which of their three contingents they will use. Each contingent may only be used in one of the three battles, but they can be used in any order. Note that players should pick a general for each of their contingents at the start of each battle (one will represent the general, and the other two represent sub-commanders assigned by the general to lead the other contingents).

THE BATTLEFIELD

Set up terrain as described in the core rules. Each battle is being fought in underground tunnels and caverns, and appropriate terrain features should be used to represent the stygian depths where they take place.

Designer's Note: Do not be put off playing this scenario if you lack terrain features that have a suitably subterranean appearance. An easy way to represent the tunnel complex is to cut out black or grey paper or cardboard into irregular shapes. These pieces can be used to represent

solid rock walls, and placed on the battlefield to create a suitably maze-like set of tunnels and caverns.

SET-UP

The players roll off, and the winner decides which territory each side will use. The territories are shown on the map below.

The players then alternate setting up units one at a time, starting with the player that won the roll-off to determine territories. Units must be set up wholly within their own territory, more than 12" from enemy territory.

Continue to set up units until both players have set up their armies. If one player finishes first, the opposing player sets up the rest of the units in their army, one after another.

GLORIOUS VICTORY

You must slay all of the models in the opposing contingent to win each individual battle. At the end of the third battle, if one player won all three games, they win a **major victory**. If one player won two of the games, they win a **minor victory**.

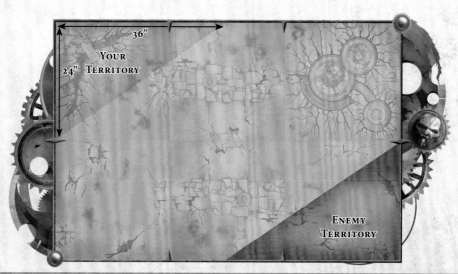

BATTLEPLAN
UNDERGROUND AMBUSH

In the darkened caverns below ground, it is possible to ambush an unwary opponent. The attackers will lurk in the darkness on the edges of a cavern that is commonly used as a route of passage, waiting for the foe to march through on their way to their destination. At a given command, the ambushers will spring from hiding, attacking the enemy from two directions at once.

DARKEST DEPTHS
Use the Darkest Depths rules from pages 298-299.

THE ARMIES
Each player picks an army as described in the core rules, and then the players roll off. The winner is the ambusher, and the loser is the defender.

THE BATTLEFIELD
Set up terrain as described in the core rules. The battle is being fought in a large underground cavern, and appropriate terrain features should be used to represent the stygian depths where they take place.

SET-UP
The defender sets up first. All of their units must be set up in a column, facing in the same direction, wholly within 3" of the centre line of the battlefield.

The ambusher can set up their units anywhere wholly within 12" of either long edge of the battlefield. Units can be deployed on both sides of the defender's army column if desired.

FIRST TURN
The ambusher has the first turn in the first battle round.

SURPRISE ATTACK
It is hard for the ambusher to co-ordinate an ambush, and difficult for the defender to respond. To represent this, each player must roll 2D6 before making a normal move with a unit in the first battle round. If the roll is greater than the unit's Bravery characteristic, it may not move in that movement phase or attempt a charge in the charge phase.

GLORIOUS VICTORY
The battle continues until one player has no units left on the battlefield, or at the end of the fifth battle round should this occur sooner.

Wiping out the opposing army does not guarantee victory – you must do so without letting your opponent cause more wounds than you inflict in return. When the battle ends, each player calculates a victory score by adding up the Wounds characteristics of all the models from the opposing army that were slain during the battle. If one player beats their opponent's score by 50% or more, they can claim a **major victory**. Otherwise the defender can claim a **minor victory**.

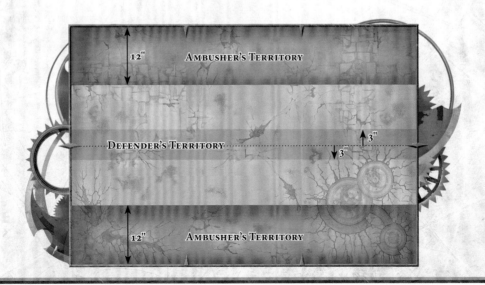

TRIUMPH & TREACHERY!

Several armies converge on the same battlefield, each determined to capture it for themselves. All are hated foes, and there can be only one winner. Each general must use their resources wisely, choosing the best time to make an alliance, and the best time to break it.

The Triumph & Treachery rules allow three or more players to take part in a multi-sided battle. Each player commands their own force and takes on all the other players involved to prove themselves the ultimate champion.

In this section we have included all the rules you need to play a Triumph & Treachery game, as well as two battleplans designed to be used with these rules (pg 304-305).

FIGHTING A TRIUMPH & TREACHERY BATTLE
Triumph & Treachery games follow the core rules, with the following exceptions.

ROLLING OFF
Sometimes the players in a Triumph & Treachery battle will be required to roll off. To do so, all of the players roll a dice, and the player that rolls highest wins the roll-off. If several players are tied for the highest roll, the tied players roll off again, until only one player remains with the highest dice roll.

DETERMINING TURN ORDER
A Triumph & Treachery battle has three or more sides. Because of this, all the players roll off at the start of each battle round (including the first battle round), and the winner decides which player will take the

first turn. The player that has been chosen takes their turn, and then all of the remaining players roll off again, and the winner decides who will have the second turn. This carries on until there is only one player that has not yet taken a turn – that player takes their turn and the battle round is then over.

PLAYER TURNS
At the start of each phase, the player whose turn it is must pick one opponent to be their 'enemy' for that phase. A different enemy player may be selected in each phase if desired. When it's your turn, picking the right opponent to attack in each phase is vital. You may want to attack two or more foes, but as you can only pick one, make sure you pick the right one!

NEUTRAL MODELS
In games of Warhammer Age of Sigmar, models and units are either considered 'friendly' or 'enemy' – models in your army are friendly

and models in your opponent's army are enemy. In Triumph & Treachery battles, models and units can also be 'neutral'.

Once you have chosen which player will be your enemy in a phase, all models in that player's army are enemy models for all rules purposes for that phase.

All models belonging to any other players are neutral models, and cannot be affected by abilities or spells, or attacked in any way for that phase. Neutral units cannot use abilities.

GAME PHASES
The following rules apply, depending on which phase is being played:

Hero Phase
In your hero phase, only enemy models can unbind spells. Neutral models are never affected by spells, even if they are within the radius of effect of a spell.

Movement Phase

Treat neutral models as if they were enemy models in your movement phase (so you can't move within 3" of them, must retreat if you want to move away from them, and so on).

Shooting Phase

In your shooting phase, only enemy units may be selected as the target of a shooting attack. Attacks that affect models within a certain distance of a target point do not affect neutral models.

Charge Phase

In your charge phase, the first model moved from a charging unit must finish the charge move within ½" of an enemy model.

Combat Phase

If your models are within 3" of models from any opposing armies at the start of the combat phase, then one of these armies must be chosen as the enemy. Attacks are only made between friendly models and enemy models.

Battleshock Phase

All units, including neutral units, have to take battleshock tests if they suffered casualties during the turn. You must still choose an enemy at the start of your battleshock phase, however, in case any of your models have any abilities that affect enemy models in this phase. Neutral players can use abilities that affect units from their own army in this phase.

VICTORY POINTS

Victory points are used in Triumph & Treachery games both to determine the winner and as a form of currency that can be used to bribe other players.

You can keep track of your victory points (sometimes referred to as VPs) on a piece of paper, but it is much more fun to use coins or some other form of suitable marker. For example, you can use a small coin to represent 1 victory point, and a larger coin to represent 3 victory points, and so on.

The victory points a player has scored are not secret, and players are free to ask an opponent how many victory points they have at any time. At the end of a Triumph & Treachery battle, the player with the most victory points is the winner.

BRIBERY & TREACHERY

Players may give one or more of their command points and/or victory points to other players if they wish. For example, you can 'pay' a player a command point or a victory point not to attack you.

Note that deals and arrangements that are struck before any points are handed over are not binding, so be careful that you don't give away any points to a player you cannot trust to honour their end of a deal – the name of the game is Triumph & Treachery, after all!

SECRET OBJECTIVES (OPTIONAL)

If all of the players agree, you can use the following Secret Objectives rules in your games of Triumph & Treachery. If you decide to do so, every player is given a secret objective, and will earn extra victory points if they can achieve it.

The players must determine their secret objective at the start of the game, before the armies are set up. To do so, each player needs to secretly roll a dice, hiding the roll from the rest of the players (we recommend using a mug or tumbler to hide the dice roll), and consult the table below.

Where the objective requires you to inflict 1 or more wounds on a unit from a certain player's army, the wound(s) must be inflicted by an attack, spell or ability used by a unit from your army, and can be a mortal wound.

When the objective is achieved, reveal the hidden dice to the other players, and score the appropriate number of victory points (VPs). Alternatively, a player can spend 1 command point in their hero phase to discard their current secret objective. In either of these cases, generate a new secret objective in the same way.

SECRET OBJECTIVES		
D6	**Secret Objective**	**VPs**
1	**Secret Agenda:** *Your devious schemes have finally borne fruit.* Inflict 1 or more wounds on a unit from the army of the player that set up on your right or your left.	1 VP
2	**Pick on the Weak:** *Crush your enemies when they are at their most vulnerable.* Inflict 1 or more wounds on a unit from the army of a player that has fewer victory points than you.	1 VP
3	**Retribution:** *Revenge is a dish best served in blood!* Inflict 1 or more wounds on a unit from the army of the player that last chose you as an enemy.	2 VPs
4	**Counter-attack:** *The time has come for you to fight back.* Inflict 1 or more wounds on a unit from the army of a player that has more victory points than you, or the same number of victory points as you.	2 VPs
5	**Topple:** *Sometimes you must risk attacking a mighty foe.* Inflict 1 or more wounds on a unit from the army of the player that has the most victory points.	3 VPs
6	**Kingslayer:** *Kill the upstart ruler that dared to insult you.* Slay the general of an opposing player's army.	3 VPs

BATTLEPLAN
RIGHT OF CONQUEST

The battlefield is a vital piece of land that lies between several kingdoms. Each kingdom insists that the land is theirs, and theirs alone.

TRIUMPH AND TREACHERY!

This is a Triumph & Treachery battle for three to six players. Use the rules on pages 302-303.

SET-UP

The players roll off, and the winner decides the order in which the players pick their territories. The territories for the armies are shown on the map below.

The players then alternate setting up units one at a time, starting with the player that won the roll-off. Units must be set up wholly within their own territory, more than 12" from any enemy models, and more than 6" from the centre of the battlefield. Continue to set up units until all players have set up their armies.

If a player desires, they may place any of their units in reserve instead of setting it up on the battlefield. Reserve units can enter play in any of their player's movement phases

starting from the second battle round. All of the models in the unit must be set up in the player's starting territory, wholly within 6" of the table edge, and more than 9" from any enemy models. This counts as their move for that movement phase.

THE TIME IS NIGH!

Roll a dice at the end of each battle round, starting from the end of the fourth battle round. If the dice roll is equal to or more than the number of players taking part in the battle, the battle continues. If the dice roll is less than the number of players taking part in the battle, the battle ends and the winner is determined.

GLORIOUS VICTORY

The player with the most victory points at the end of the battle wins a **major victory**. In the case of a tie, each tied player wins a **minor victory**.

VICTORY POINTS

Victory points are scored as follows:

If a player achieves a secret objective, they gain the relevant number of victory points.

1 victory point is scored in each phase for every 5 wounds you inflicted in that phase.

At the end of the battle, each player scores D3 victory points for each territory in which one of their models is closer to the centre of the territory than any models belonging to the other players. If several players have models equally close to the centre of the territory, each scores 1 victory point.

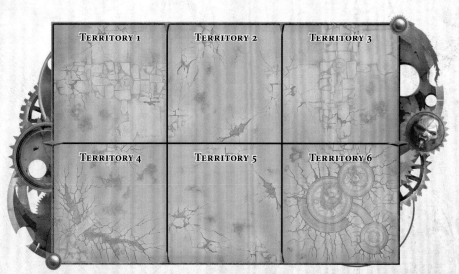

BATTLEPLAN
ARGUMENT OF KINGS

A battleground stands where the borders of several kingdoms meet. The rulers of the kingdoms are determined to keep their borders secure, while stealing as much territory as they can.

TRIUMPH AND TREACHERY!

This is a Triumph & Treachery battle for three to six players. Use the rules on pages 302-303.

SET-UP

The players roll off, and the winner decides the order in which the players pick their territories. The territories for the armies are shaded on the map below.

The players then alternate setting up units one at a time, starting with the player that won the roll-off. Units must be set up wholly within 12" of the centre of a table edge or a corner, as shown on the map below. Continue to set up units until all players have set up their armies.

If a player desires, they may place any of their units in reserve instead of setting them up on the battlefield. Reserve units can enter play in any of their player's movement phases starting from the second battle round. All of the models in the unit must be set up in the player's starting territory, wholly within 6" of the table edge, and more than 9" from any enemy models. This counts as their move for that movement phase.

GLORIOUS VICTORY

The player with the most victory points at the end of the fifth battle round wins a **major victory**. In the case of a tie, each tied player wins a **minor victory**.

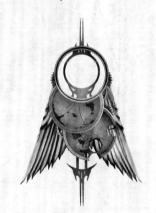

VICTORY POINTS

Victory points are scored as follows:

If a player achieves a secret objective, they gain the relevant number of victory points.

1 victory point is scored in each phase for every 5 wounds you inflicted in that phase.

At the end of each turn, the player whose turn is taking place scores 3 victory points if there are no enemy models wholly within their starting territory. They score D3 additional victory points for each other territory that only has their models wholly within it (including any territories that were not used by a player at the start of the battle).

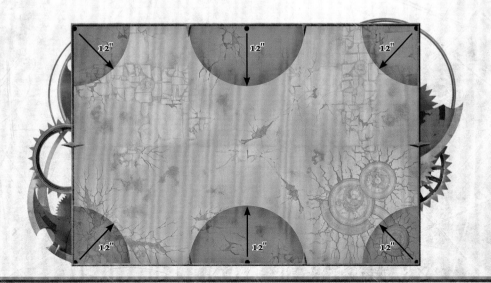

MATCHED PLAY GAMES

People play Warhammer Age of Sigmar for all kinds of reasons. Many want to play games that test their skill as the commander of an army, in as evenly balanced a competition as possible. If the thought of games like this appeals to you, then read through the matched play rules detailed on the following pages to learn more.

There are countless benefits to matched play games. While narrative play games allow you to assemble your army based on a theme or story, and open play games enable you to include any models you like, matched play games give you the option to fight battles with forces that are intentionally balanced against one another.

A battle between armies that are equally balanced makes for a decisive test of your skill as a player, and the outcome of such a clash will always be hard to predict. Once you have settled on an army to use, you essentially have a pick-up-and-play force that you can bring to any table, against any opponent, and there's no need to agree on the setting and story of a battle as you would in an open or narrative play game. Matched play is ideal for tournaments and school leagues, as it provides clear guidelines on the size and strength of the armies taking part, as well as ensuring that all battles are as fair as they can be. Also, putting limits on both sides makes it easier to control how long a game will last, and as such, matched play is perfect for a quick battle in your local club or games store.

The following section offers more details on playing matched play games, providing inspiring methods for building and expanding your army, and additional rules to make your games all the more challenging. But however fascinating and enjoyable it is to design a perfect army, a true general will only be satisfied after their force has sallied forth and proven its worth on the battlefield. Matched play beckons – and glory awaits you!

INTRODUCING MATCHED PLAY

In the Mortal Realms, armies come in all shapes and sizes, each with its unique strengths and weaknesses. To truly test a general's mettle as a commander, there needs to be a level playing field that accounts for the variety of forces abroad in the Age of Sigmar. This is the goal of matched play.

The main differences between matched play and open play lie in army selection and battleplan design. Matched play games include rules that allow players to pick armies of equal power, and the battleplans written for matched play games are designed to provide tactically challenging games where each side has a more-or-less equal chance of winning.

The emphasis of matched play gaming is on planning, tactics and military nous, so it is the perfect format for those who consider themselves accomplished strategists and savvy commanders. While narrative and open play games can vary greatly in scope and content, presenting you with all manner of scenarios to battle through, matched play games are all about you and your army, the models you select and the tactics you use. They are driven by every player's desire for a satisfying and well-earned victory.

MATCHED PLAY ARMIES

As you will see, there are a number of ways to choose an army for a matched play game. Later in this section you will find our Pitched Battle rules, which can be used to pit your matched play army against those of fellow players. It uses a comprehensive points-based system that assigns a value to every unit available in the Warhammer Age of Sigmar range. Using this system, you and your opponent can assemble your armies based on a prearranged total of points so as to ensure that your forces are as equally matched as possible. Also included in this section are six battleplans designed to be used as part of a Pitched Battle game, which have been designed to provide players with different sets of tactical challenges to overcome.

There are other methods of choosing an army that don't involve adding up points, but still suit the matched play format. For example, you could use the Wounds characteristics listed on each unit's warscroll as a guideline, either setting an upper limit for the number of wounds a unit can have, or a fixed total of wounds that an army can have as a whole.

Whichever method you use, assembling an army for a matched play game is an important part of the process, and an interesting challenge in its own right. Do you spend a lot of points on one high-powered model and risk being overrun by a larger force? Do you allocate your points evenly on a versatile middleweight force? Your knowledge of the units available to you will be pivotal in this selection process, and knowledge of your opponent's force can be just as vital. These choices may be hard to make at first, but once you've found the perfect balance, you'll be able to use the same formula again and again to great effect, and this in turn can guide you when it comes to expanding your collection.

MATCHED PLAY BATTLEPLANS

In order to create a fair and balanced contest, matched play games have a method of setting up terrain, deploying armies, and determining the winner that is as even as possible for both sides.

Because of the desire to create an even contest, the battleplans for matched play tend to be quite simple, and both armies will usually be set up in a territory near one table edge.

Victory conditions can be more complex, but will almost always be the same for both sides (a process called 'mirroring'). Some common victory conditions in matched play battleplans include determining which side has slain the most enemy units after a certain number of battle rounds, and assigning victory points to players who are able to take control of objectives set up at the start of the game.

The Pitched Battle battleplans you'll find later on in this section use a combination of these two methods, with players winning points for destroying the enemy and capturing objectives to determine the winner.

However, whatever rules are actually used, the aim is always to create as even a contest as possible between the two armies, and this usually leads to fairly straightforward 'line up and fight' battles with mirrored victory conditions for both sides. The overall effect of this is a format that is ideal for 'pick-up' games between two players that have not met each other before. Matched play battleplans allow a player to simply go ahead and collect an army, choosing whichever models they like within the constraints of the army list, and then turn up at a club or gaming event, find an opponent, and play – knowing that the game will be as fair and even as possible.

GAMING CLUBS

A wonderful feature of the Games Workshop hobby is the degree to which it enables collectors to socialise. Hobbyists can connect via organised clubs, meet up, make friends, and play games of Warhammer Age of Sigmar in a friendly and supportive environment. The Internet makes this process easier than ever, especially for those who can't easily get to a Games Workshop store.

A good start would be to search the Internet for 'Warhammer clubs' and the name of your town. You'll see which are popular, and chances are there's one close to you.

TOURNAMENTS

Throughout the wargaming hobby world, gaming events and tournaments take place virtually every weekend. Wherever you are, you're likely to find a tournament you can reach in the near future, and they're well worth attending.

Not only will you get to meet up with a warm and welcoming community of fellow hobbyists, but you'll get to play some great games, and see some truly amazing-looking armies. Often, special 'house' rules will have been created for the event, and no two tournaments are ever the same, keeping things exciting and interesting.

To find one near you, simply type 'Age of Sigmar tournament' and your town or area into an Internet search engine and get ready to go to war.

Warhammer Age of Sigmar tournaments are fantastic fun. Typically using the matched play format, they allow gamers to test their skills against one another in a series of competitive games.

PITCHED BATTLES

The following rules allow you to play a Pitched Battle, either as a one-off game, or as part of a tournament. These rules are designed to allow players to take part with the minimum of fuss, making them ideal for matched play pick-up games at clubs or gaming events.

To play a Pitched Battle, you and your opponent will first need to decide what type of Pitched Battle game you want to fight, and then pick your armies. The type of game you pick will determine how big the battle will be – the larger the battle, the more points you will have to spend on units for your army, but the longer the game will take.

There are three different types of Pitched Battle to choose from:

Game Type	Game Length
Vanguard	Up to 1 ½ hours
Battlehost	2 to 2 ½ hours
Warhost	3 or more hours

After you have agreed what type of game you want to play, look it up on the chart above. The chart lists the number of points each player has to spend on the units for their army, and what limitations apply to the types of unit you can bring. Each player must pick the units they will use for their army as described next.

PICKING YOUR ARMY

Each unit in a Pitched Battle is assigned a points value and a minimum and maximum unit size in its Pitched Battle profile. Pitched Battle profiles can be found in the *General's Handbook* or the book where the warscroll for the unit appears. The game type you have chosen for your battle determines how many points you can spend on the units in your army. The combined points of the units in your army must not exceed the number of points shown on the chart. For example, in a Battlehost game, you can each field up to 2,000 points worth of units.

In a Pitched Battle game you must pick an allegiance for your army (pg 242). All of the units in the army must either have that allegiance, or be allied to that allegiance (see Allied Units, below).

PITCHED BATTLE CHART	Vanguard	Battlehost	Warhost
Points	1,000	2,000	2,500
Leaders	1-4	1-6	1-8
Battleline	2+	3+	4+
Artillery	0-2	0-4	0-5
Behemoths	0-2	0-4	0-5
Other Units	Any number	Any number	Any number
Allied Units (pts)	≤ 200	≤ 400	≤ 500

Endless spells (pg 262) have Pitched Battle profiles and a points cost. By paying the spell's points cost, all **WIZARDS** in the player's army know that endless spell, and the player can use (and re-use) one endless spell model of the appropriate type in the battle. A player cannot take the same endless spell model more than once for their army, but can take any number of different endless spell models (for example, you could not take two Balewind Vortex models).

BATTLEFIELD ROLES

Some units are assigned a battlefield role in their Pitched Battle profile. A unit's battlefield role is based on how it is used in a battle.

The Pitched Battle chart above lists the minimum number of Leaders and Battleline units you must include in a Pitched Battle army, and the maximum number of Leaders, Artillery, and Behemoth units it can include. A model that is a Leader and a Behemoth counts as one Leader and one Behemoth in your army.

ALLIED UNITS

In a Pitched Battle, the number of points that can be spent on allies from the player's total points allowance is shown on the Pitched Battle chart above. For example, a player playing a Battlehost game can spend up to 400 of their 2,000 points on allied units. This is in addition to

the restrictions that normally apply to taking allied units (pg 242).

Allied units are not included when working out the number of Battleline units in the army. They do count towards the maximum number of Leader, Behemoth and Artillery units that can be included in the army

WARSCROLL BATTALIONS

If a player's army includes the units needed to field a warscroll battalion, then the player can include the battalion as part of their army by paying the points cost for it as shown on its Pitched Battle profile. You must pay the cost of the units in the battalion normally – the points value listed for each battalion is an extra cost that allows you to use it.

PITCHED BATTLE VARIATIONS

If both players agree, you can use either or both of the following variations to the way that the armies are picked:

You can agree to modify the points allowed for a Pitched Battle by plus or minus 250 points. For example, you might agree to play a 750 point Vanguard game, or a 2,750 point Warhost game.

You can agree to use points on their own. When playing a points-only game, ignore the limits on

the number of Leader, Battleline, Behemoth and Artillery units you can take – you can take any units you like as long as they do not exceed the points limit you have set for your game.

ARMY ROSTER
Once you have picked your army, record the details on a piece of paper (your army roster), and show it to your opponent before setting up your army at the start of the battle. See page 320 for an army roster you can photocopy.

The roster must include a list of the units, warscroll battalions and endless spells included in your army, what size the units are, details of weapons and equipment they have, the army's allegiance, which units are allies, the number of command points you have, and which model is the army's general. In a Pitched Battle, your general must be a Leader, and may not be an ally.

If your general is slain in a Pitched Battle game, do not select a new one.

If your army includes any units that are given keywords when they are set up, such as units with a Mark of Chaos, then these must be written down when the unit is added to the roster.

You must also record the allegiance abilities you have chosen for your army, the spells that are known by the wizards in your army, any artefacts or other items wielded by heroes in your army, and what command trait you have chosen for your general.

TRIUMPHS & COMMAND POINTS
Do not roll on the Triumph table in the core rules if you won your last battle. Instead, if one player has more points left over than their opponent after selecting their army, then they can roll on the Triumph table after both armies have been set up.

In a Pitched Battle, an army receives 1 extra command point for every 50 points that were not spent on units

for the army. For example, if you are fighting a Battlehost game and spend 1,895 points on units, then you will receive an extra 2 command points.

BATTLEPLANS
We have provided six battleplans designed for use in Pitched Battles (pg 312-317). Each offers a unique set of tactical challenges, and will provide each player with a chance to show their skill. To pick a battleplan, roll a dice on the table below, and use the battleplan that corresponds to the dice roll.

D6	Battleplan
1	Blood and Glory (pg 312)
2	Escalation (pg 313)
3	Border War (pg 314)
4	Three Places of Power (pg 315)
5	Gifts from the Heavens (pg 316)
6	Take and Hold (pg 317)

The Grand Tournament, held annually at Warhammer World in Nottingham, is a prestigious event comprising several heats that build up to a hotly contested grand final. Here we see two veteran gamers engaged in battle during Heat Three.

BATTLEPLAN
BLOOD AND GLORY

Two armies meet upon a battlefield, each ready to deal death and destruction upon their hated foe. The conflict will be settled in blood between the two rivals, with spoils going to the victor, and death and dishonour to the loser.

PITCHED BATTLE

Use the Pitched Battle rules on pages 310-311.

SET-UP

The players roll off, and the winner decides which territory each side will use. The territories are shown on the map below.

The players then alternate setting up units one at a time, starting with the player that won the roll-off. Units must be set up wholly within their own territory, more than 12" from enemy territory.

Continue to set up units until both players have set up their armies. If one player finishes first, the opposing player sets up the rest of the units in their army, one after another.

GLORIOUS VICTORY

This battle is fought to control four objectives. The objectives are located at the centre of each quarter of the field of battle, as shown on the map.

Starting from the third battle round, one player immediately wins a **major victory** if they have control of all four objectives.

If neither player has won by the end of the fifth battle round, or the amount of time allocated for the battle runs out, then the player that controls the most objectives wins a **minor victory**. If both players control the same number of objectives, each must add up the points value of any enemy units that have been destroyed during

the battle (excluding any new units that were added to the armies after the battle started). If one player has a higher total, they win a **minor victory**.

'Too long has this sacred ground been sullied by Chaos filth. The land itself keens in anguish. Can you hear it? Even the sky bleeds, wounded by the presence of creatures that do not belong here. We shall give our blades, our arrows, our hatred and our outrage – even our very souls – to free this paradise from the clutches of the Cursed Ones. Whatever happens this day, the sun will set on the fallen corpses of these blasphemers.'

– The Lady of Vines,
at the Shimmerfalls of Gloriphus

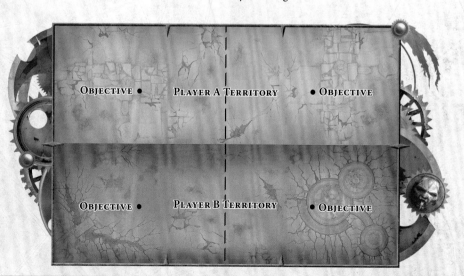

OBJECTIVE ●   PLAYER A TERRITORY   ● OBJECTIVE

OBJECTIVE ●   PLAYER B TERRITORY   ● OBJECTIVE

BATTLEPLAN
ESCALATION

Sometimes, two deadly foes will stumble across each other, and a bloody engagement will start.

PITCHED BATTLE
Use the Pitched Battle rules on pages 310-311.

SET-UP
The players roll off, and the winner decides which territory each side will use. The territories are shown on the map below.

The players then alternate setting up their units, starting with the player that determined territories. Units must be set up wholly within their own territory. Battleline units must be set up more than 9" from enemy territory. Behemoths and Artillery must be set up more than 24" from enemy territory. Units that are both Battleline and Behemoth can be set up within 24" of enemy territory, but they must still be more than 9" from it, as above. All other units must be set up more than 18" from enemy territory.

Continue to set up units until both players have set up their units. If one player finishes first, the opposing player sets up the rest of their units, one after another.

GLORIOUS VICTORY
This battle is fought to control three objectives. The objectives are located on the border between the player's territories, one in the middle of the battlefield and the others 12" from each corner, as shown on the map below.

Starting from the second battle round, at the end of each of their turns a player scores 1 victory point for each objective they control. The player with the most victory points at the end of the fifth battle round (or when the amount of time allocated for the battle runs out), wins a **major victory**. If the players are tied on victory points at the end of the game, then each player adds up the points value of any enemy units that have been destroyed during the battle (excluding any new units that were added to the armies after the battle started). If one player has a higher total, they win a **minor victory**.

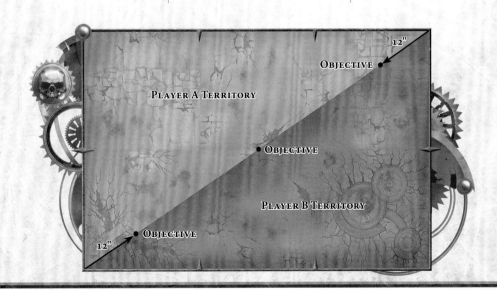

BATTLEPLAN
BORDER WAR

Two armies approach the same battlefield, determined to capture the vital ground that separates their territories and, if possible, strike deep into enemy territory.

PITCHED BATTLE
Use the Pitched Battle rules on pages 310-311.

SET-UP
The players roll off, and the winner decides which territory each side will use. The territories are shown on the map below.

The players then alternate setting up units one at a time, starting with the player that won the roll-off. Units must be set up wholly within their own territory, more than 12" from enemy territory.

Continue to set up units until both players have set up their armies. If one player finishes first, the opposing player sets up the rest of the units in their army, one after another.

GLORIOUS VICTORY
This battle is fought to control four objectives. Two are located at the centre of each player's territory. The other two are located on the border between the players' territories, one at the centre of the left half of the battlefield, and one at the centre of the right half as shown on the map.

You score victory points for each objective you control at the end of each of your turns. The number of points you receive varies depending on the objective's location, as follows.

Objective is in your own territory: 1 victory point

Objective is on the border between the territories: 2 victory points

Objective is in enemy territory: 4 victory points

The player with the most victory points at the end of the fifth battle round (or when the amount of time allocated for the battle runs out), wins a **major victory**. If the players are tied on victory points at the end of the game, then each player adds up the points value of any enemy units that have been destroyed during the battle (excluding any new units that were added to the armies after the battle started). If one player has a higher total, they win a **minor victory**.

PLAYER A TERRITORY

● OBJECTIVE

OBJECTIVE ●   ● OBJECTIVE

● OBJECTIVE

PLAYER B TERRITORY

BATTLEPLAN
THREE PLACES OF POWER

The leaders of two rival armies have learned the location of three places of great power. If a mighty warrior stands upon such a location, they can leech some of the energy and siphon it away. The longer they can remain upon the place of power, the more energy they can steal!

PITCHED BATTLE

Use the Pitched Battle rules on pages 310-311.

SET-UP

The players roll off, and the winner decides which territory each side will use. The territories are shown on the map below.

The players then alternate setting up units one at a time, starting with the player that won the roll-off. Units must be set up wholly within their own territory, more than 12" from enemy territory.

Continue to set up units until both players have set up their armies. If one player finishes first, the opposing player sets up the rest of the units in their army, one after another.

THE PLACES OF POWER

The three places of power are located upon the border between the two territories. One lies at the centre of the battlefield, and the others lie halfway between the central place of power and each narrow edge of the battlefield, as shown on the map.

A player controls a place of power if a friendly **HERO** finishes a move within 3" of it. The player loses control of the place of power if the hero finishes a subsequent move more than 3" from the place of power or is slain. Only one hero can control each place of power at a time – if more than one hero is eligible, then the first to arrive controls it. If a hero slays an enemy hero that is controlling a place of power, then they immediately gain control of the place of power if they are within 3" of it.

GLORIOUS VICTORY

At the end of each of your turns, you score victory points for each place of power controlled by one of your **HEROES**. The number of victory points is equal to the number of your turns that the hero has controlled the place of power for: 1 on the turn they gained control, 2 if they controlled it in your last turn as well as this one, and so on.

For example, a **HERO** controls the same place of power for 3 turns without losing control of it. They score 1 victory point at the end of their first turn, 2 victory points at the end of their second turn and 3 victory points at the end of their third turn, making 6 victory points in total.

The player with the most victory points at the end of the fifth battle round (or when the amount of time allocated for the battle runs out) wins a **major victory**. If the players are tied on victory points at the end of the game, then each player adds up the points value of any enemy units that have been destroyed during the battle (excluding any new units that were added to the armies after the battle started). If one player has a higher total, they win a **minor victory**.

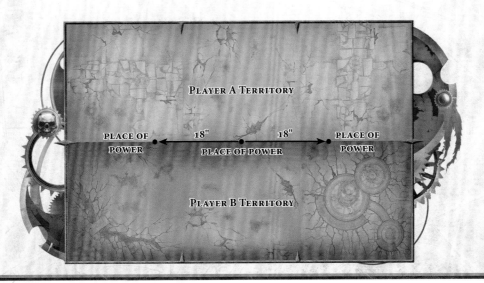

BATTLEPLAN
GIFTS FROM THE HEAVENS

The battlefield is frequently bombarded by meteors of sigmarite and warpstone that fall from the skies. Ambitious warlords are willing to sacrifice any number of their followers to gain control of such a valuable substance. As time goes on, the prize only becomes more coveted.

PITCHED BATTLE
Use the Pitched Battle rules on pages 310-311.

SET-UP
The players roll off, and the winner decides which territory each side will use. The territories are shown on the map below.

The players then alternate setting up units one at a time, starting with the player that won the roll-off. Units must be set up wholly within their own territory, more than 12" from enemy territory.

Continue to set up units until both players have set up their armies. If one player finishes first, the opposing player sets up the rest of the units in their army, one after another.

THE METEOR STRIKE
Two meteors strike the battlefield in the second battle round, one landing in each player's territory. Each player rolls a dice in their second hero phase, and a meteor lands at the centre of the board section in their territory that has the corresponding number. The locations of the meteors are treated as objectives for the rest of the battle.

GLORIOUS VICTORY
At the end of each of your turns you score a number of victory points equal to the number of the current battle round for each objective you control. For example, if you control 1 objective at the end of your turn in the third battle round, you score 3 victory points.

The player with the most victory points at the end of the fifth battle round (or when the amount of time allocated for the battle runs out), wins a **major victory**. If the players are tied on victory points at the end of the game, then each player adds up the points value of any enemy units that have been destroyed during the battle (excluding any new units that were added to the armies after the battle started). If one player has a higher total, they win a **minor victory**.

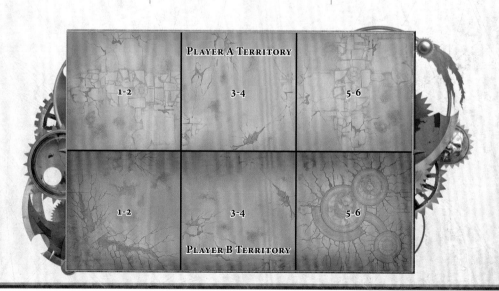

BATTLEPLAN
TAKE AND HOLD

Battles are often fought over territory. In such a battle neither side can afford to give an inch of ground, and must ruthlessly wipe out any enemy incursion while at the same time thrusting deep into the enemy heartland.

PITCHED BATTLE
Use the Pitched Battle rules on pages 310-311.

SET-UP
The players roll off, and the winner decides which territory each side will use. The territories are shown on the map below.

The players then alternate setting up units one at a time, starting with the player that won the roll-off. Units must be set up wholly within their own territory, more than 12" from enemy territory.

Continue to set up units until both players have set up their armies. If one player finishes first, the opposing player sets up the rest of the units in their army, one after another.

HOLDING FORCE
This battle is fought to control two objectives. The objectives are located at the centre of each player's territory, 9" from the edge of the battlefield, as shown on the map below.

In this battle, a player only controls an objective if they have 5 or more friendly models within 6" of the centre of the objective, in addition to needing to have more models within 6" than their opponent. The 5 models can belong to different units.

GLORIOUS VICTORY
Starting from the third battle round, one player immediately wins a **major victory** if they have control of both objectives.

If neither player has won by the end of the fifth battle round, or the amount of time allocated for the battle runs out, then each player adds up the points value of any enemy units that have been destroyed during the battle (excluding any new units that were added to the armies after the battle started). If one player has a higher total, they win a **minor victory**.

BATTLE STRATEGIES

War is unpredictable and fluid, and opportunities to dominate and win a battle may appear at a moment's notice. A good general must be flexible, prepared to take advantage of any opportunity, and ever able to adapt their plans to react to changing circumstances.

The following Battle Strategies can be used to determine the winner of games of Warhammer Age of Sigmar. Pick armies and set up terrain as described in the core rules, and use the map table on page 270 to determine which map will be used in your game. Next, follow the instructions below to determine which Battle Strategies each side will need to achieve in order to win.

OBJECTIVES

After the map for the battle has been generated and the territories chosen, the players roll off. Starting with the winner, the players alternate setting up three objectives each as follows. Each objective set up by each player should be labelled A, B or C, so that each player sets up one objective A, one objective B and one objective C.

Stormcast Eternals
Lord-Relictor

Each objective should be represented by a suitable marker, such as a coin.

The objectives you set up are friendly objectives, and the objectives set up by your opponent are enemy objectives. Set the objectives up in order (A, B, C), placing A and C in your own territory and B in your opponent's territory. Each objective must be set up more than 9" from any other objectives and more than 9" from the edge of the battlefield. Measure from the centre of each objective marker.

At the end of each player's turn, check to see if either player has gained control of any objectives. A player controls an objective if they have more models within 6" of the centre of it than their opponent does. A unit cannot be used to gain control of more than one objective in the same turn. Once you gain control of an objective, it remains under your control until the enemy is able to gain control of it.

GENERATING BATTLE STRATEGIES

After the objectives have been set up, both players must generate two Battle Strategies as described below. In addition, during the battle, each player generates one additional Battle Strategy at the start of each of their hero phases.

To generate a Battle Strategy, roll two dice, one after the other: the first dice represents tens, and the second represents digits, giving you a result between 11 and 66. Look up the result on the table opposite and make a note of the strategy you have generated. Note that the results are not secret; both players should be able to see which Battle Strategies the other has.

Battle Strategies that have been generated are said to be active until they are achieved. Once a Battle

Strategy has been achieved, it ceases to be active. You can have any number of active Battle Strategies at the same time.

Note that while there are several Battle Strategies with the same name, they are all uniquely numbered. When generating your Battle Strategies, keep a note of the numbers you roll. If you generate the same numbered Battle Strategy more than once for the same game, roll again until a different number is generated. In addition, generate a new strategy if you roll a strategy that is impossible to achieve (for example, you cannot achieve the Slayer of Beasts strategy if your opponent has no **MONSTERS** in their army).

ACHIEVING BATTLE STRATEGIES

The description for each Battle Strategy tells you what the requirements are to achieve the Battle Strategy, at which stage in a turn this requirement must be achieved, and how many victory points (VPs) are scored for achieving the Battle Strategy. For example, a roll of 11 on the Battle Strategy table generates the Capture (11) strategy, which requires you to control enemy objective A at the end of your turn in order to receive 1 victory point.

Only active Battle Strategies can be achieved. If you can achieve a Battle Strategy, you must immediately score the victory points for it – you cannot choose not to do so. Players can achieve any number of their Battle Strategies in the same turn.

VICTORY

At the end of the fifth battle round, the player that has scored the most victory points is the winner. Alternatively, a player can win by achieving a sudden death victory condition as normal.

BATTLE STRATEGIES TABLE

D66	Name	Requirement	When	VPs
11	Capture	Control enemy objective A	End of your turn	1
12	Capture	Control enemy objective B	End of your turn	1
13	Capture	Control enemy objective C	End of your turn	1
14	Hold	Control friendly objective A	End of opponent's turn	1
15	Hold	Control friendly objective B	End of opponent's turn	1
16	Hold	Control friendly objective C	End of opponent's turn	1
21	Capture	Control enemy objective A	End of your turn	1
22	Capture	Control enemy objective B	End of your turn	1
23	Capture	Control enemy objective C	End of your turn	1
24	Hold	Control friendly objective A	End of opponent's turn	1
25	Hold	Control friendly objective B	End of opponent's turn	1
26	Hold	Control friendly objective C	End of opponent's turn	1
31	Invade	Control two enemy objectives	End of your turn	3
32	Conquer	Control all enemy objectives	End of your turn	6
33	No Retreat	Control all friendly objectives	End of opponent's turn	3
34	Take & Hold	Control both A objectives	End of your turn	2
35	Take & Hold	Control both B objectives	End of your turn	2
36	Take & Hold	Control both C objectives	End of your turn	2
41	Dominate	Control at least two more objectives than your opponent	End of your turn	2
42	Overrun	Control at least four objectives	End of opponent's turn	2
43	Hold Out	Control an enemy objective	End of opponent's turn	2
44	Thrust	Control the enemy objective furthest from your territory	End of your turn	2
45	Front Line Defence	Control the friendly objective closest to (but not within) enemy territory	End of your opponent's turn	2
46	Retake	Control a friendly objective that was held by your opponent at the start of your turn	End of your turn	2
51	Blood Debt	Slay the last model in an enemy unit	At any time during either player's turn	1
52	Blood on the Ground	Slay the last model in an enemy unit, when the last model is in your opponent's territory	At any time during either player's turn	2
53	Blood on the Ground	Slay the last model in an enemy unit, when the last model is in your territory	At any time during either player's turn	2
54	Bloody Retribution	Slay the last model in an enemy unit, when the last model is within 6" of an objective	At any time during either player's turn	2
55	Blood Tithe	Slay the last model in two enemy units in the same turn	At any time during either player's turn	2
56	River of Blood	Slay the last model in three enemy units in the same turn	At any time during either player's turn	3
61	Slayer	Slay a model in an enemy unit using attacks made with melee weapons	At any time during either player's turn	1
62	Mighty Slayer	Slay a model in two enemy units using attacks made with melee weapons	In the same phase during either player's turn	2
63	Exalted Slayer	Slay a model in three enemy units using attacks made with melee weapons	In the same phase during either player's turn	3
64	Slayer of Beasts	Slay an enemy **Monster**	At any time during either player's turn	2
65	Slayer of Champions	Slay an enemy **Hero**	At any time during either player's turn	2
66	Slayer of Kings	Slay the enemy general	At any time during either player's turn	3

PITCHED BATTLE ARMY ROSTER

PLAYER: .... GAME SIZE: ....

GENERAL: .... ALLEGIANCE: ....

SIZE	TYPE	ROLE	POINTS
....	....	....	....
....	....	....	....
....	....	....	....
....	....	....	....
....	....	....	....
....	....	....	....
....	....	....	....
....	....	....	....
....	....	....	....
....	....	....	....
....	....	....	....

BATTALIONS	UNITS	POINTS
....	....	....
....	....	....
....	....	....

ALLEGIANCE ABILITIES

....

....

....

....

TOTAL POINTS:...

LEFTOVER POINTS:...................................

LEADERS: ....

ARTILLERY:..

BEHEMOTHS:...